ZENESCOPE ENTERTAINMENT PRESENTS

Grimm Fairy Tales
presents:

ZOMBIES
&
DEMONS

zenescope   UNLEASHED TIE-IN

Grimm Fairy Tales Zombies & Demons

GRIMM FAIRY TALES CREATED BY
JOE BRUSHA AND RALPH TEDESCO

STORY
**PAT SHAND
RAVEN GREGORY
JOE BRUSHA
RALPH TEDESCO**

WRITERS
**PAT SHAND
TROY BROWNFIELD**

ART DIRECTOR
ANTHONY SPAY

TRADE DESIGN
**CHRISTOPHER COTE
STEPHEN SCHAFFER**

EDITOR
RALPH TEDESCO

THIS VOLUME REPRINTS THE
COMIC SERIES GRIMM FAIRY TALES
PRESENTS ZOMBIES: THE CURSED
ISSUES #1-3 AND DEMONS: THE
UNSEEN ISSUES #1-3 PUBLISHED BY
ZENESCOPE ENTERTAINMENT.

WWW.ZENESCOPE.COM

FIRST EDITION, OCTOBER 2013
ISBN: 978-1-939683-14-4

ZENESCOPE ENTERTAINMENT, INC.

Joe Brusha • President & Chief Creative Officer
Ralph Tedesco • Editor-in-Chief
Jennifer Bermel • Director of Licensing & Business Development
Raven Gregory • Executive Editor
Anthony Spay • Art Director
Christopher Cote • Senior Designer/Production Manager
Dave Franchini • Direct Market Sales & Customer Service
Stephen Haberman • Marketing Manager

WWW.ZENESCOPE.COM
FACEBOOK.COM/ZENESCOPE

Grimm Fairy Tales
presents:

ZOMBIES
&
DEMONS

Zombies: The Cursed Part One   4

Zombies: The Cursed Part Two   26

Zombies: The Cursed Part Three   48

Demons: The Unseen Part One   72

Demons: The Unseen Part Two   98

Demons: The Unseen Part Three   124

Cover Gallery   148

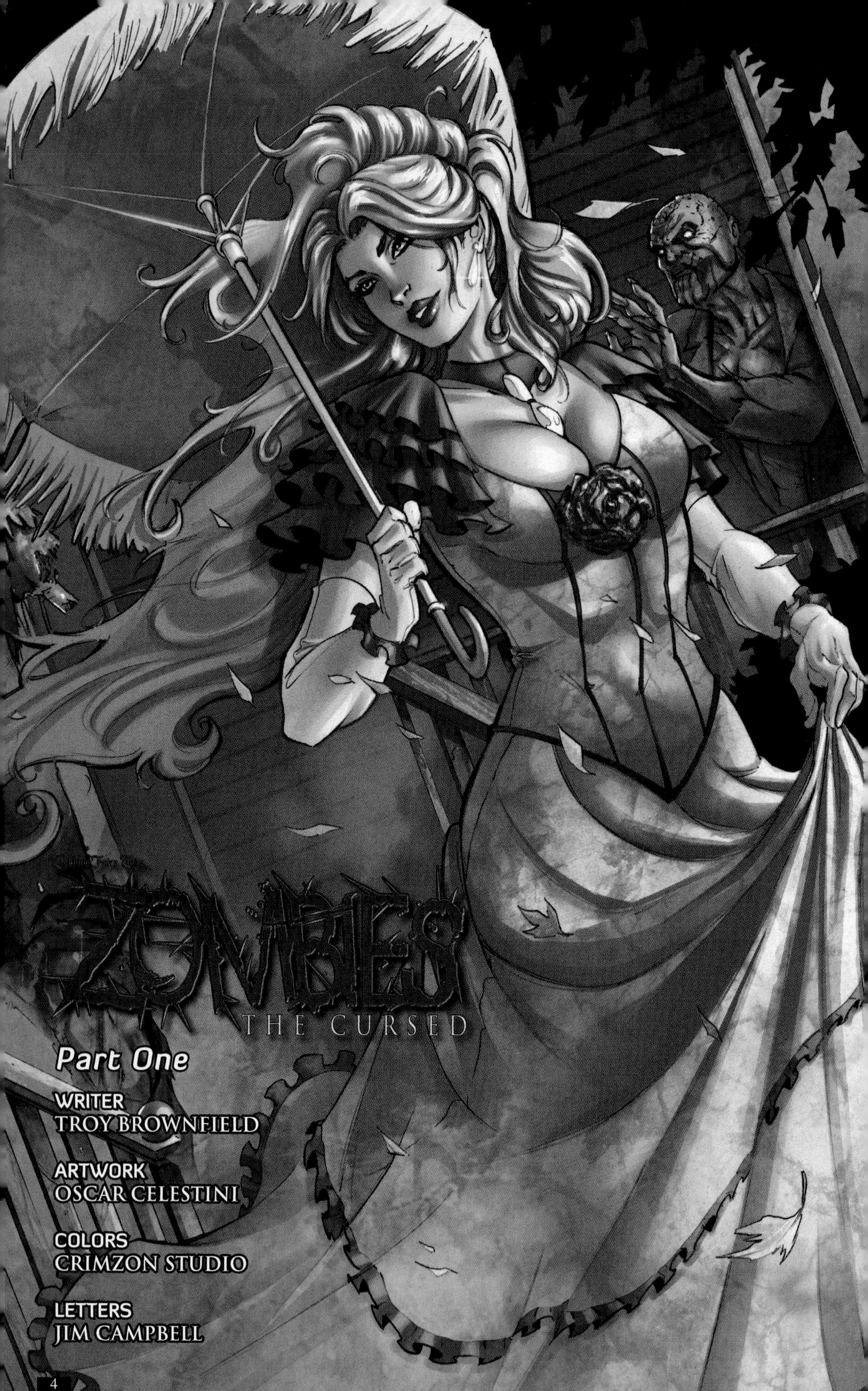
ZOMBIES
THE CURSED
Part One
WRITER
TROY BROWNFIELD
ARTWORK
OSCAR CELESTINI
COLORS
CRIMZON STUDIO
LETTERS
JIM CAMPBELL

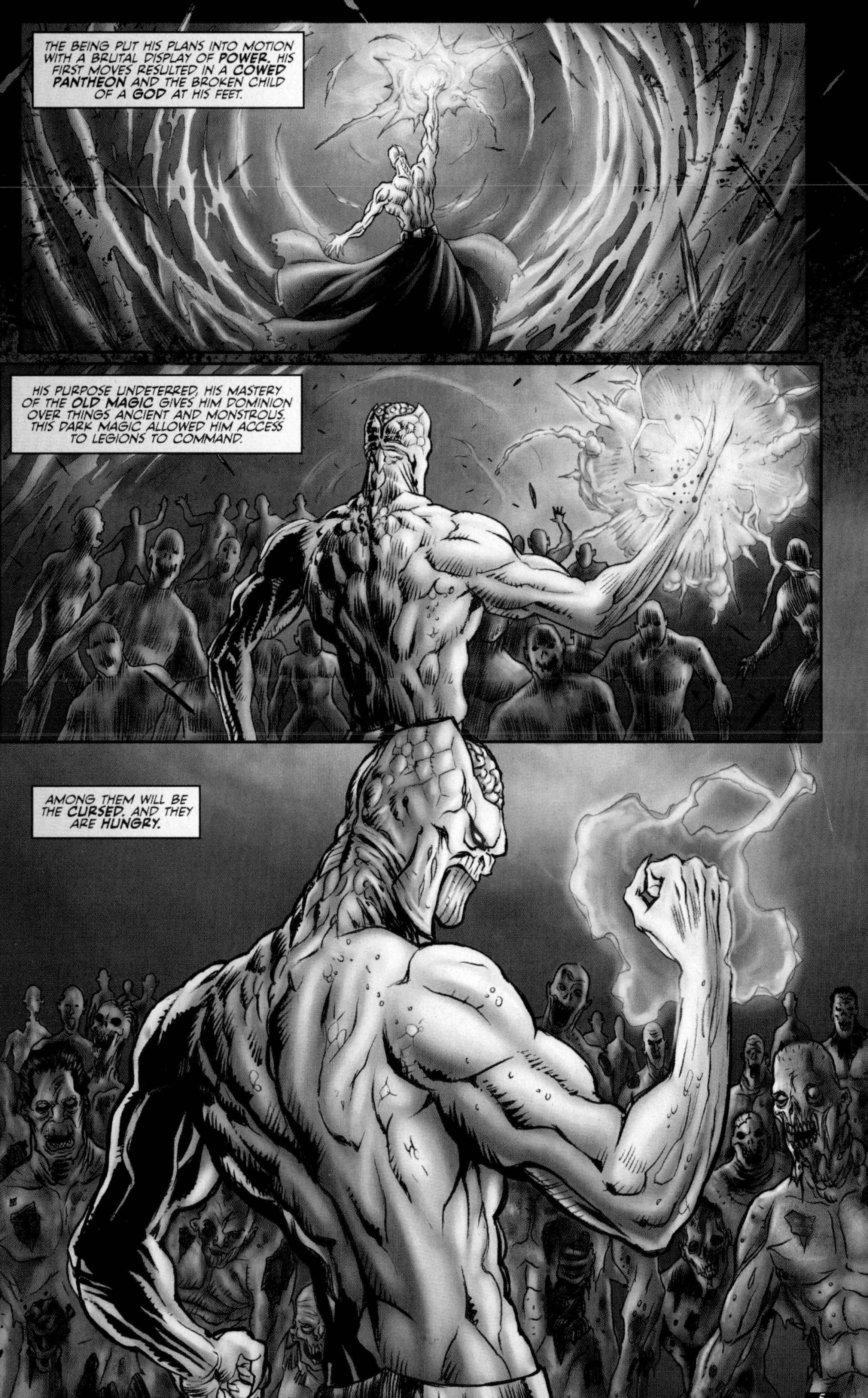
THE BEING PUT HIS PLANS INTO MOTION WITH A BRUTAL DISPLAY OF **POWER.** HIS FIRST MOVES RESULTED IN A **COWED PANTHEON** AND THE BROKEN CHILD OF A **GOD** AT HIS FEET.
HIS PURPOSE UNDETERRED, HIS MASTERY OF THE **OLD MAGIC** GIVES HIM DOMINION OVER THINGS ANCIENT AND MONSTROUS. THIS DARK MAGIC ALLOWED HIM ACCESS TO LEGIONS TO COMMAND.
AMONG THEM WILL BE THE **CURSED.** AND THEY ARE **HUNGRY.**

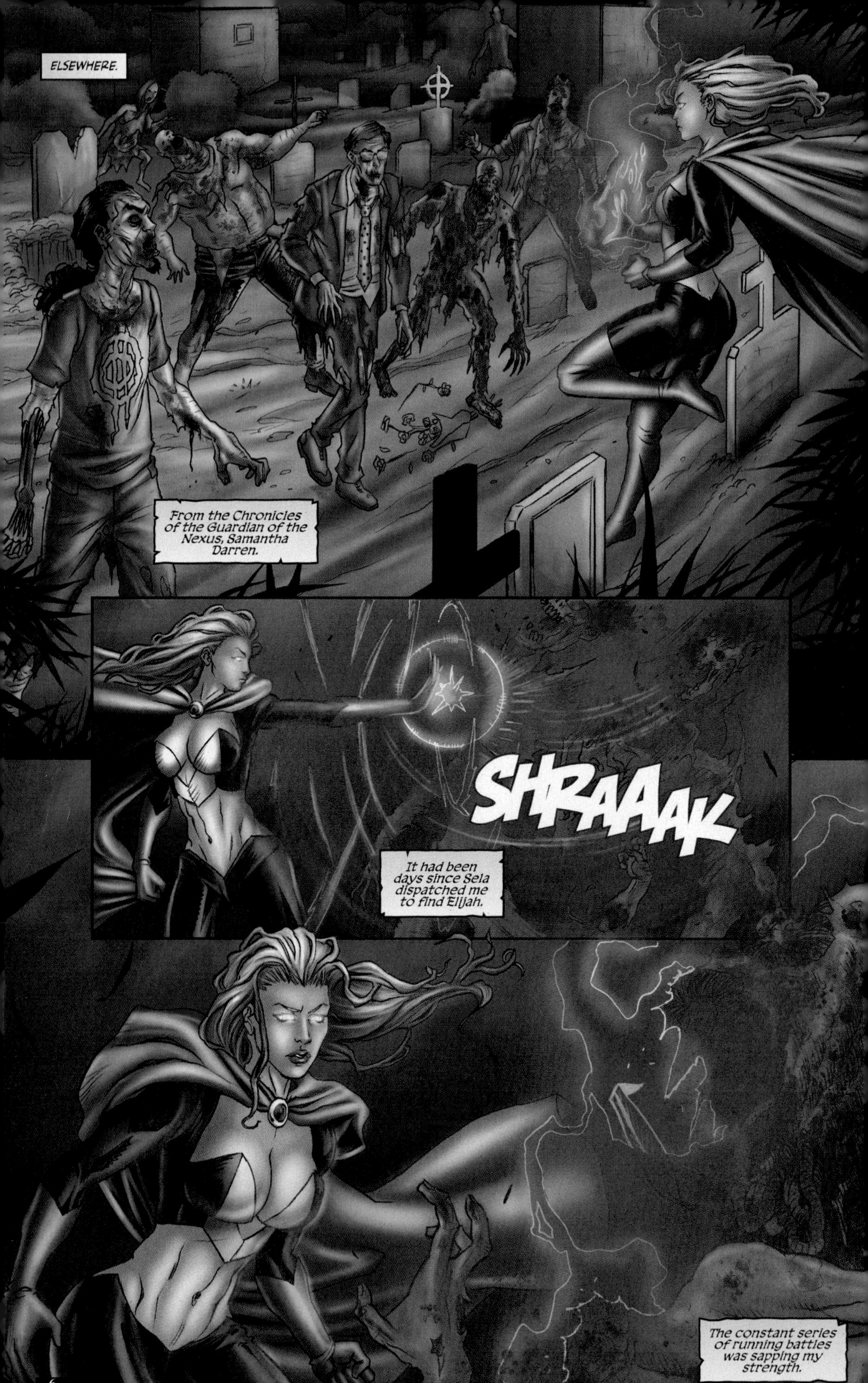
ELSEWHERE.
From the Chronicles of the Guardian of the Nexus, Samantha Darren.
SHRAAAK
It had been days since Sela dispatched me to find Elijah.
The constant series of running battles was sapping my strength.

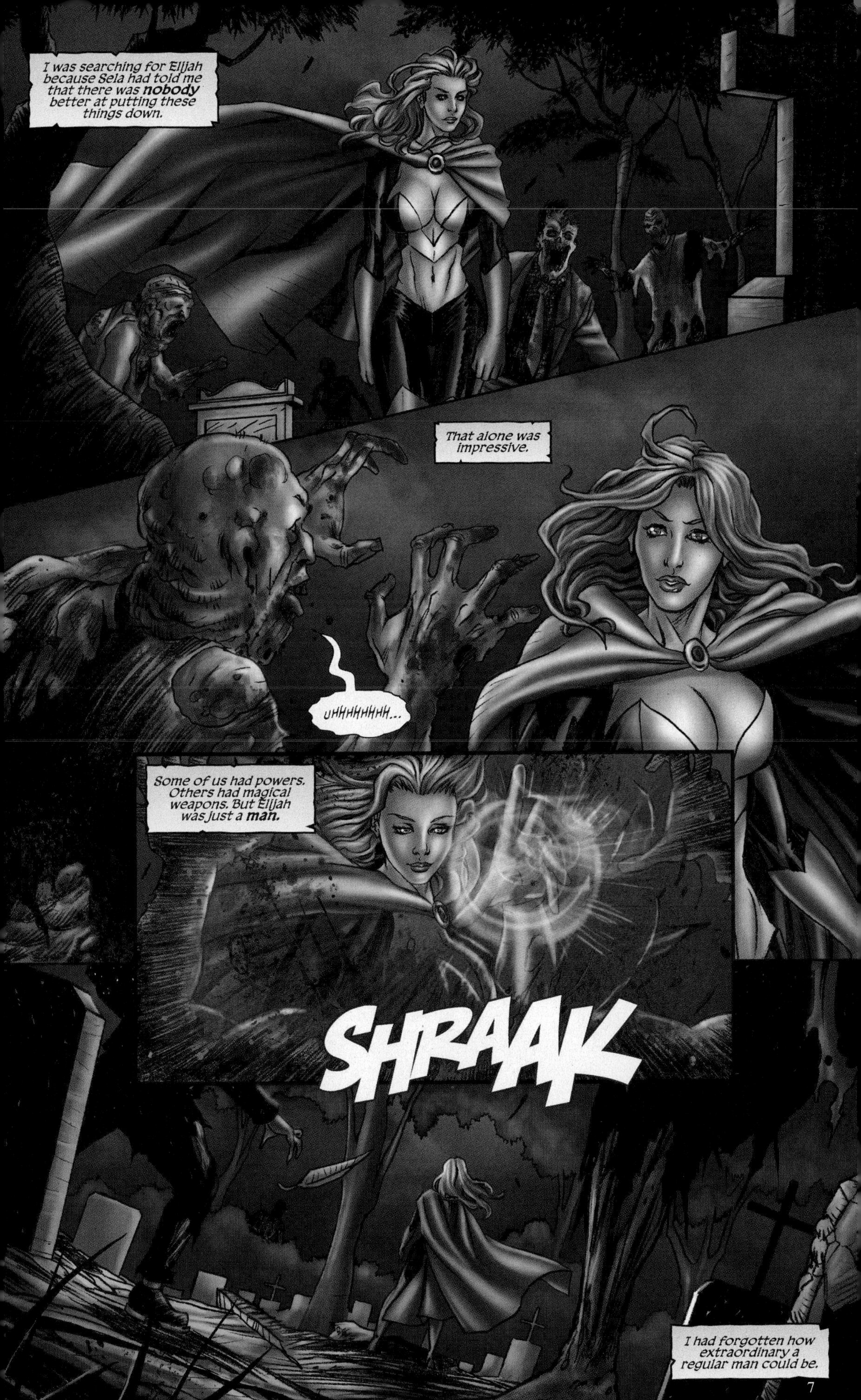
I was searching for Elijah because Sela had told me that there was **nobody** better at putting these things down.
That alone was impressive.
UHHHHHHHH...
Some of us had powers. Others had magical weapons. But Elijah was just a **man.**
SHRAAK
I had forgotten how extraordinary a regular man could be.

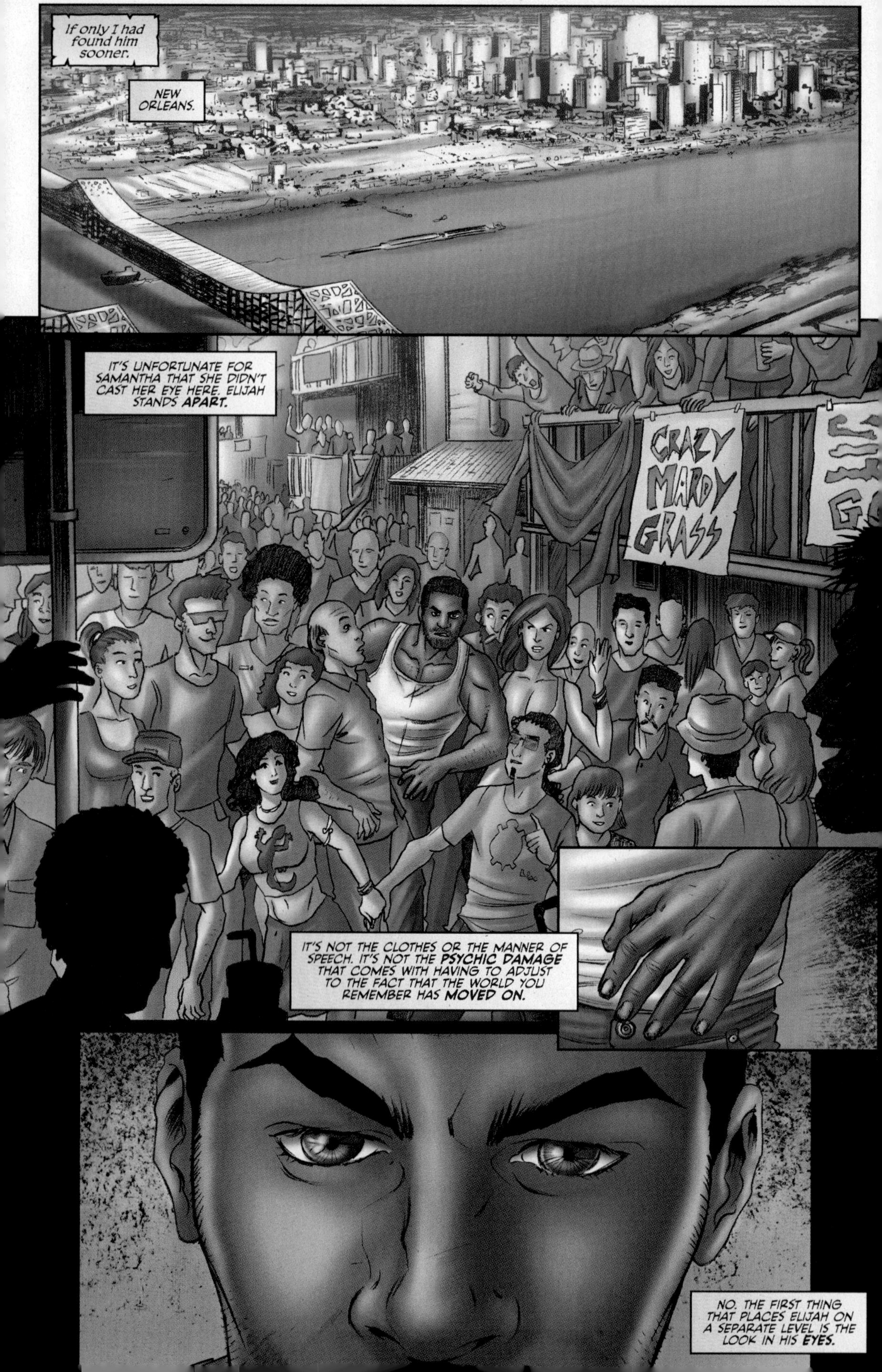
If only I had found him sooner.
NEW ORLEANS.
IT'S UNFORTUNATE FOR SAMANTHA THAT SHE DIDN'T CAST HER EYE HERE. ELIJAH STANDS APART.
CRAZY MARDY GRASS
IT'S NOT THE CLOTHES OR THE MANNER OF SPEECH. IT'S NOT THE PSYCHIC DAMAGE THAT COMES WITH HAVING TO ADJUST TO THE FACT THAT THE WORLD YOU REMEMBER HAS MOVED ON.
NO. THE FIRST THING THAT PLACES ELIJAH ON A SEPARATE LEVEL IS THE LOOK IN HIS EYES.

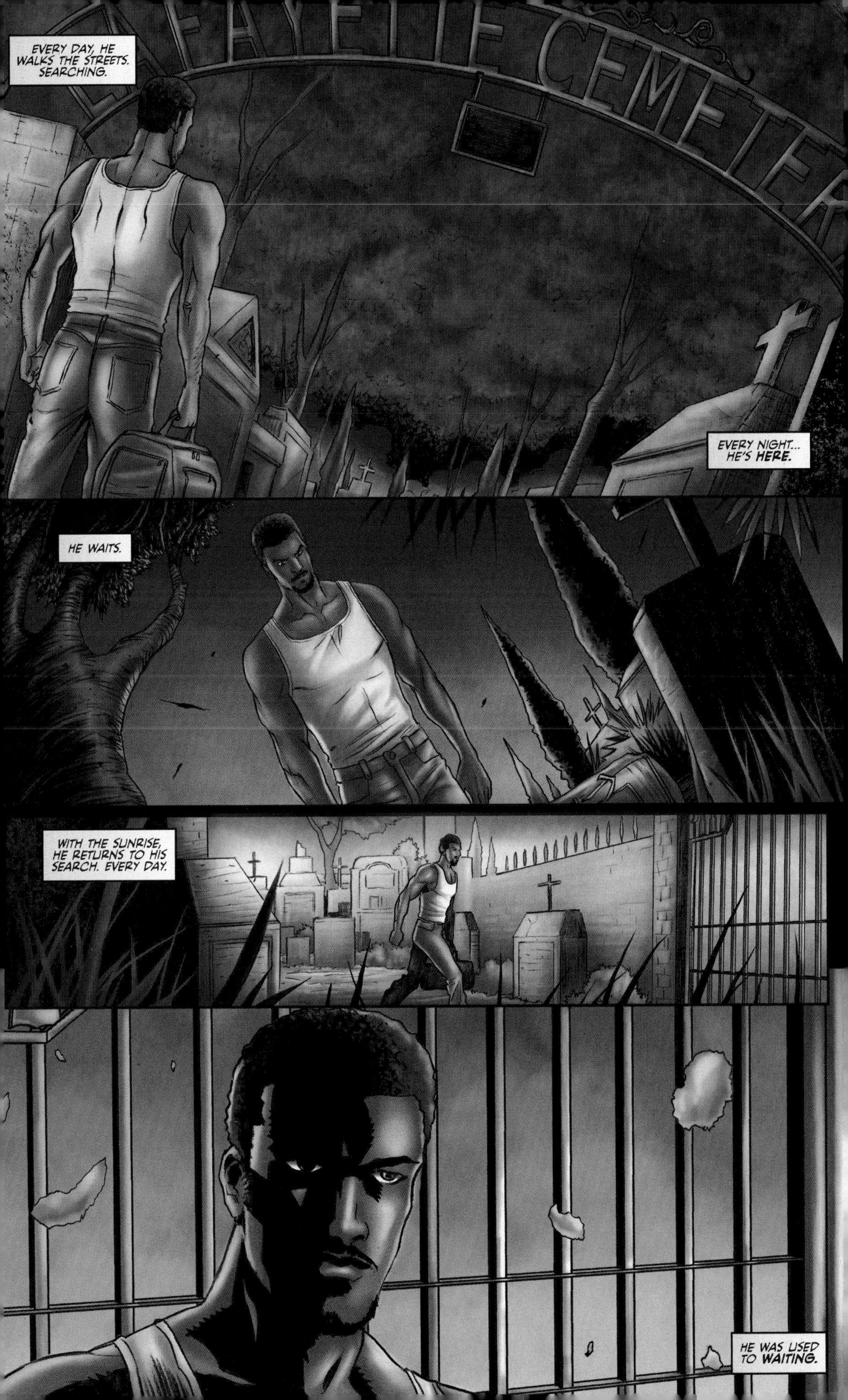

LAFAYETTE CEMETERY
EVERY DAY, HE WALKS THE STREETS. SEARCHING.
EVERY NIGHT... HE'S **HERE.**
HE WAITS.
WITH THE SUNRISE, HE RETURNS TO HIS SEARCH. EVERY DAY.
HE WAS USED TO **WAITING.**

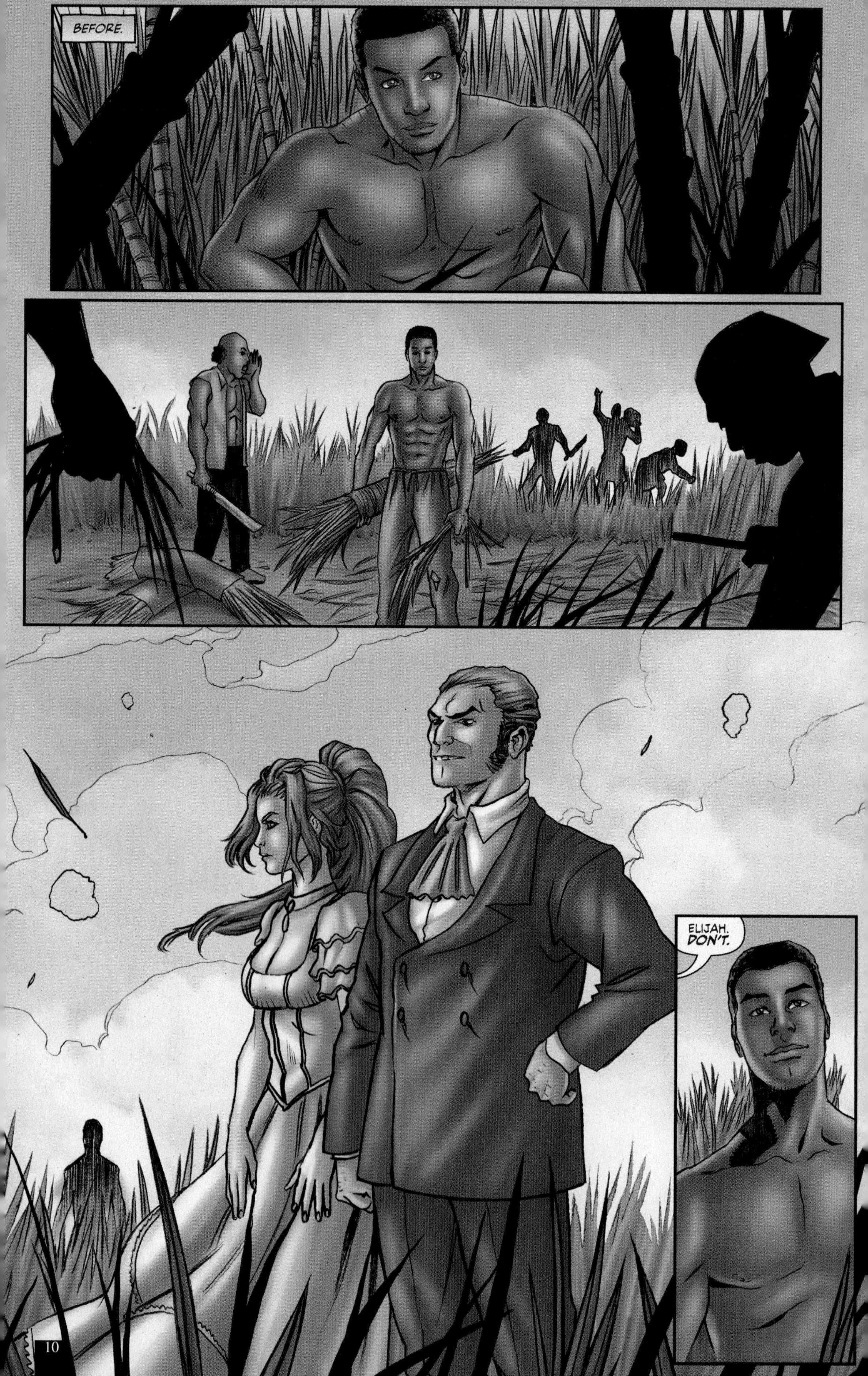
BEFORE.
ELIJAH. DON'T.

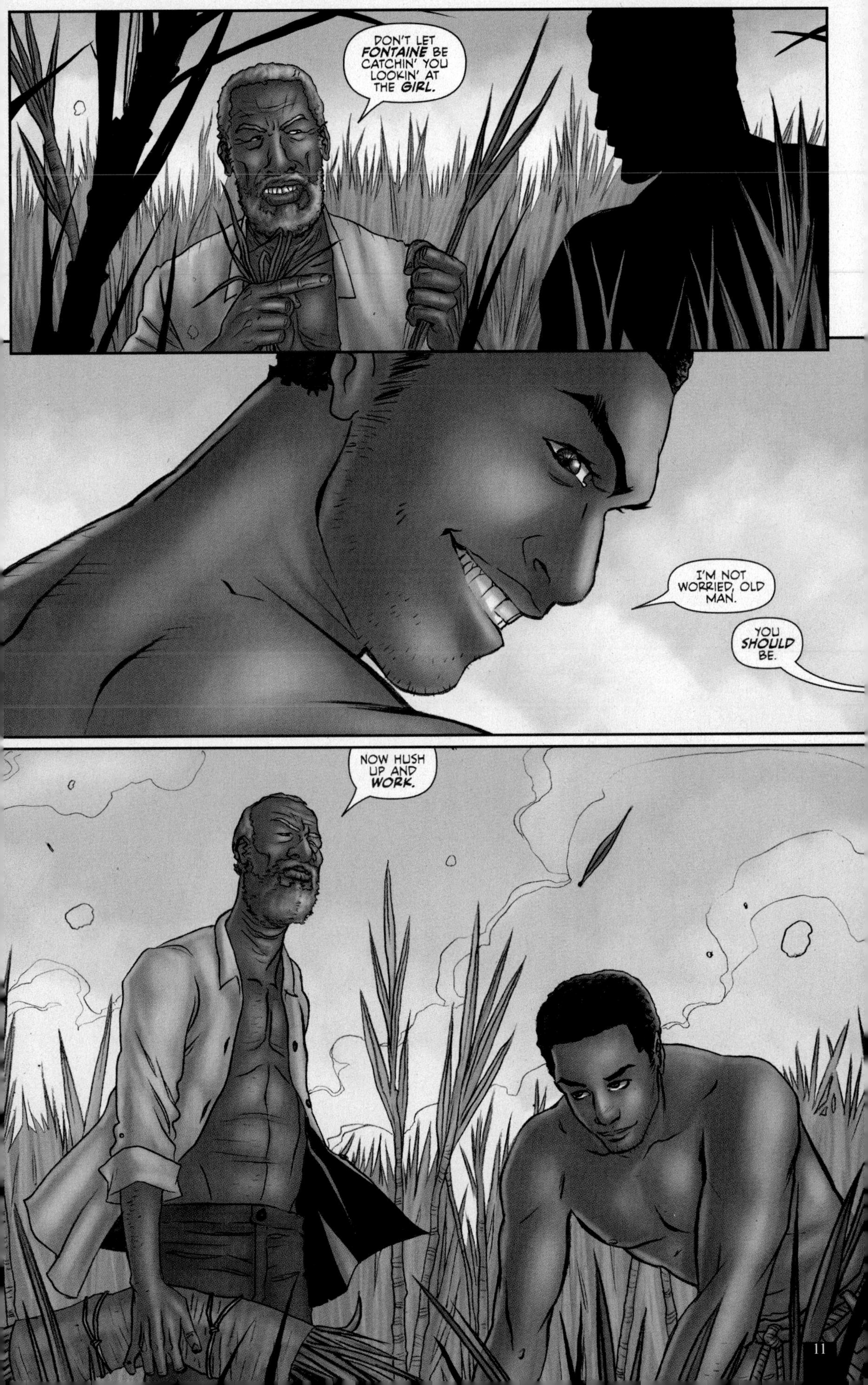
DON'T LET FONTAINE BE CATCHIN' YOU LOOKIN' AT THE GIRL.
I'M NOT WORRIED, OLD MAN.
YOU SHOULD BE.
NOW HUSH UP AND WORK.

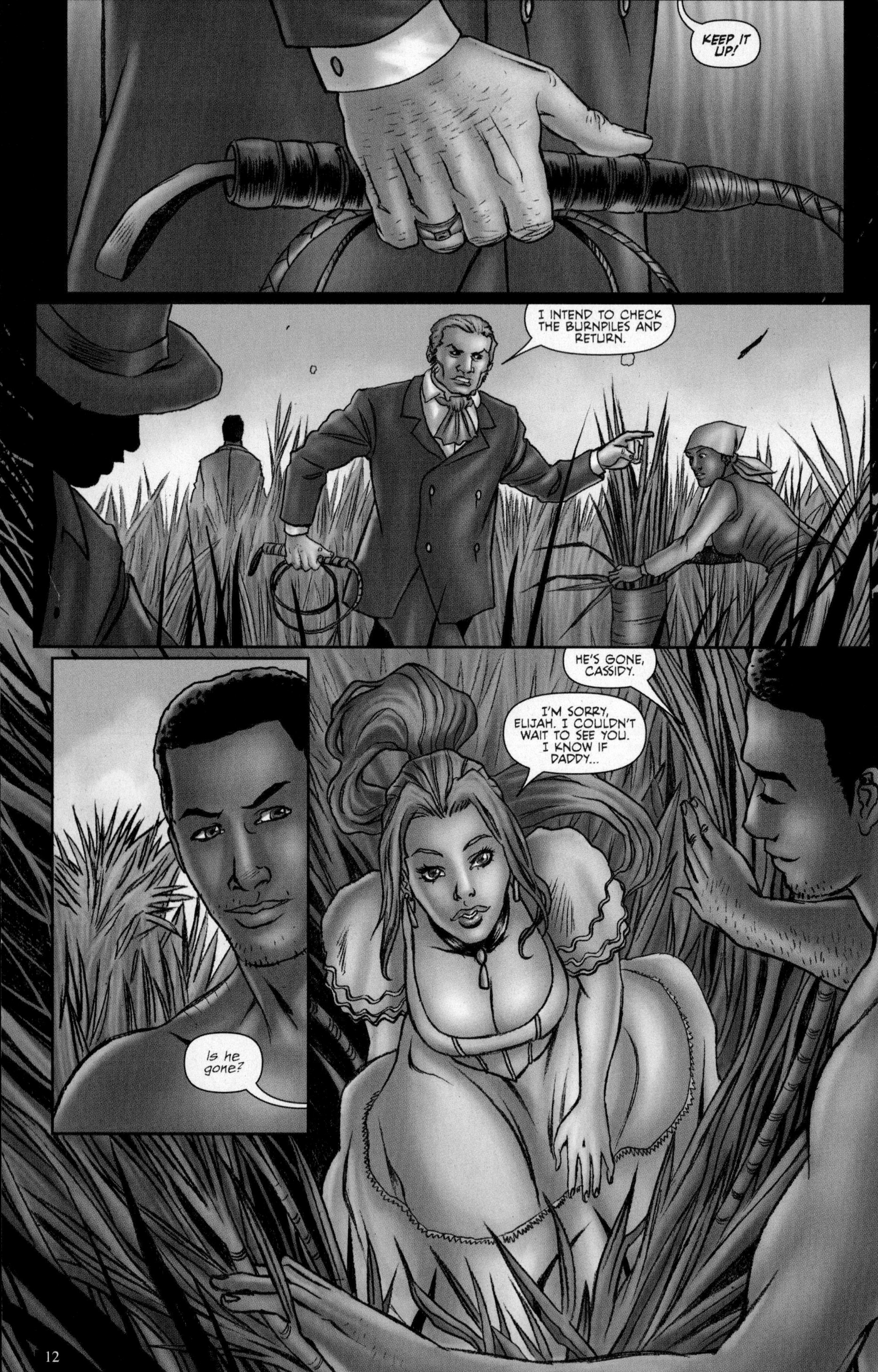
KEEP IT UP!
I INTEND TO CHECK THE BURNPILES AND RETURN.
Is he gone?
HE'S GONE, CASSIDY.
I'M SORRY, ELIJAH. I COULDN'T WAIT TO SEE YOU. I KNOW IF DADDY...

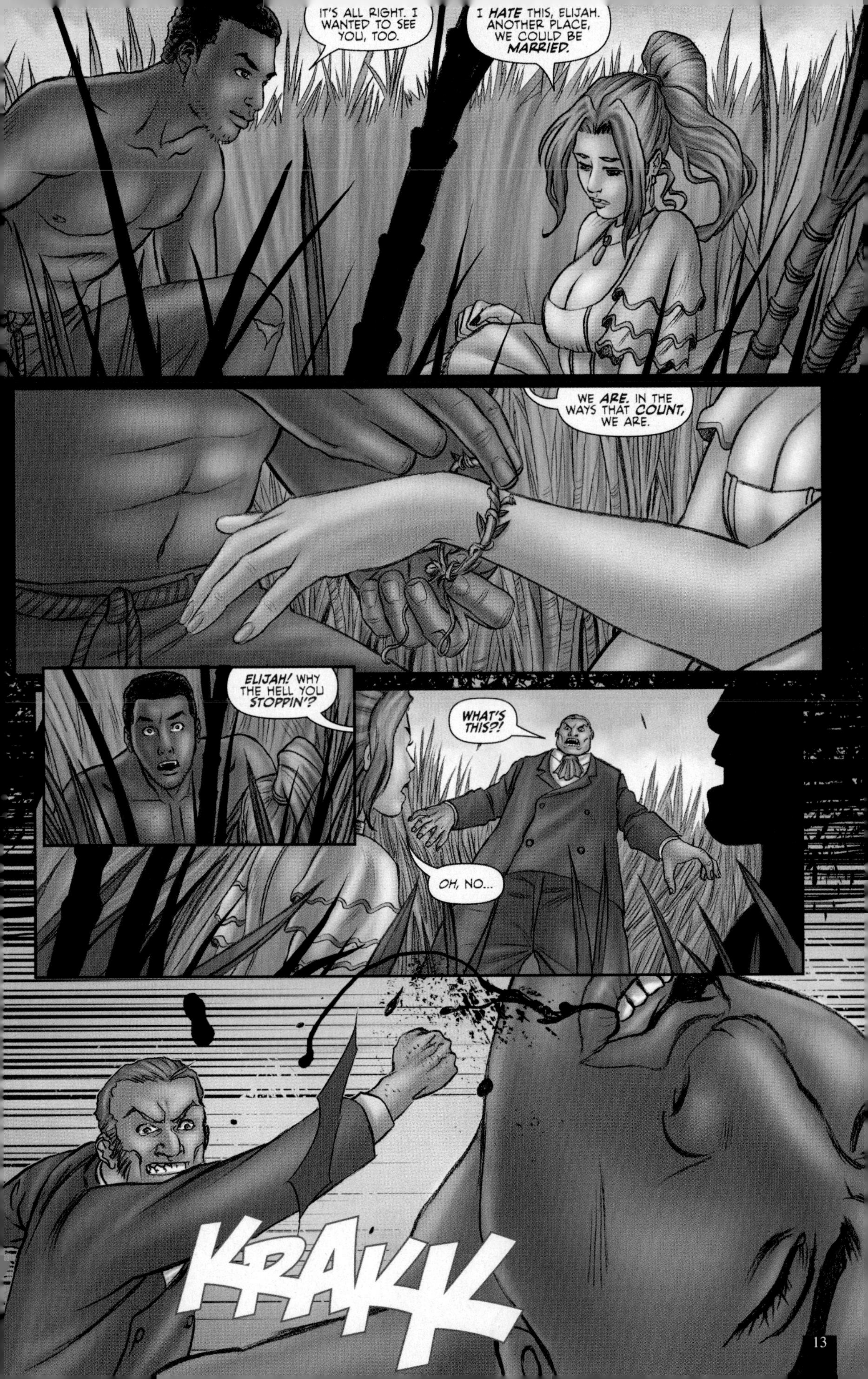
IT'S ALL RIGHT. I WANTED TO SEE YOU, TOO.
I *HATE* THIS, ELIJAH. ANOTHER PLACE, WE COULD BE *MARRIED.*
WE *ARE.* IN THE WAYS THAT *COUNT,* WE ARE.
ELIJAH! WHY THE HELL YOU *STOPPIN'?*
WHAT'S THIS?!
OH, NO...
KRAKK

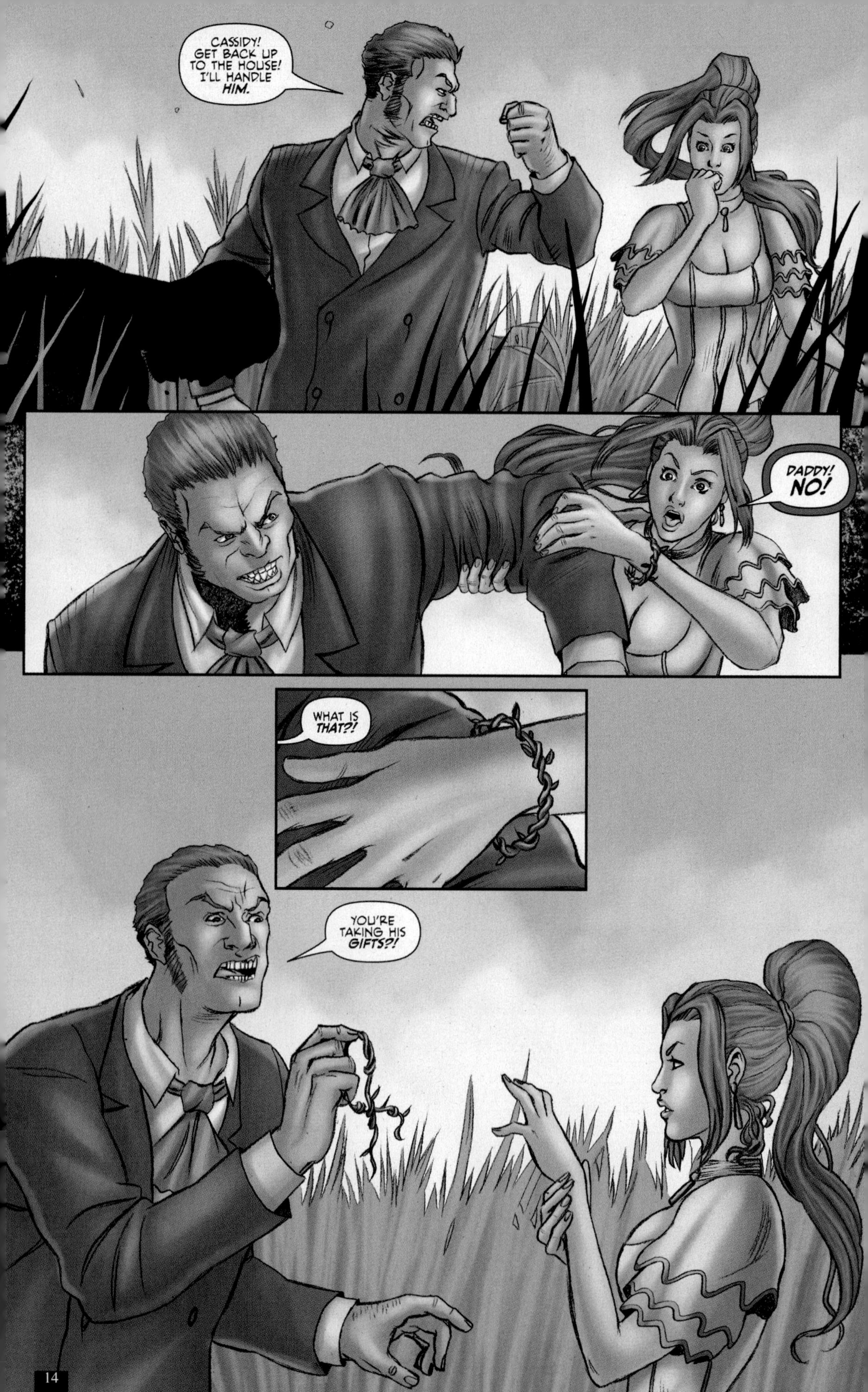
CASSIDY! GET BACK UP TO THE HOUSE! I'LL HANDLE *HIM.*
DADDY! NO!
WHAT IS *THAT?!*
YOU'RE TAKING HIS *GIFTS?!*

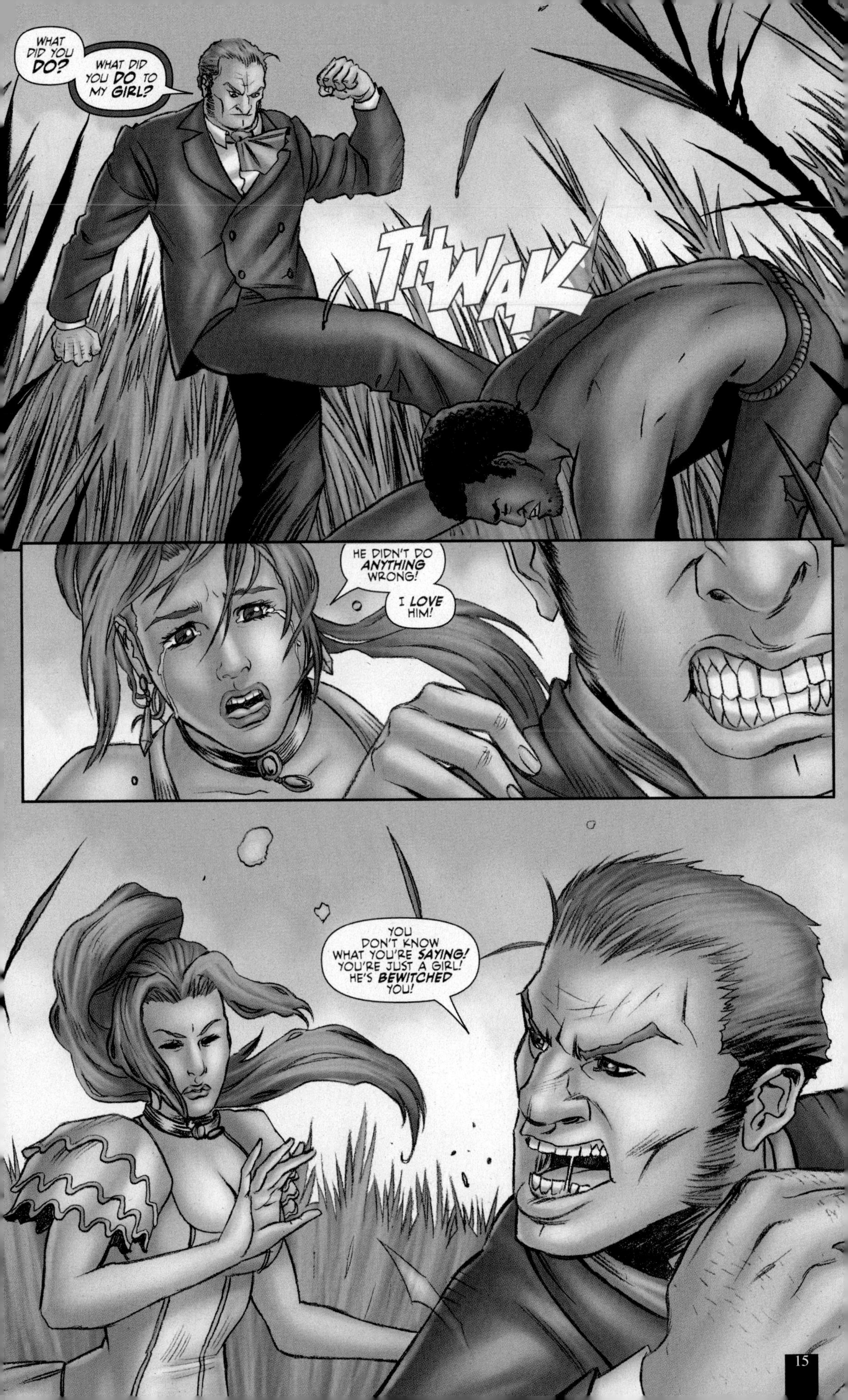
WHAT DID YOU DO?
WHAT DID YOU DO TO MY GIRL?
THWAK
HE DIDN'T DO ANYTHING WRONG!
I LOVE HIM!
YOU DON'T KNOW WHAT YOU'RE SAYING! YOU'RE JUST A GIRL! HE'S BEWITCHED YOU!

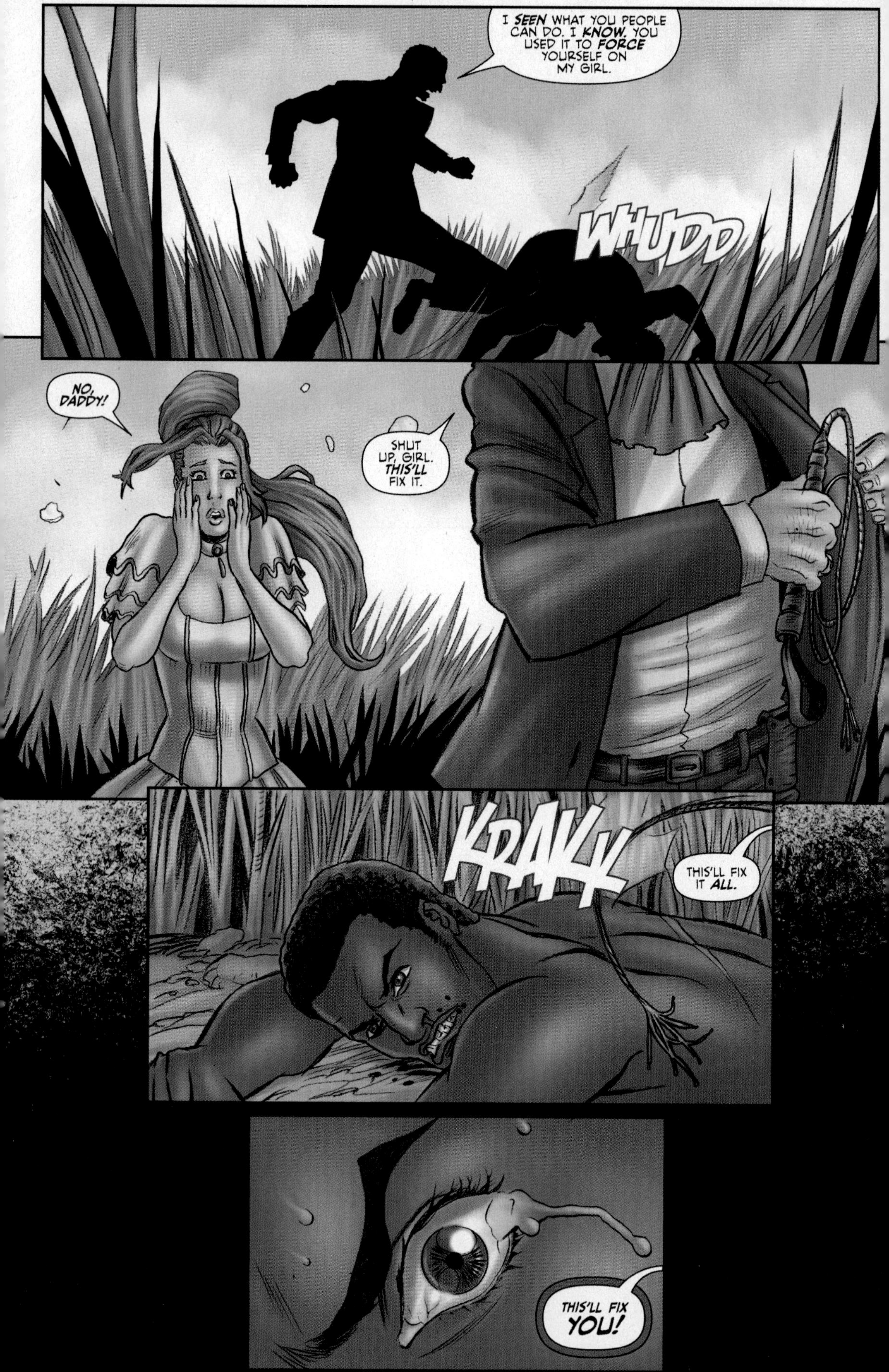
I SEEN WHAT YOU PEOPLE CAN DO. I KNOW. YOU USED IT TO FORCE YOURSELF ON MY GIRL.
WHUDD
NO, DADDY!
SHUT UP, GIRL. THIS'LL FIX IT.
KRAKK
THIS'LL FIX IT ALL.
THIS'LL FIX YOU!

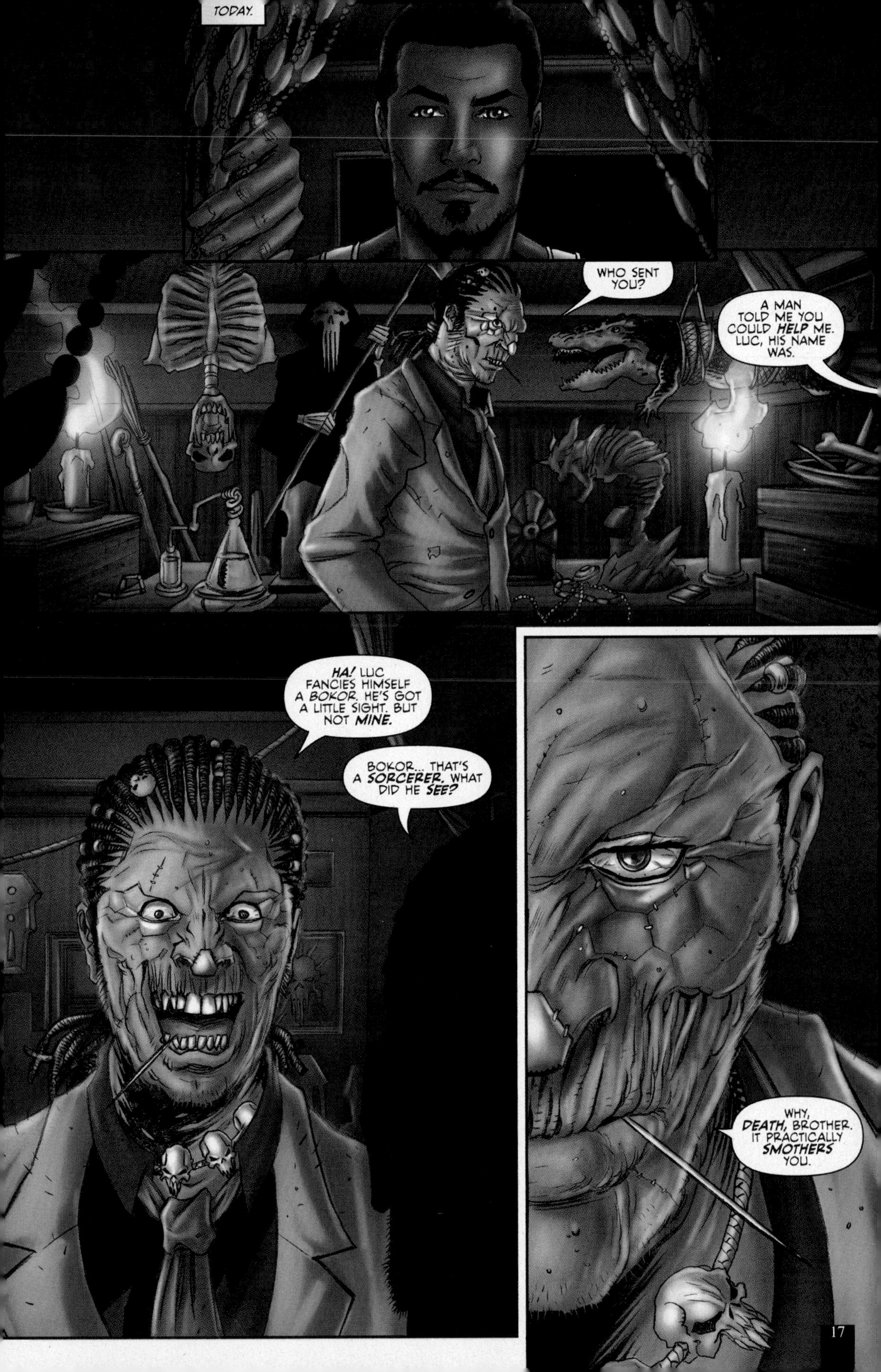
TODAY.
WHO SENT YOU?
A MAN TOLD ME YOU COULD HELP ME. LUC, HIS NAME WAS.
HA! LUC FANCIES HIMSELF A BOKOR. HE'S GOT A LITTLE SIGHT. BUT NOT MINE.
BOKOR... THAT'S A SORCERER. WHAT DID HE SEE?
WHY, DEATH, BROTHER. IT PRACTICALLY SMOTHERS YOU.

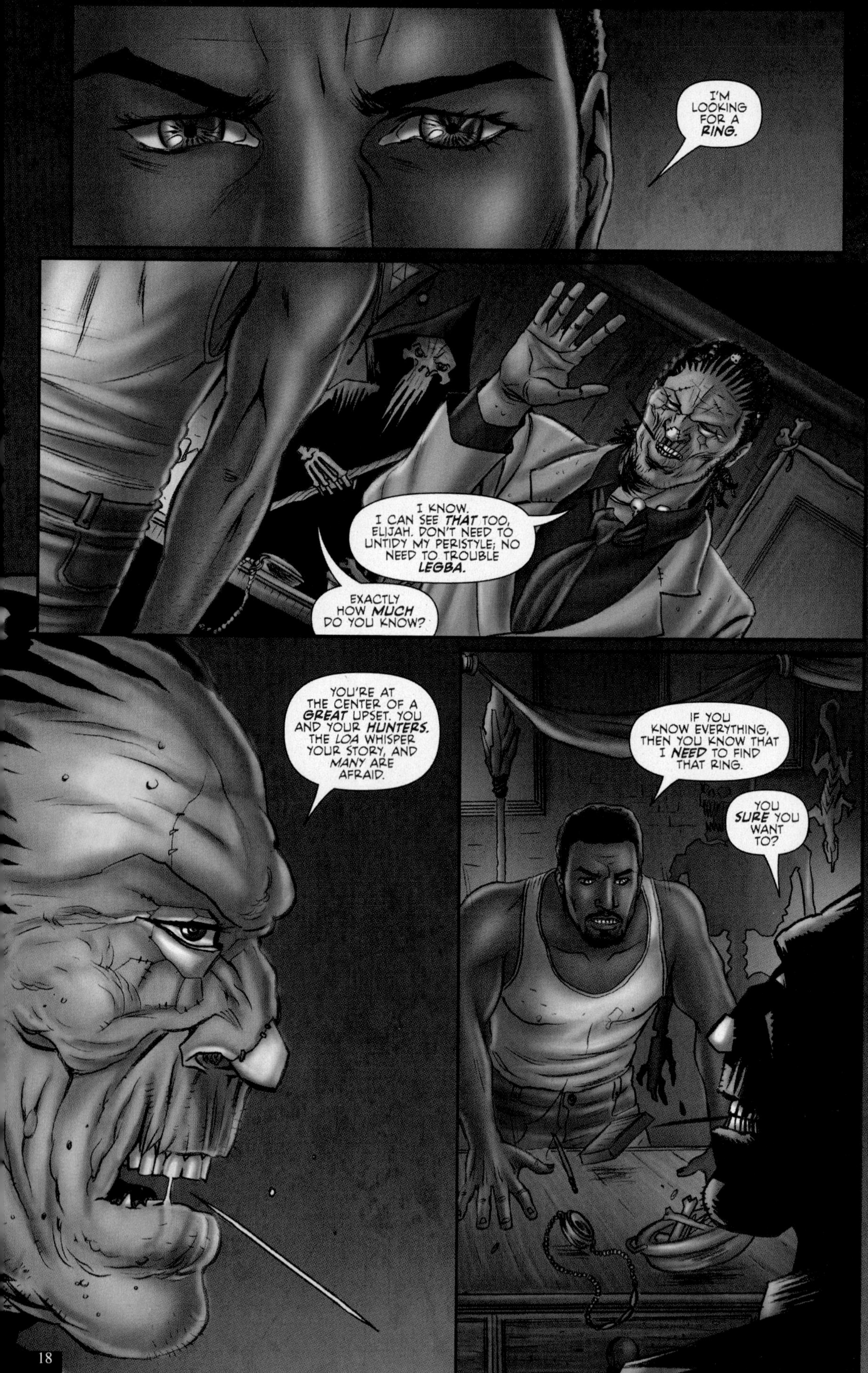
I'M LOOKING FOR A RING.
I KNOW. I CAN SEE THAT TOO, ELIJAH. DON'T NEED TO UNTIDY MY PERISTYLE; NO NEED TO TROUBLE LEGBA.
EXACTLY HOW MUCH DO YOU KNOW?
YOU'RE AT THE CENTER OF A GREAT UPSET. YOU AND YOUR HUNTERS. THE LOA WHISPER YOUR STORY, AND MANY ARE AFRAID.
IF YOU KNOW EVERYTHING, THEN YOU KNOW THAT I NEED TO FIND THAT RING.
YOU SURE YOU WANT TO?

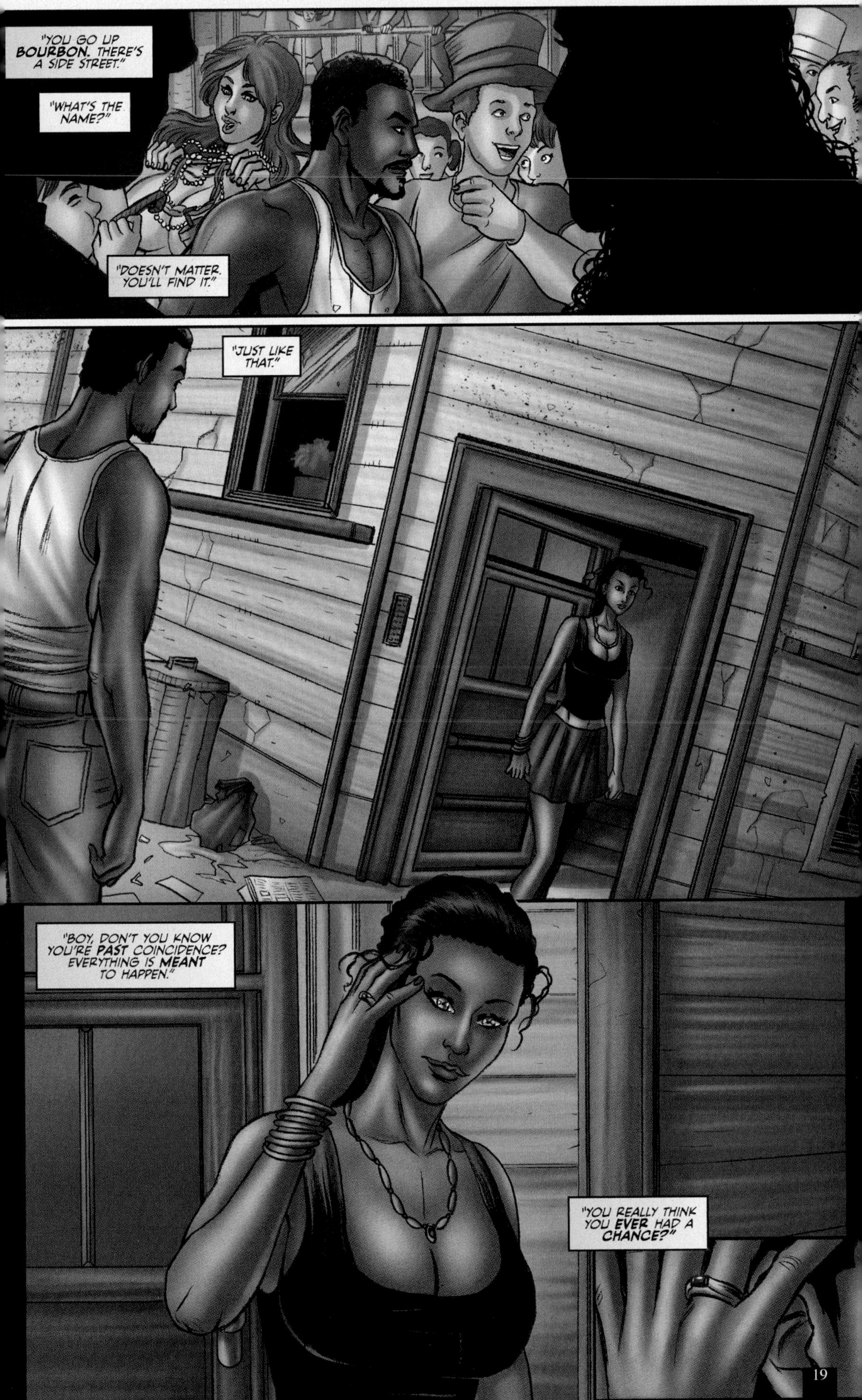
"YOU GO UP BOURBON. THERE'S A SIDE STREET."
"WHAT'S THE NAME?"
"DOESN'T MATTER. YOU'LL FIND IT."
"JUST LIKE THAT."
"BOY, DON'T YOU KNOW YOU'RE PAST COINCIDENCE? EVERYTHING IS MEANT TO HAPPEN."
"YOU REALLY THINK YOU EVER HAD A CHANCE?"

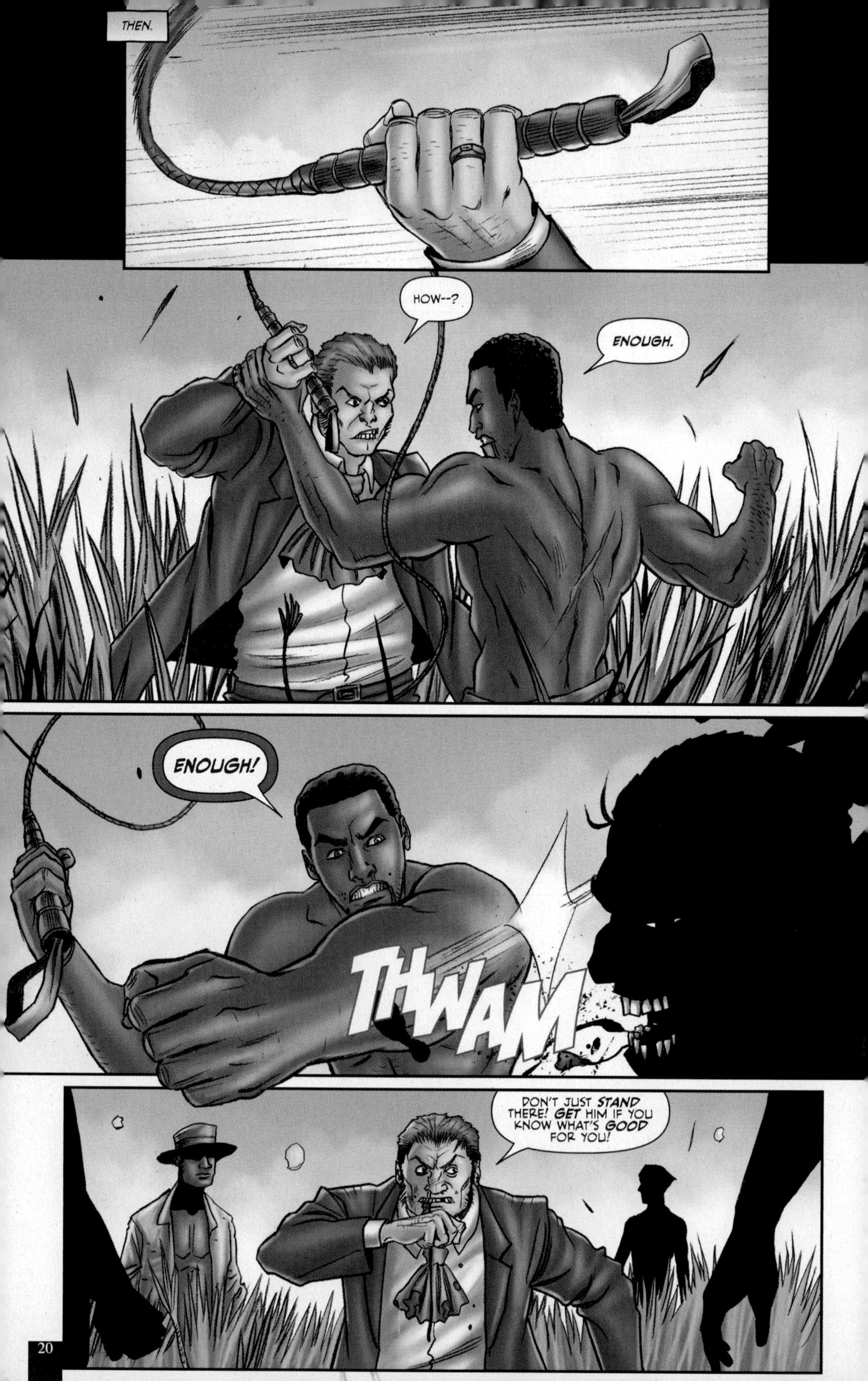
THEN.
HOW--?
ENOUGH.
ENOUGH!
THWAM
DON'T JUST STAND THERE! GET HIM IF YOU KNOW WHAT'S GOOD FOR YOU!

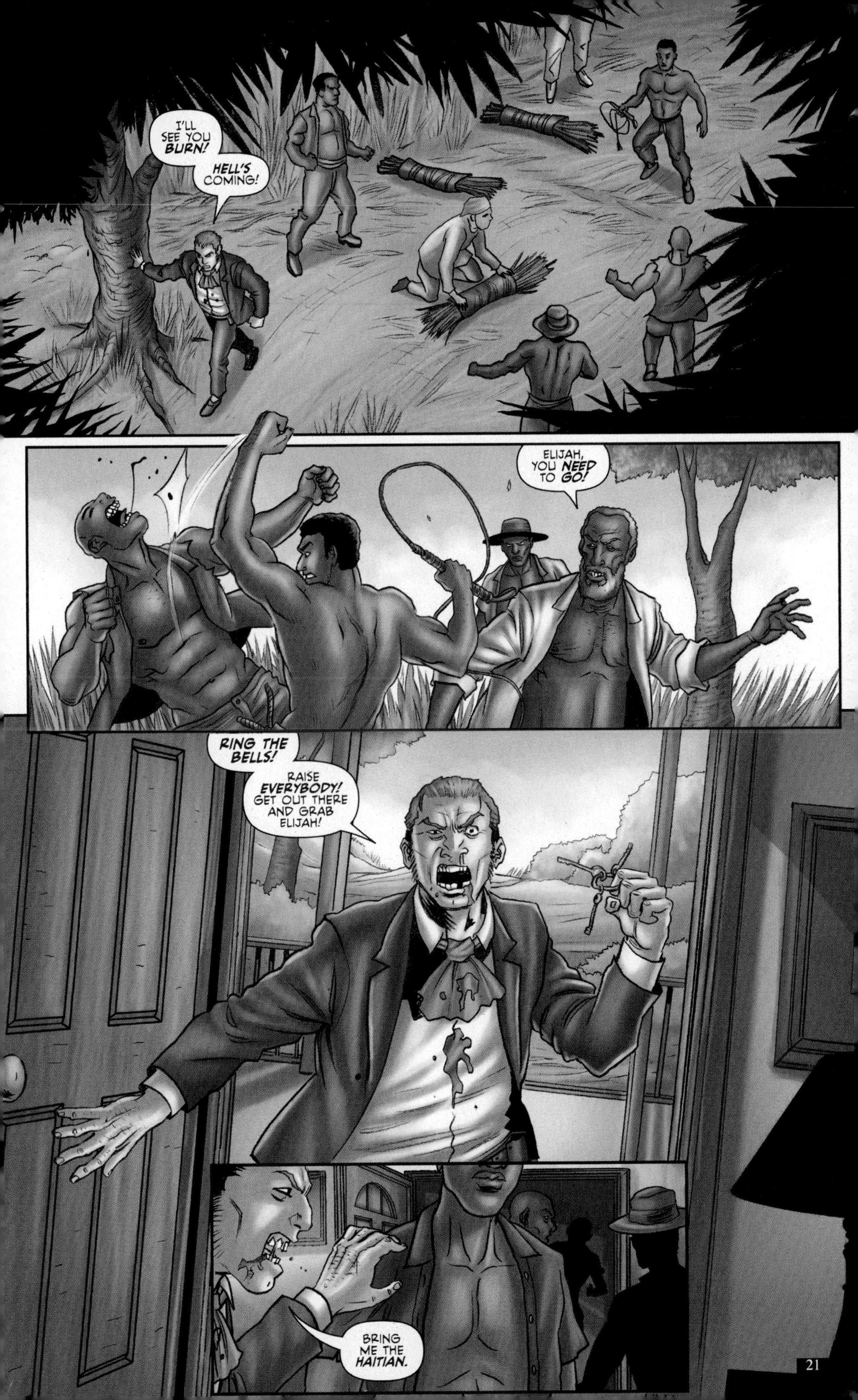
I'LL SEE YOU BURN!
HELL'S COMING!
ELIJAH, YOU NEED TO GO!
RING THE BELLS!
RAISE EVERYBODY! GET OUT THERE AND GRAB ELIJAH!
BRING ME THE HAITIAN.

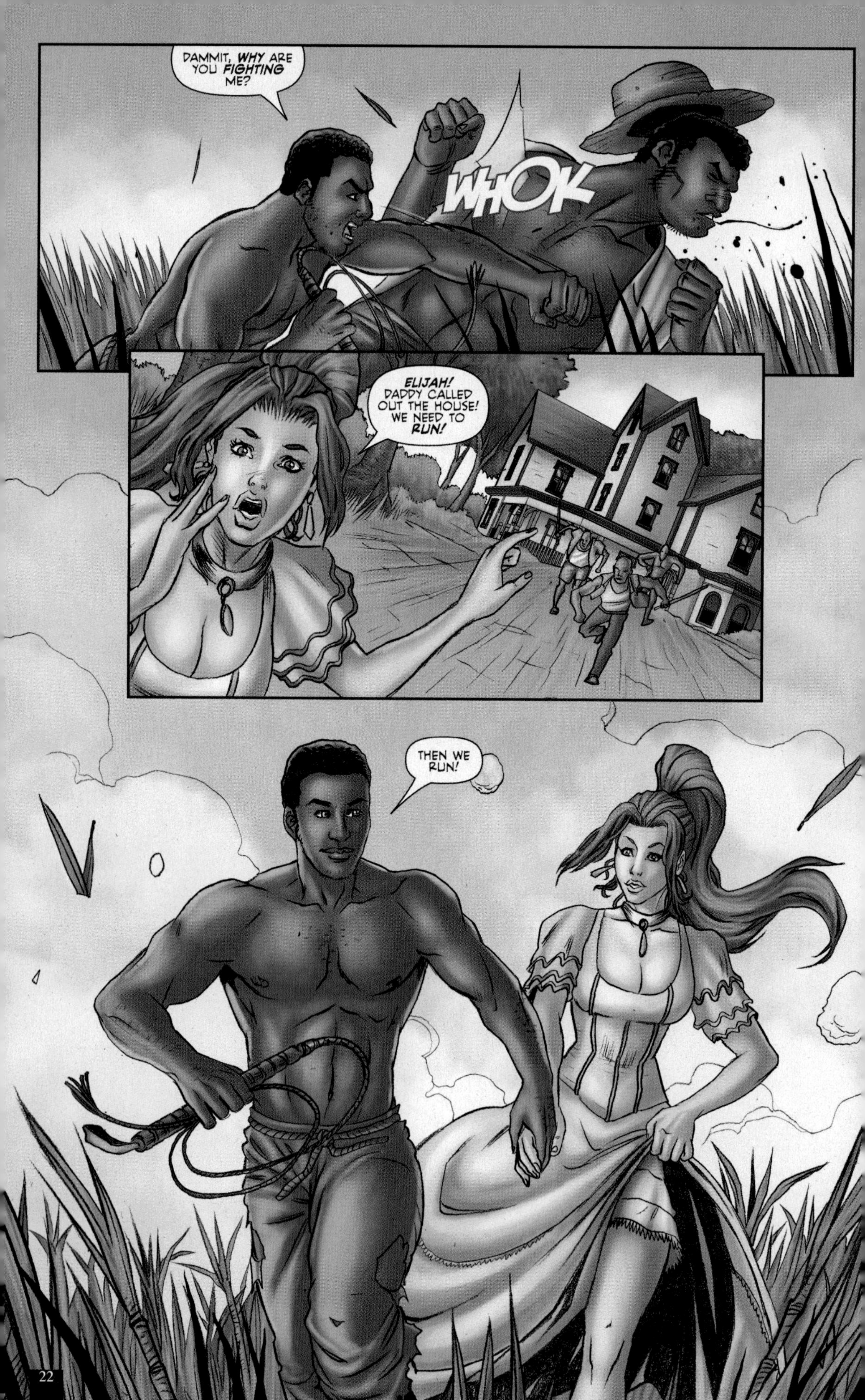
DAMMIT, WHY ARE YOU FIGHTING ME?
WHOK
ELIJAH! DADDY CALLED OUT THE HOUSE! WE NEED TO RUN!
THEN WE RUN!

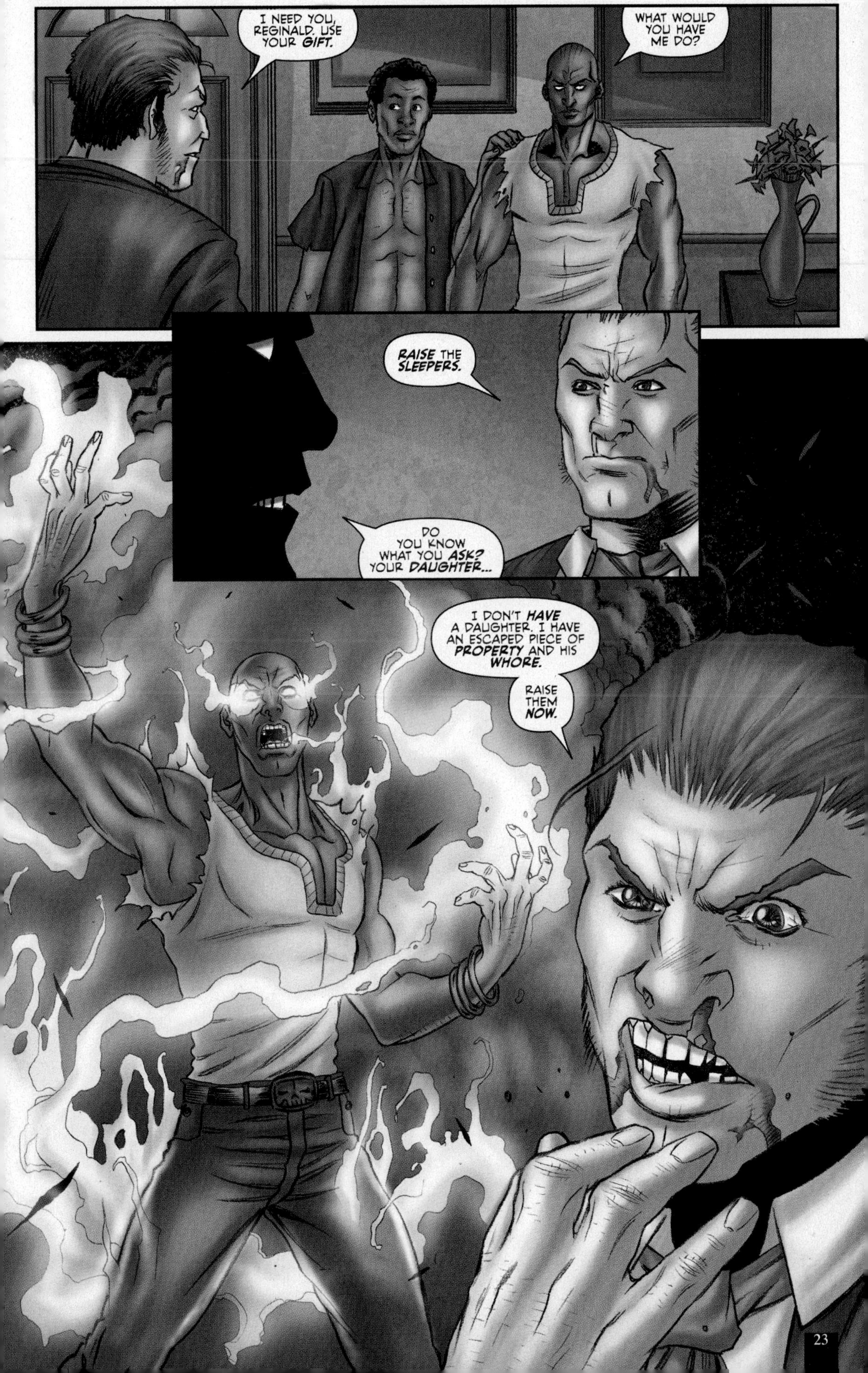
I NEED YOU, REGINALD. USE YOUR GIFT.
WHAT WOULD YOU HAVE ME DO?
RAISE THE SLEEPERS.
DO YOU KNOW WHAT YOU ASK? YOUR DAUGHTER...
I DON'T HAVE A DAUGHTER. I HAVE AN ESCAPED PIECE OF PROPERTY AND HIS WHORE.
RAISE THEM NOW.

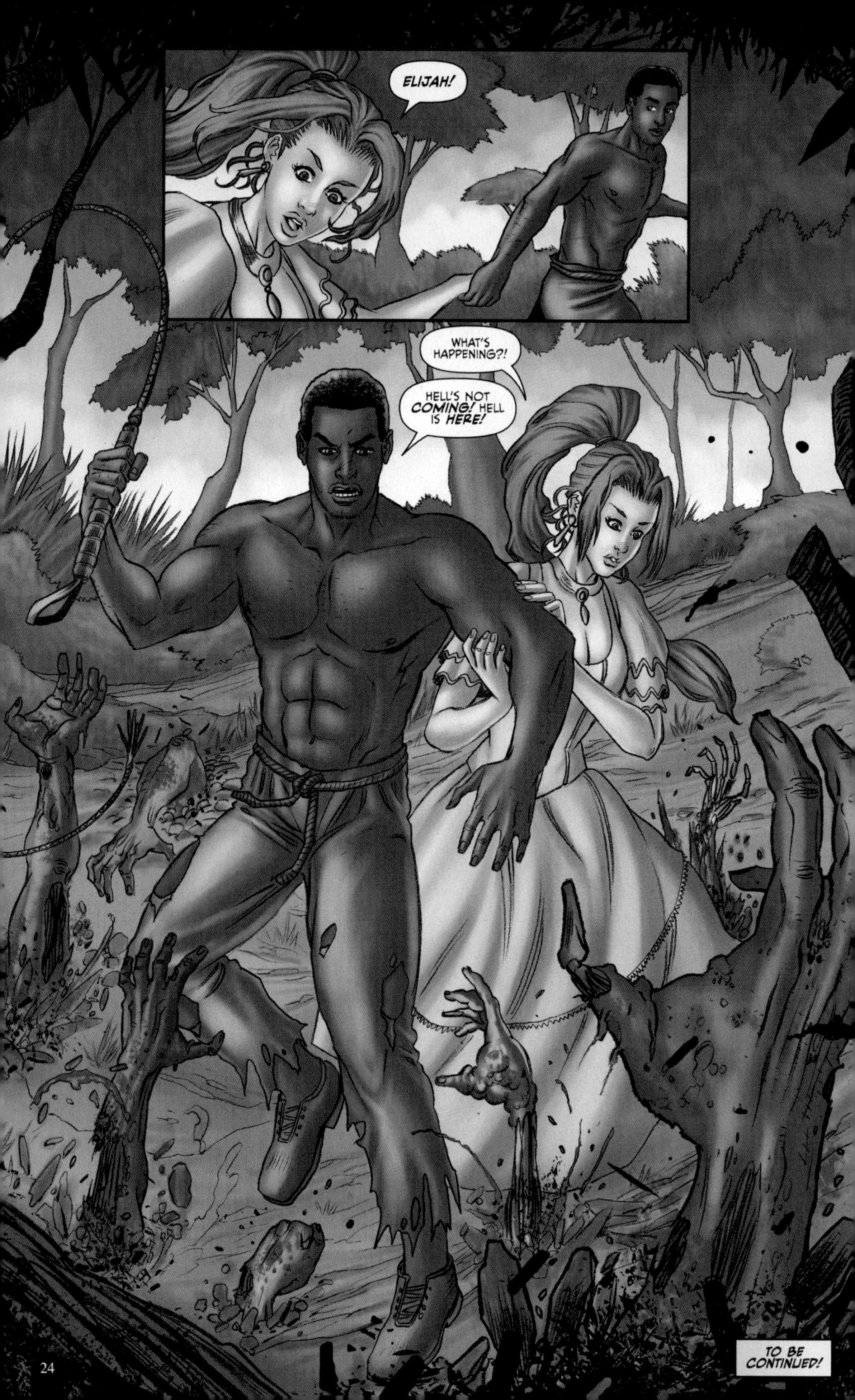
ELIJAH!
WHAT'S HAPPENING?!
HELL'S NOT COMING! HELL IS HERE!
TO BE CONTINUED!

Grimm Fairy Tales presents:

Zombies & Demons

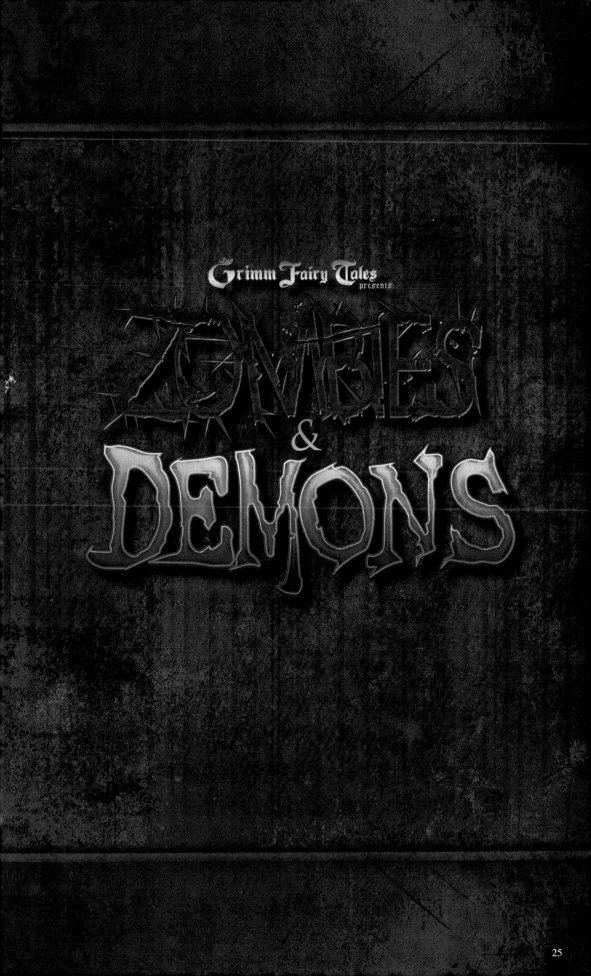

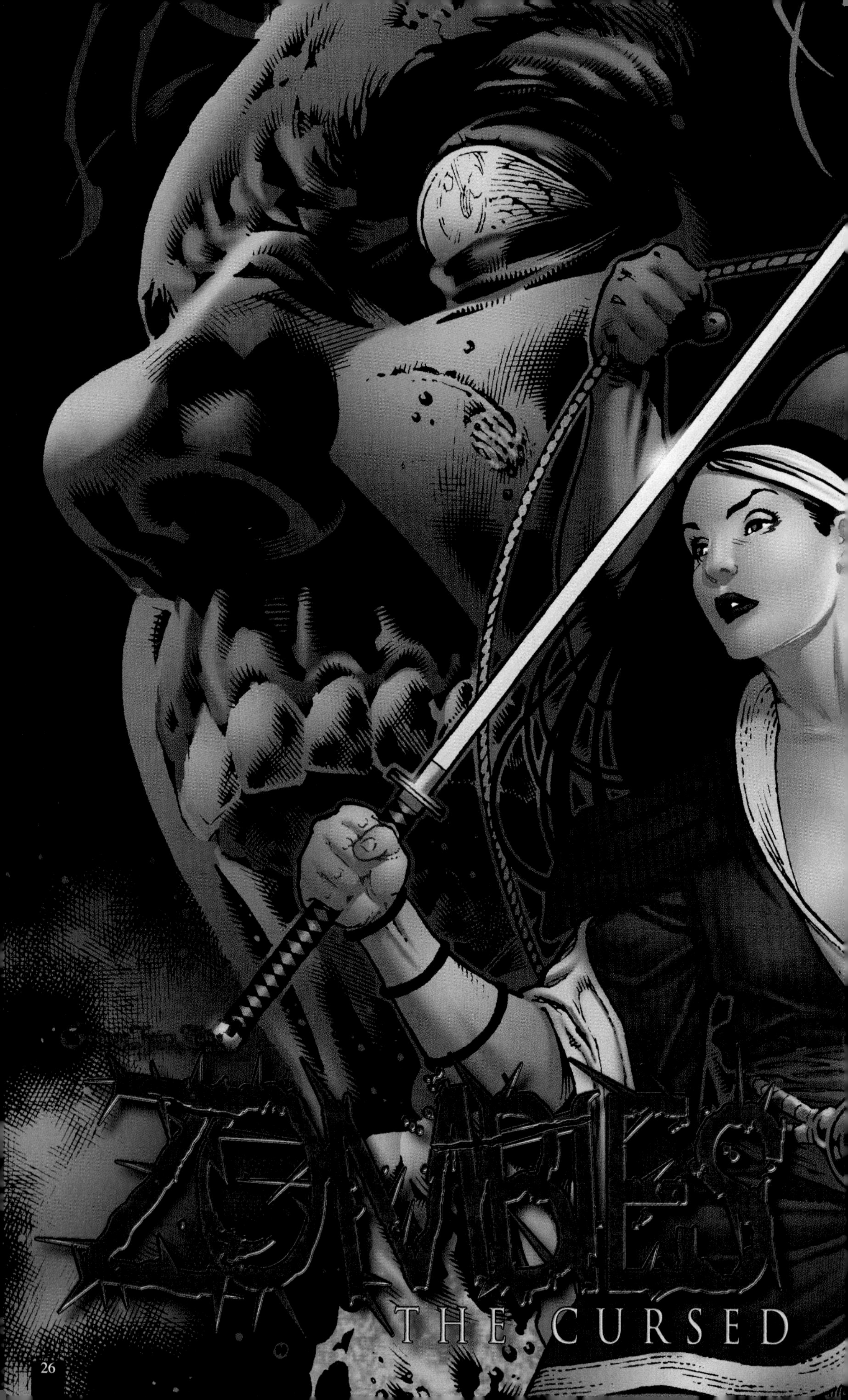
ZOMBIES
THE CURSED

Part Two

WRITER
TROY BROWNFIELD

ARTWORK
OSCAR CELESTINI

COLORS
3MARTSTUDIO

LETTERS
JIM CAMPBELL

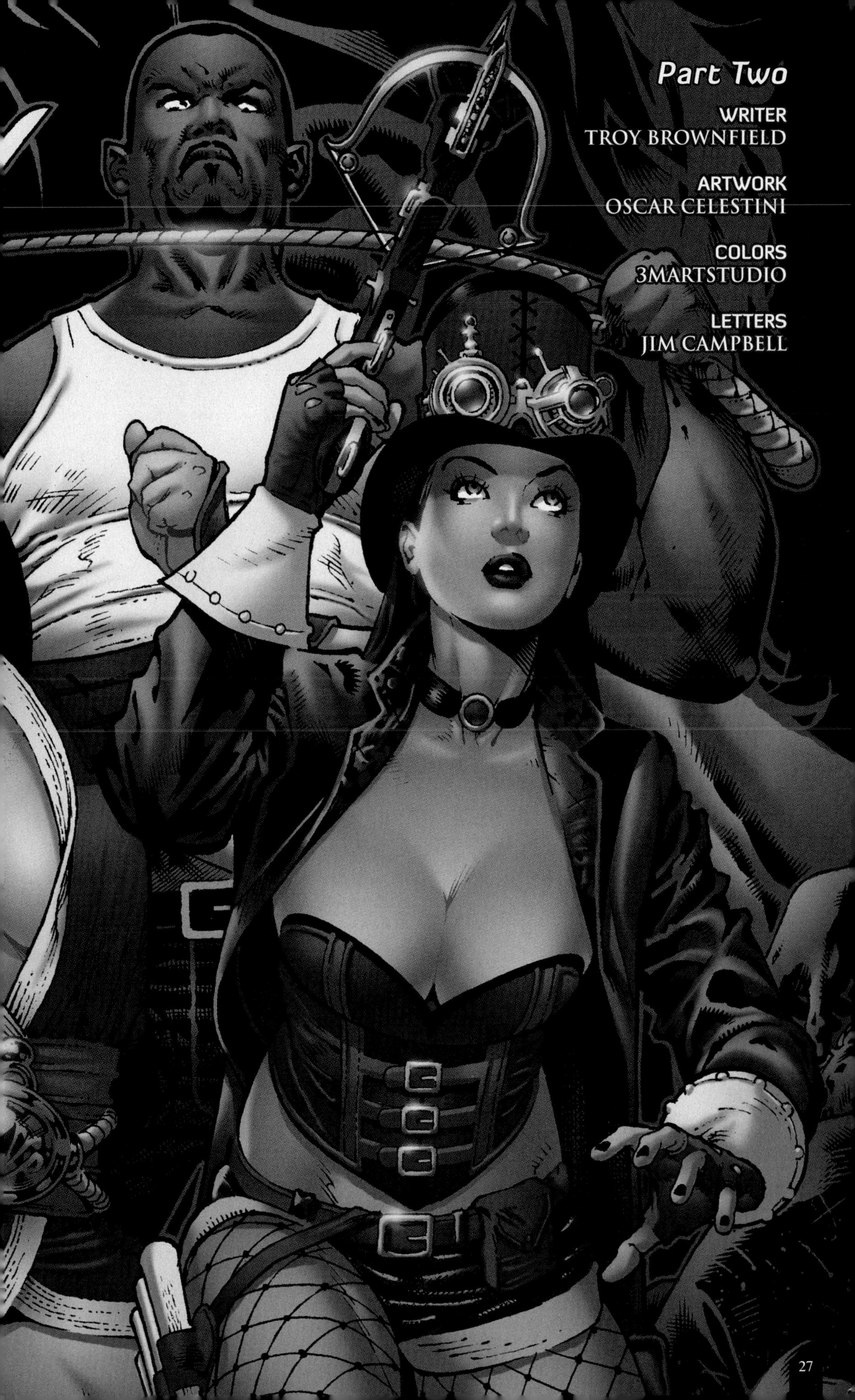

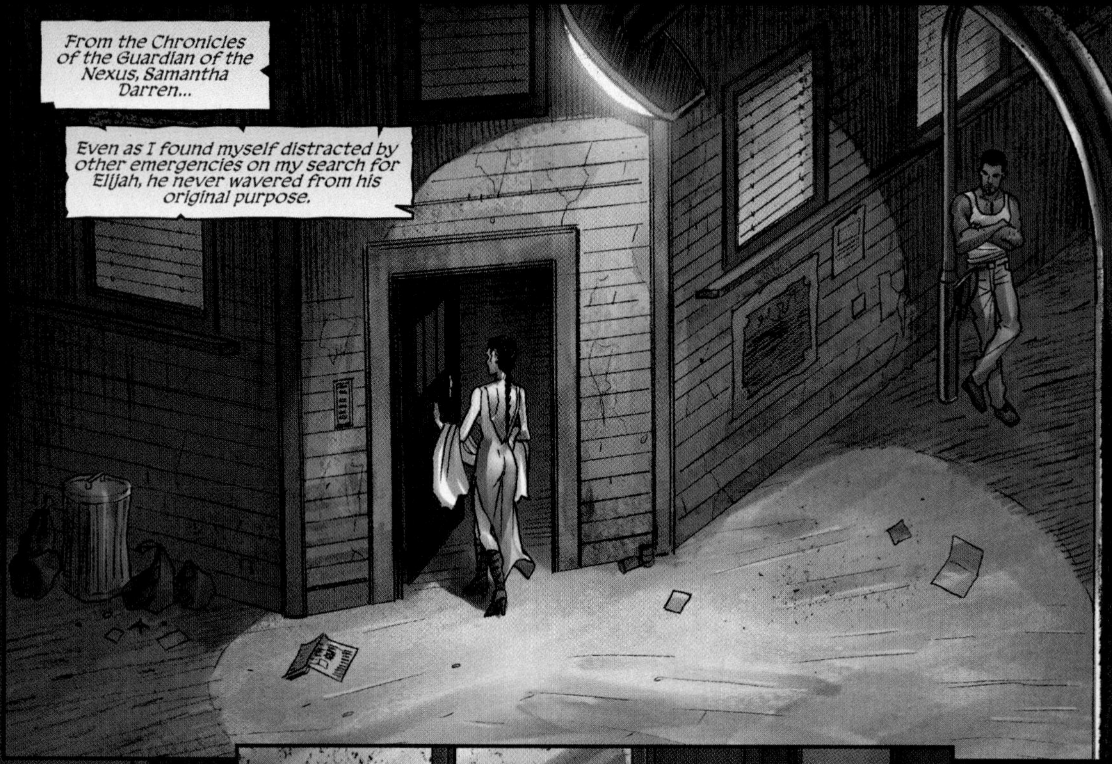
From the Chronicles of the Guardian of the Nexus, Samantha Darren...
Even as I found myself distracted by other emergencies on my search for Elijah, he never wavered from his original purpose.

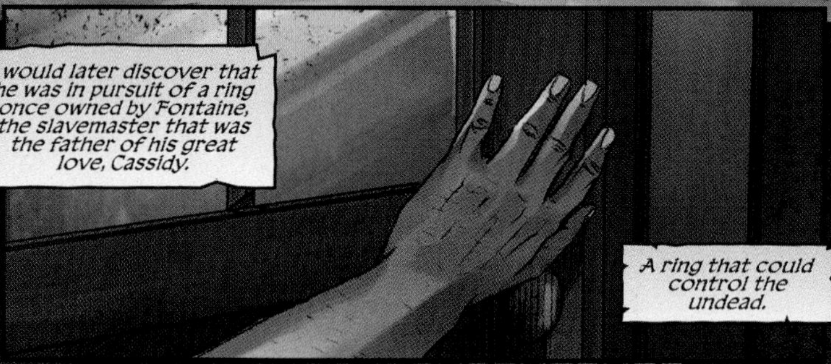
I would later discover that he was in pursuit of a ring once owned by Fontaine, the slavemaster that was the father of his great love, Cassidy.
A ring that could control the undead.

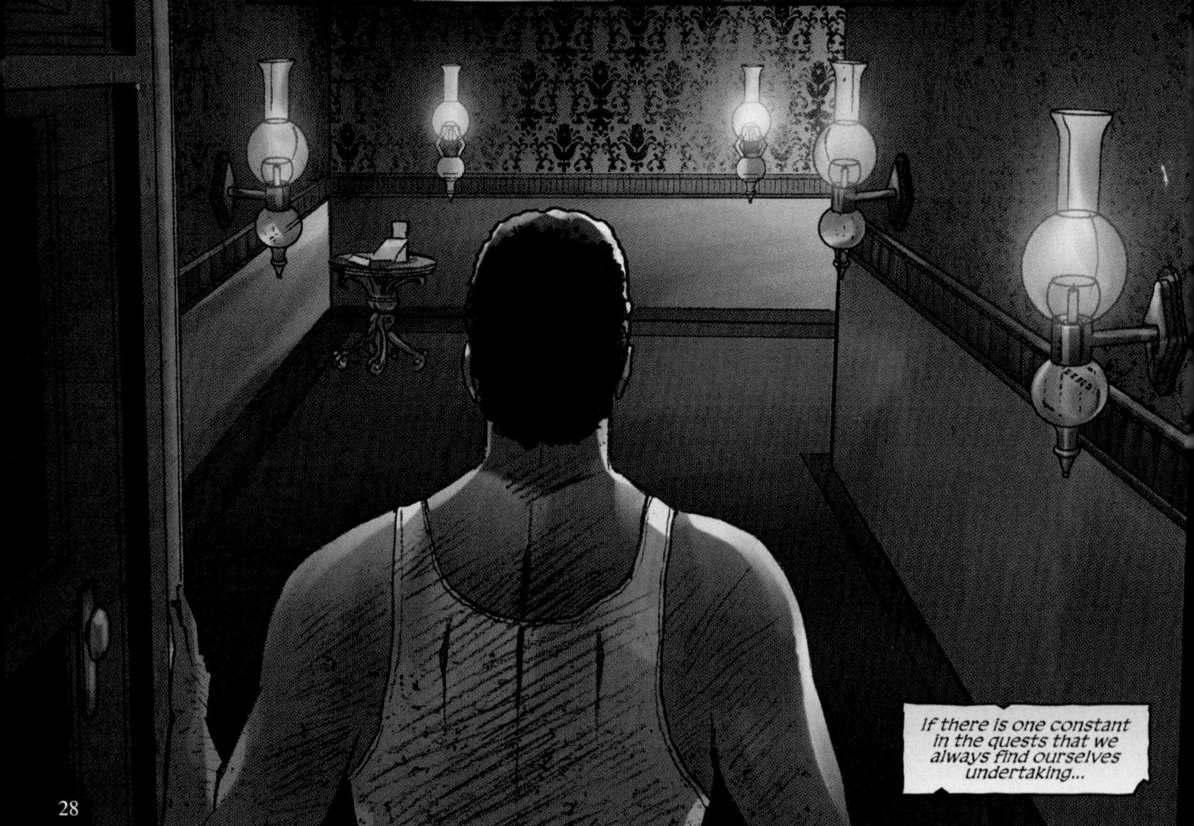
If there is one constant in the quests that we always find ourselves undertaking...

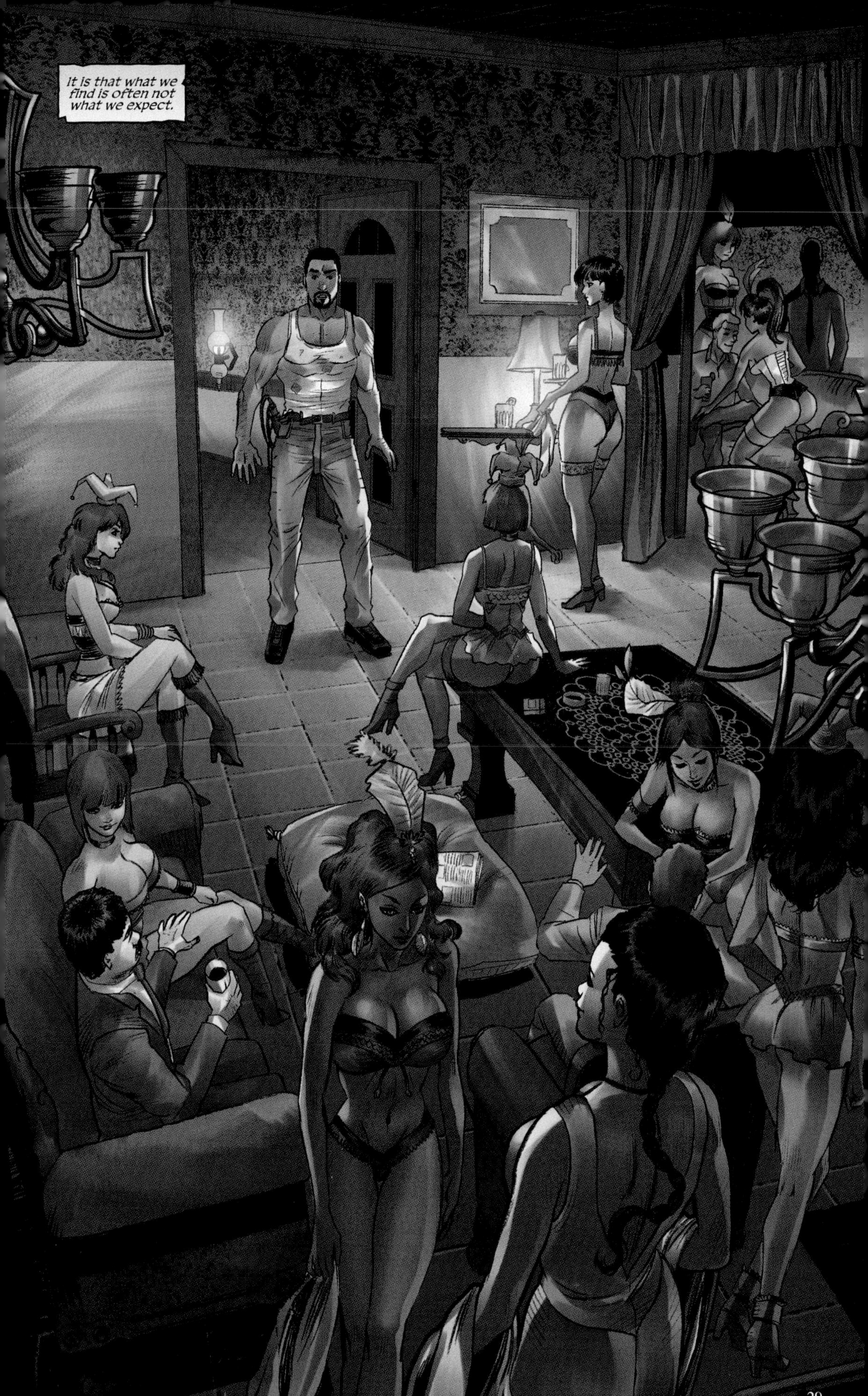
It is that what we find is often not what we expect.

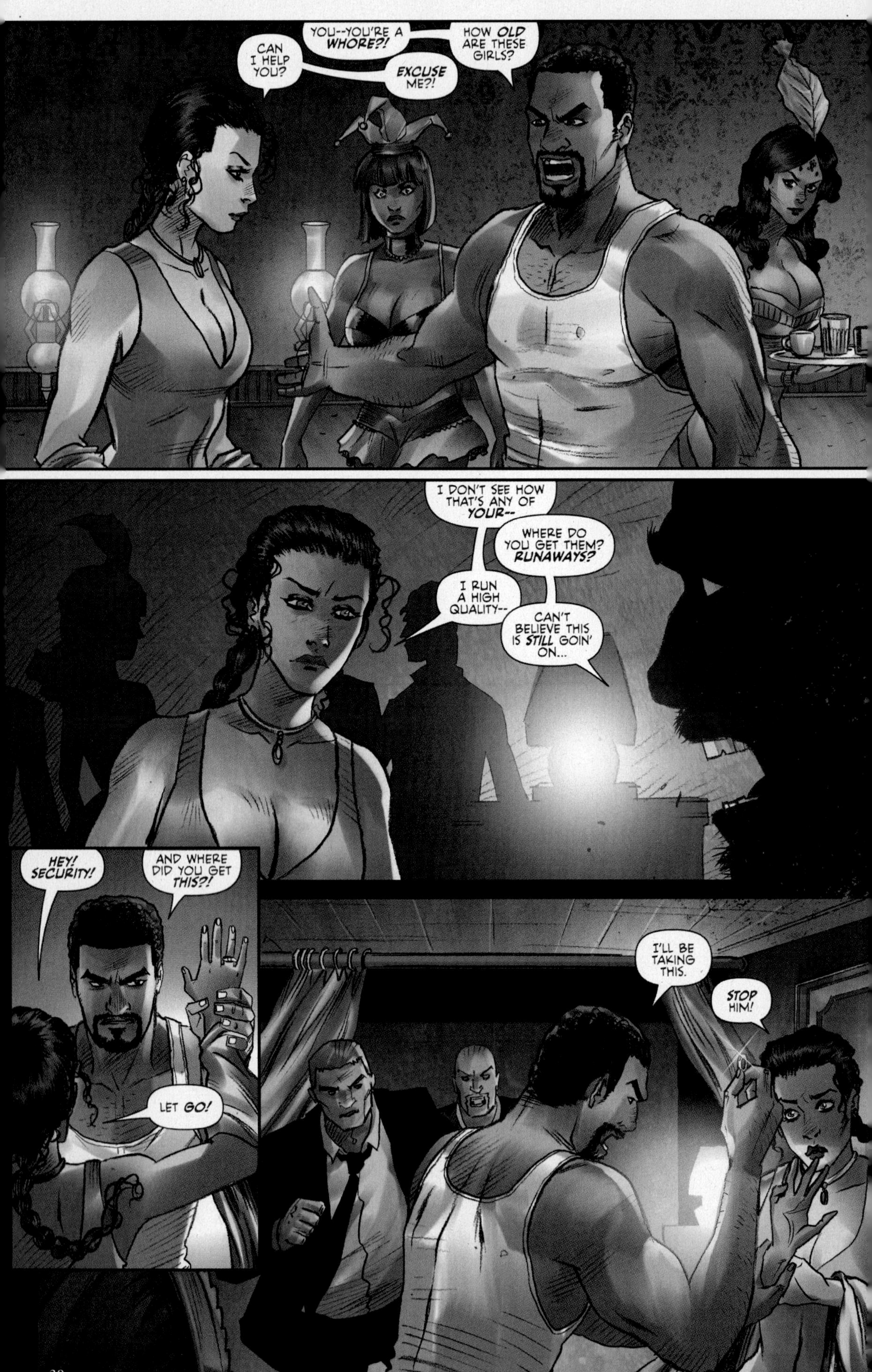

CAN I HELP YOU?
YOU--YOU'RE A WHORE?!
EXCUSE ME?!
HOW OLD ARE THESE GIRLS?
I DON'T SEE HOW THAT'S ANY OF YOUR--
WHERE DO YOU GET THEM? RUNAWAYS?
I RUN A HIGH QUALITY--
CAN'T BELIEVE THIS IS STILL GOIN' ON...
HEY! SECURITY!
AND WHERE DID YOU GET THIS?!
LET GO!
I'LL BE TAKING THIS.
STOP HIM!

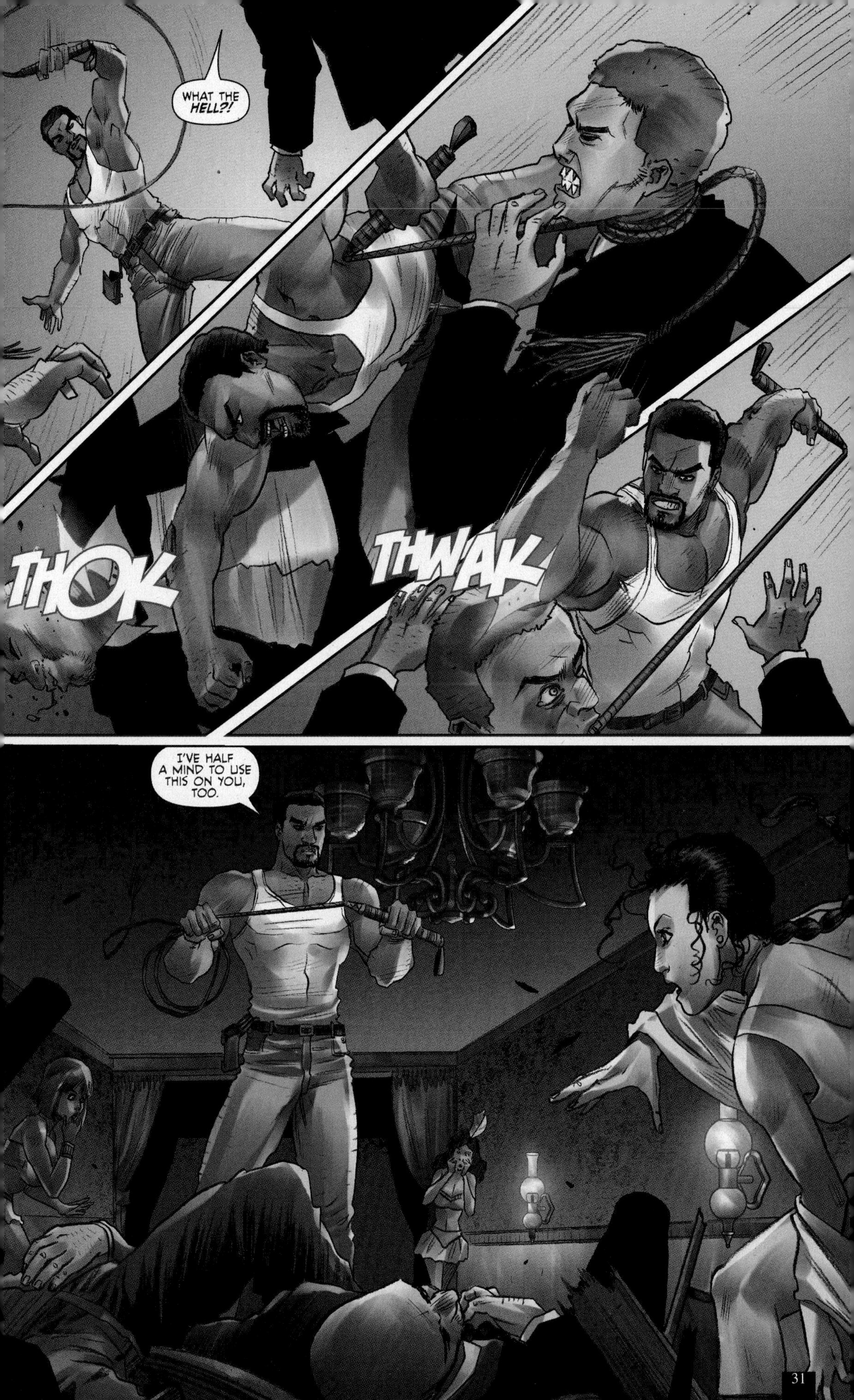
WHAT THE HELL?!
THOK
THWAK
I'VE HALF A MIND TO USE THIS ON YOU, TOO.

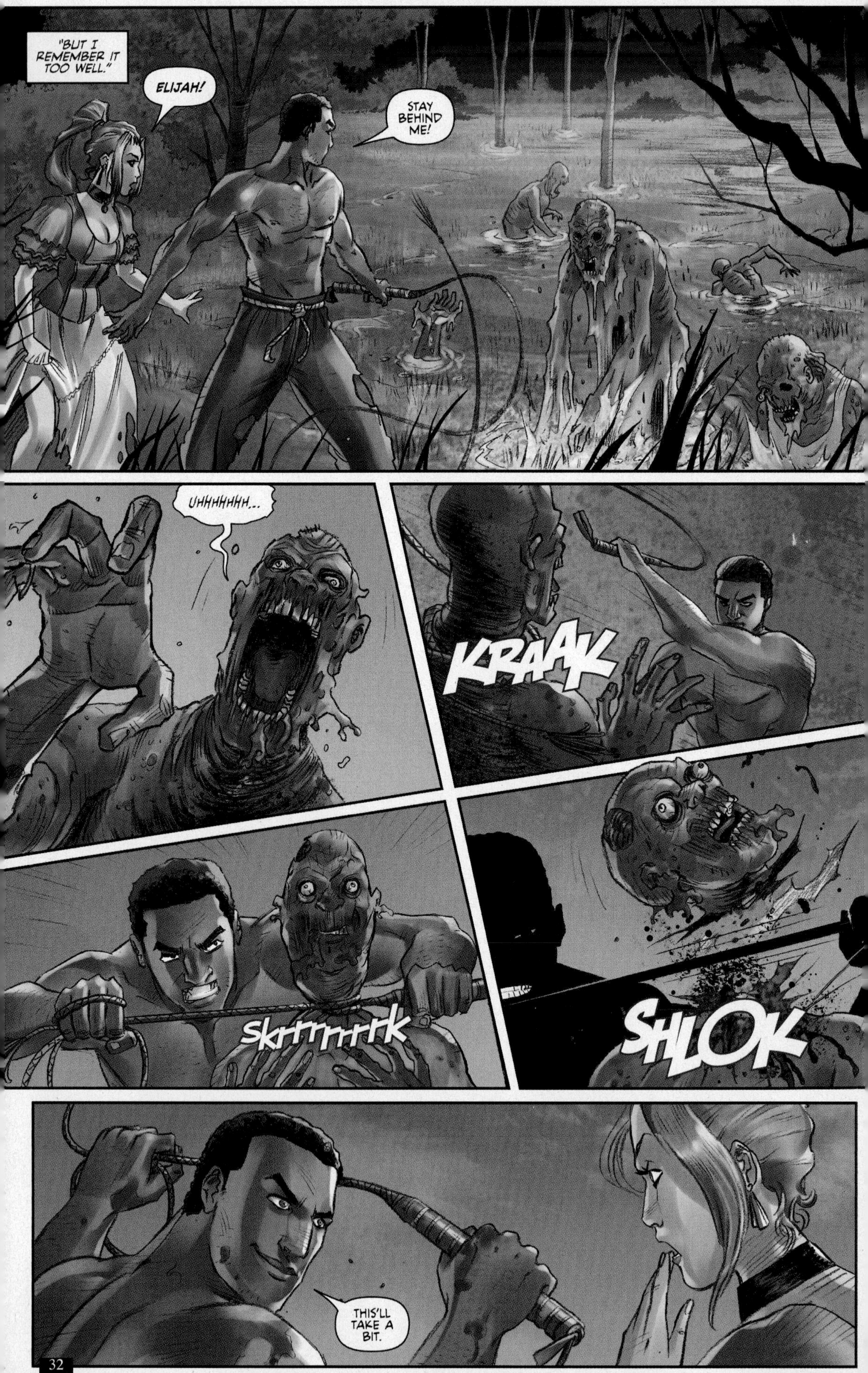
"BUT I REMEMBER IT TOO WELL."
ELIJAH!
STAY BEHIND ME!
UHHHHHHH...
KRAAK
SKRRRRRRK
SHLOK
THIS'LL TAKE A BIT.

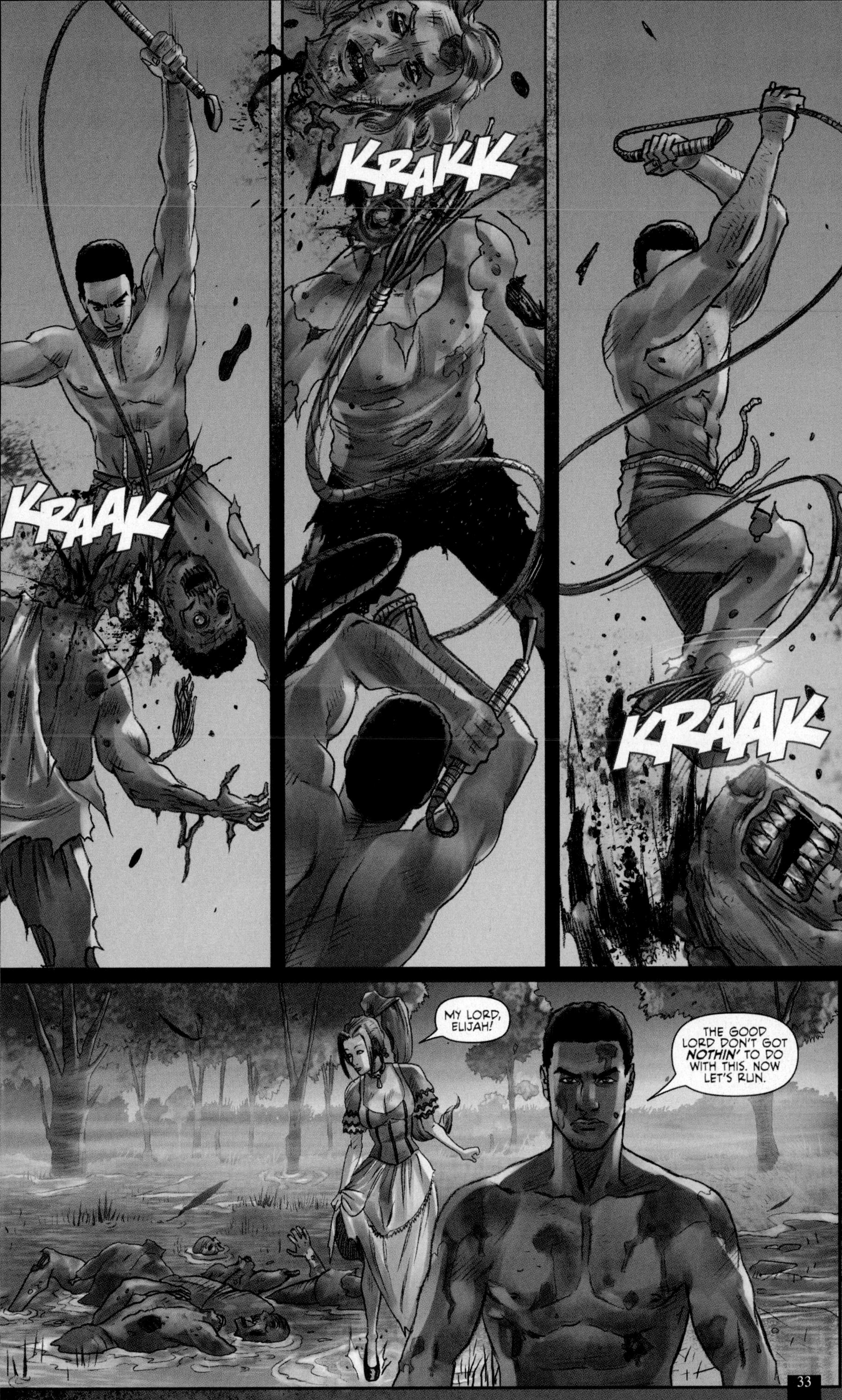
KRAAK
KRAKK
KRAAK
MY LORD, ELIJAH!
THE GOOD LORD DON'T GOT NOTHIN' TO DO WITH THIS. NOW LET'S RUN.

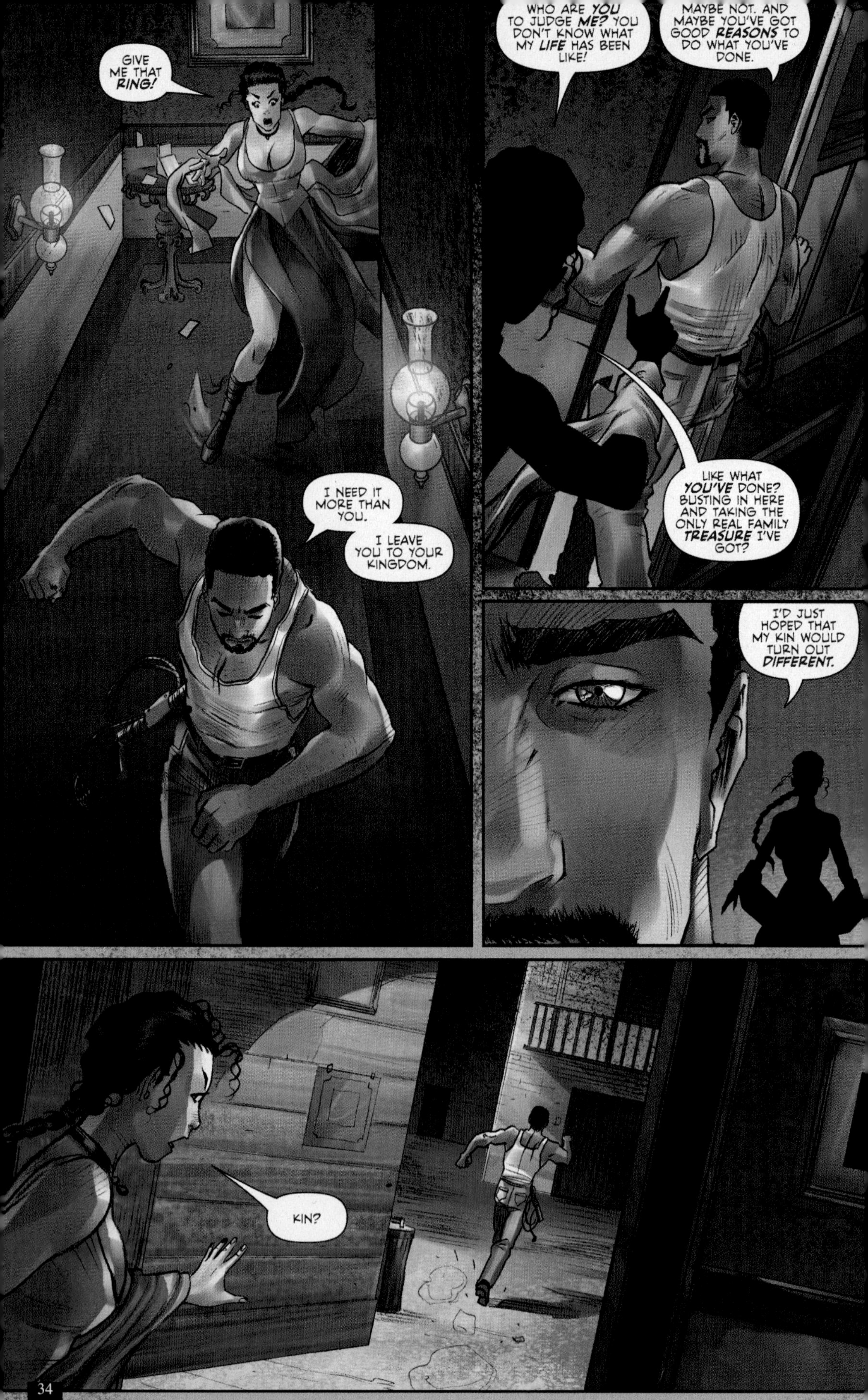
GIVE ME THAT RING!
I NEED IT MORE THAN YOU.
I LEAVE YOU TO YOUR KINGDOM.
WHO ARE YOU TO JUDGE ME? YOU DON'T KNOW WHAT MY LIFE HAS BEEN LIKE!
MAYBE NOT. AND MAYBE YOU'VE GOT GOOD REASONS TO DO WHAT YOU'VE DONE.
LIKE WHAT YOU'VE DONE? BUSTING IN HERE AND TAKING THE ONLY REAL FAMILY TREASURE I'VE GOT?
I'D JUST HOPED THAT MY KIN WOULD TURN OUT DIFFERENT.
KIN?

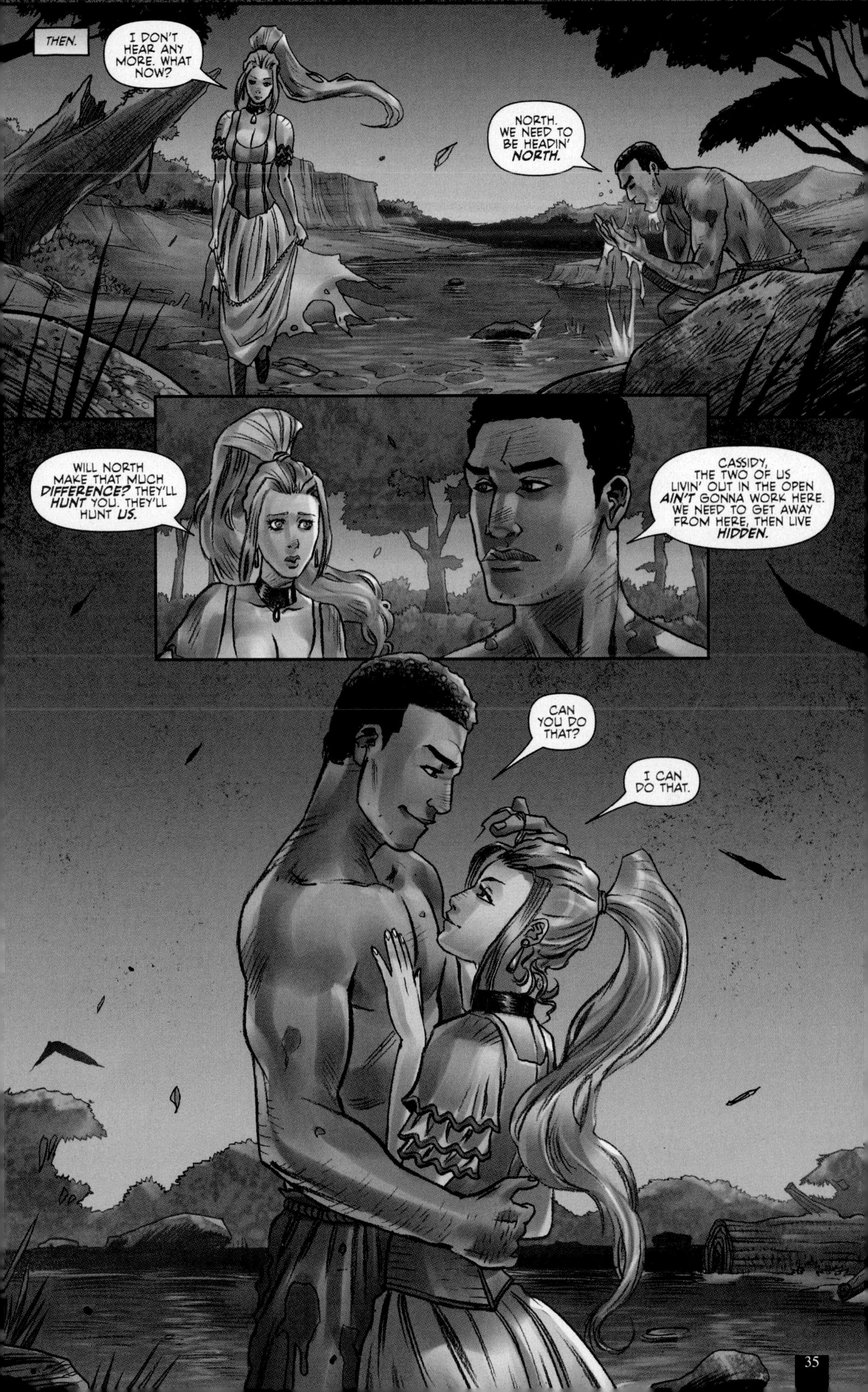
THEN.
I DON'T HEAR ANY MORE. WHAT NOW?
NORTH. WE NEED TO BE HEADIN' NORTH.
WILL NORTH MAKE THAT MUCH DIFFERENCE? THEY'LL HUNT YOU. THEY'LL HUNT US.
CASSIDY, THE TWO OF US LIVIN' OUT IN THE OPEN AIN'T GONNA WORK HERE. WE NEED TO GET AWAY FROM HERE, THEN LIVE HIDDEN.
CAN YOU DO THAT?
I CAN DO THAT.

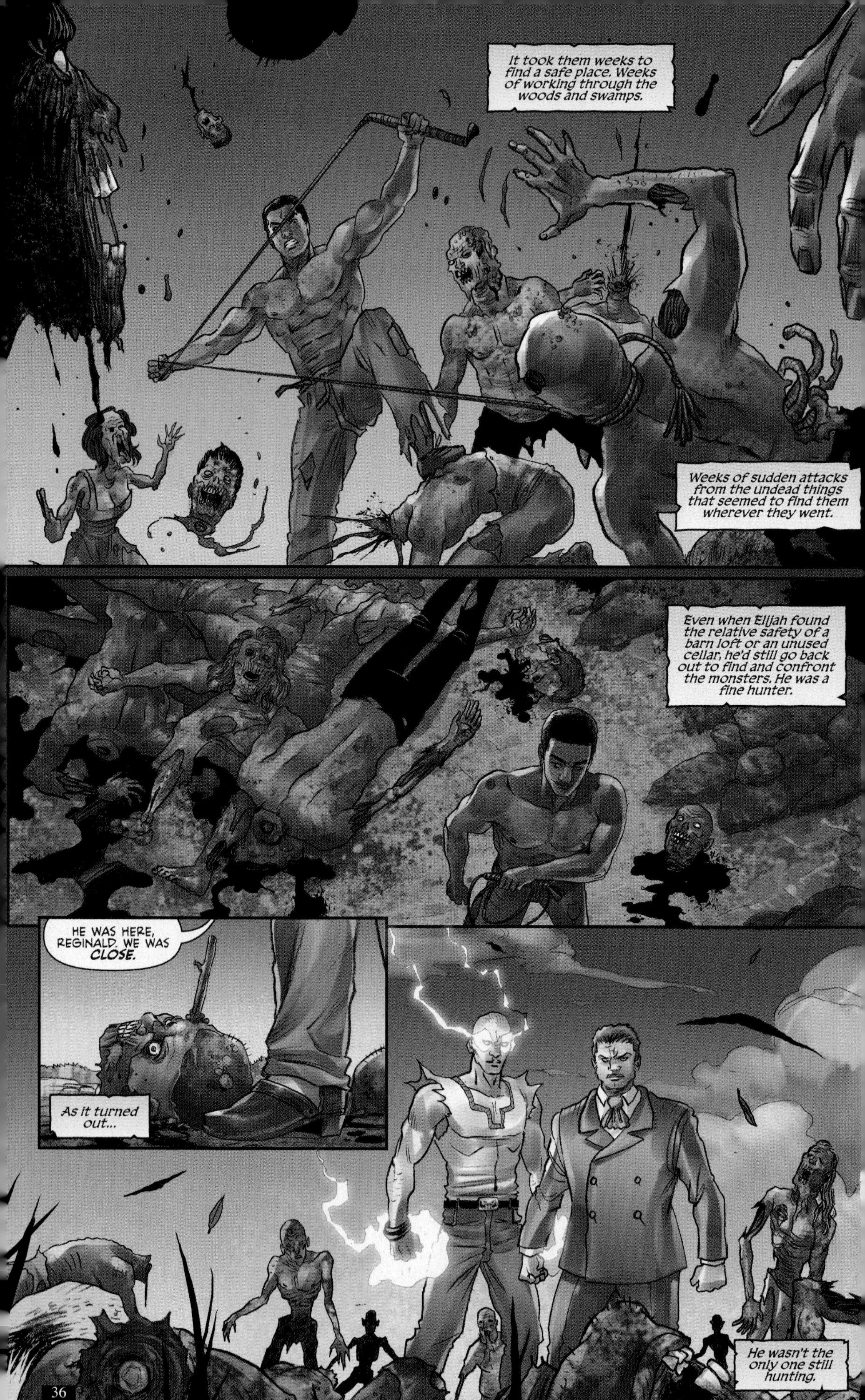
It took them weeks to find a safe place. Weeks of working through the woods and swamps.
Weeks of sudden attacks from the undead things that seemed to find them wherever they went.
Even when Elijah found the relative safety of a barn loft or an unused cellar, he'd still go back out to find and confront the monsters. He was a fine hunter.
HE WAS HERE, REGINALD. WE WAS CLOSE.
As it turned out...
He wasn't the only one still hunting.

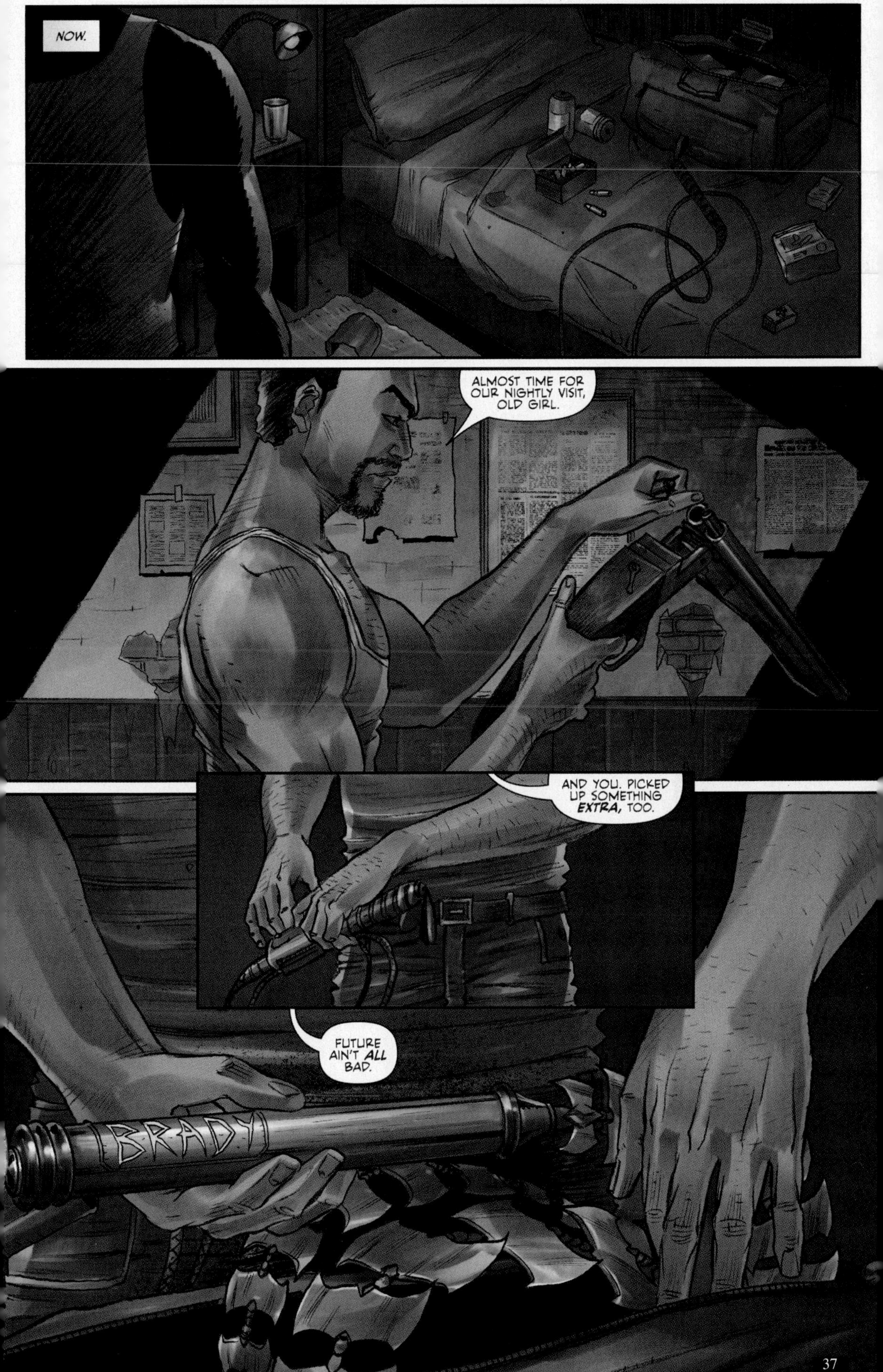
NOW.
ALMOST TIME FOR OUR NIGHTLY VISIT, OLD GIRL.
AND YOU. PICKED UP SOMETHING EXTRA, TOO.
FUTURE AIN'T ALL BAD.
BRADY

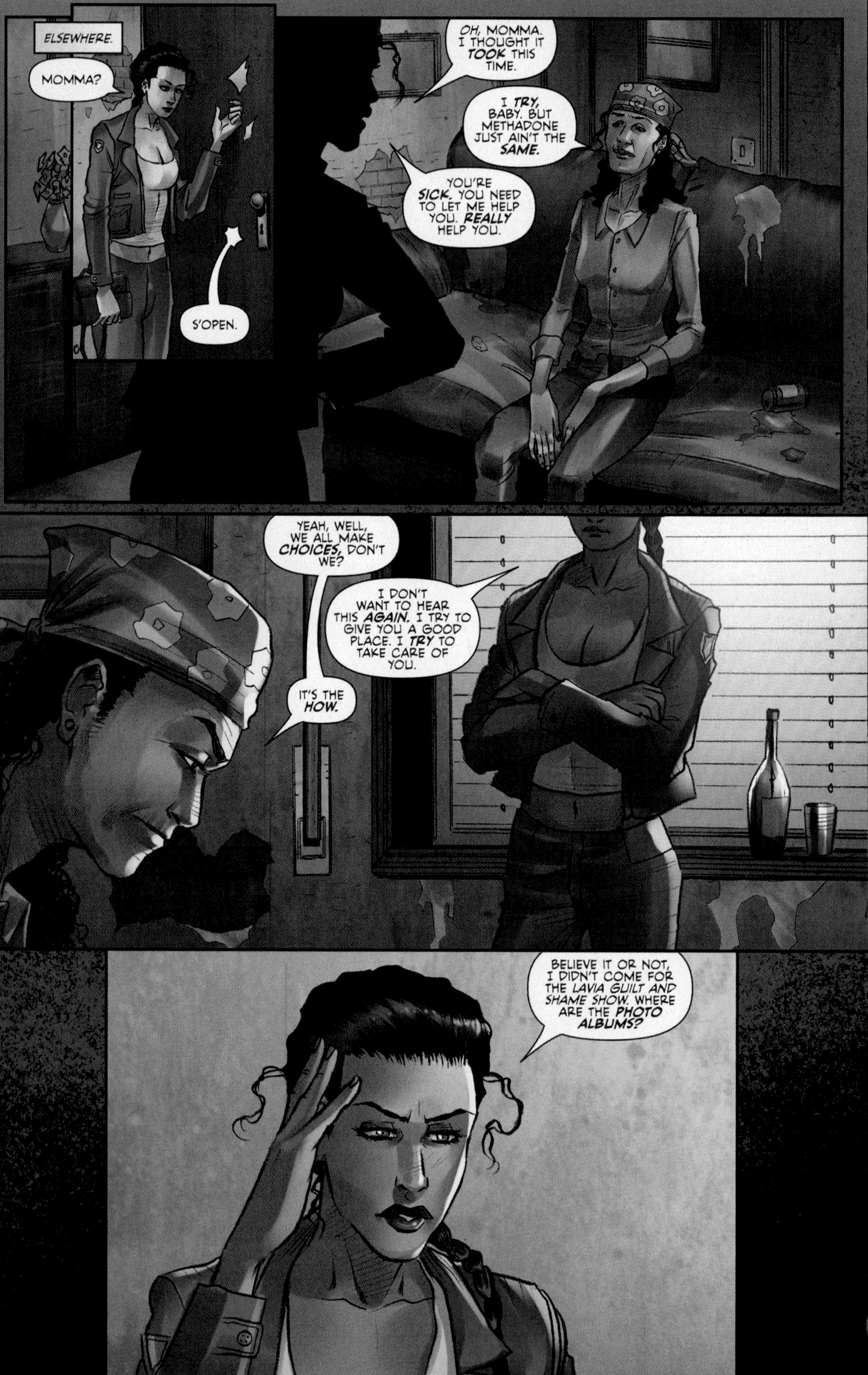

ELSEWHERE.
MOMMA?
S'OPEN.
OH, MOMMA. I THOUGHT IT TOOK THIS TIME.
I TRY, BABY. BUT METHADONE JUST AIN'T THE SAME.
YOU'RE SICK. YOU NEED TO LET ME HELP YOU. REALLY HELP YOU.
YEAH, WELL, WE ALL MAKE CHOICES, DON'T WE?
I DON'T WANT TO HEAR THIS AGAIN. I TRY TO GIVE YOU A GOOD PLACE. I TRY TO TAKE CARE OF YOU.
IT'S THE HOW.
BELIEVE IT OR NOT, I DIDN'T COME FOR THE LAVIA GUILT AND SHAME SHOW. WHERE ARE THE PHOTO ALBUMS?

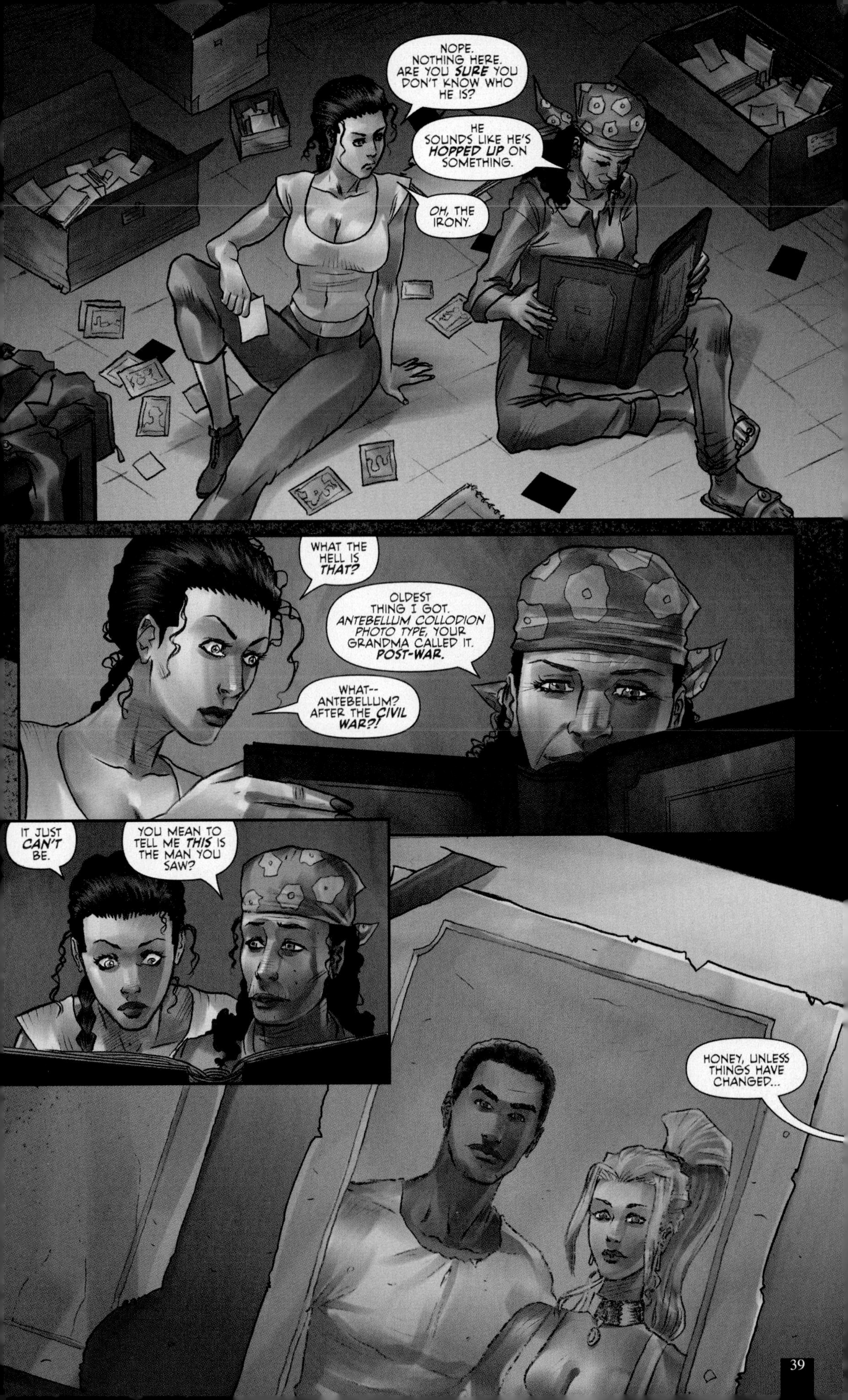

NOPE. NOTHING HERE. ARE YOU SURE YOU DON'T KNOW WHO HE IS?
HE SOUNDS LIKE HE'S HOPPED UP ON SOMETHING.
OH, THE IRONY.
WHAT THE HELL IS THAT?
OLDEST THING I GOT. ANTEBELLUM COLLODION PHOTO TYPE, YOUR GRANDMA CALLED IT. POST-WAR.
WHAT-- ANTEBELLUM? AFTER THE CIVIL WAR?!
IT JUST CAN'T BE.
YOU MEAN TO TELL ME THIS IS THE MAN YOU SAW?
HONEY, UNLESS THINGS HAVE CHANGED...

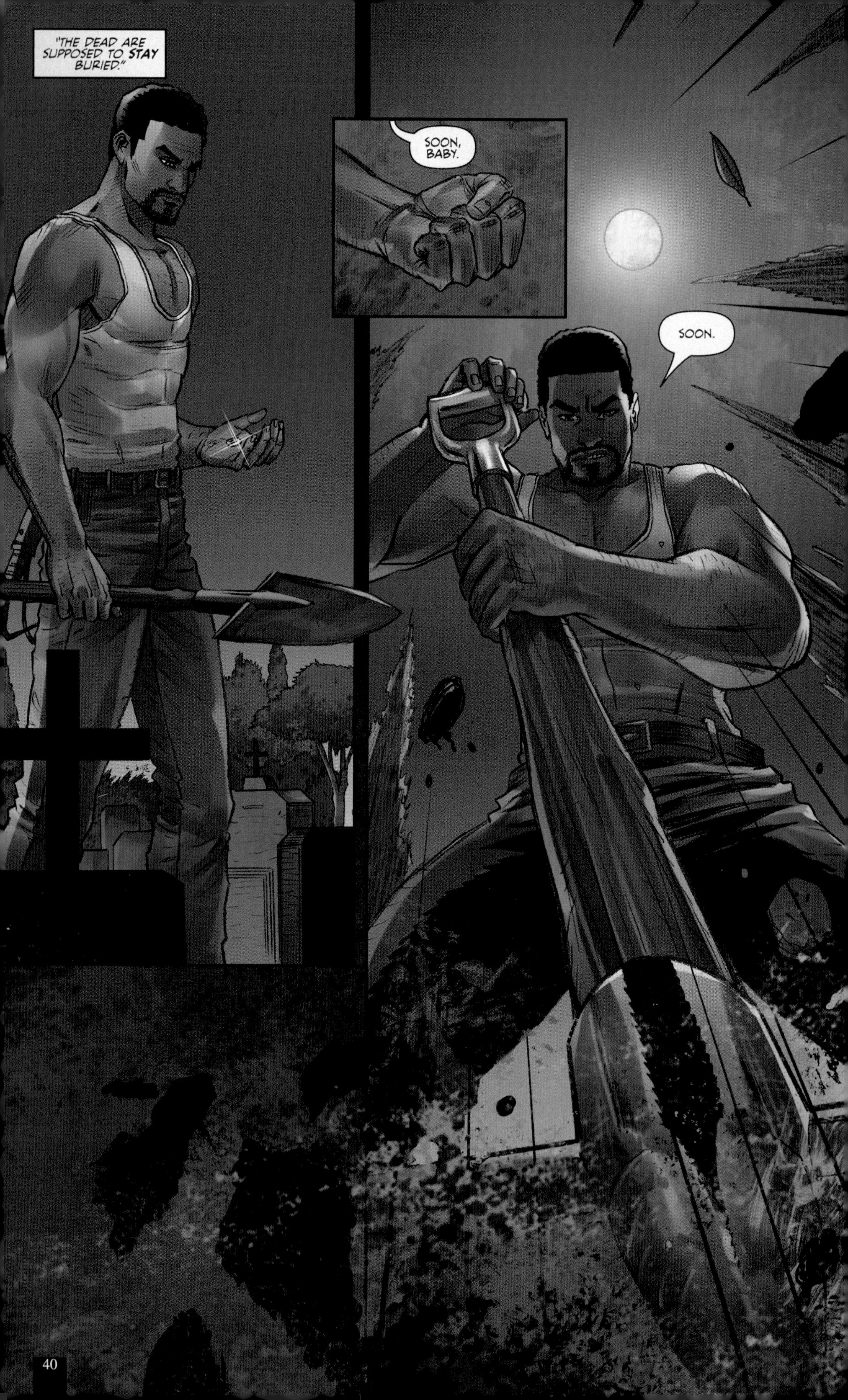
"THE DEAD ARE SUPPOSED TO STAY BURIED."
SOON, BABY.
SOON.

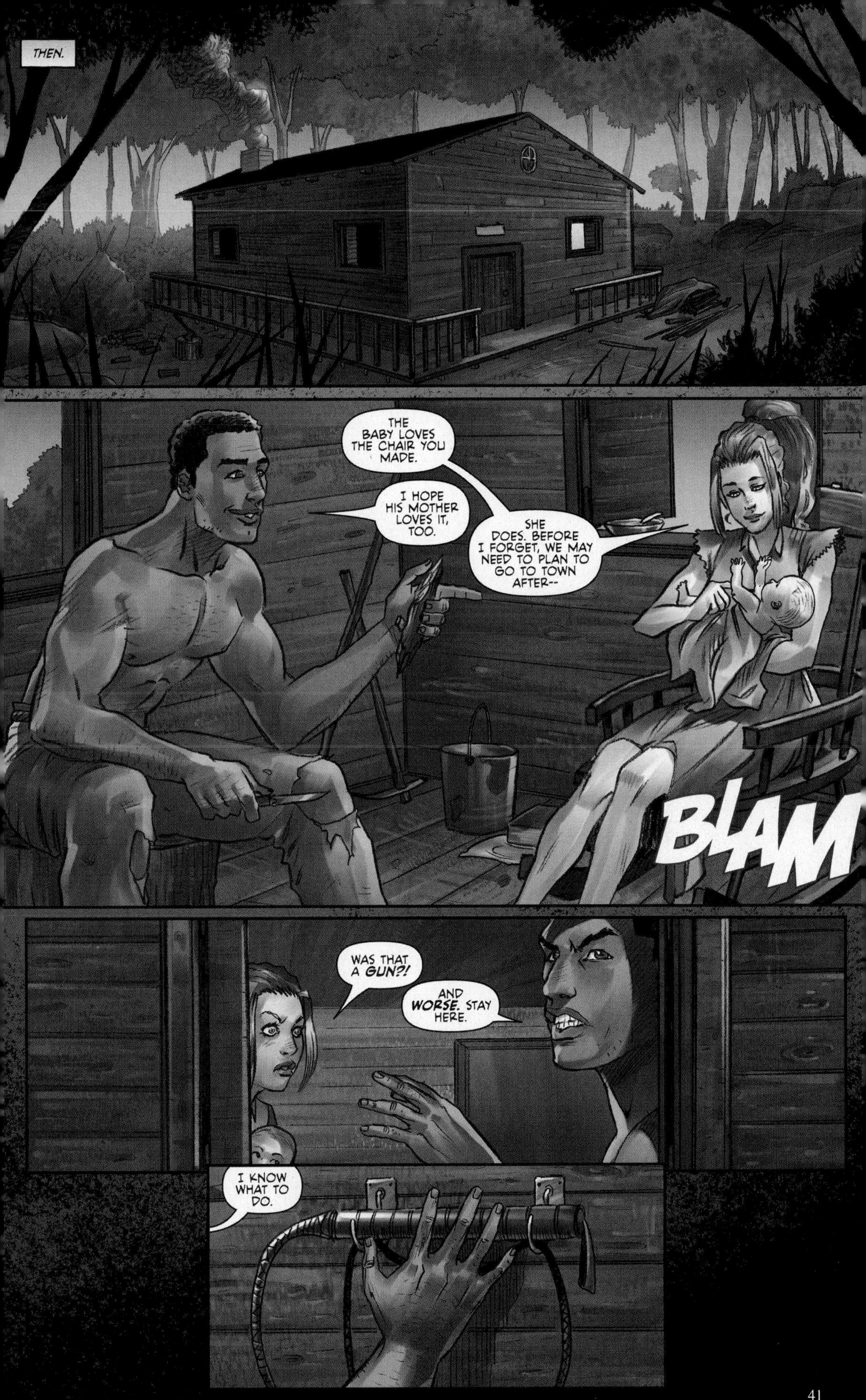
THEN.
THE BABY LOVES THE CHAIR YOU MADE.
I HOPE HIS MOTHER LOVES IT, TOO.
SHE DOES. BEFORE I FORGET, WE MAY NEED TO PLAN TO GO TO TOWN AFTER--
BLAM
WAS THAT A GUN?!
AND WORSE. STAY HERE.
I KNOW WHAT TO DO.

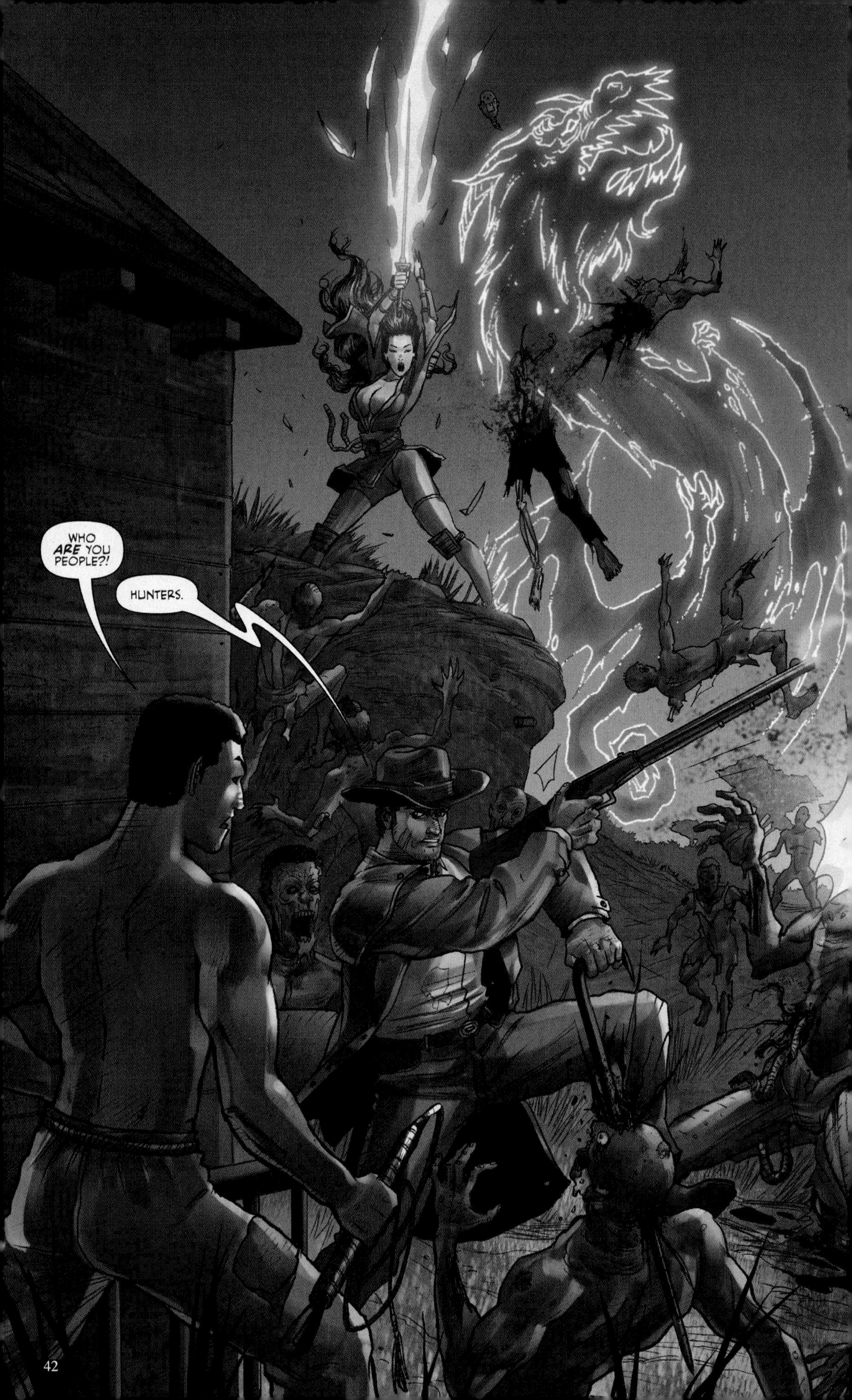
WHO *ARE* YOU PEOPLE?!
HUNTERS.

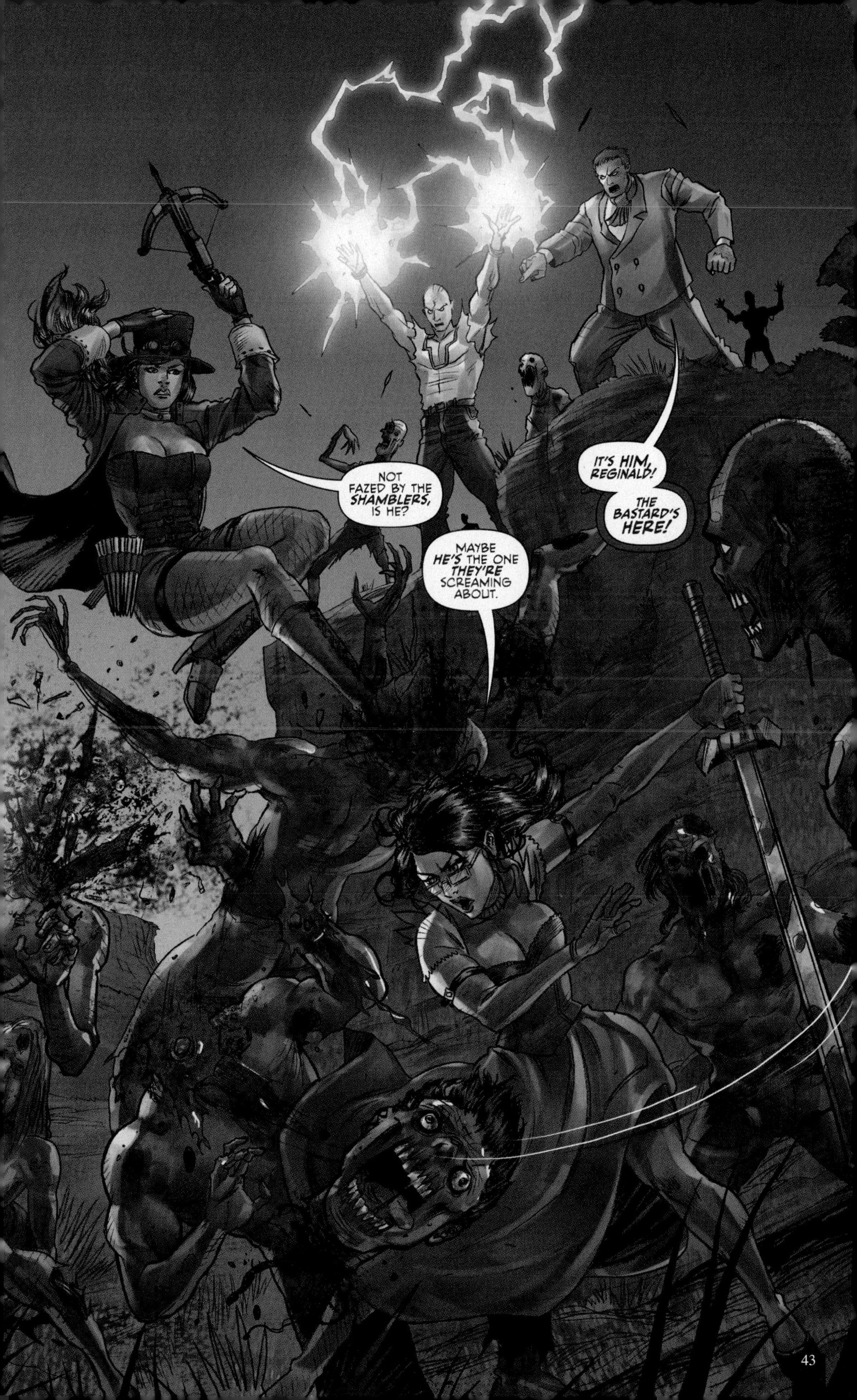
NOT FAZED BY THE SHAMBLERS, IS HE?
IT'S HIM, REGINALD!
THE BASTARD'S HERE!
MAYBE HE'S THE ONE THEY'RE SCREAMING ABOUT.

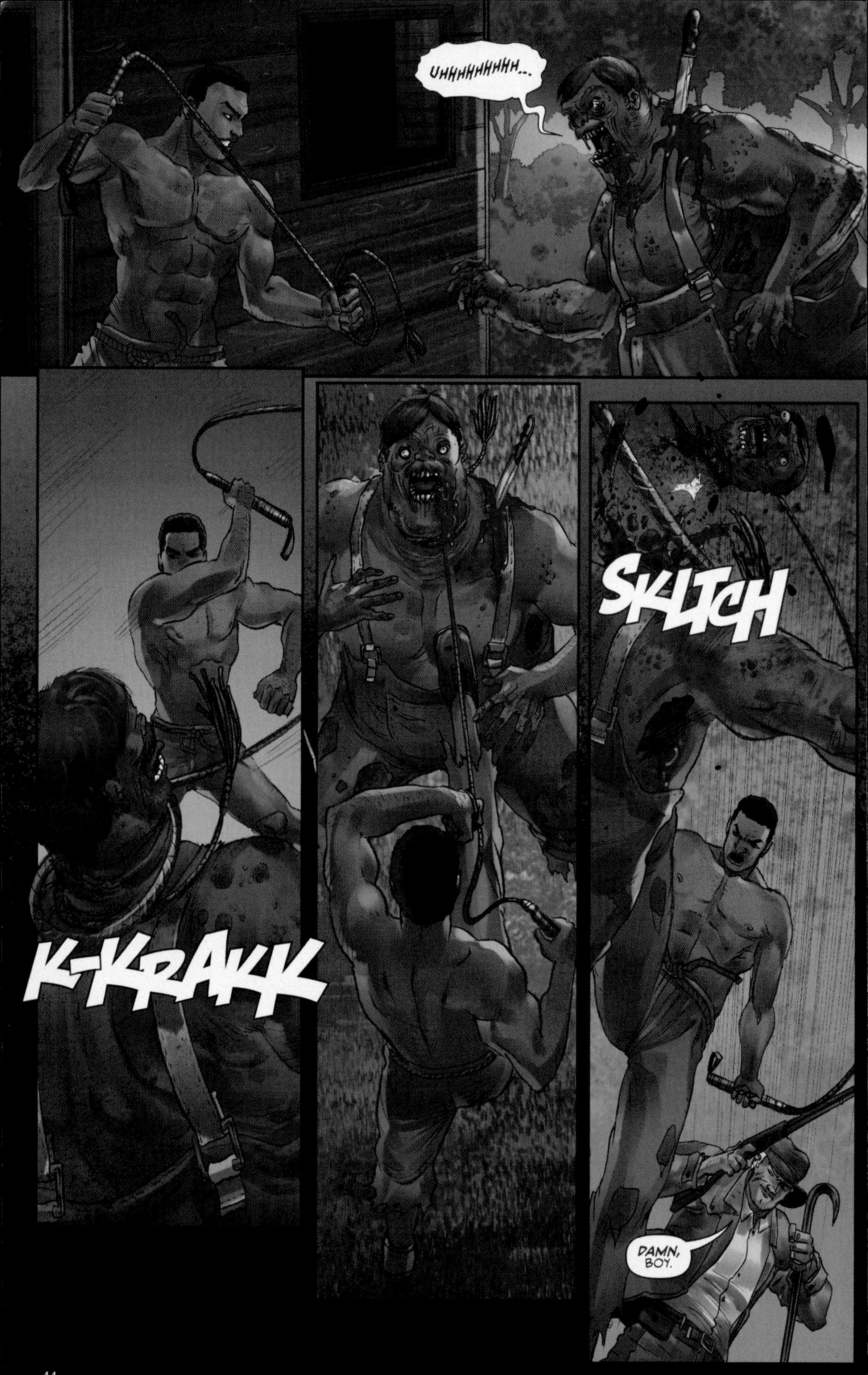
UHHHHHHHHH...
K-KRAKK
SKLTCH
DAMN, BOY.

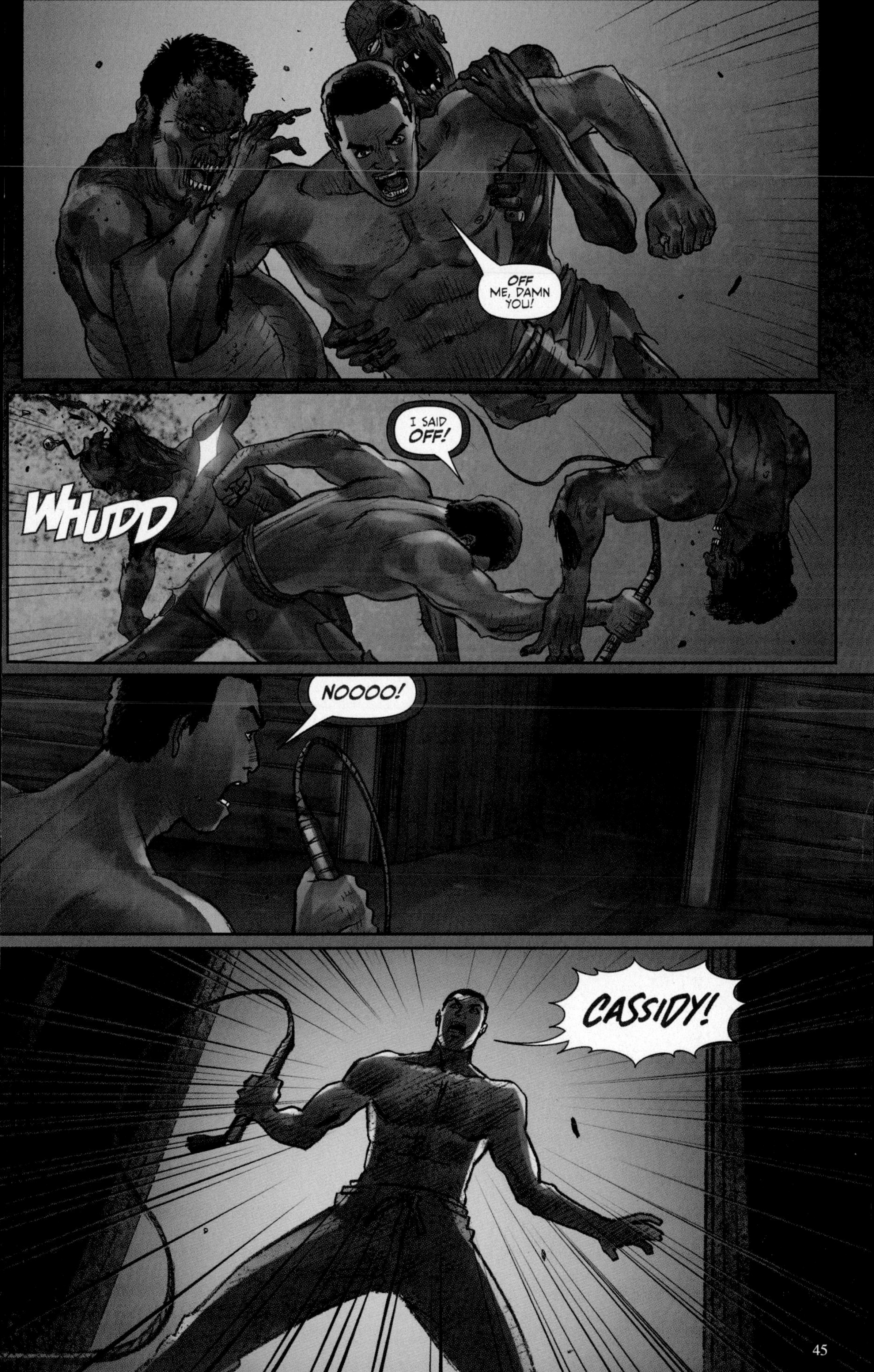
OFF ME, DAMN YOU!
WHUDD
I SAID OFF!
NOOOO!
CASSIDY!

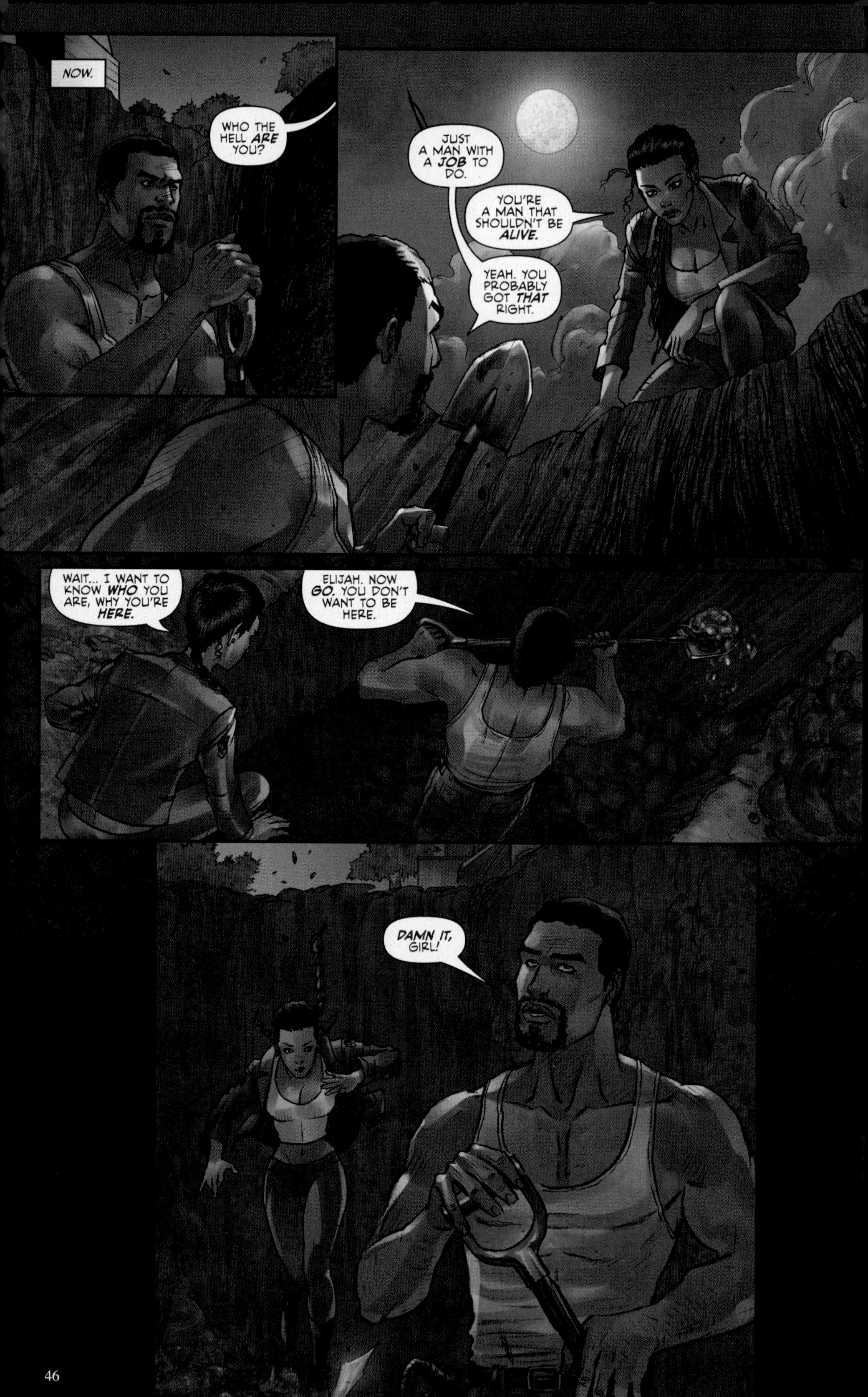
NOW.
WHO THE HELL ARE YOU?
JUST A MAN WITH A JOB TO DO.
YOU'RE A MAN THAT SHOULDN'T BE ALIVE.
YEAH. YOU PROBABLY GOT THAT RIGHT.
WAIT... I WANT TO KNOW WHO YOU ARE, WHY YOU'RE HERE.
ELIJAH. NOW GO. YOU DON'T WANT TO BE HERE.
DAMN IT, GIRL!

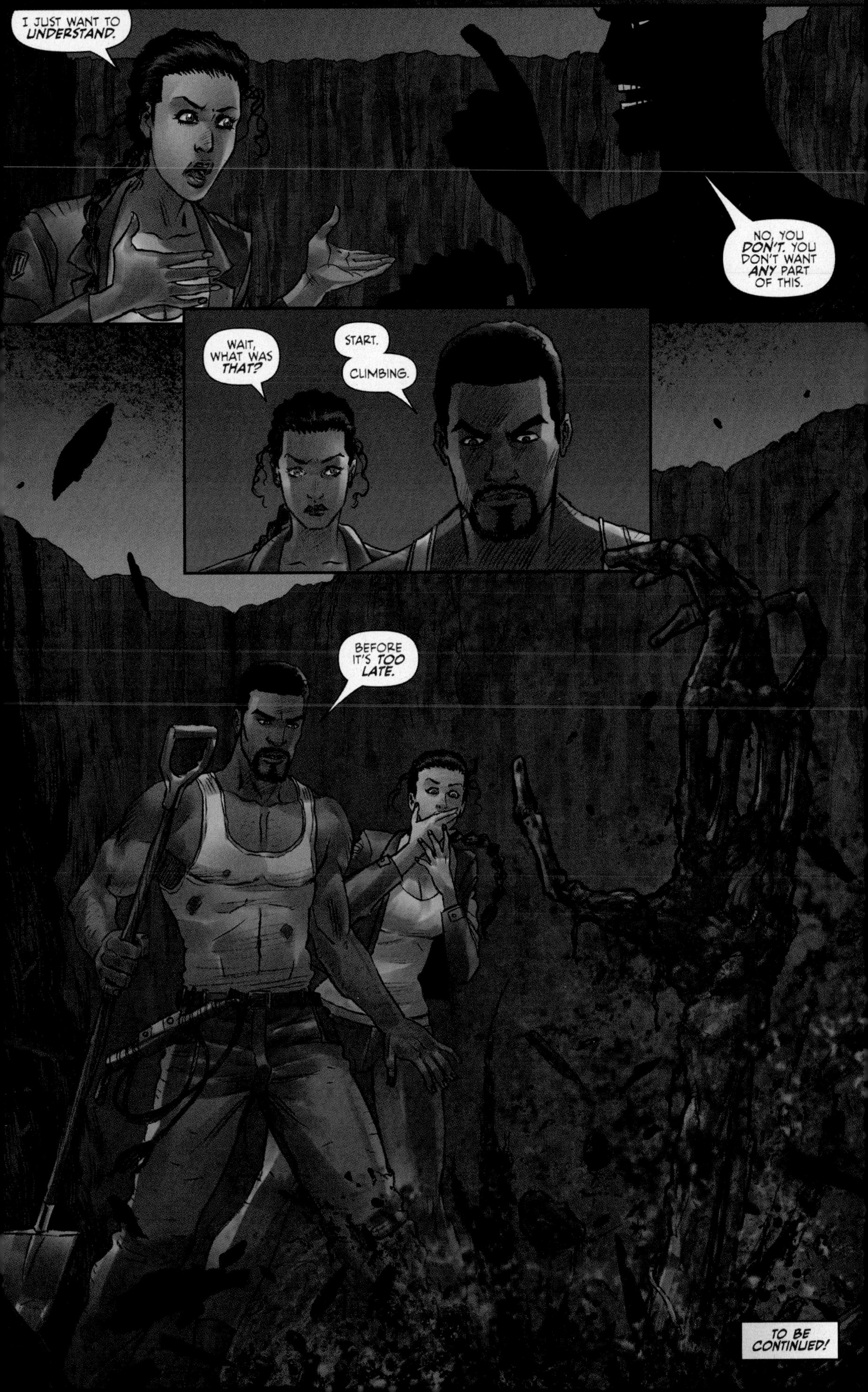
I JUST WANT TO *UNDERSTAND.*
NO, YOU *DON'T.* YOU DON'T WANT *ANY* PART OF THIS.
WAIT, WHAT WAS *THAT?*
START.
CLIMBING.
BEFORE IT'S *TOO LATE.*
TO BE CONTINUED!

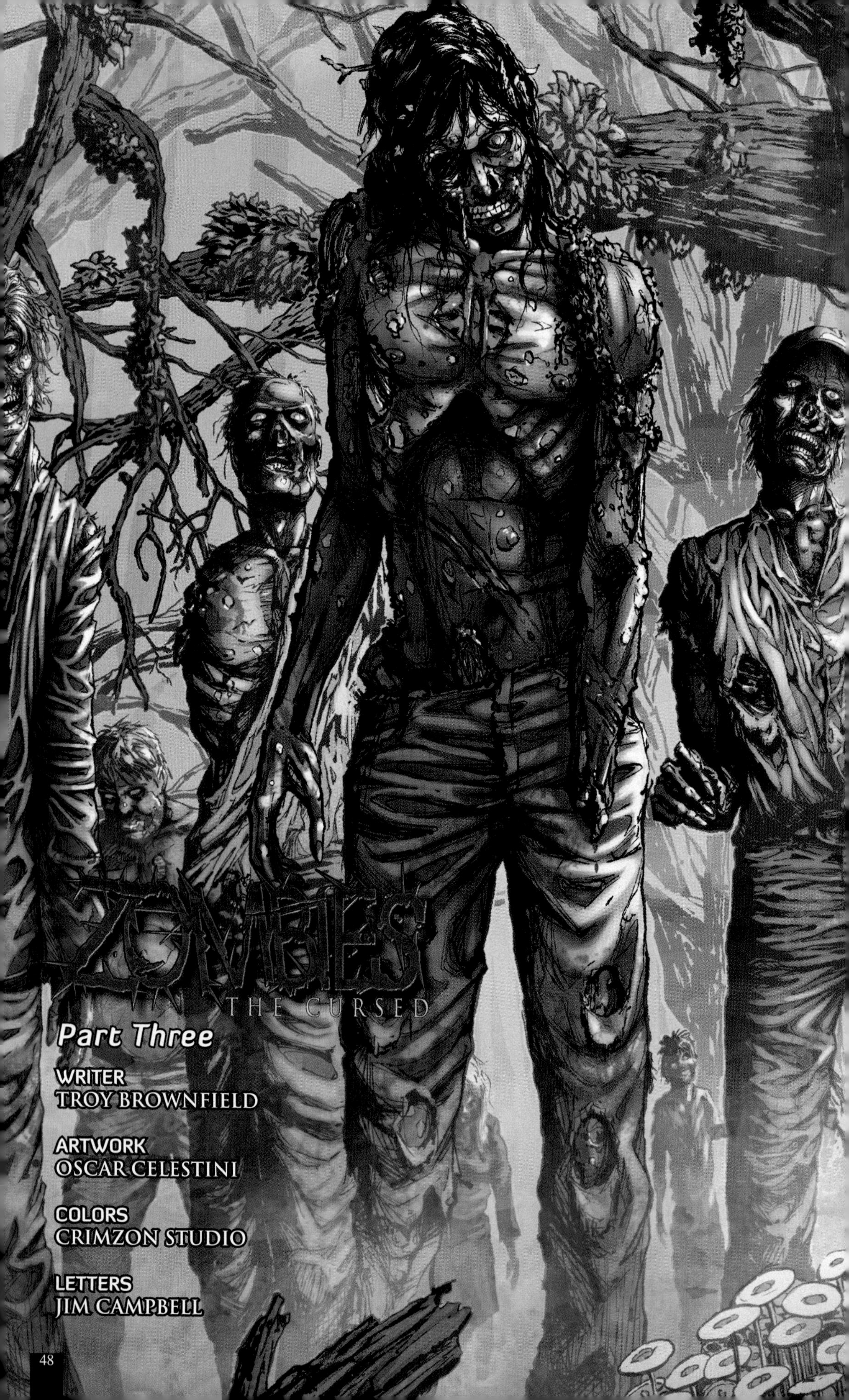
ZOMBIES
THE CURSED
Part Three
WRITER
TROY BROWNFIELD
ARTWORK
OSCAR CELESTINI
COLORS
CRIMZON STUDIO
LETTERS
JIM CAMPBELL

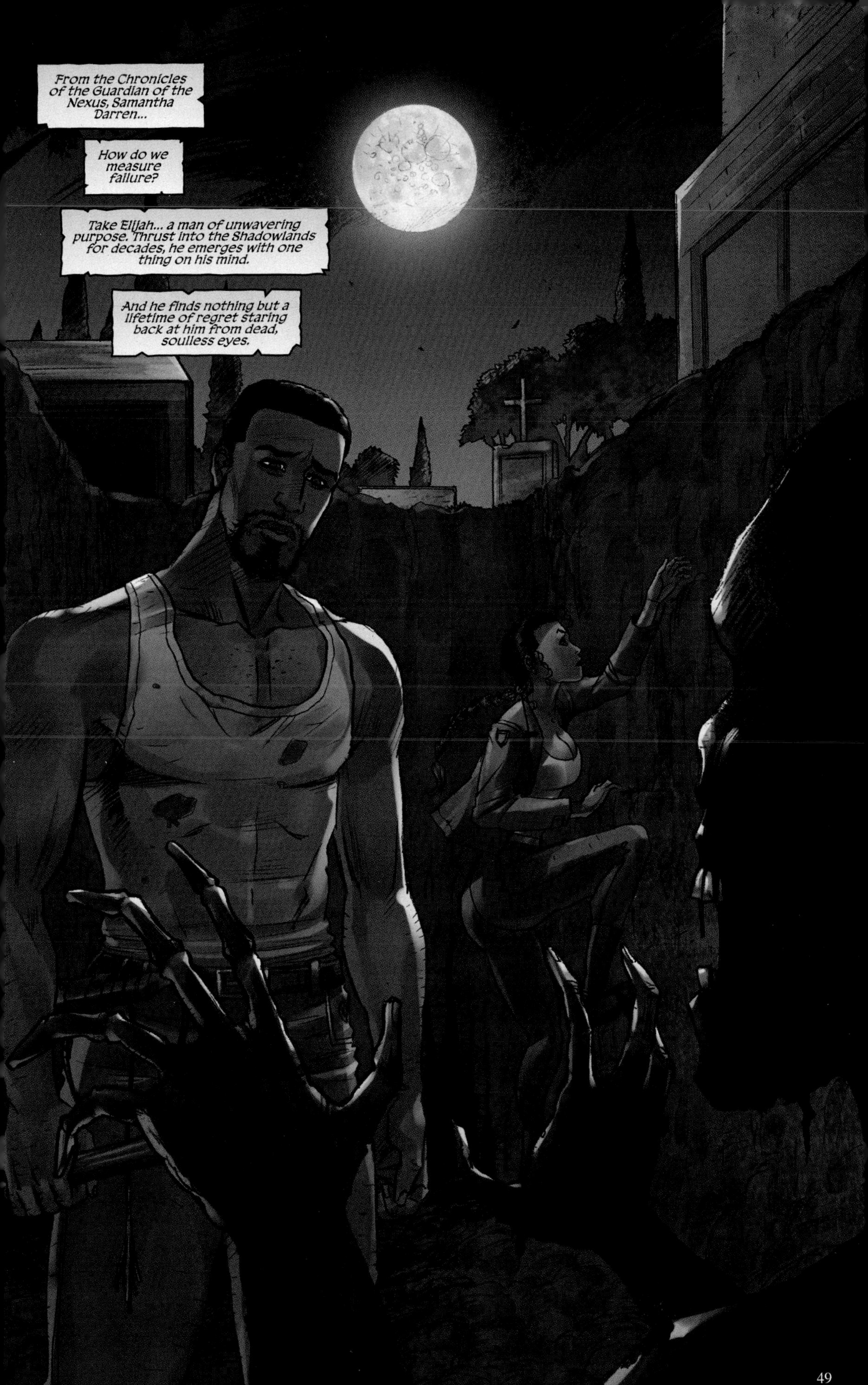
From the Chronicles of the Guardian of the Nexus, Samantha Darren...
How do we measure failure?
Take Elijah... a man of unwavering purpose. Thrust into the Shadowlands for decades, he emerges with one thing on his mind.
And he finds nothing but a lifetime of regret staring back at him from dead, soulless eyes.

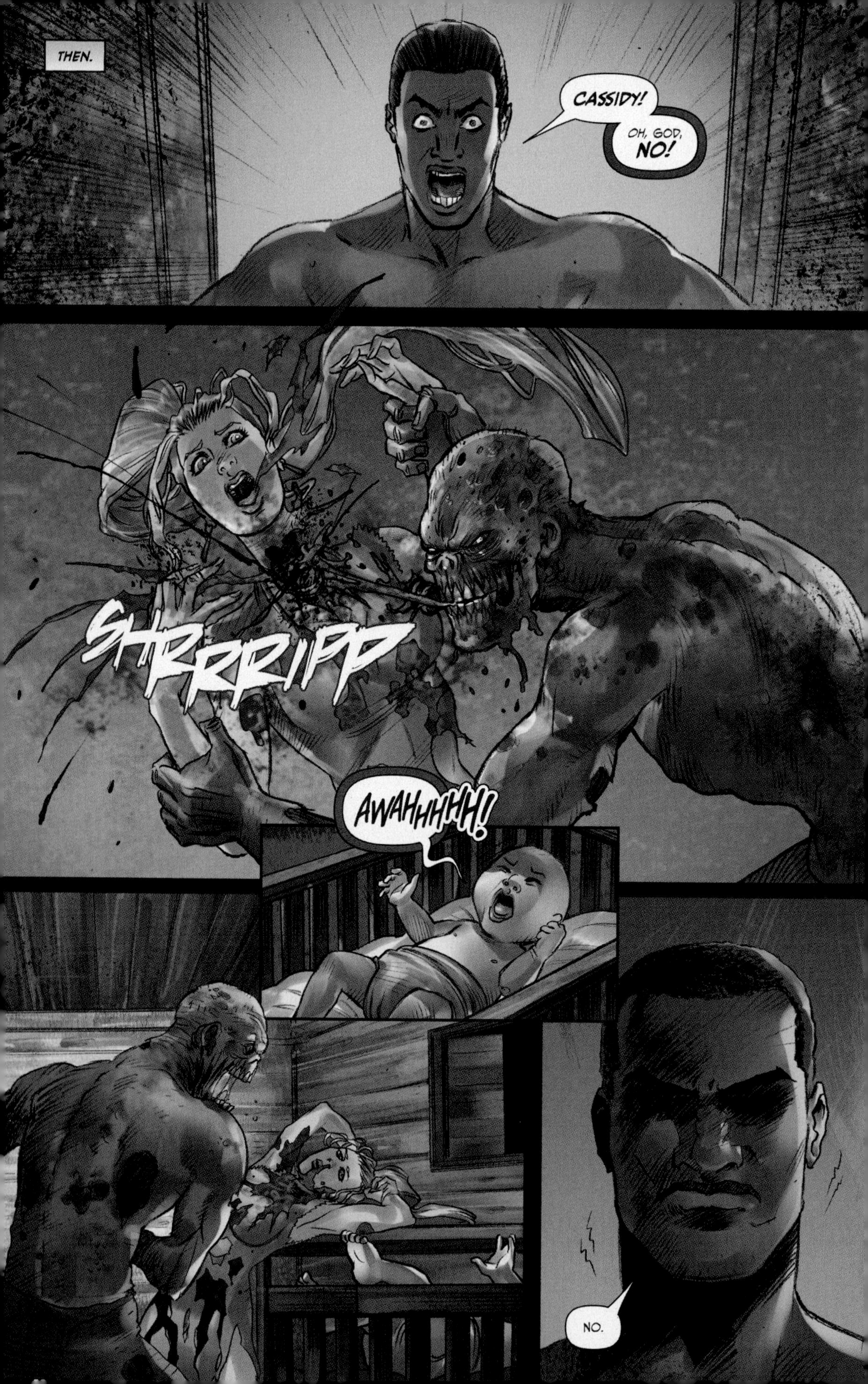
THEN.
CASSIDY!
OH, GOD, NO!
SHRRRIPP
AWAHHHHH!
NO.

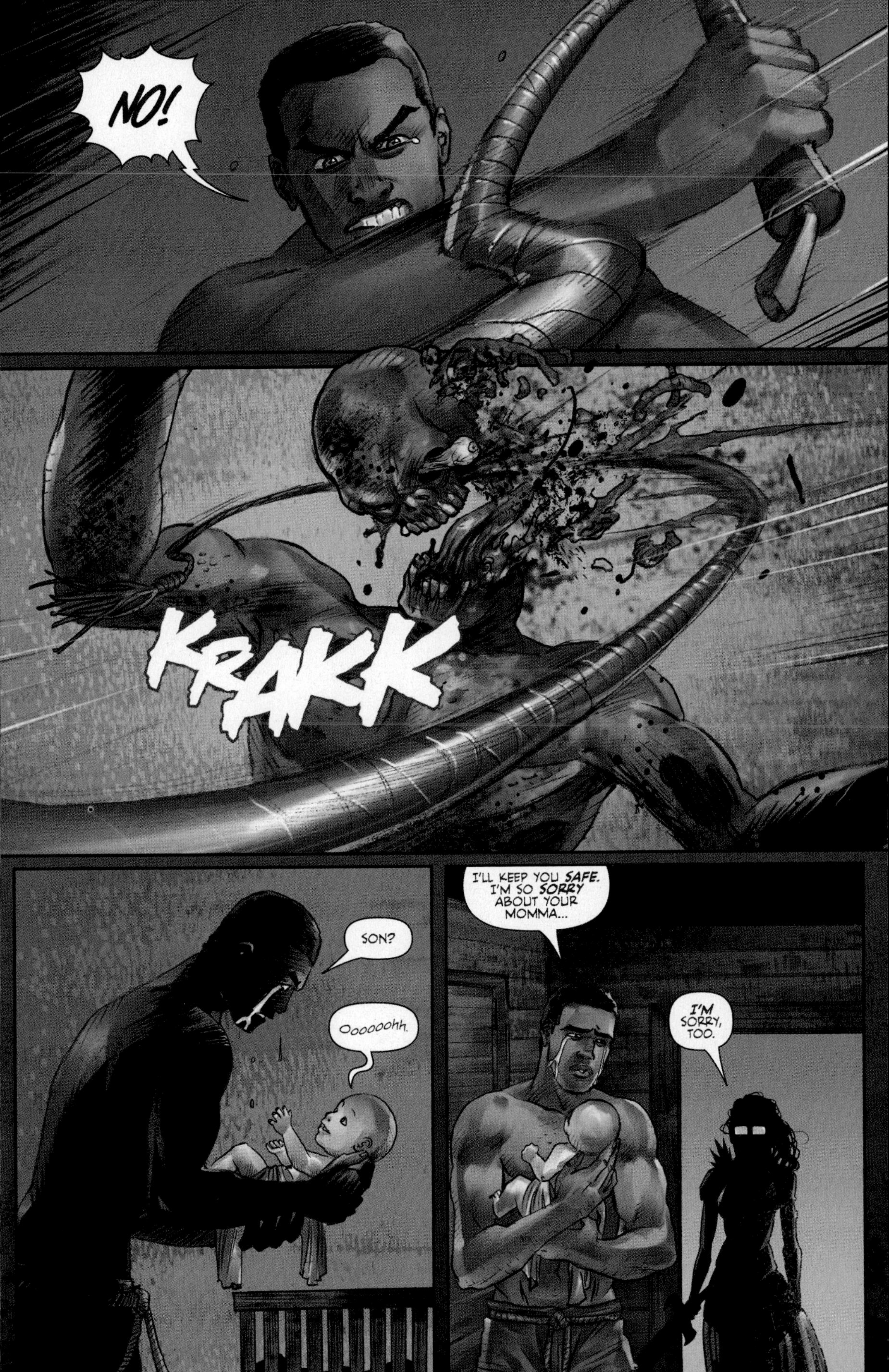
NO!
KRAKK
SON?
Oooooohh.
I'LL KEEP YOU SAFE. I'M SO SORRY ABOUT YOUR MOMMA...
I'M SORRY, TOO.

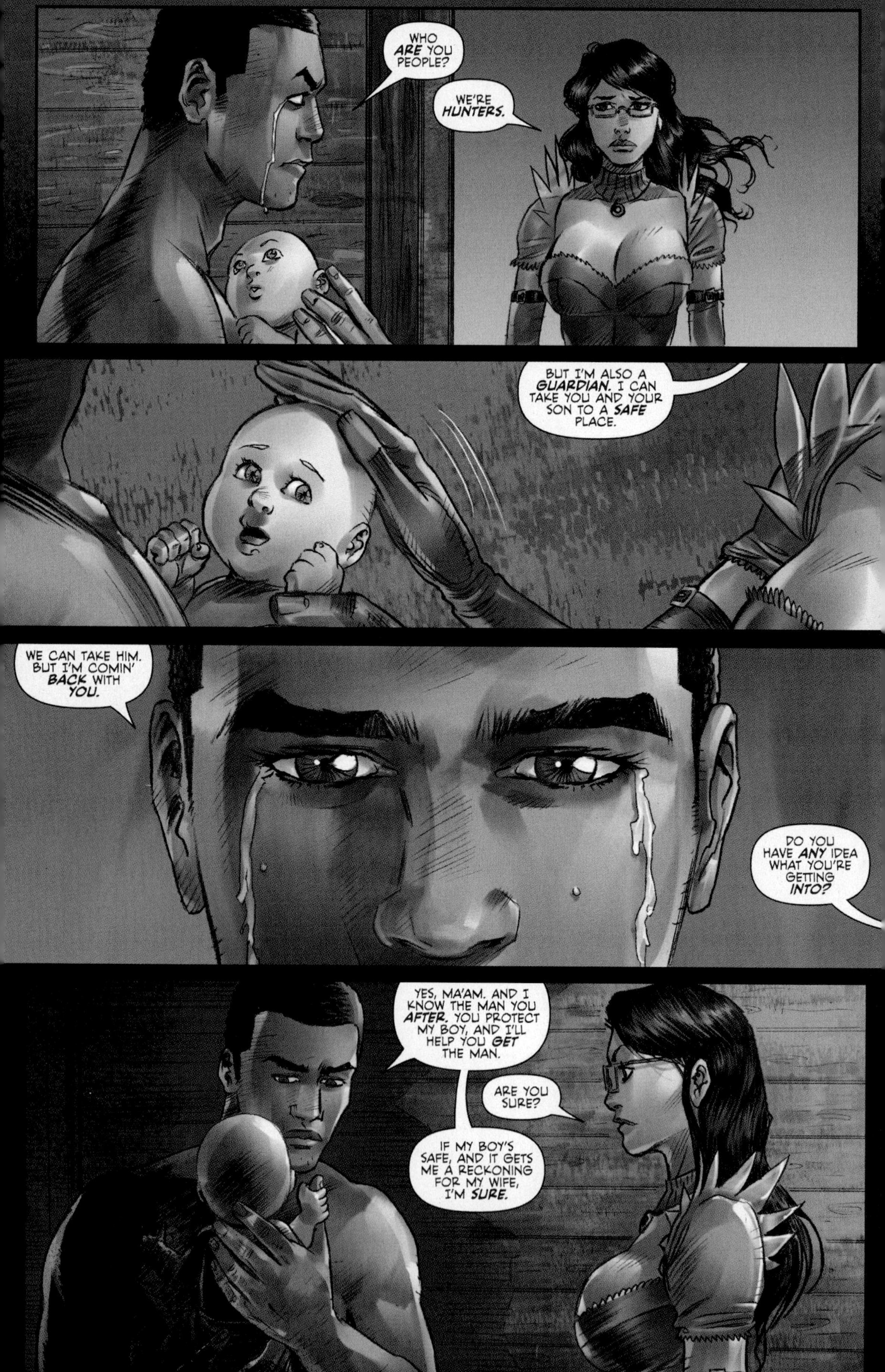
WHO ARE YOU PEOPLE?
WE'RE HUNTERS.
BUT I'M ALSO A GUARDIAN. I CAN TAKE YOU AND YOUR SON TO A SAFE PLACE.
WE CAN TAKE HIM. BUT I'M COMIN' BACK WITH YOU.
DO YOU HAVE ANY IDEA WHAT YOU'RE GETTING INTO?
YES, MA'AM. AND I KNOW THE MAN YOU AFTER. YOU PROTECT MY BOY, AND I'LL HELP YOU GET THE MAN.
ARE YOU SURE?
IF MY BOY'S SAFE, AND IT GETS ME A RECKONING FOR MY WIFE, I'M SURE.

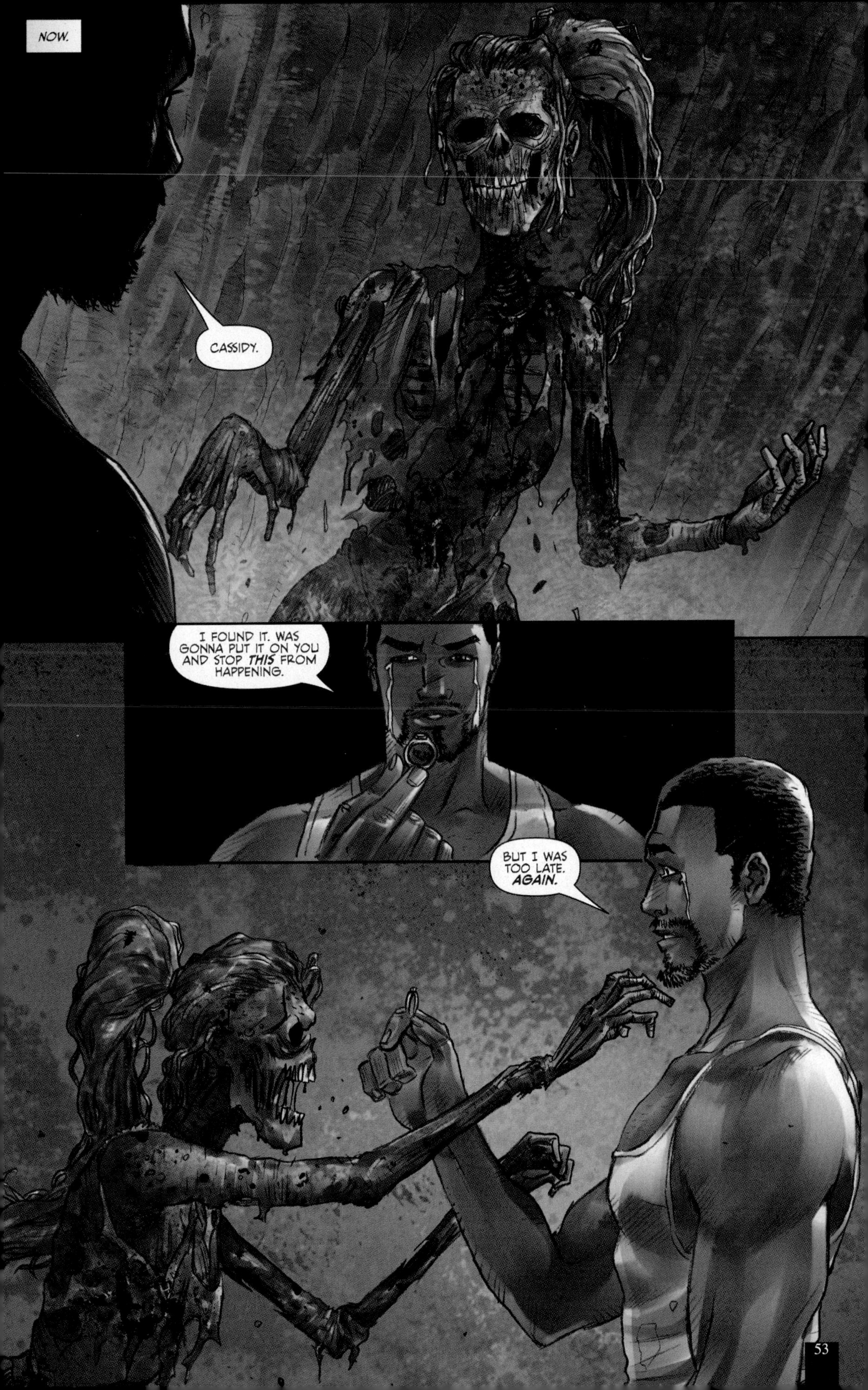
NOW.
CASSIDY.
I FOUND IT. WAS GONNA PUT IT ON YOU AND STOP THIS FROM HAPPENING.
BUT I WAS TOO LATE. AGAIN.

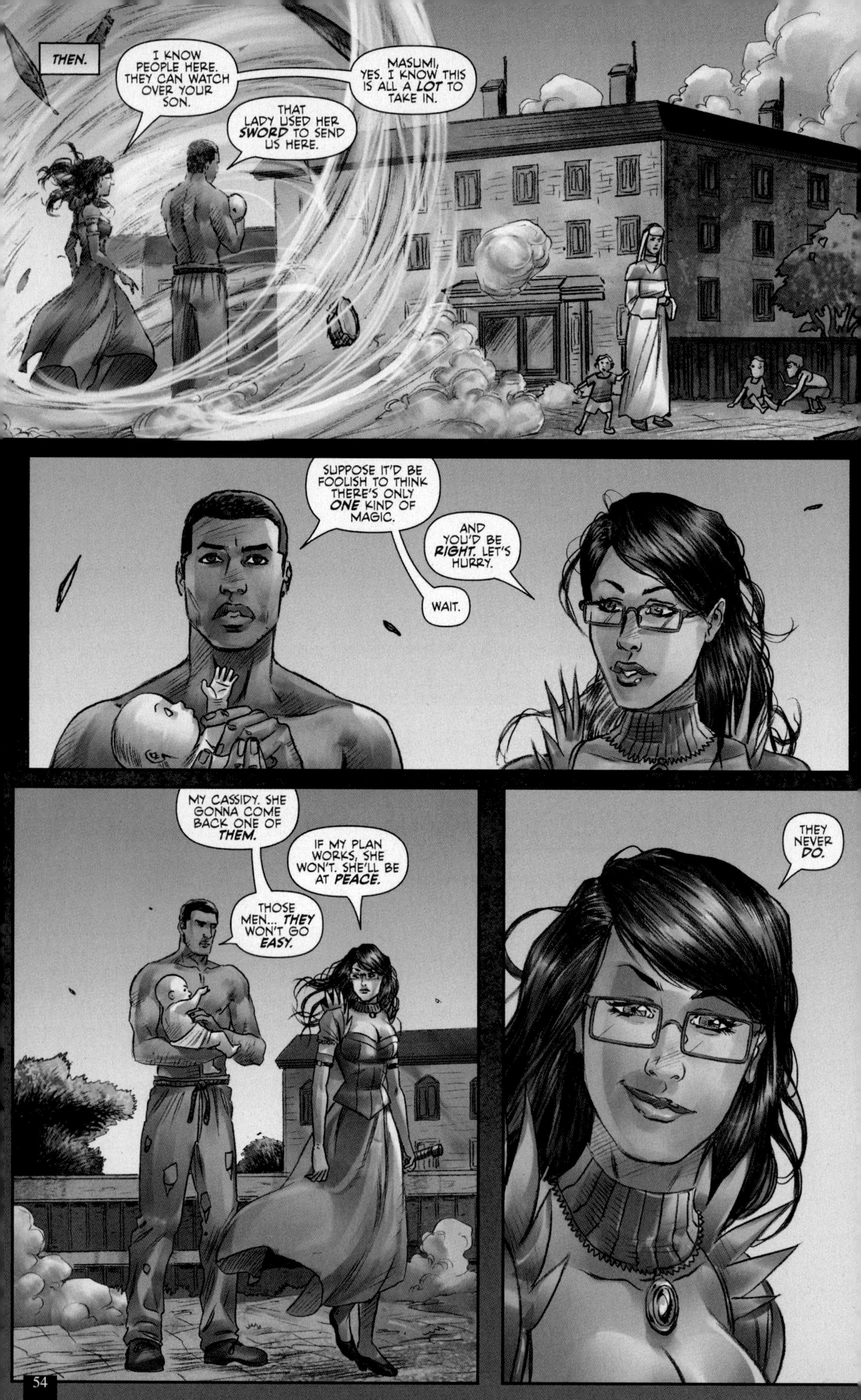
THEN.
I KNOW PEOPLE HERE. THEY CAN WATCH OVER YOUR SON.
MASUMI, YES. I KNOW THIS IS ALL A LOT TO TAKE IN.
THAT LADY USED HER SWORD TO SEND US HERE.
SUPPOSE IT'D BE FOOLISH TO THINK THERE'S ONLY ONE KIND OF MAGIC.
AND YOU'D BE RIGHT. LET'S HURRY.
WAIT.
MY CASSIDY. SHE GONNA COME BACK ONE OF THEM.
IF MY PLAN WORKS, SHE WON'T. SHE'LL BE AT PEACE.
THOSE MEN... THEY WON'T GO EASY.
THEY NEVER DO.

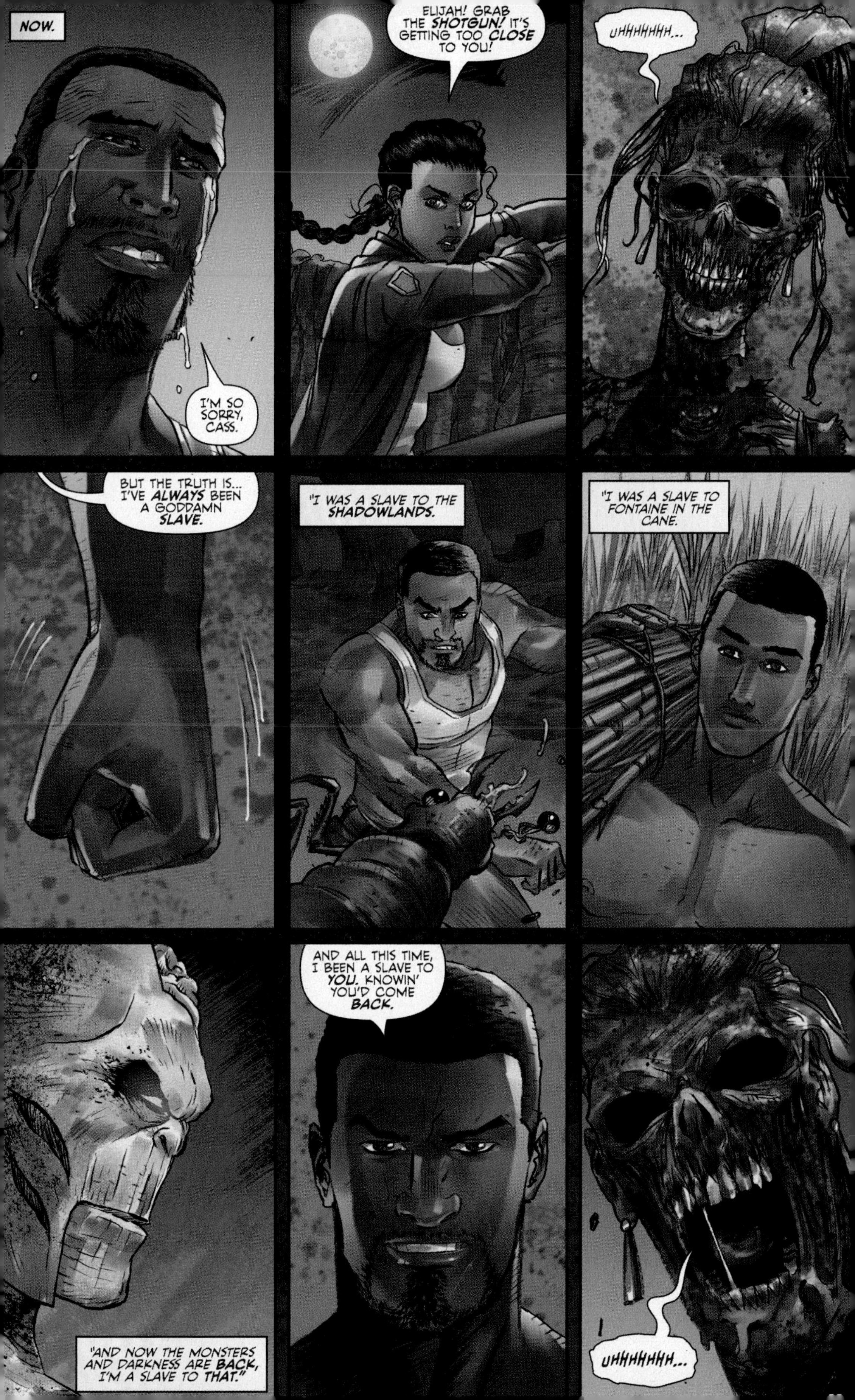
NOW.
I'M SO SORRY, CASS.
ELIJAH! GRAB THE SHOTGUN! IT'S GETTING TOO CLOSE TO YOU!
UHHHHHHH...
BUT THE TRUTH IS... I'VE ALWAYS BEEN A GODDAMN SLAVE.
"I WAS A SLAVE TO THE SHADOWLANDS.
"I WAS A SLAVE TO FONTAINE IN THE CANE.
"AND NOW THE MONSTERS AND DARKNESS ARE BACK, I'M A SLAVE TO THAT."
AND ALL THIS TIME, I BEEN A SLAVE TO YOU. KNOWIN' YOU'D COME BACK.
UHHHHHHH...

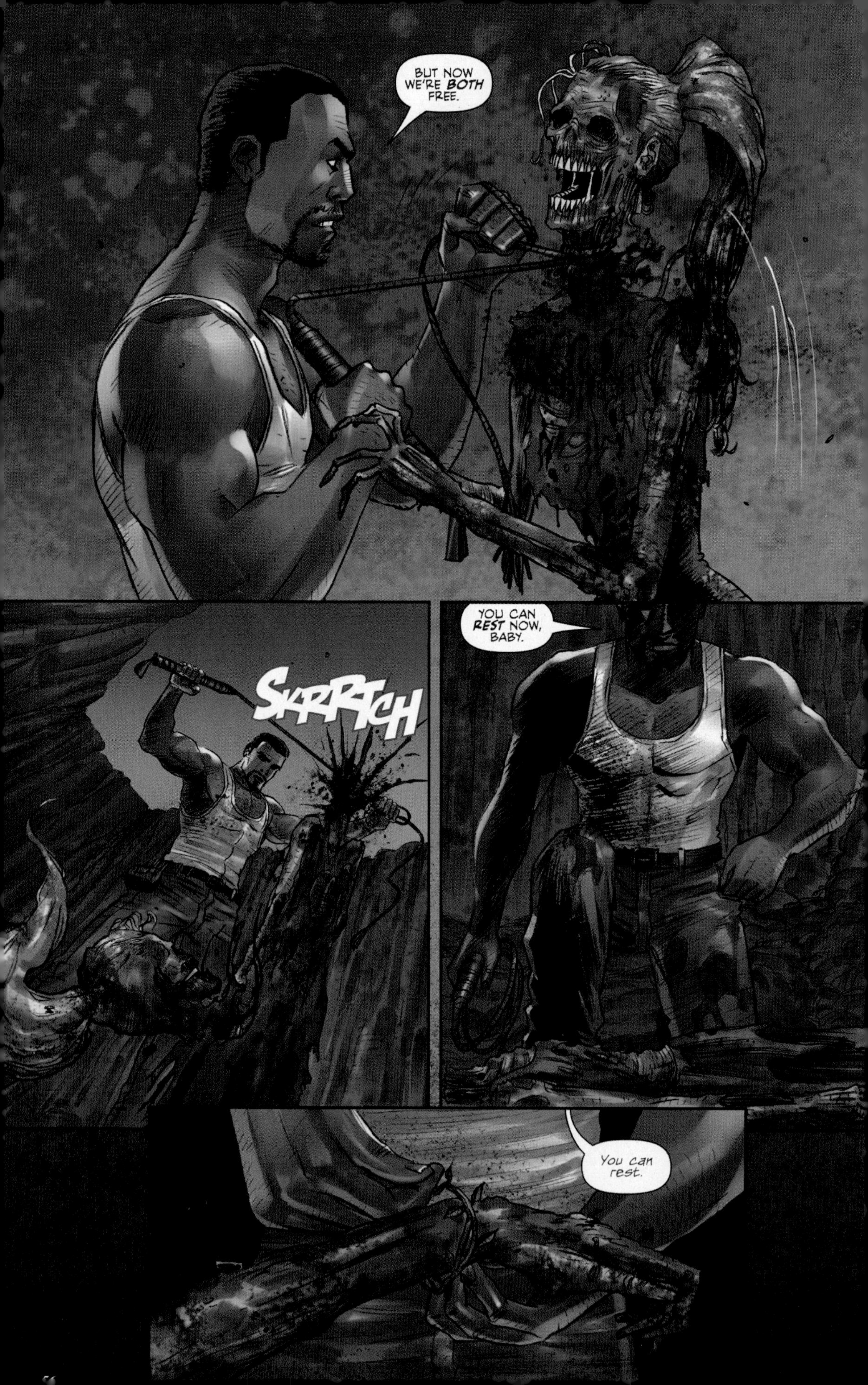
BUT NOW WE'RE BOTH FREE.
SKRRTCH
YOU CAN REST NOW, BABY.
You can rest.

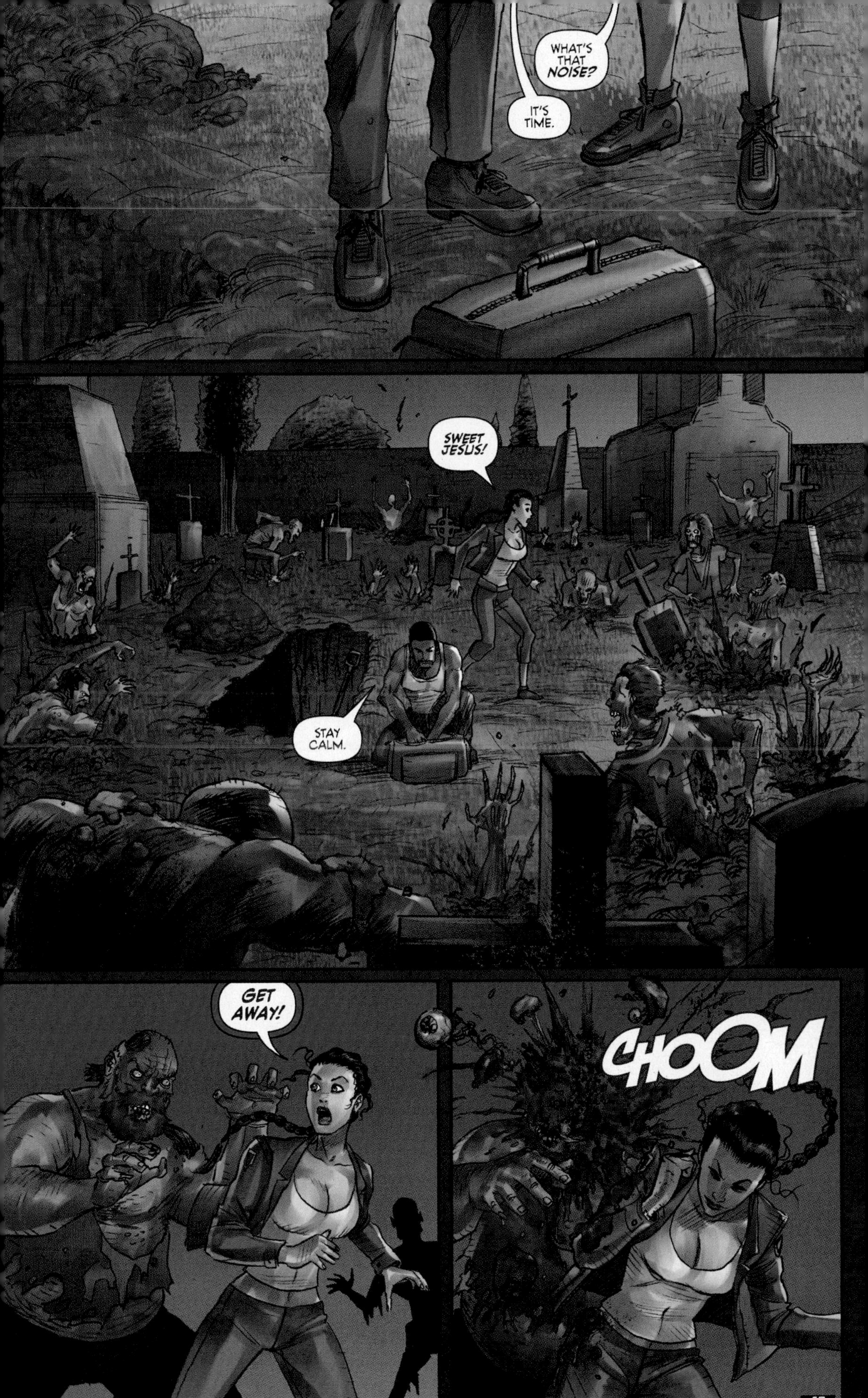
WHAT'S THAT NOISE?
IT'S TIME.
SWEET JESUS!
STAY CALM.
GET AWAY!
CHOOM

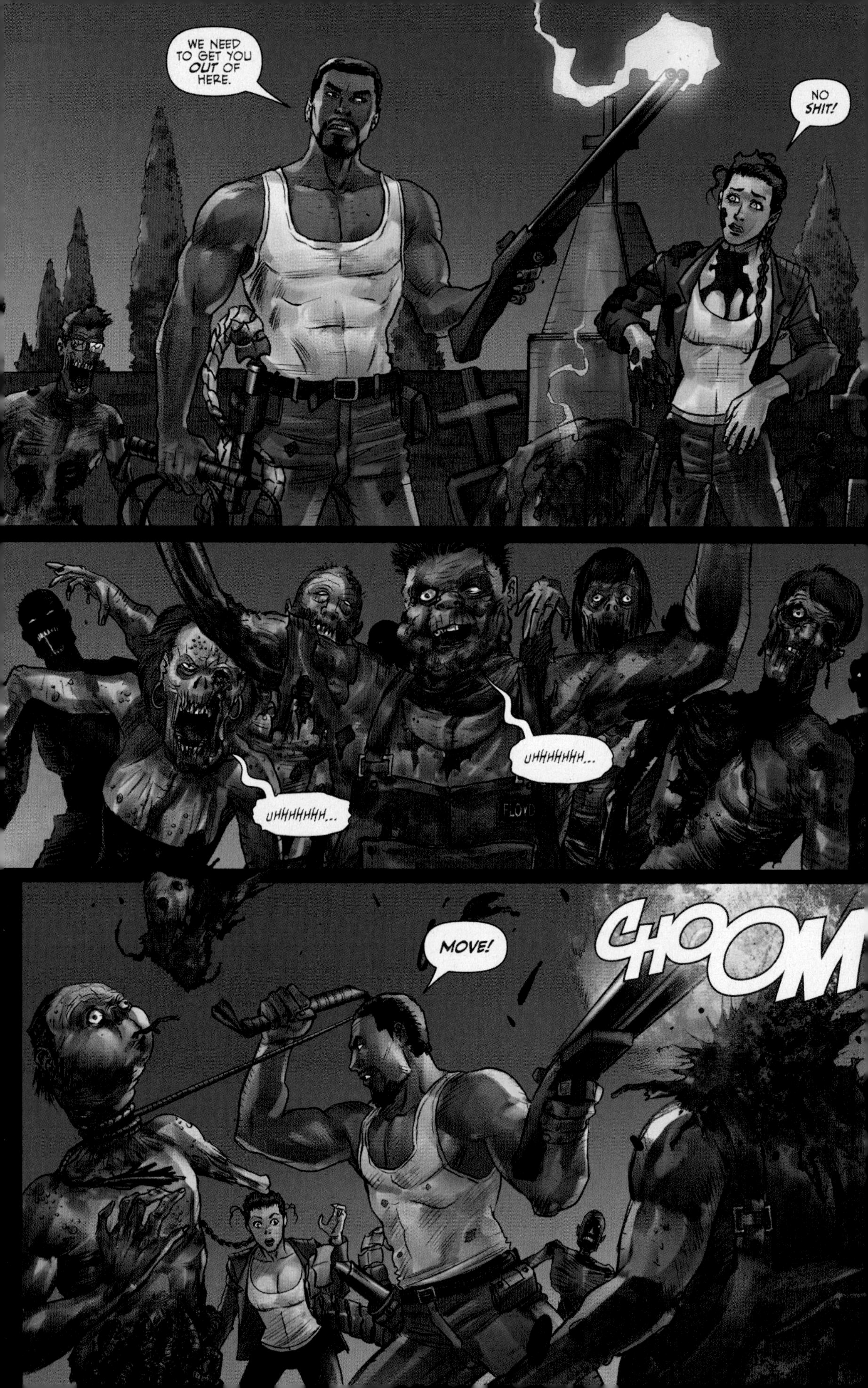
WE NEED TO GET YOU OUT OF HERE.
NO SHIT!
UHHHHHHH...
UHHHHHHH...
FLOYD
MOVE!
CHOOM

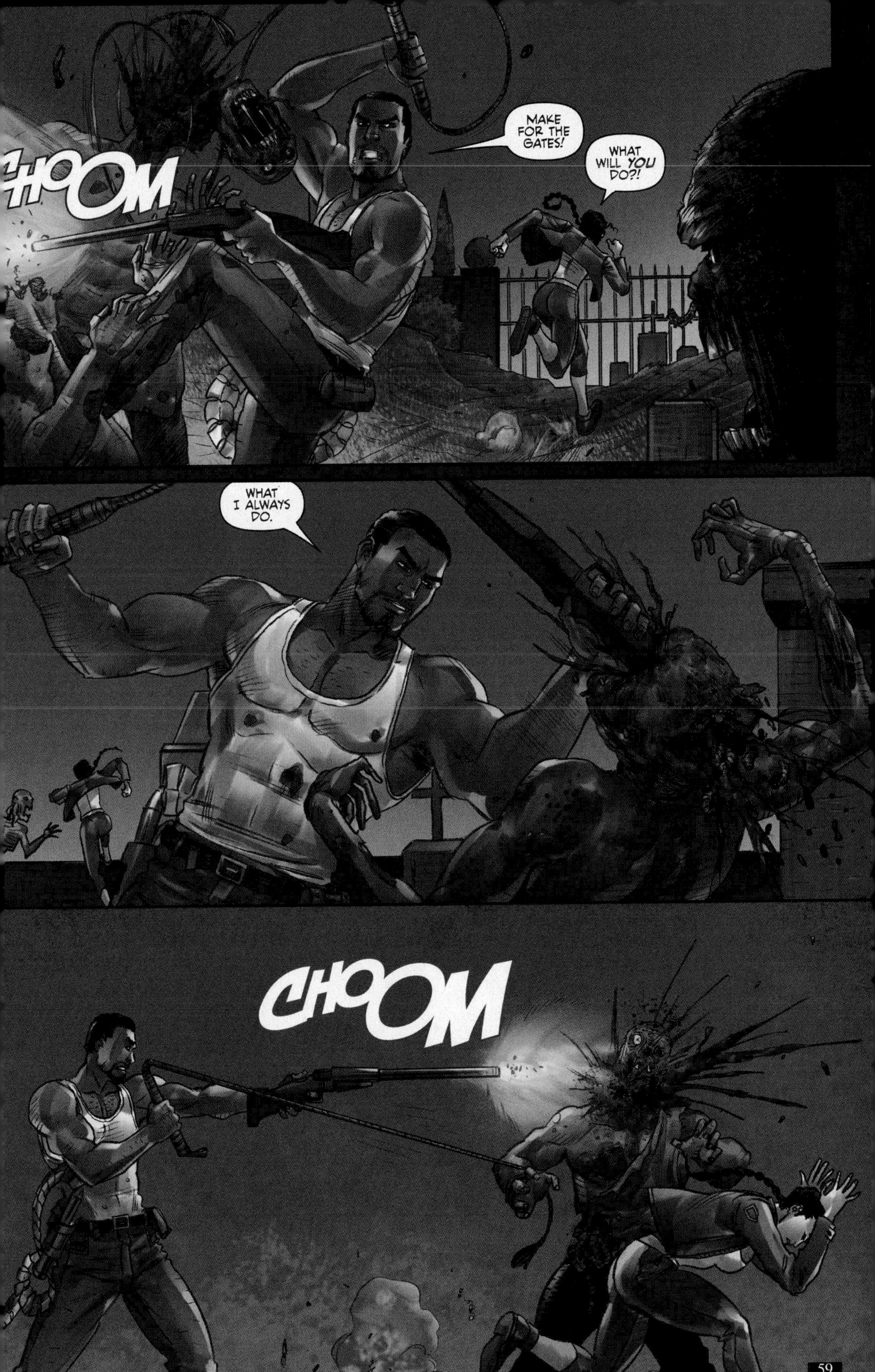
CHOOM
MAKE FOR THE GATES!
WHAT WILL YOU DO?!
WHAT I ALWAYS DO.
CHOOM

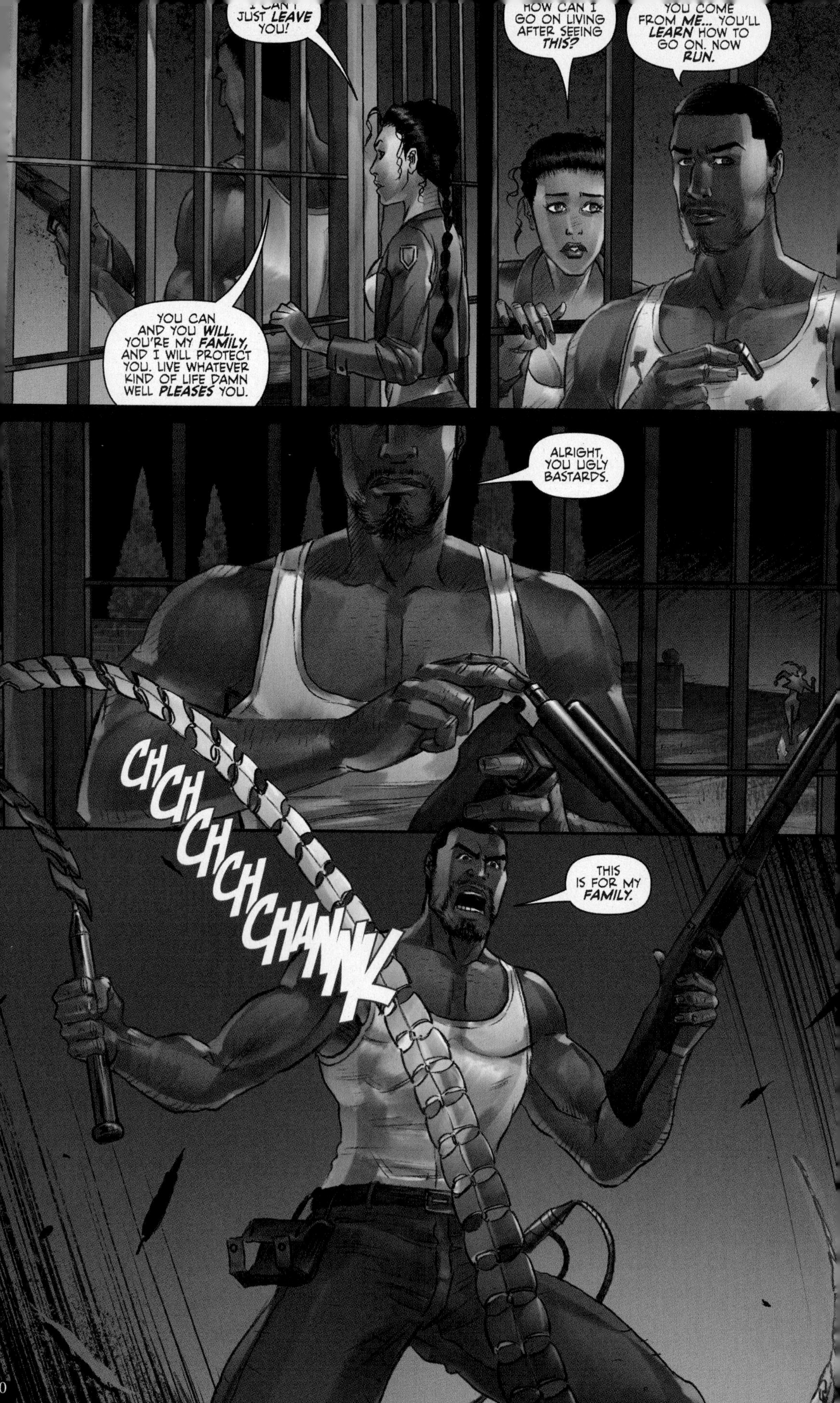
I CAN'T JUST LEAVE YOU!
YOU CAN AND YOU WILL. YOU'RE MY FAMILY, AND I WILL PROTECT YOU. LIVE WHATEVER KIND OF LIFE DAMN WELL PLEASES YOU.
HOW CAN I GO ON LIVING AFTER SEEING THIS?
YOU COME FROM ME... YOU'LL LEARN HOW TO GO ON. NOW RUN.
ALRIGHT, YOU UGLY BASTARDS.
CHCHCHCHCHANNK
THIS IS FOR MY FAMILY.

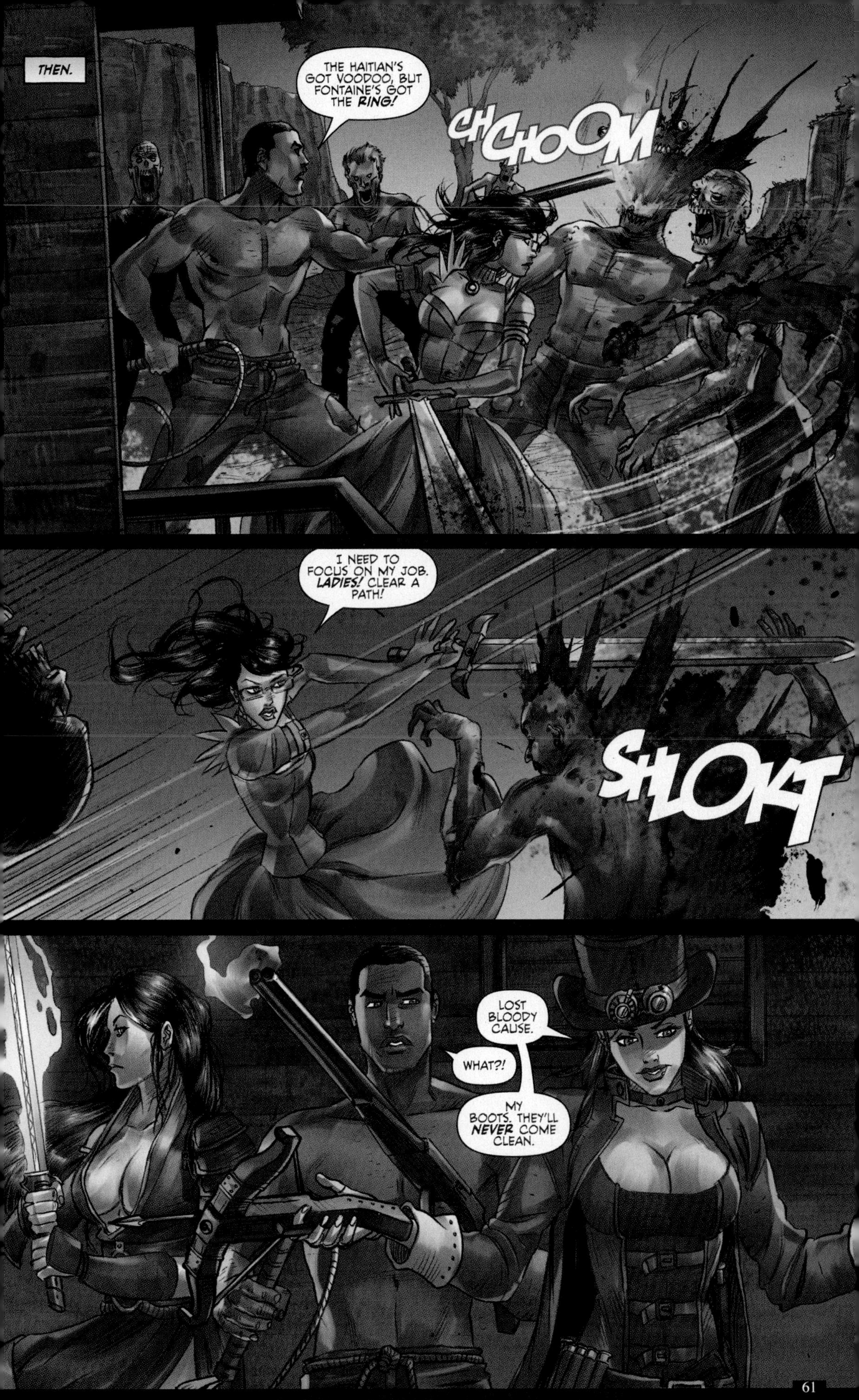
THEN.
THE HAITIAN'S GOT VOODOO, BUT FONTAINE'S GOT THE RING!
CH CHOOM
I NEED TO FOCUS ON MY JOB. LADIES! CLEAR A PATH!
SHLOKT
LOST BLOODY CAUSE.
WHAT?!
MY BOOTS. THEY'LL NEVER COME CLEAN.

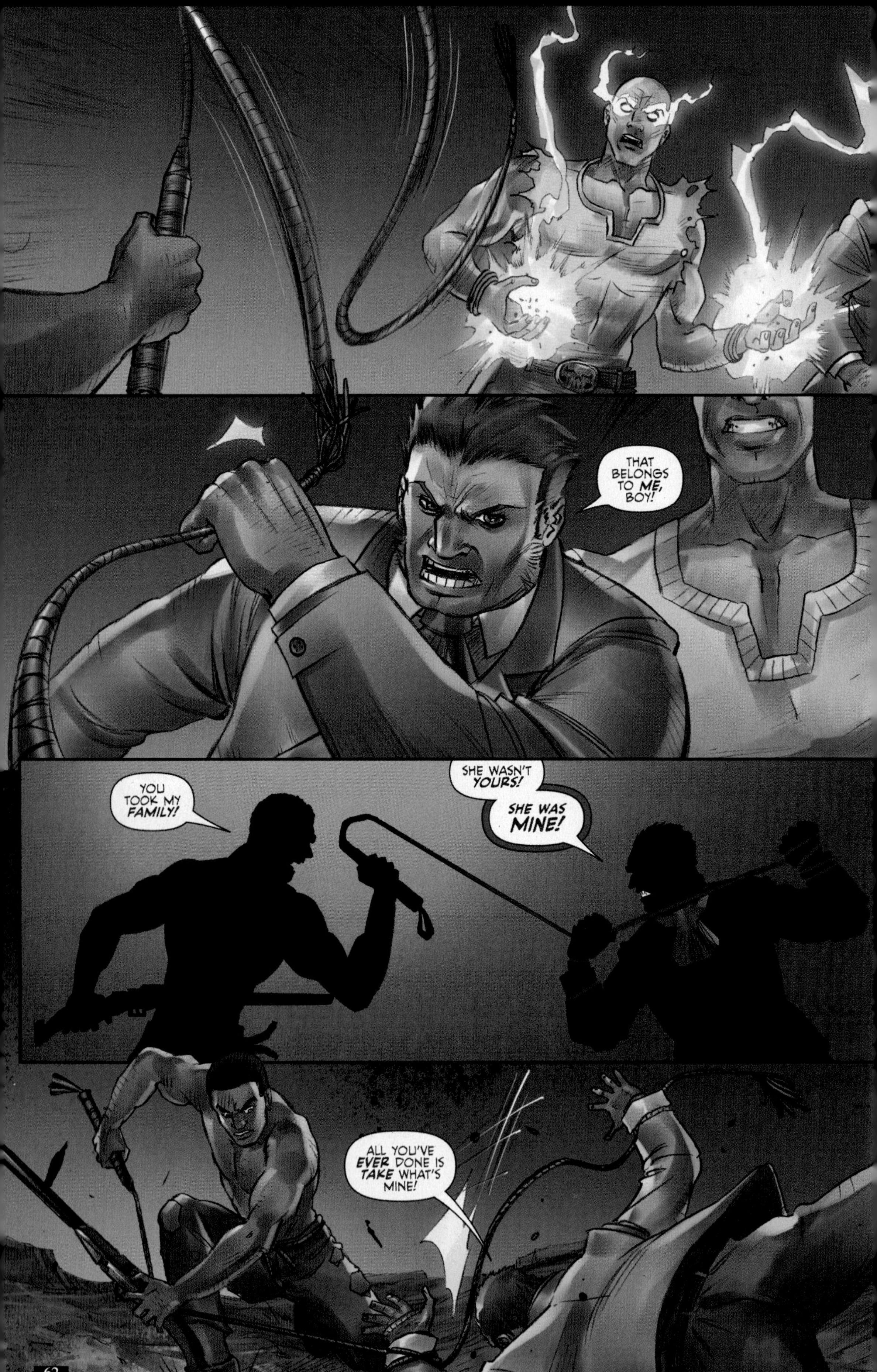
THAT BELONGS TO ME, BOY!
YOU TOOK MY FAMILY!
SHE WASN'T YOURS!
SHE WAS MINE!
ALL YOU'VE EVER DONE IS TAKE WHAT'S MINE!

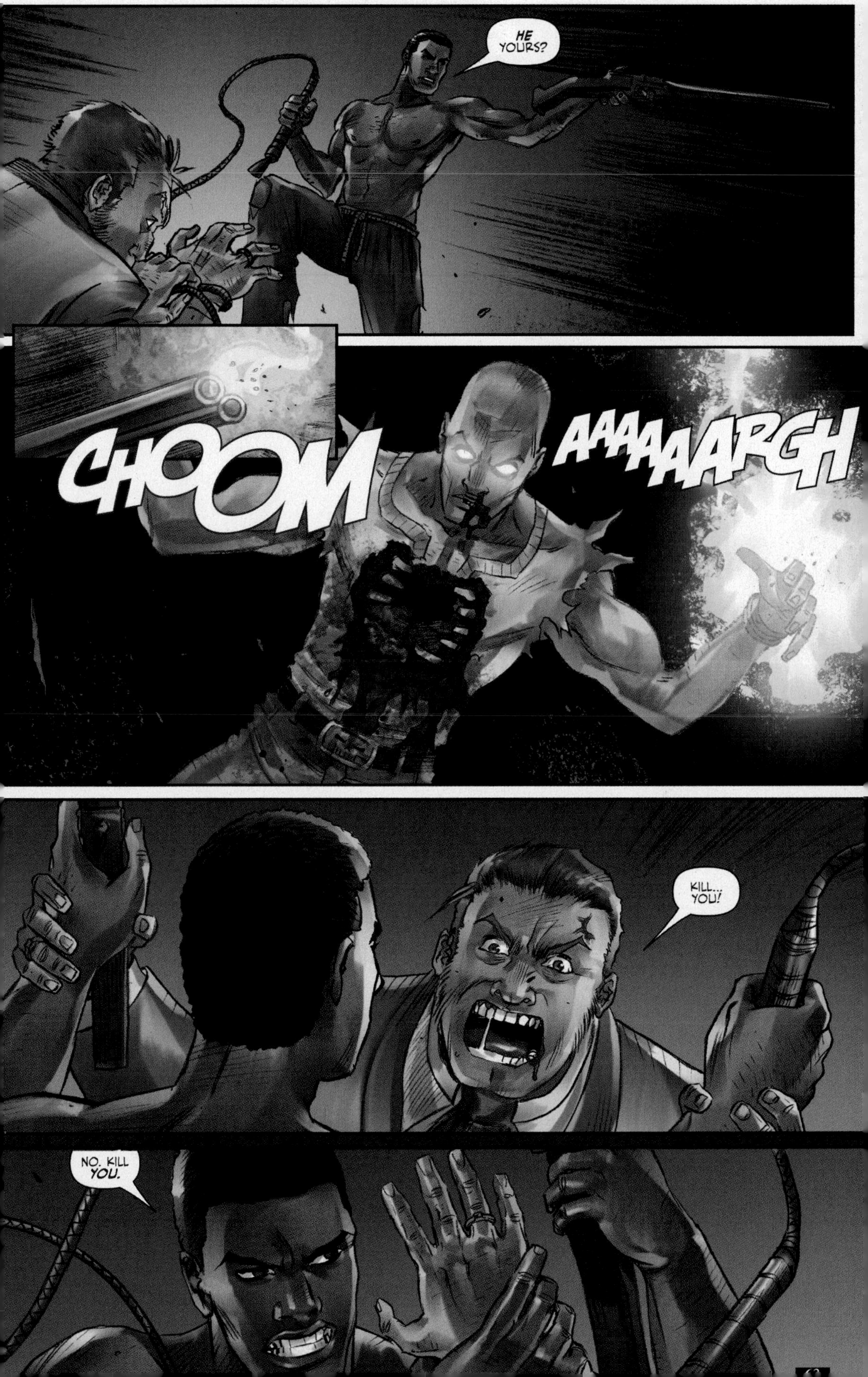
HE YOURS?
CHOOM
AAAAAARGH
KILL... YOU!
NO. KILL YOU.

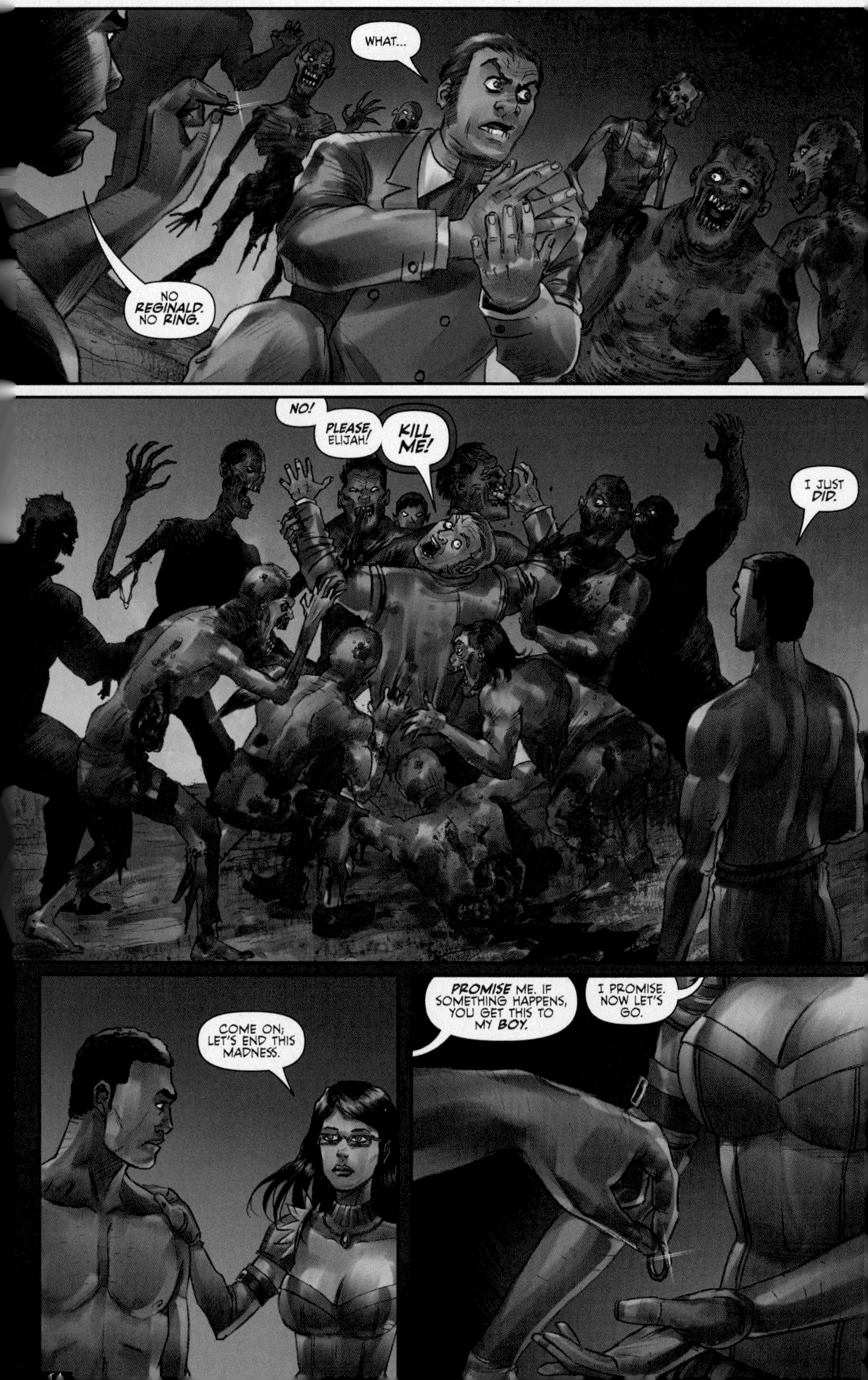
WHAT...
NO *REGINALD.* NO *RING.*
NO!
PLEASE, ELIJAH!
KILL ME!
I JUST *DID.*
COME ON; LET'S END THIS MADNESS.
PROMISE ME. IF SOMETHING HAPPENS, YOU GET THIS TO MY *BOY.*
I PROMISE. NOW LET'S GO.

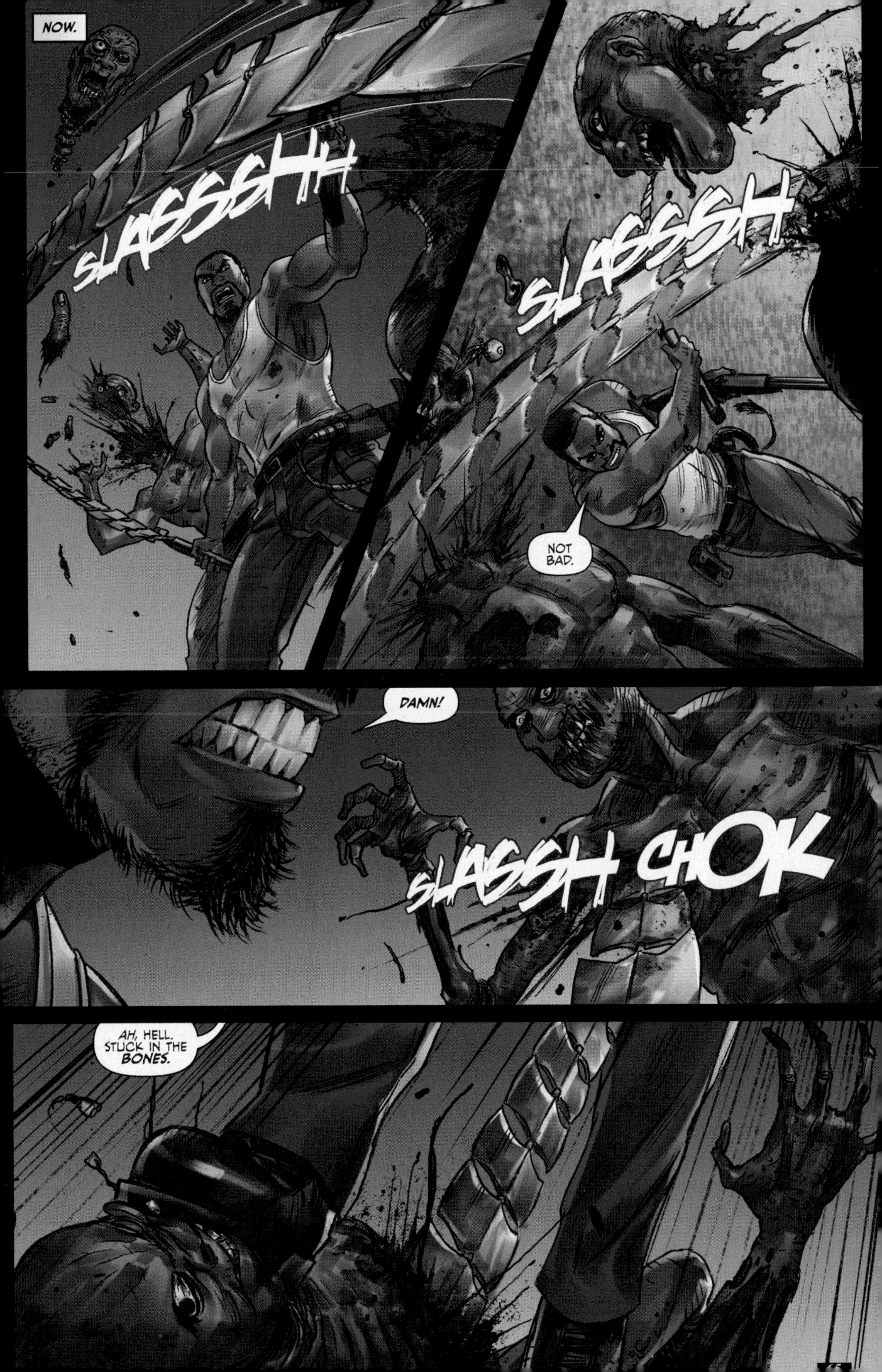
NOW.
SLASSSHH
SLASSSH
NOT BAD.
DAMN!
SLASSSH CHOK
AH, HELL. STUCK IN THE BONES.

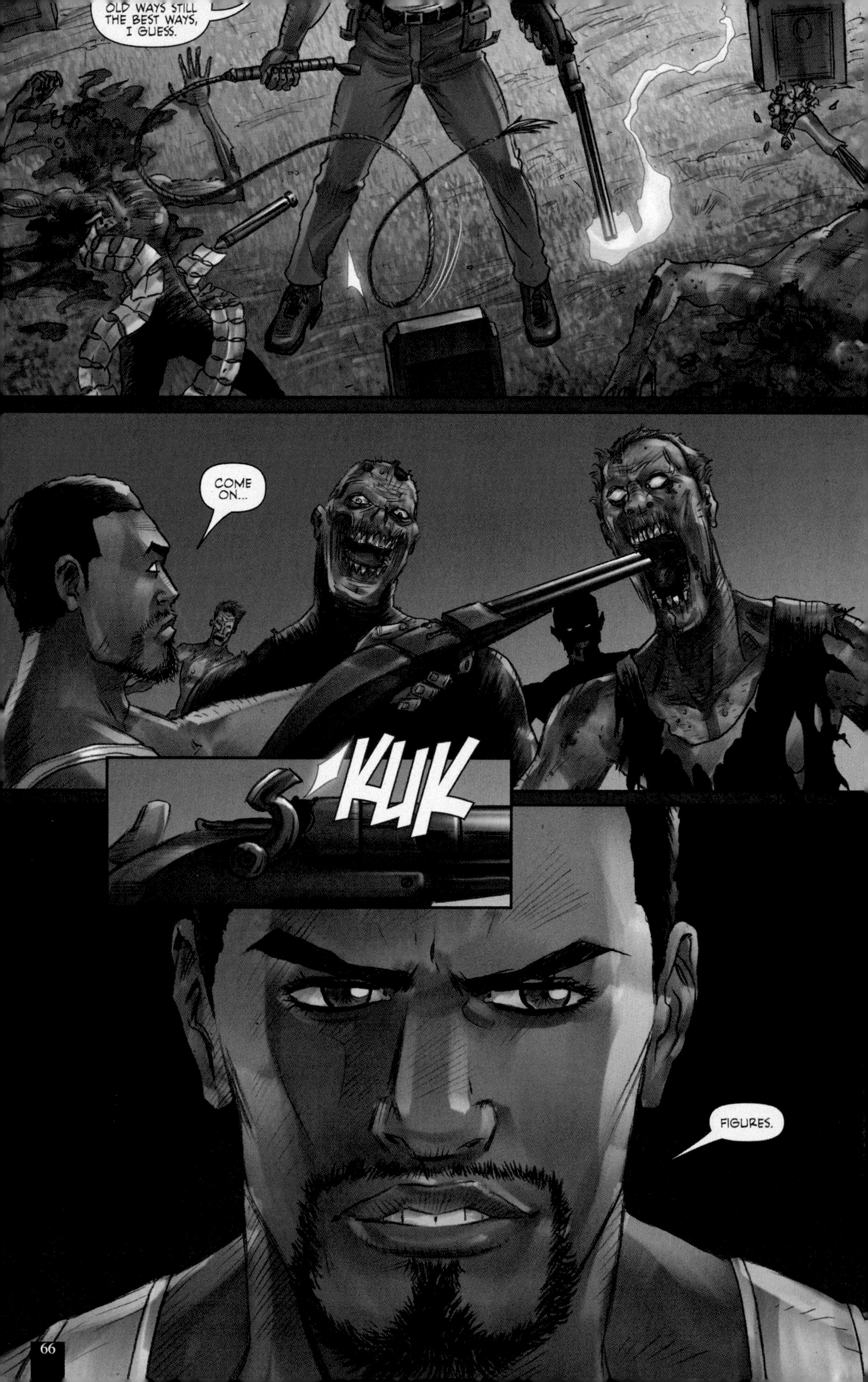
OLD WAYS STILL THE BEST WAYS, I GUESS.
COME ON...
KUK
FIGURES.

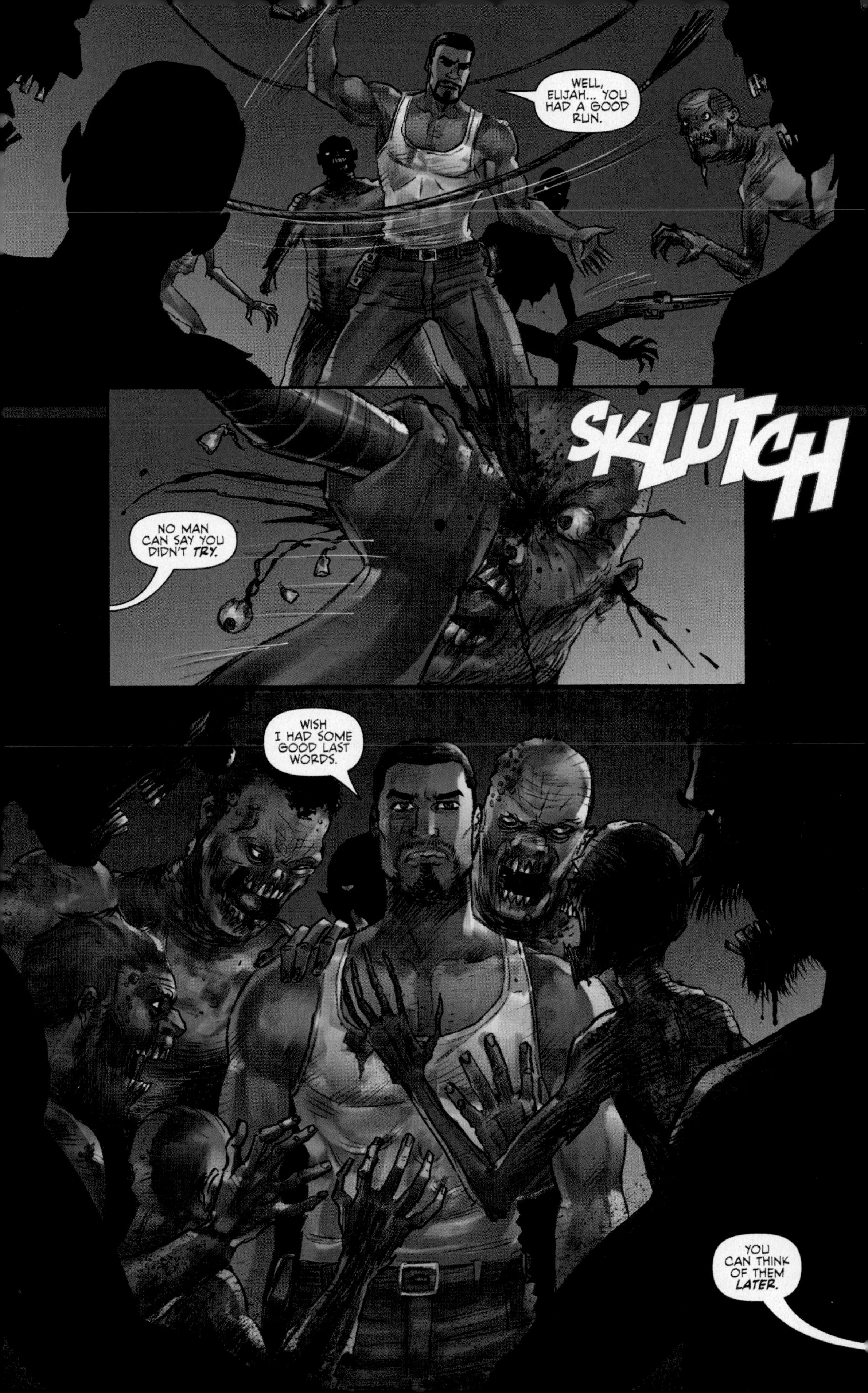
WELL, ELIJAH... YOU HAD A GOOD RUN.
SKLUTCH
NO MAN CAN SAY YOU DIDN'T *TRY*.
WISH I HAD SOME GOOD LAST WORDS.
YOU CAN THINK OF THEM *LATER*.

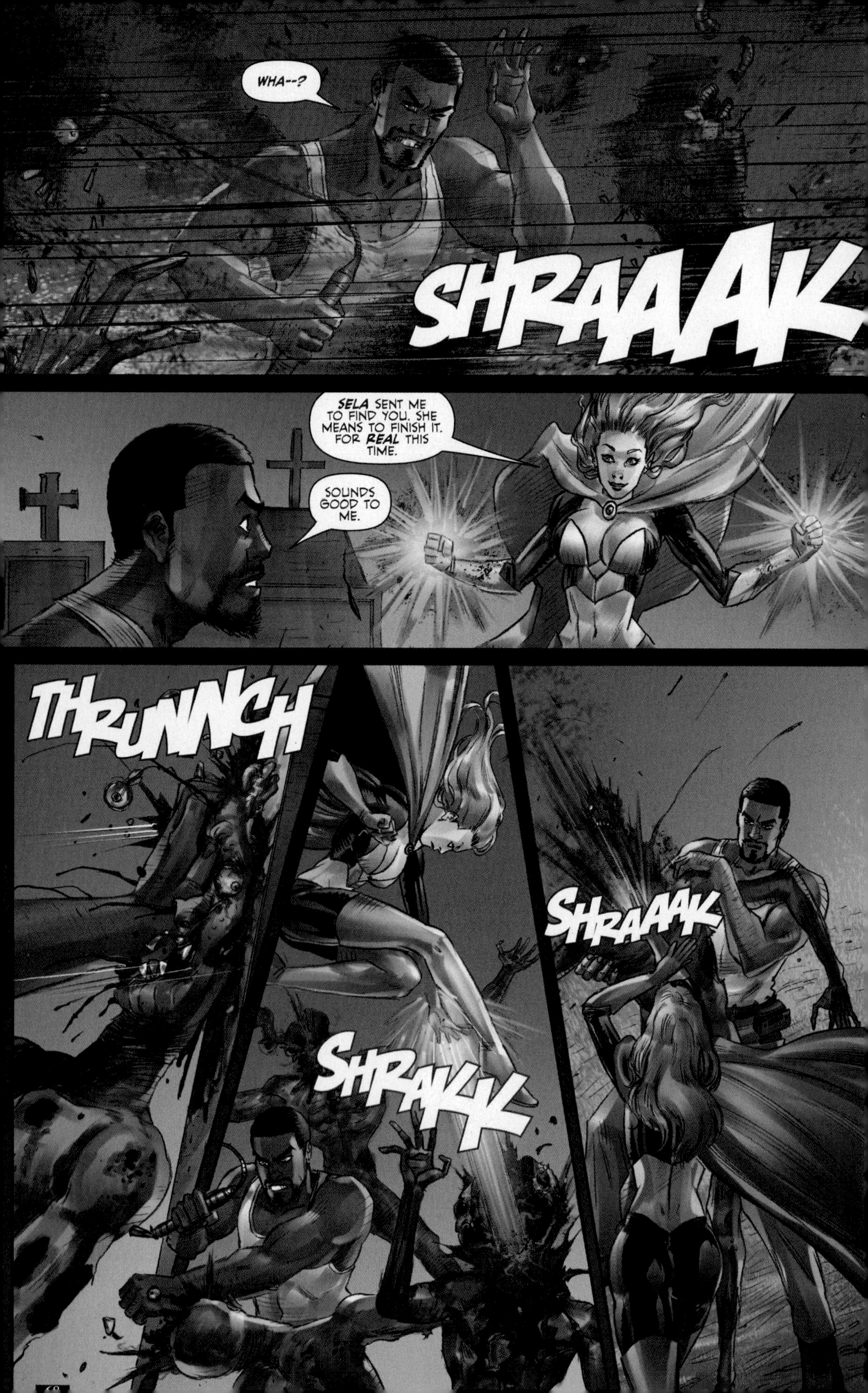
WHA--?
SHRAAAK
SELA SENT ME TO FIND YOU. SHE MEANS TO FINISH IT. FOR REAL THIS TIME.
SOUNDS GOOD TO ME.
THRUNNCH
SHRAKK
SHRAAAK

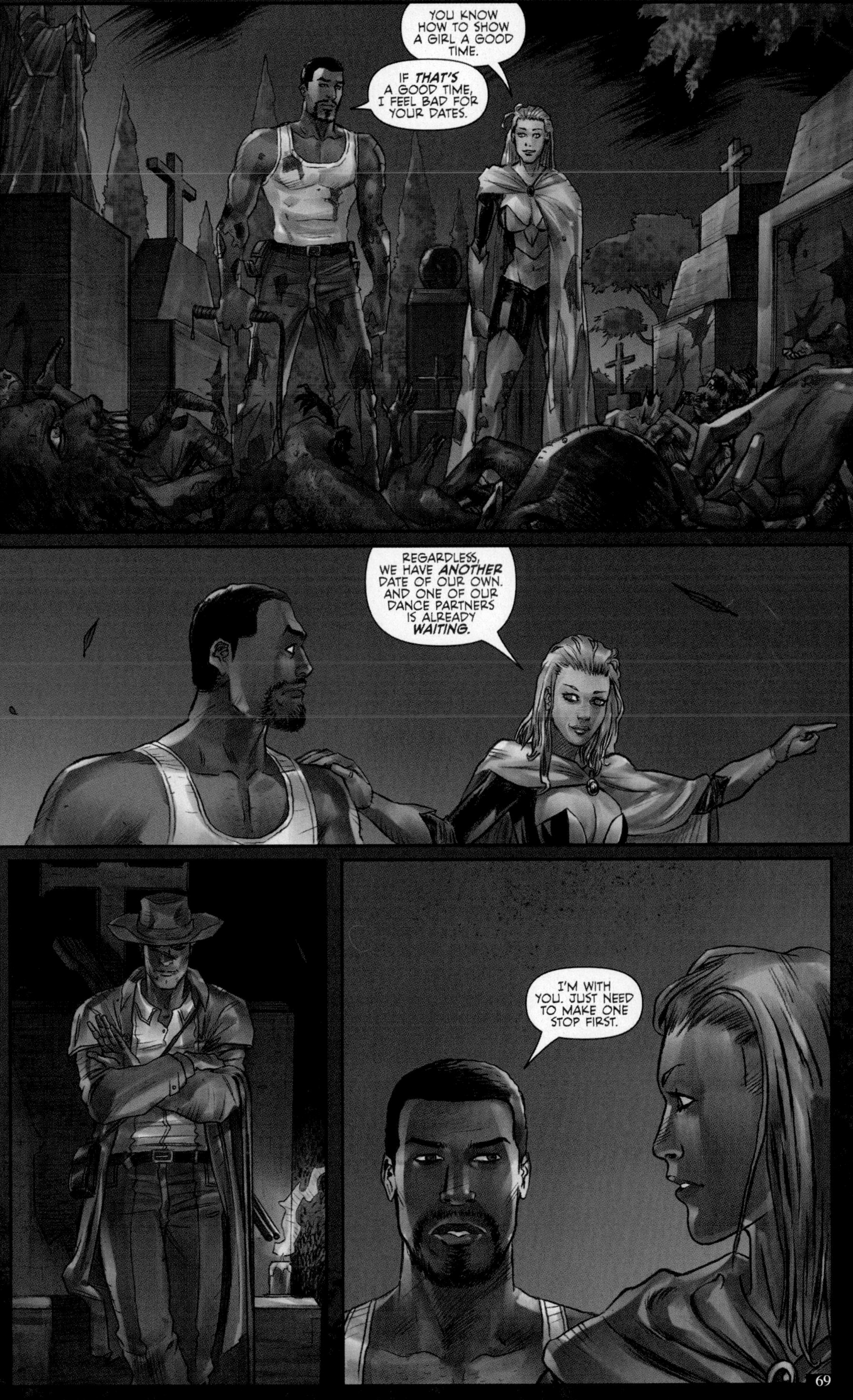
YOU KNOW HOW TO SHOW A GIRL A GOOD TIME.
IF THAT'S A GOOD TIME, I FEEL BAD FOR YOUR DATES.
REGARDLESS, WE HAVE ANOTHER DATE OF OUR OWN. AND ONE OF OUR DANCE PARTNERS IS ALREADY WAITING.
I'M WITH YOU. JUST NEED TO MAKE ONE STOP FIRST.

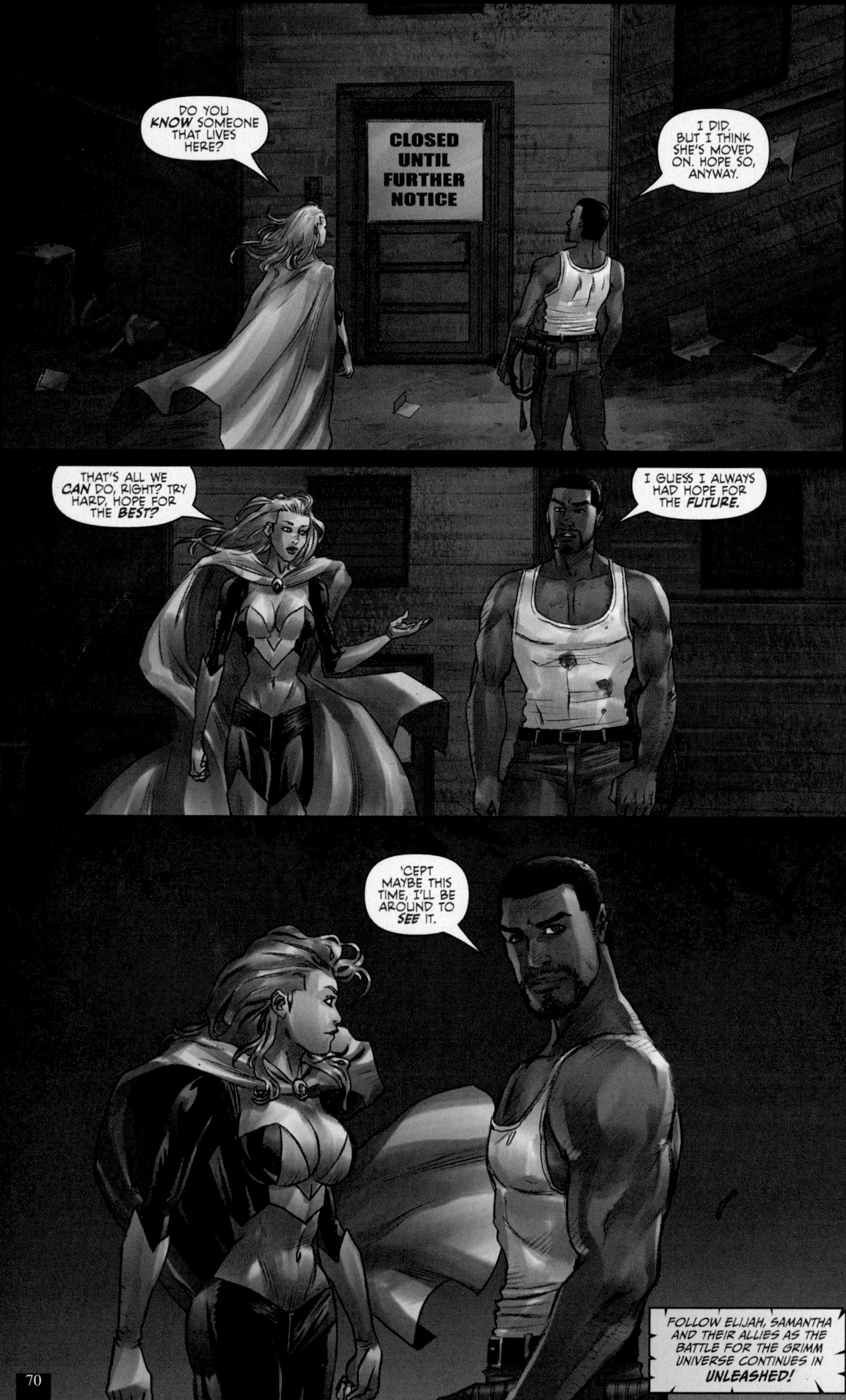
DO YOU KNOW SOMEONE THAT LIVES HERE?
CLOSED UNTIL FURTHER NOTICE
I DID. BUT I THINK SHE'S MOVED ON. HOPE SO, ANYWAY.
THAT'S ALL WE CAN DO, RIGHT? TRY HARD, HOPE FOR THE BEST?
I GUESS I ALWAYS HAD HOPE FOR THE FUTURE.
'CEPT MAYBE THIS TIME, I'LL BE AROUND TO SEE IT.
FOLLOW ELIJAH, SAMANTHA AND THEIR ALLIES AS THE BATTLE FOR THE GRIMM UNIVERSE CONTINUES IN UNLEASHED!

Grimm Fairy Tales presents:

Zombies & Demons

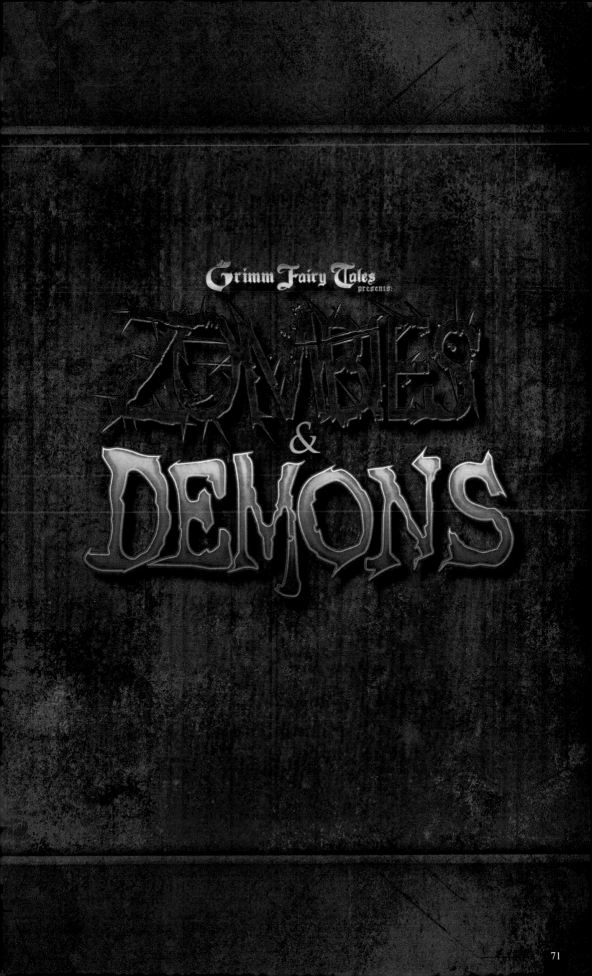

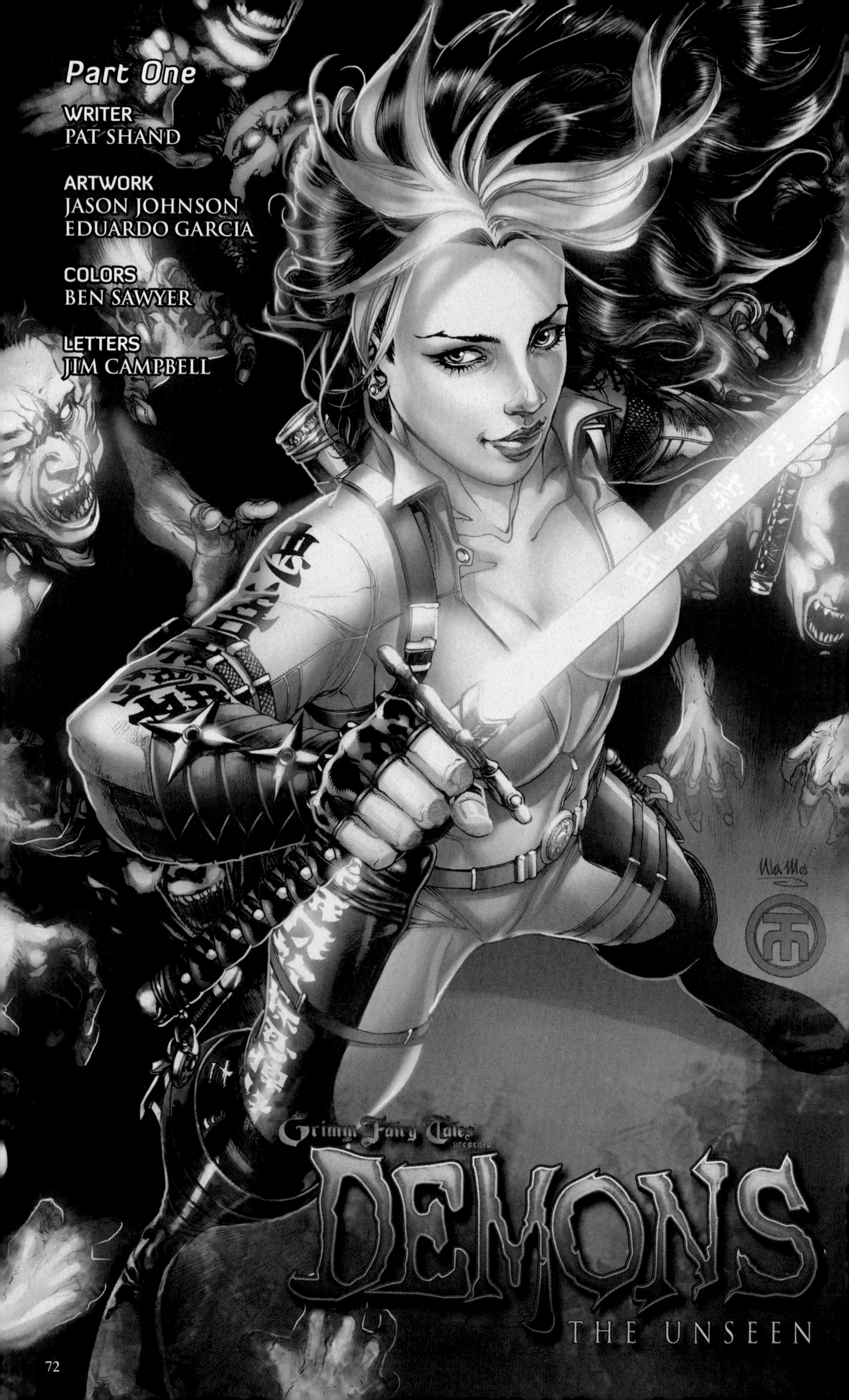
Part One
WRITER
PAT SHAND
ARTWORK
JASON JOHNSON
EDUARDO GARCIA
COLORS
BEN SAWYER
LETTERS
JIM CAMPBELL
Grimm Fairy Tales presents
DEMONS
THE UNSEEN

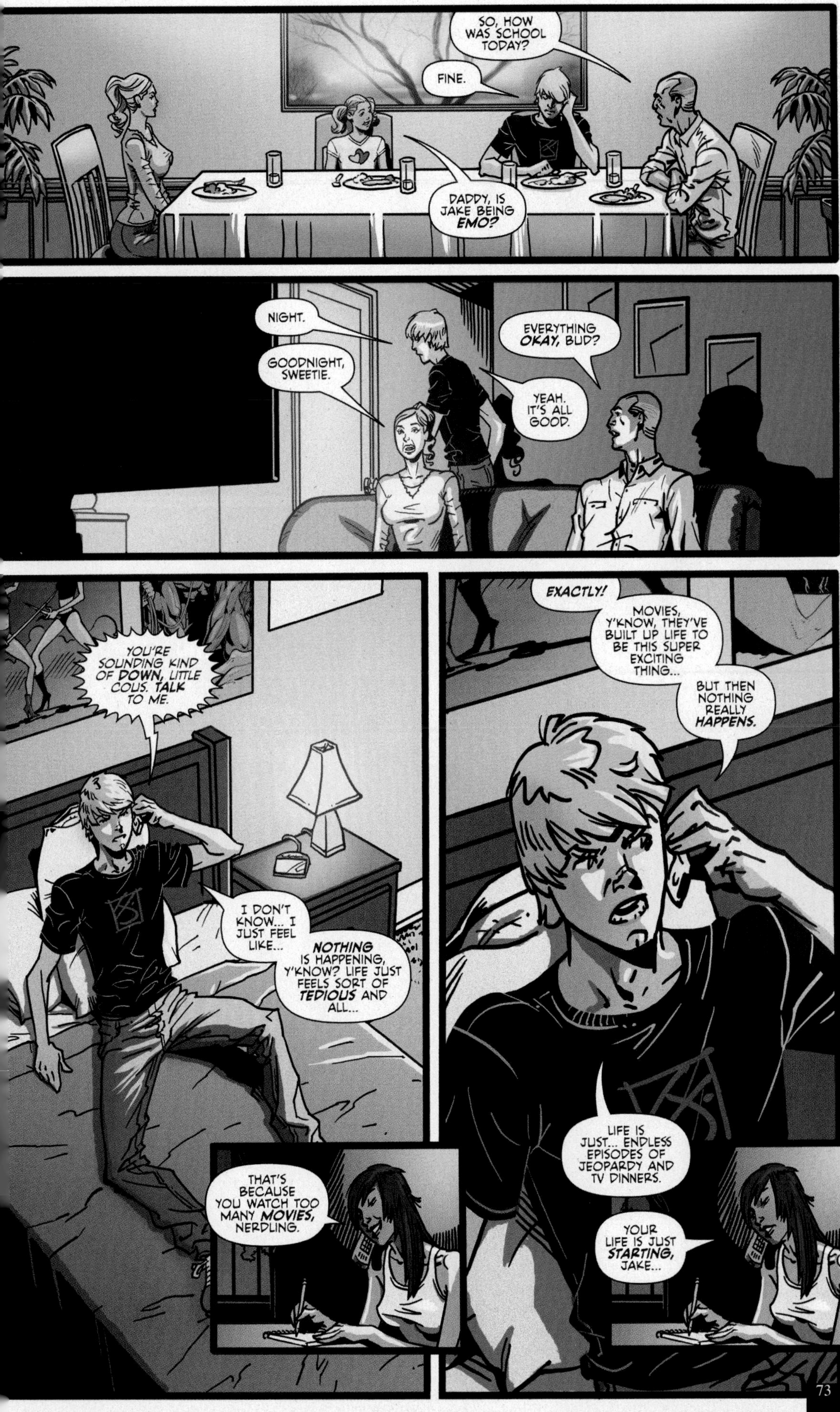
SO, HOW WAS SCHOOL TODAY?
FINE.
DADDY, IS JAKE BEING EMO?
NIGHT.
GOODNIGHT, SWEETIE.
EVERYTHING OKAY, BUD?
YEAH. IT'S ALL GOOD.
YOU'RE SOUNDING KIND OF DOWN, LITTLE COUS. TALK TO ME.
I DON'T KNOW... I JUST FEEL LIKE...
NOTHING IS HAPPENING, Y'KNOW? LIFE JUST FEELS SORT OF TEDIOUS AND ALL...
THAT'S BECAUSE YOU WATCH TOO MANY MOVIES, NERDLING.
EXACTLY!
MOVIES, Y'KNOW, THEY'VE BUILT UP LIFE TO BE THIS SUPER EXCITING THING...
BUT THEN NOTHING REALLY HAPPENS.
LIFE IS JUST... ENDLESS EPISODES OF JEOPARDY AND TV DINNERS.
YOUR LIFE IS JUST STARTING, JAKE...

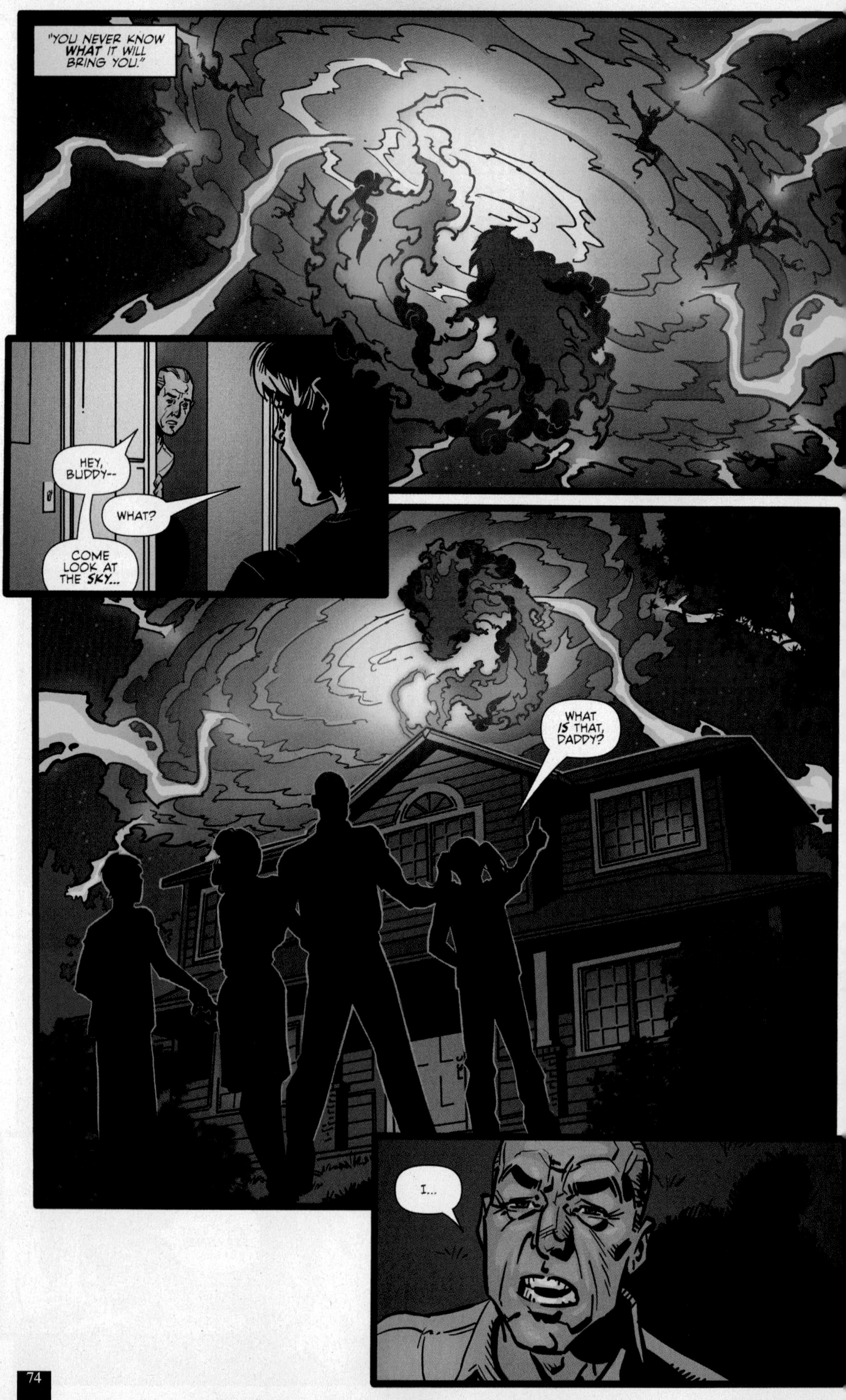
"YOU NEVER KNOW WHAT IT WILL BRING YOU."
HEY, BUDDY--
WHAT?
COME LOOK AT THE SKY...
WHAT IS THAT, DADDY?
I...

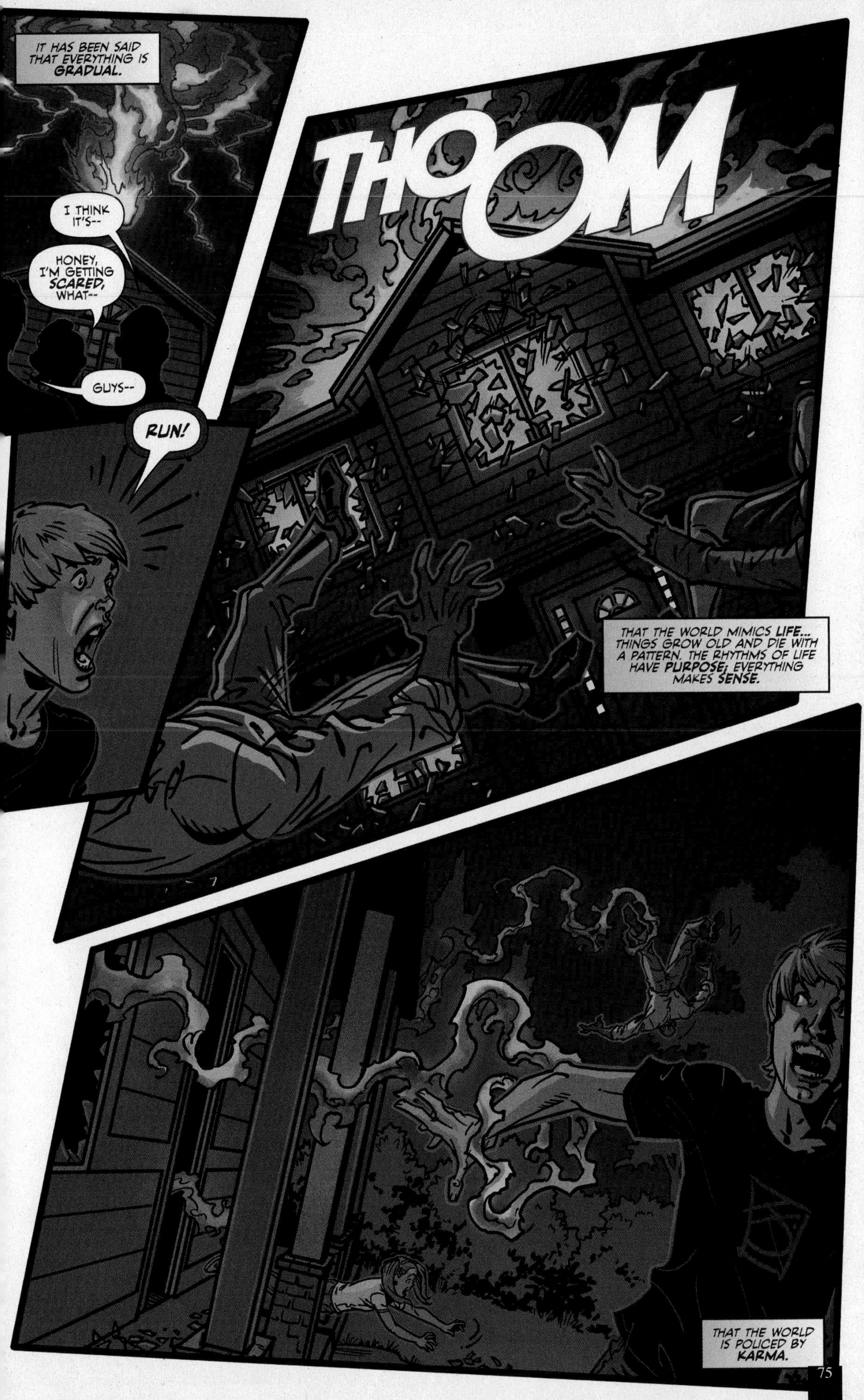

IT HAS BEEN SAID THAT EVERYTHING IS GRADUAL.
I THINK IT'S--
HONEY, I'M GETTING SCARED, WHAT--
GUYS--
RUN!
THOOM
THAT THE WORLD MIMICS LIFE... THINGS GROW OLD AND DIE WITH A PATTERN. THE RHYTHMS OF LIFE HAVE PURPOSE; EVERYTHING MAKES SENSE.
THAT THE WORLD IS POLICED BY KARMA.

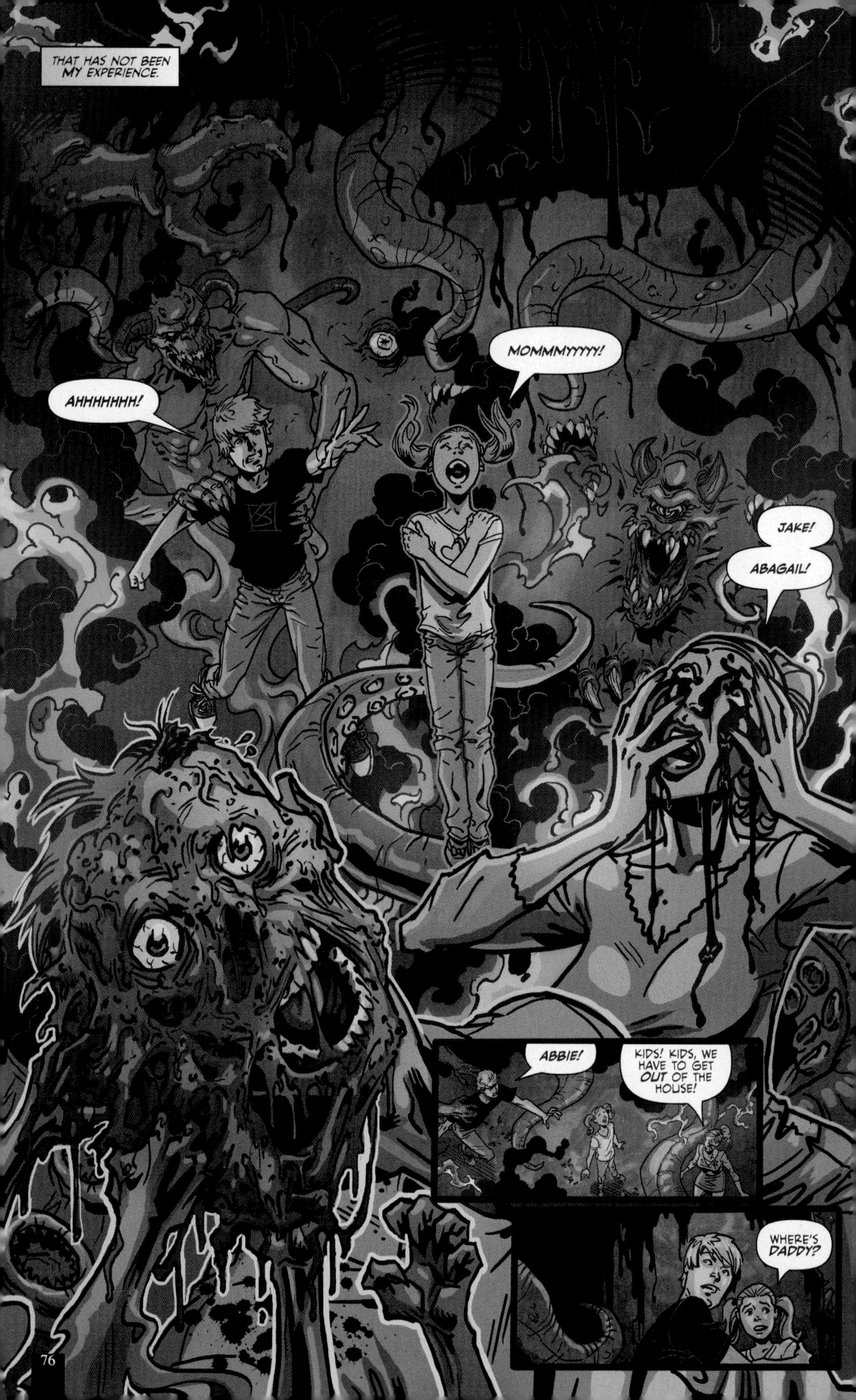
THAT HAS NOT BEEN MY EXPERIENCE.
AHHHHHHH!
MOMMMYYYYY!
JAKE!
ABAGAIL!
ABBIE!
KIDS! KIDS, WE HAVE TO GET OUT OF THE HOUSE!
WHERE'S DADDY?

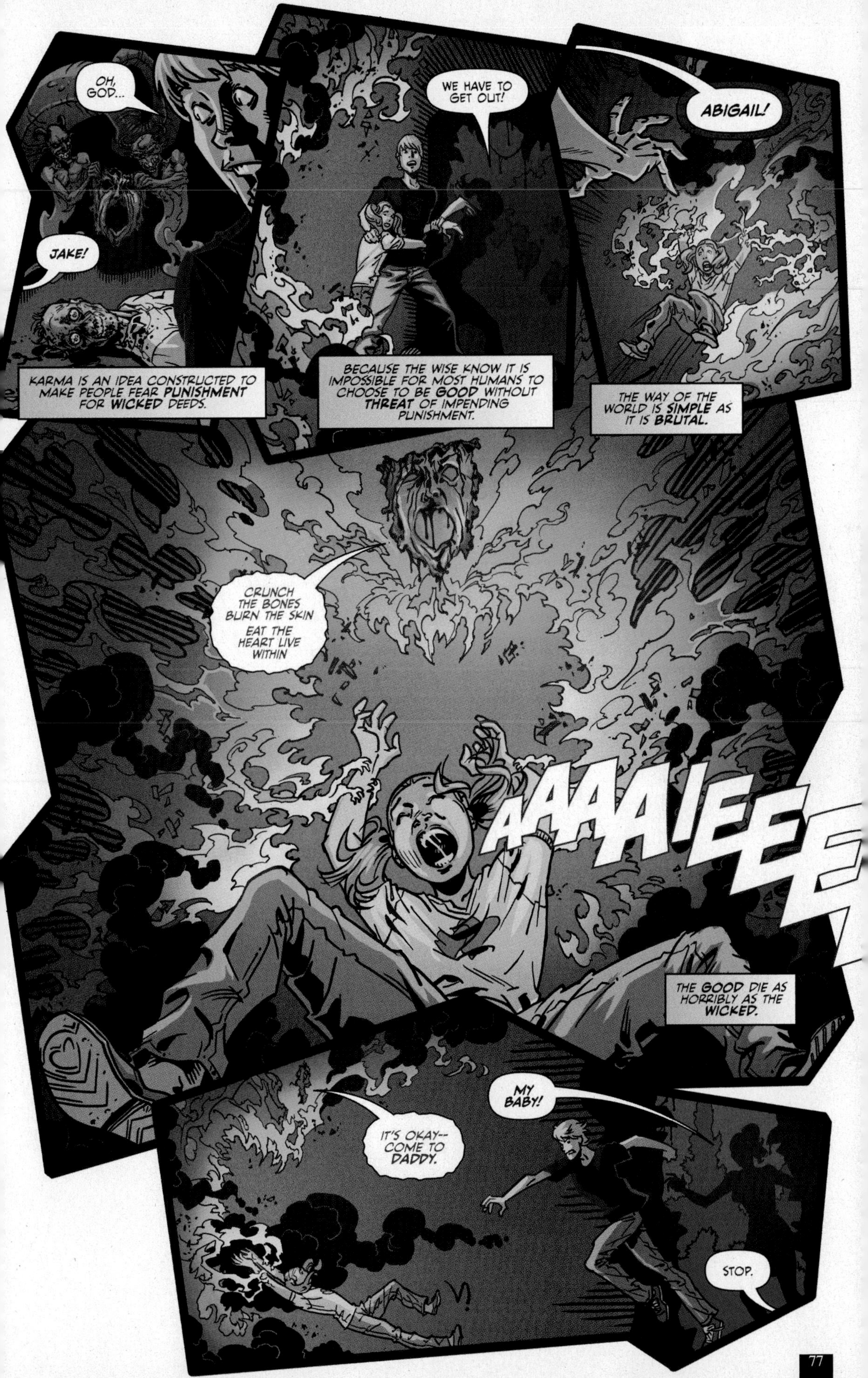
OH, GOD...
JAKE!
KARMA IS AN IDEA CONSTRUCTED TO MAKE PEOPLE FEAR PUNISHMENT FOR WICKED DEEDS.
WE HAVE TO GET OUT!
BECAUSE THE WISE KNOW IT IS IMPOSSIBLE FOR MOST HUMANS TO CHOOSE TO BE GOOD WITHOUT THREAT OF IMPENDING PUNISHMENT.
ABIGAIL!
THE WAY OF THE WORLD IS SIMPLE AS IT IS BRUTAL.
CRUNCH THE BONES BURN THE SKIN
EAT THE HEART LIVE WITHIN
AAAAIEEE
THE GOOD DIE AS HORRIBLY AS THE WICKED.
IT'S OKAY-- COME TO DADDY.
MY BABY!
STOP.

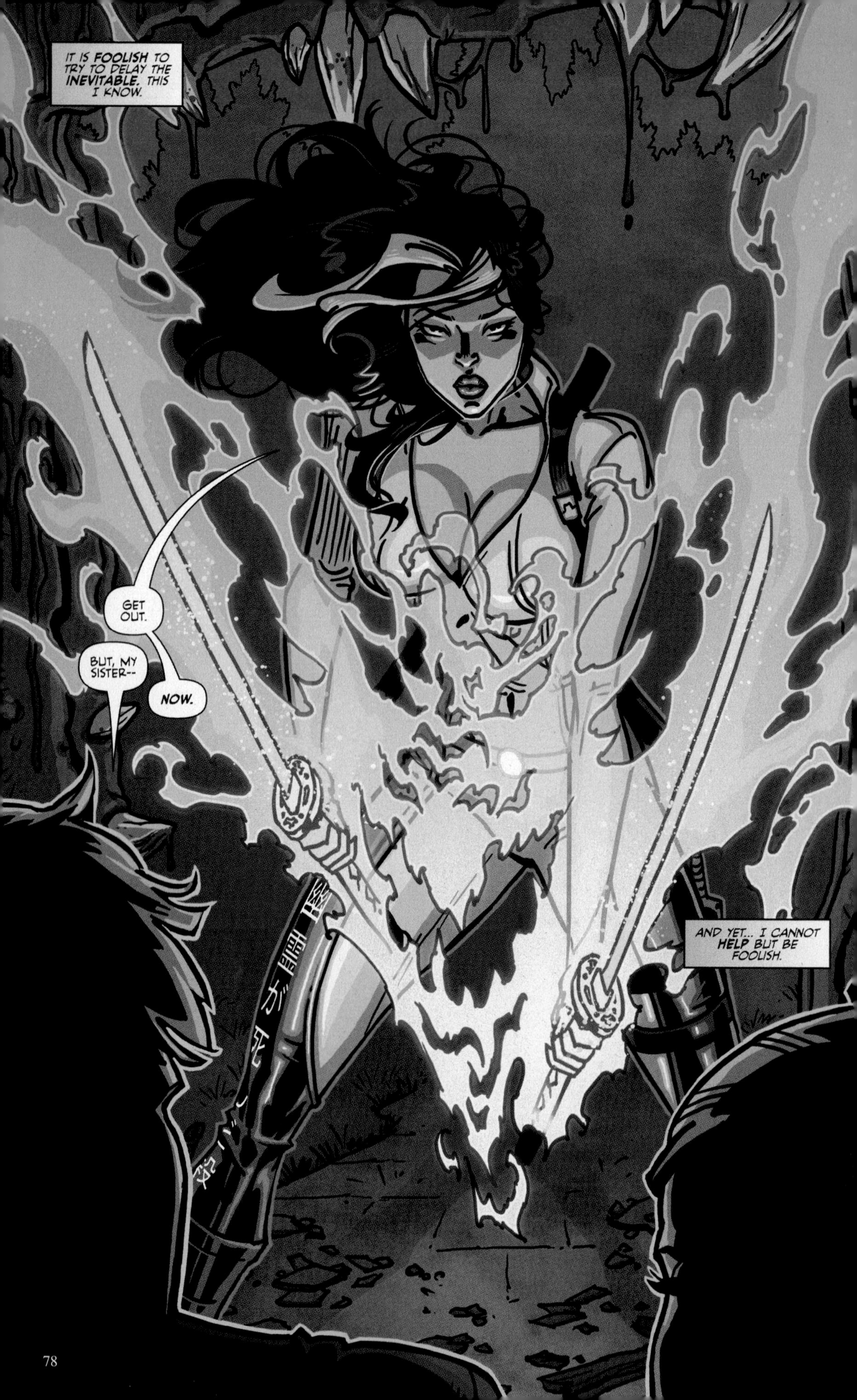
IT IS FOOLISH TO TRY TO DELAY THE INEVITABLE. THIS I KNOW.
GET OUT.
BUT, MY SISTER--
NOW.
AND YET... I CANNOT HELP BUT BE FOOLISH.

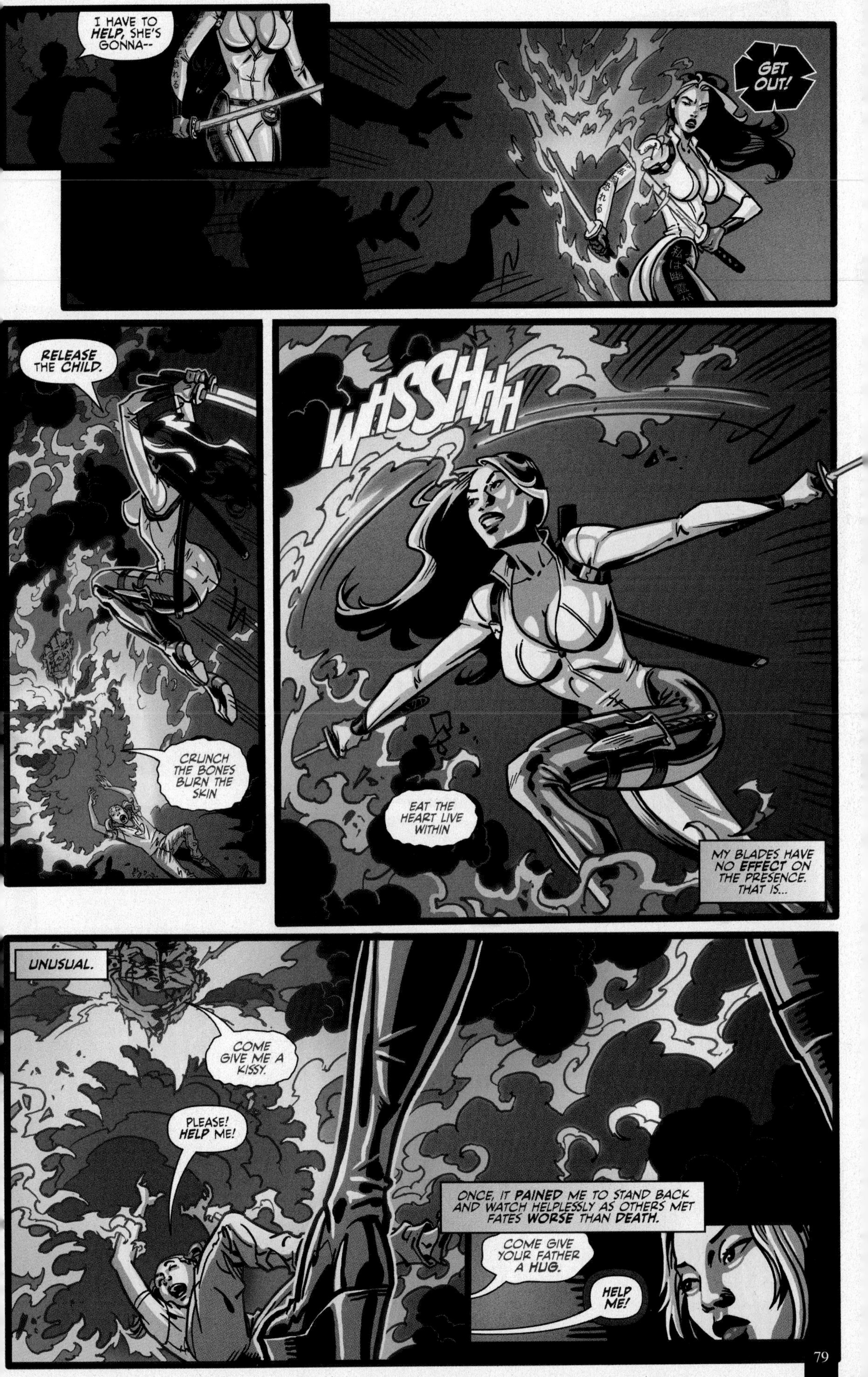

I HAVE TO HELP, SHE'S GONNA--
GET OUT!
RELEASE THE CHILD.
CRUNCH THE BONES BURN THE SKIN
WHSSHHH
EAT THE HEART LIVE WITHIN
MY BLADES HAVE NO EFFECT ON THE PRESENCE. THAT IS...
UNUSUAL.
COME GIVE ME A KISSY.
PLEASE! HELP ME!
ONCE, IT PAINED ME TO STAND BACK AND WATCH HELPLESSLY AS OTHERS MET FATES WORSE THAN DEATH.
COME GIVE YOUR FATHER A HUG.
HELP ME!

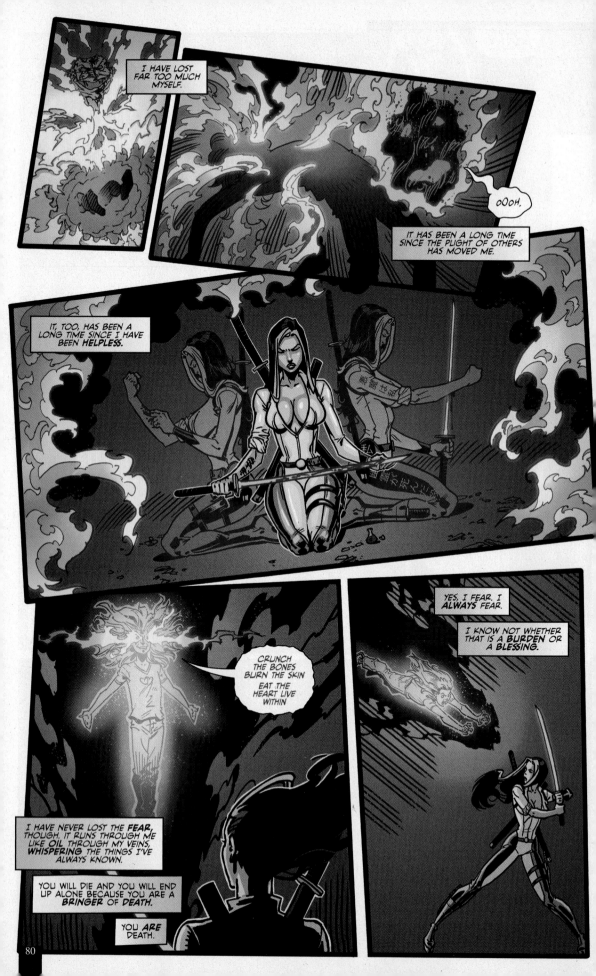

I HAVE LOST FAR TOO MUCH MYSELF.

OOOH.

IT HAS BEEN A LONG TIME SINCE THE PLIGHT OF OTHERS HAS MOVED ME.

IT, TOO, HAS BEEN A LONG TIME SINCE I HAVE BEEN **HELPLESS.**

CRUNCH THE BONES BURN THE SKIN
EAT THE HEART LIVE WITHIN

YES, I FEAR. I **ALWAYS** FEAR.

I KNOW NOT WHETHER THAT IS A **BURDEN** OR A **BLESSING.**

I HAVE NEVER LOST THE **FEAR,** THOUGH. IT RUNS THROUGH ME LIKE OIL THROUGH MY VEINS, **WHISPERING** THE THINGS I'VE ALWAYS KNOWN.

YOU WILL DIE AND YOU WILL END UP ALONE BECAUSE YOU ARE A **BRINGER** OF **DEATH.**

YOU **ARE** DEATH.

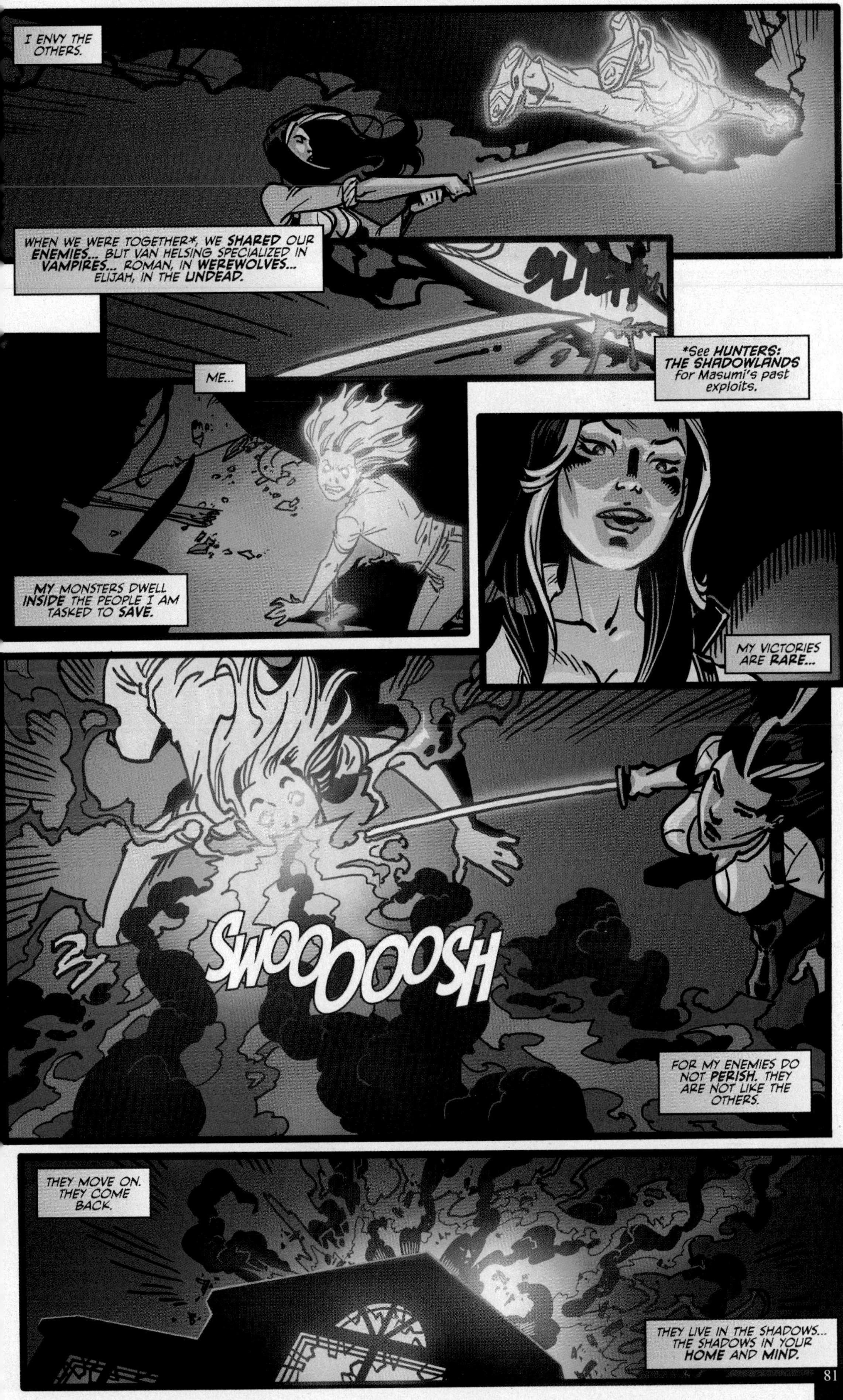
I ENVY THE OTHERS.
WHEN WE WERE TOGETHER*, WE SHARED OUR ENEMIES... BUT VAN HELSING SPECIALIZED IN VAMPIRES... ROMAN, IN WEREWOLVES... ELIJAH, IN THE UNDEAD.
*See HUNTERS: THE SHADOWLANDS for Masumi's past exploits.
ME...
MY MONSTERS DWELL INSIDE THE PEOPLE I AM TASKED TO SAVE.
MY VICTORIES ARE RARE...
SWOOOOOSH
FOR MY ENEMIES DO NOT PERISH. THEY ARE NOT LIKE THE OTHERS.
THEY MOVE ON. THEY COME BACK.
THEY LIVE IN THE SHADOWS... THE SHADOWS IN YOUR HOME AND MIND.

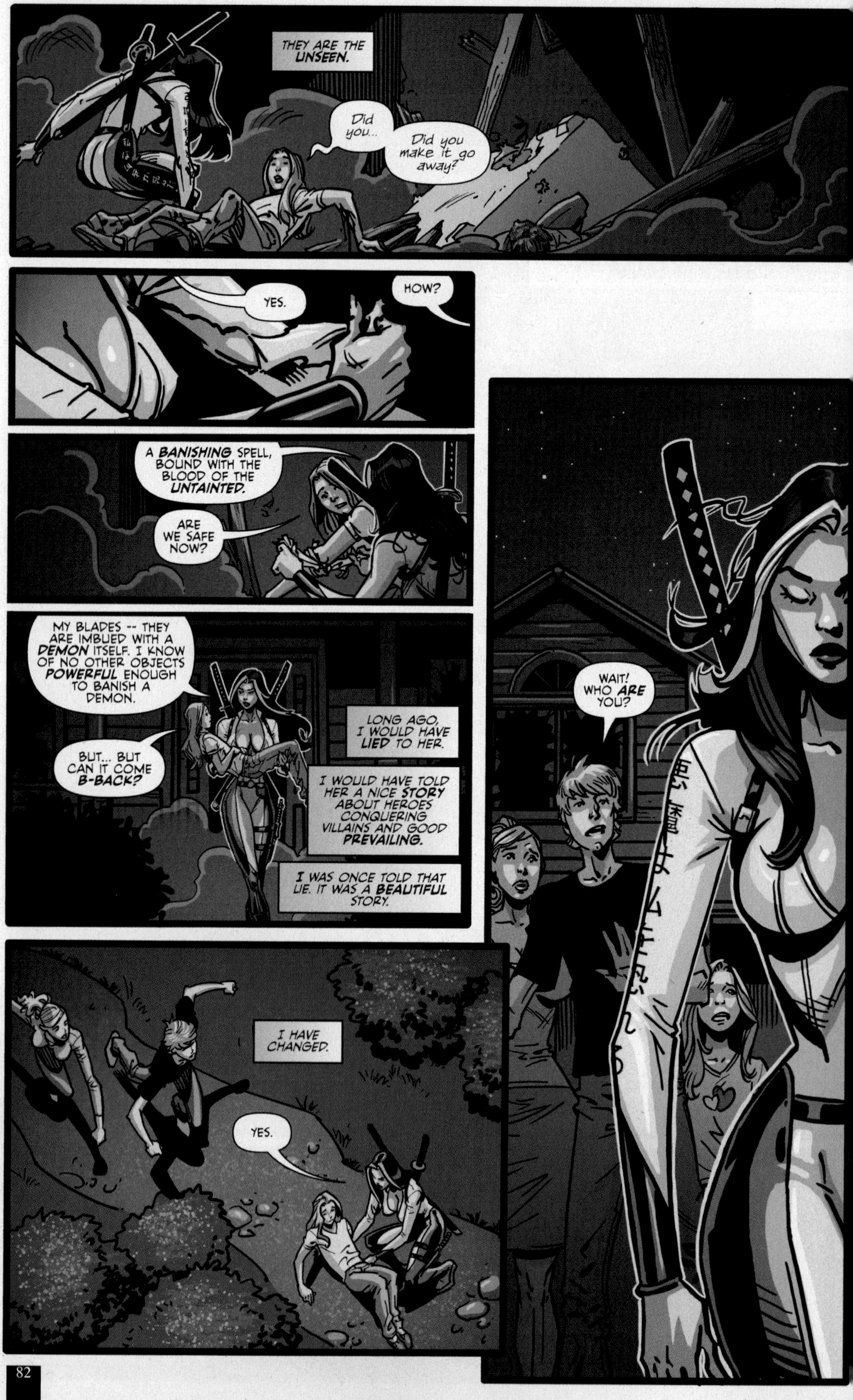
THEY ARE THE UNSEEN.
Did you...
Did you make it go away?
YES.
HOW?
A BANISHING SPELL, BOUND WITH THE BLOOD OF THE UNTAINTED.
ARE WE SAFE NOW?
MY BLADES -- THEY ARE IMBUED WITH A DEMON ITSELF. I KNOW OF NO OTHER OBJECTS POWERFUL ENOUGH TO BANISH A DEMON.
BUT... BUT CAN IT COME B-BACK?
LONG AGO, I WOULD HAVE LIED TO HER.
I WOULD HAVE TOLD HER A NICE STORY ABOUT HEROES CONQUERING VILLAINS AND GOOD PREVAILING.
I WAS ONCE TOLD THAT LIE. IT WAS A BEAUTIFUL STORY.
I HAVE CHANGED.
YES.
WAIT! WHO ARE YOU?

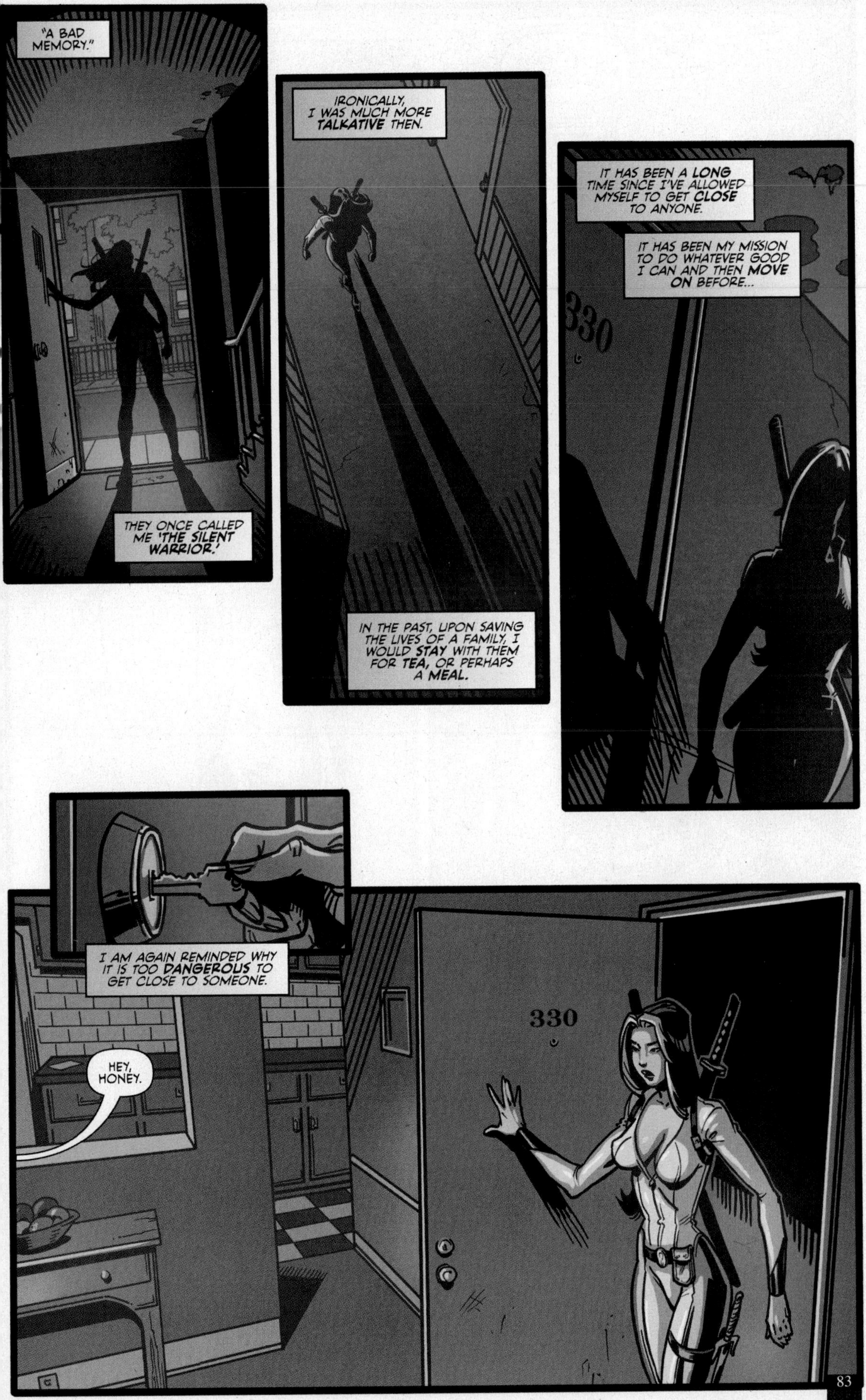
"A BAD MEMORY."
THEY ONCE CALLED ME 'THE SILENT WARRIOR.'
IRONICALLY, I WAS MUCH MORE TALKATIVE THEN.
IN THE PAST, UPON SAVING THE LIVES OF A FAMILY, I WOULD STAY WITH THEM FOR TEA, OR PERHAPS A MEAL.
IT HAS BEEN A LONG TIME SINCE I'VE ALLOWED MYSELF TO GET CLOSE TO ANYONE.
IT HAS BEEN MY MISSION TO DO WHATEVER GOOD I CAN AND THEN MOVE ON BEFORE...
330
I AM AGAIN REMINDED WHY IT IS TOO DANGEROUS TO GET CLOSE TO SOMEONE.
330
HEY, HONEY.

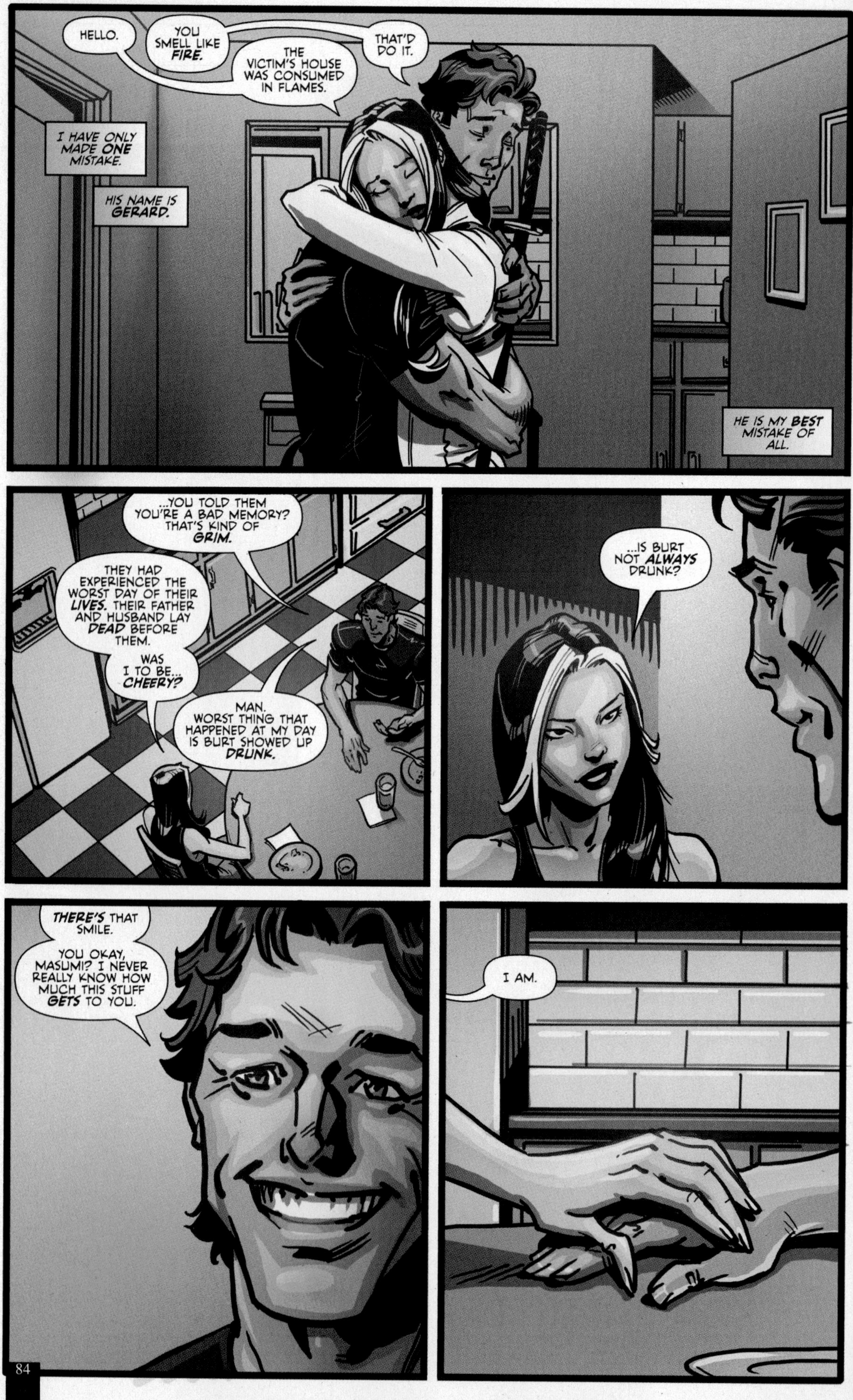
HELLO.
YOU SMELL LIKE FIRE.
THE VICTIM'S HOUSE WAS CONSUMED IN FLAMES.
THAT'D DO IT.
I HAVE ONLY MADE ONE MISTAKE.
HIS NAME IS GERARD.
HE IS MY BEST MISTAKE OF ALL.
...YOU TOLD THEM YOU'RE A BAD MEMORY? THAT'S KIND OF GRIM.
THEY HAD EXPERIENCED THE WORST DAY OF THEIR LIVES. THEIR FATHER AND HUSBAND LAY DEAD BEFORE THEM.
WAS I TO BE... CHEERY?
MAN. WORST THING THAT HAPPENED AT MY DAY IS BURT SHOWED UP DRUNK.
...IS BURT NOT ALWAYS DRUNK?
THERE'S THAT SMILE.
YOU OKAY, MASUMI? I NEVER REALLY KNOW HOW MUCH THIS STUFF GETS TO YOU.
I AM.

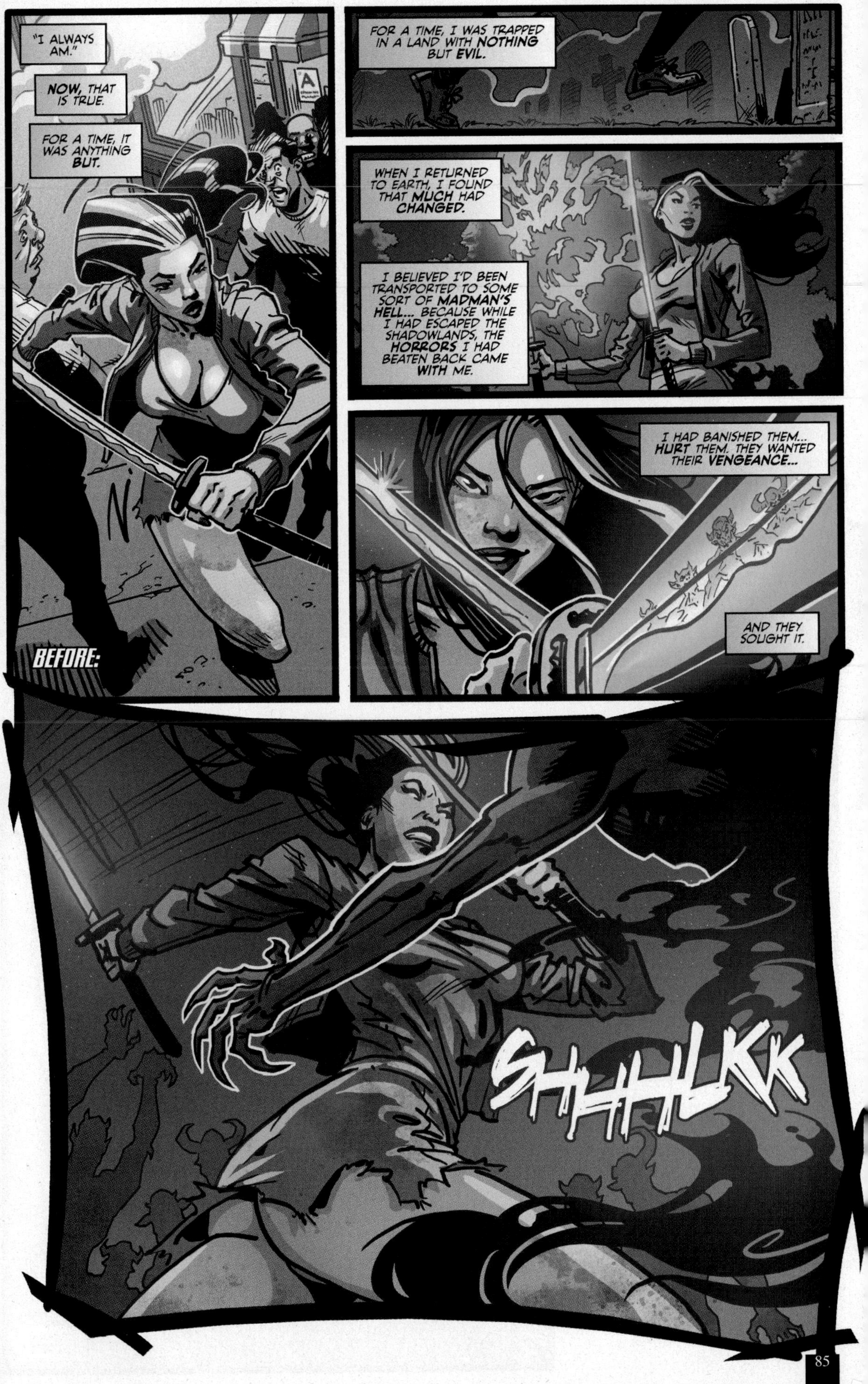

"I ALWAYS AM."
NOW, THAT IS TRUE.
FOR A TIME, IT WAS ANYTHING BUT.
BEFORE:
FOR A TIME, I WAS TRAPPED IN A LAND WITH NOTHING BUT EVIL.
WHEN I RETURNED TO EARTH, I FOUND THAT MUCH HAD CHANGED.
I BELIEVED I'D BEEN TRANSPORTED TO SOME SORT OF MADMAN'S HELL... BECAUSE WHILE I HAD ESCAPED THE SHADOWLANDS, THE HORRORS I HAD BEATEN BACK CAME WITH ME.
I HAD BANISHED THEM... HURT THEM. THEY WANTED THEIR VENGEANCE...
AND THEY SOUGHT IT.
SHHHLKK

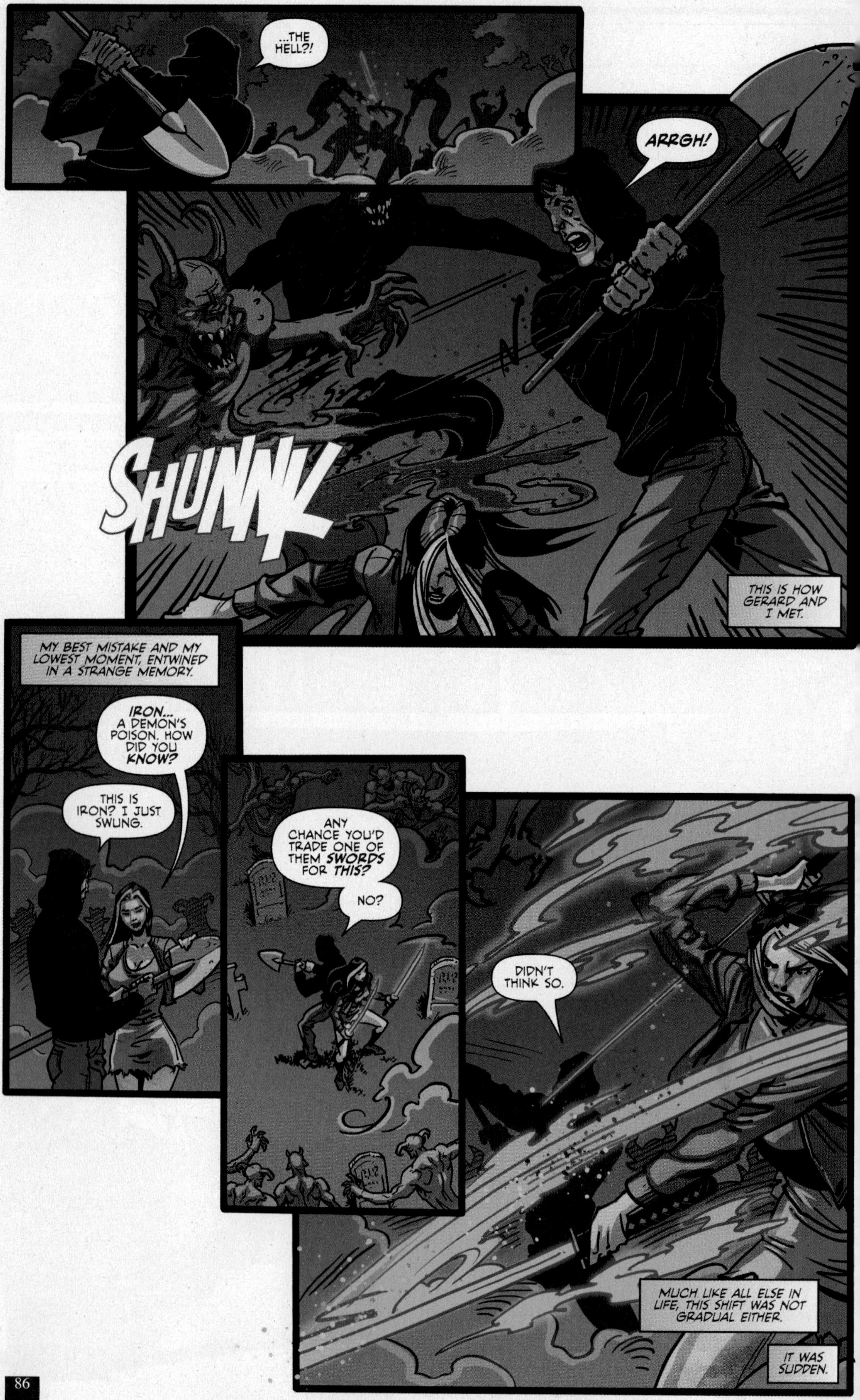
...THE HELL?!
ARRGH!
SHUNNK
THIS IS HOW GERARD AND I MET.
MY BEST MISTAKE AND MY LOWEST MOMENT, ENTWINED IN A STRANGE MEMORY.
IRON... A DEMON'S POISON. HOW DID YOU KNOW?
THIS IS IRON? I JUST SWUNG.
ANY CHANCE YOU'D TRADE ONE OF THEM SWORDS FOR THIS?
NO?
DIDN'T THINK SO.
MUCH LIKE ALL ELSE IN LIFE, THIS SHIFT WAS NOT GRADUAL EITHER.
IT WAS SUDDEN.

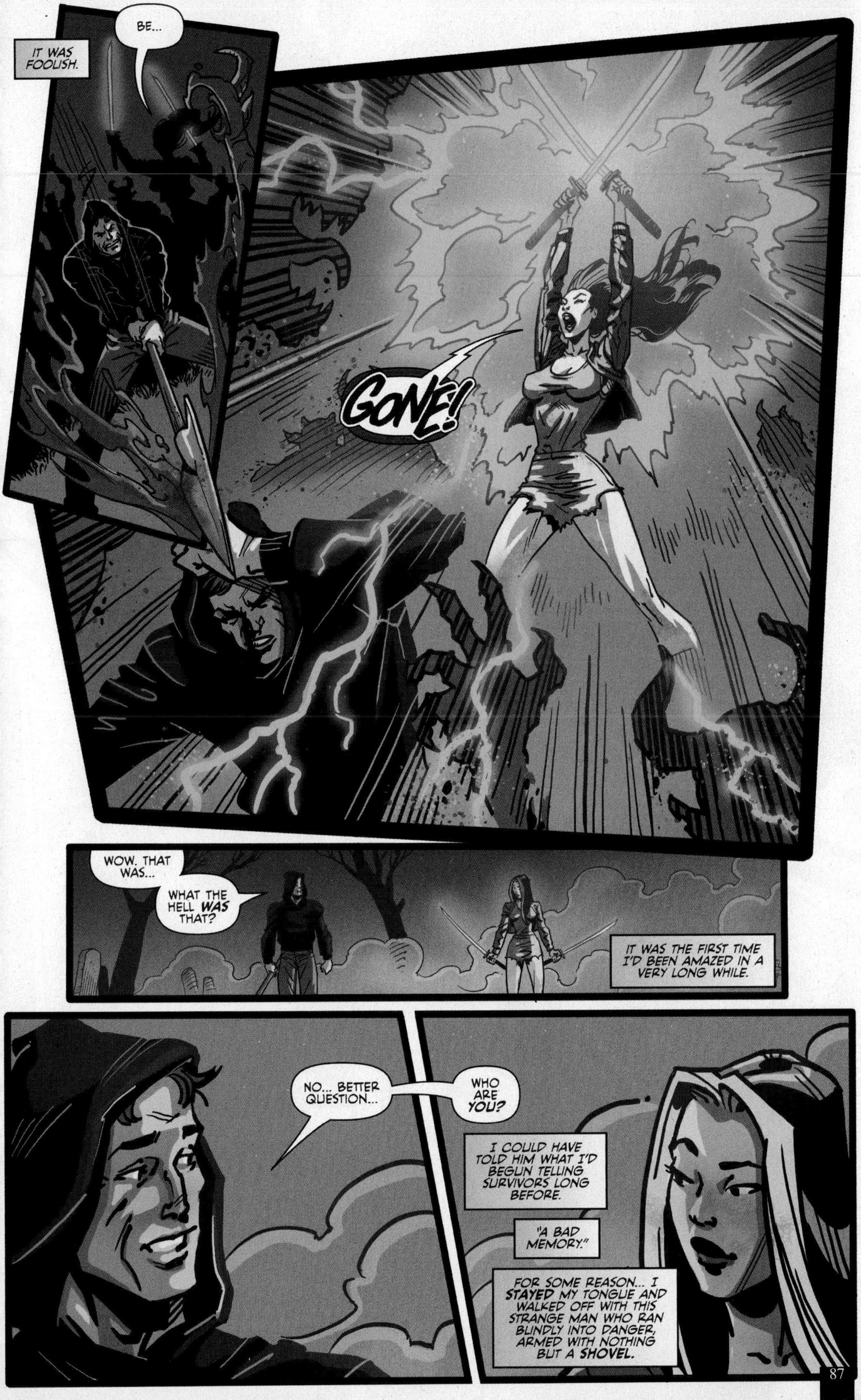
IT WAS FOOLISH.
BE...
GONE!
WOW. THAT WAS...
WHAT THE HELL WAS THAT?
IT WAS THE FIRST TIME I'D BEEN AMAZED IN A VERY LONG WHILE.
NO... BETTER QUESTION...
WHO ARE YOU?
I COULD HAVE TOLD HIM WHAT I'D BEGUN TELLING SURVIVORS LONG BEFORE.
"A BAD MEMORY."
FOR SOME REASON... I STAYED MY TONGUE AND WALKED OFF WITH THIS STRANGE MAN WHO RAN BLINDLY INTO DANGER, ARMED WITH NOTHING BUT A SHOVEL.

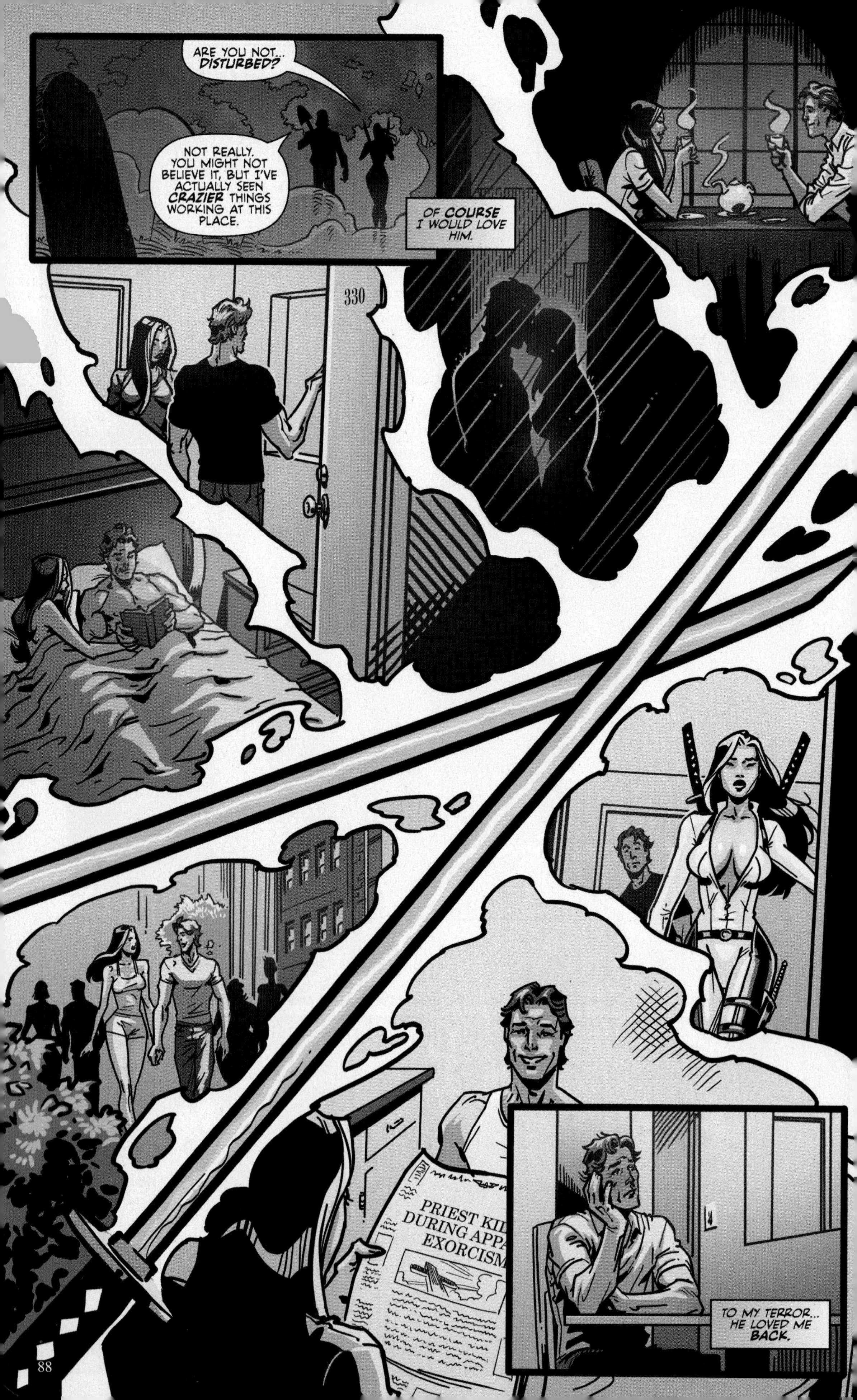
ARE YOU NOT... DISTURBED?
NOT REALLY. YOU MIGHT NOT BELIEVE IT, BUT I'VE ACTUALLY SEEN CRAZIER THINGS WORKING AT THIS PLACE.
OF COURSE I WOULD LOVE HIM.
330
PRIEST KIL
DURING APPA
EXORCISM
TO MY TERROR... HE LOVED ME BACK.

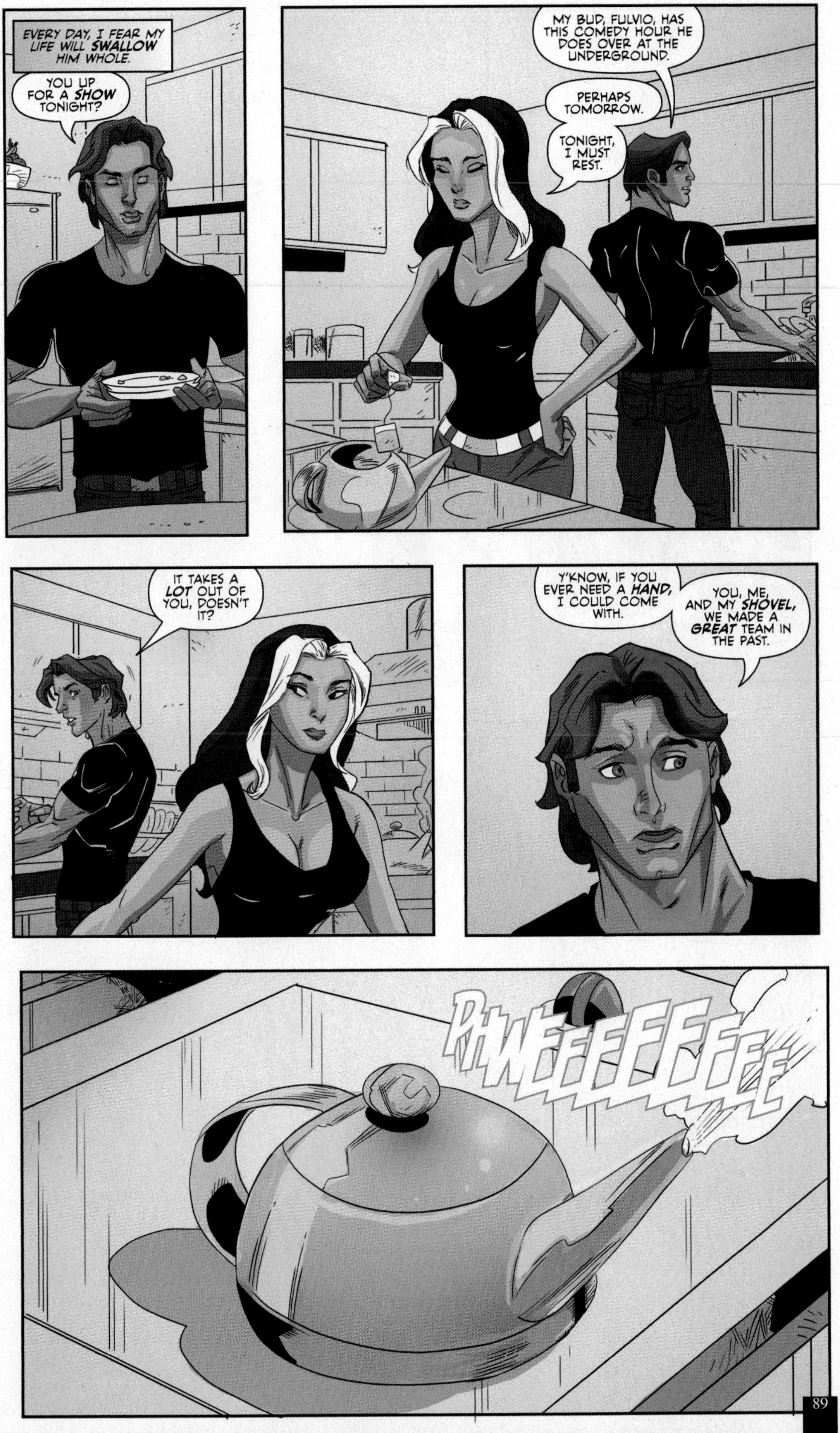
EVERY DAY, I FEAR MY LIFE WILL SWALLOW HIM WHOLE.
YOU UP FOR A SHOW TONIGHT?
MY BUD, FULVIO, HAS THIS COMEDY HOUR HE DOES OVER AT THE UNDERGROUND.
PERHAPS TOMORROW.
TONIGHT, I MUST REST.
IT TAKES A LOT OUT OF YOU, DOESN'T IT?
Y'KNOW, IF YOU EVER NEED A HAND, I COULD COME WITH.
YOU, ME, AND MY SHOVEL, WE MADE A GREAT TEAM IN THE PAST.
PHWEEEEEEEEE

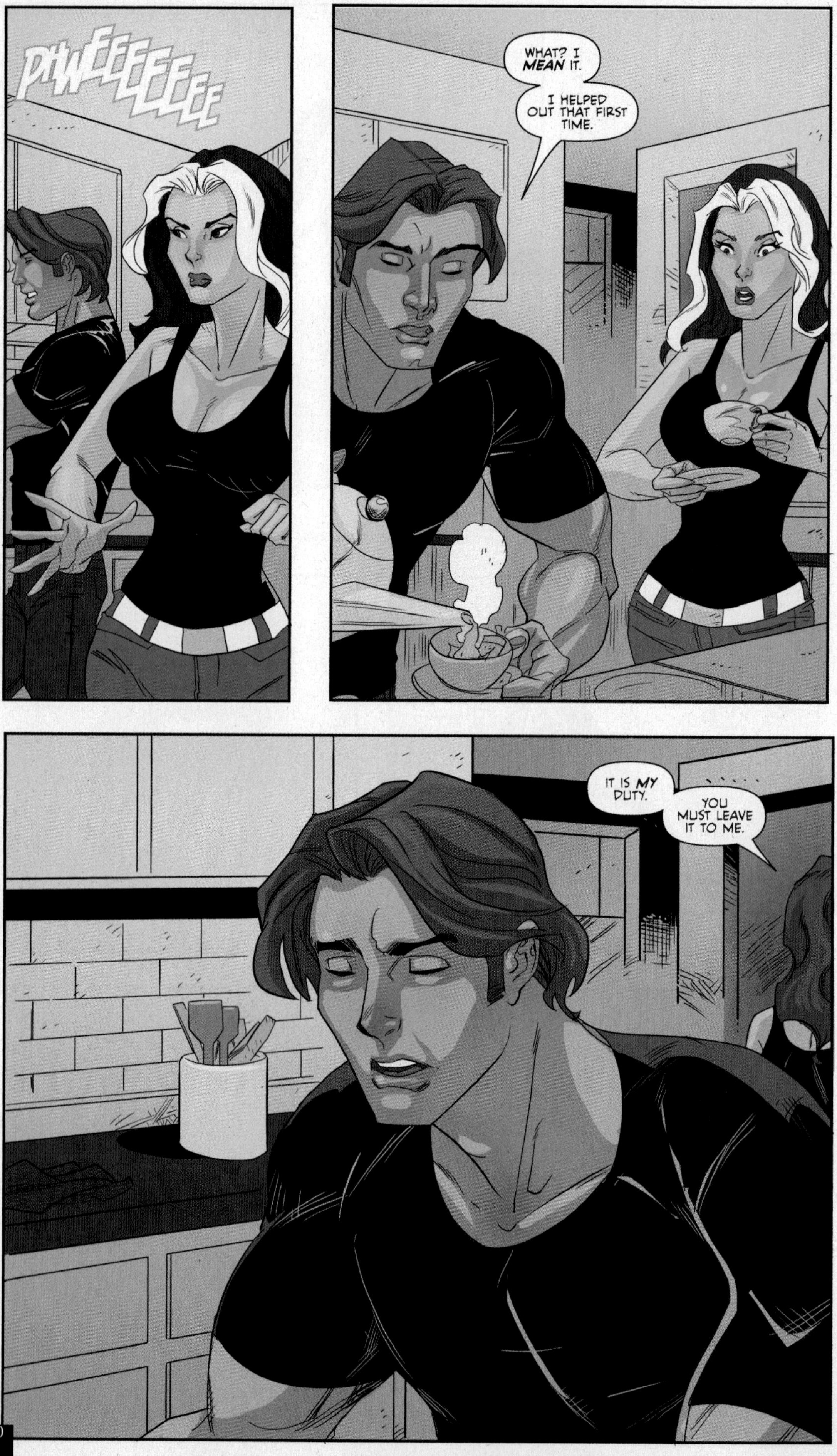
PHWEEEEEEEE
WHAT? I MEAN IT.
I HELPED OUT THAT FIRST TIME.
IT IS MY DUTY.
YOU MUST LEAVE IT TO ME.

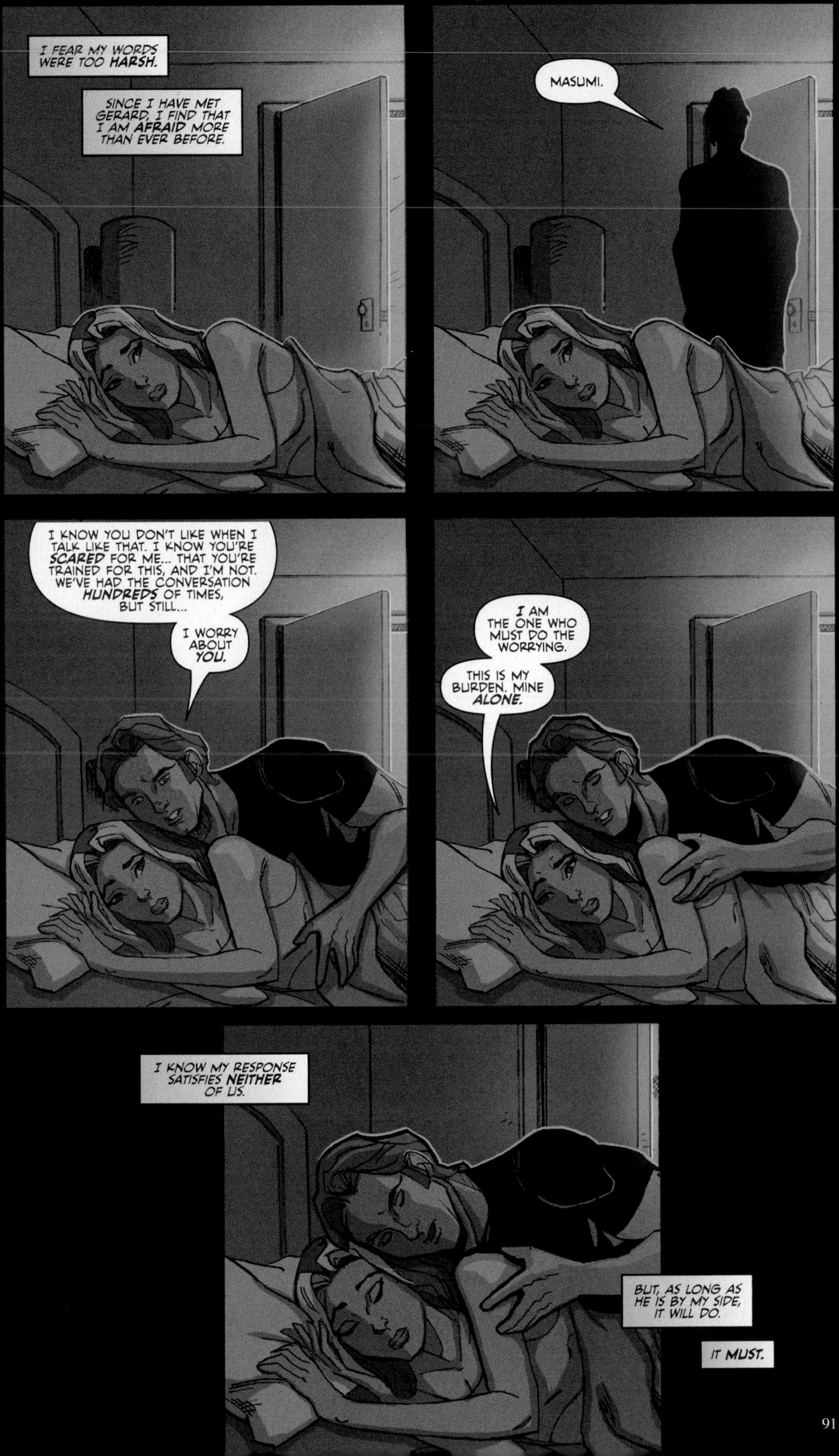
I FEAR MY WORDS WERE TOO HARSH.
SINCE I HAVE MET GERARD, I FIND THAT I AM AFRAID MORE THAN EVER BEFORE.
MASUMI.
I KNOW YOU DON'T LIKE WHEN I TALK LIKE THAT. I KNOW YOU'RE SCARED FOR ME... THAT YOU'RE TRAINED FOR THIS, AND I'M NOT. WE'VE HAD THE CONVERSATION HUNDREDS OF TIMES, BUT STILL...
I WORRY ABOUT YOU.
I AM THE ONE WHO MUST DO THE WORRYING.
THIS IS MY BURDEN. MINE ALONE.
I KNOW MY RESPONSE SATISFIES NEITHER OF US.
BUT, AS LONG AS HE IS BY MY SIDE, IT WILL DO.
IT MUST.

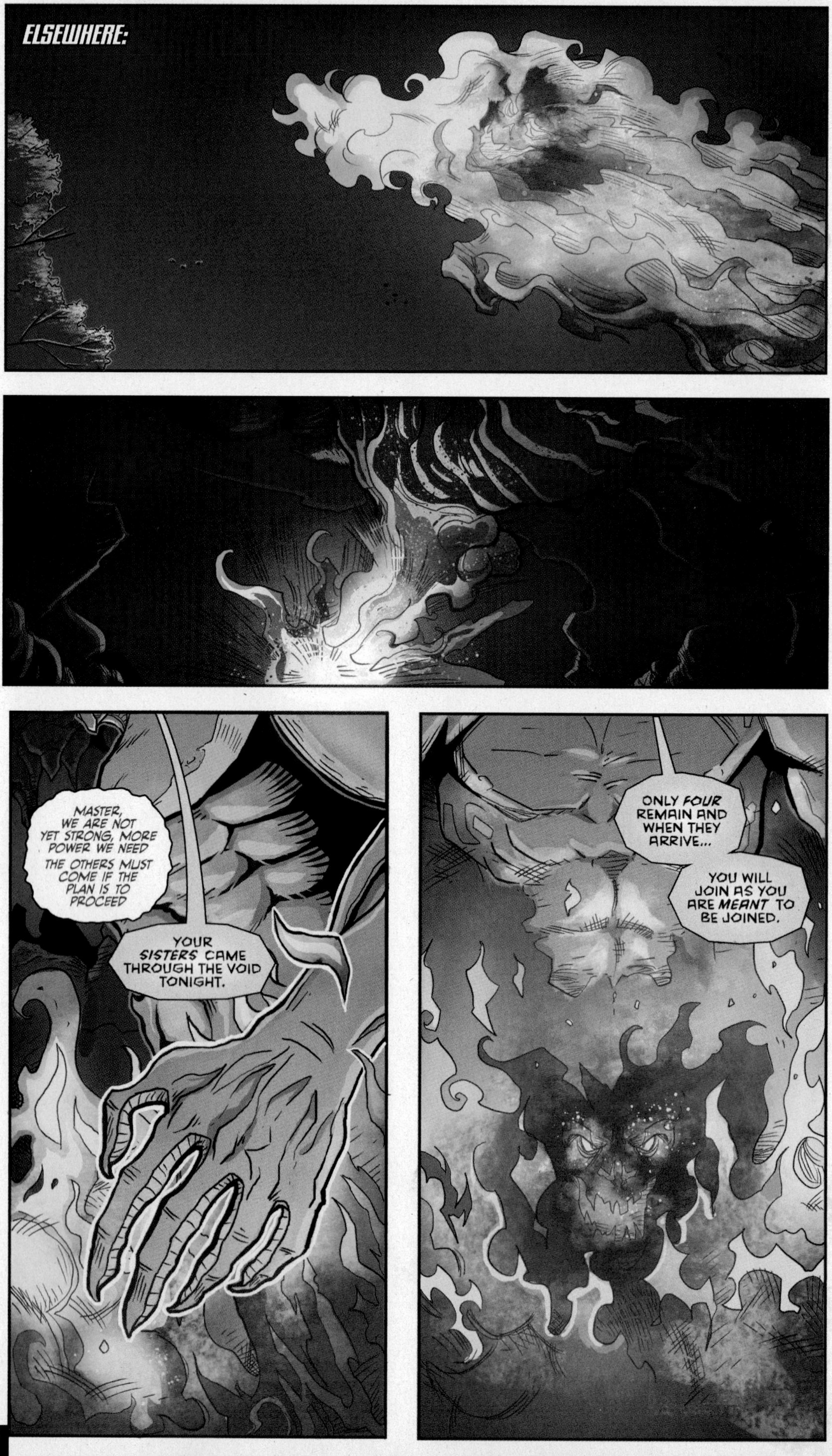
ELSEWHERE:
MASTER, WE ARE NOT YET STRONG, MORE POWER WE NEED
THE OTHERS MUST COME IF THE PLAN IS TO PROCEED
YOUR SISTERS CAME THROUGH THE VOID TONIGHT.
ONLY FOUR REMAIN AND WHEN THEY ARRIVE...
YOU WILL JOIN AS YOU ARE MEANT TO BE JOINED.

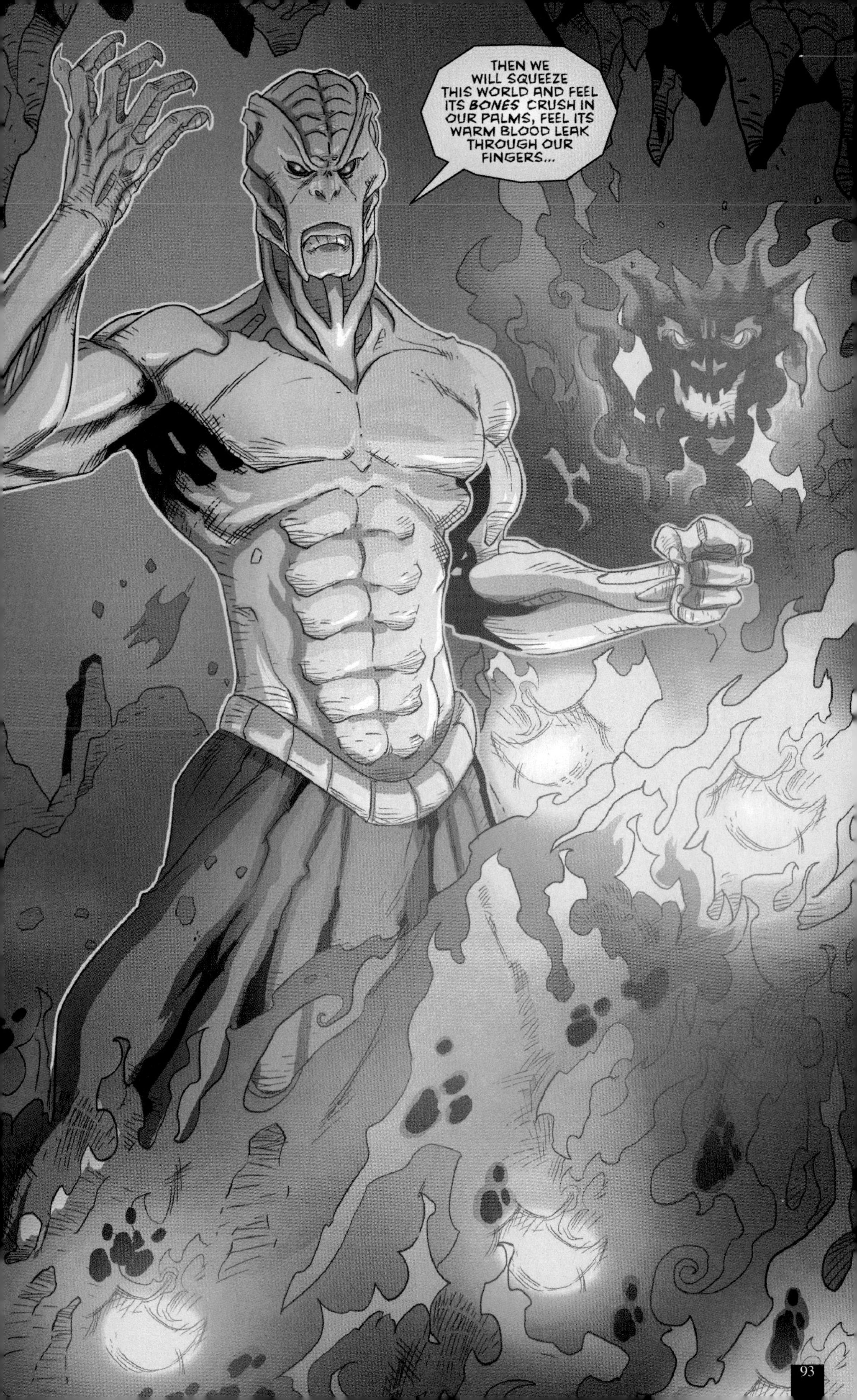
THEN WE WILL SQUEEZE THIS WORLD AND FEEL ITS BONES CRUSH IN OUR PALMS, FEEL ITS WARM BLOOD LEAK THROUGH OUR FINGERS...

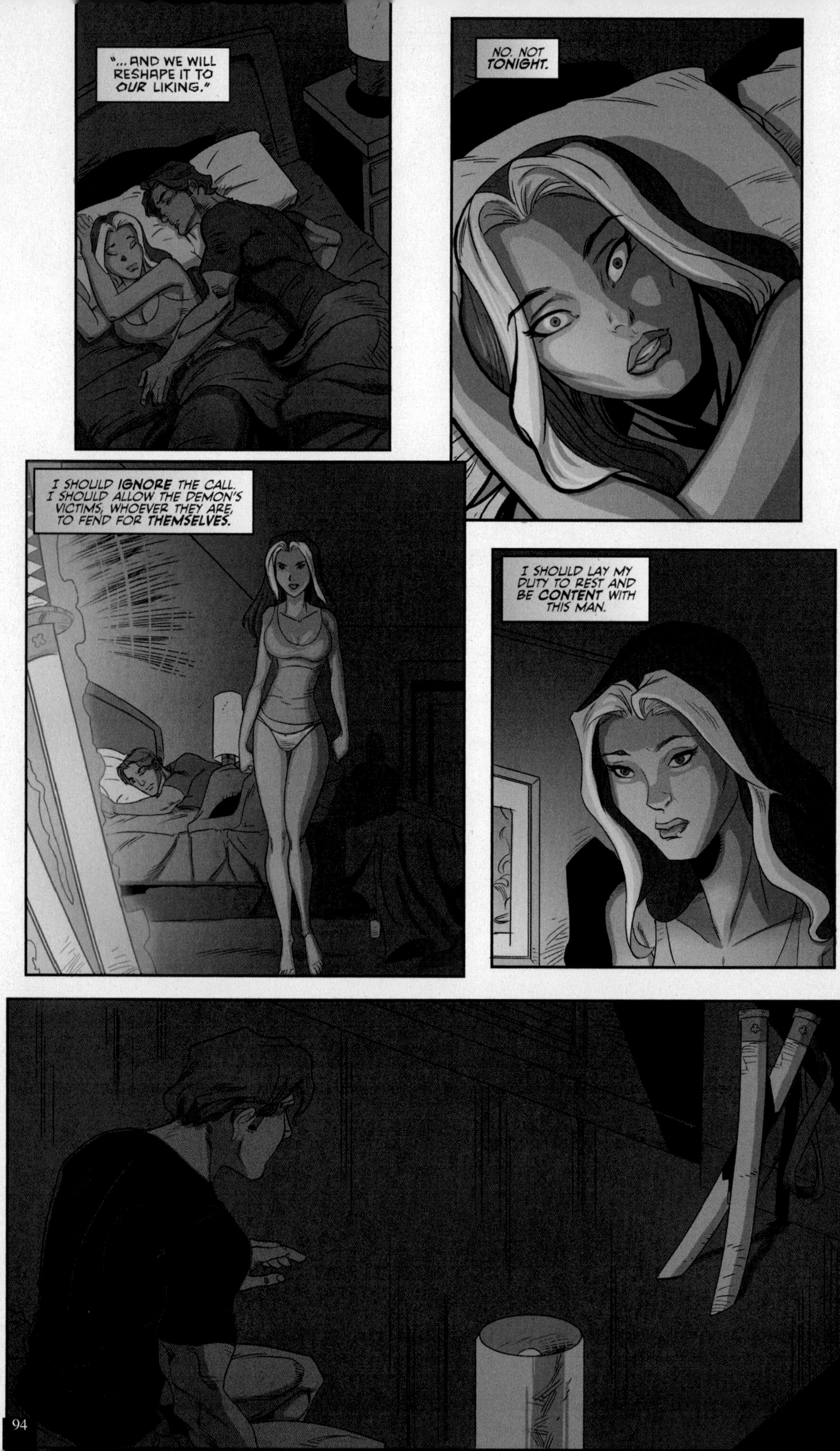
"...AND WE WILL RESHAPE IT TO OUR LIKING."
NO. NOT TONIGHT.
I SHOULD IGNORE THE CALL. I SHOULD ALLOW THE DEMON'S VICTIMS, WHOEVER THEY ARE, TO FEND FOR THEMSELVES.
I SHOULD LAY MY DUTY TO REST AND BE CONTENT WITH THIS MAN.

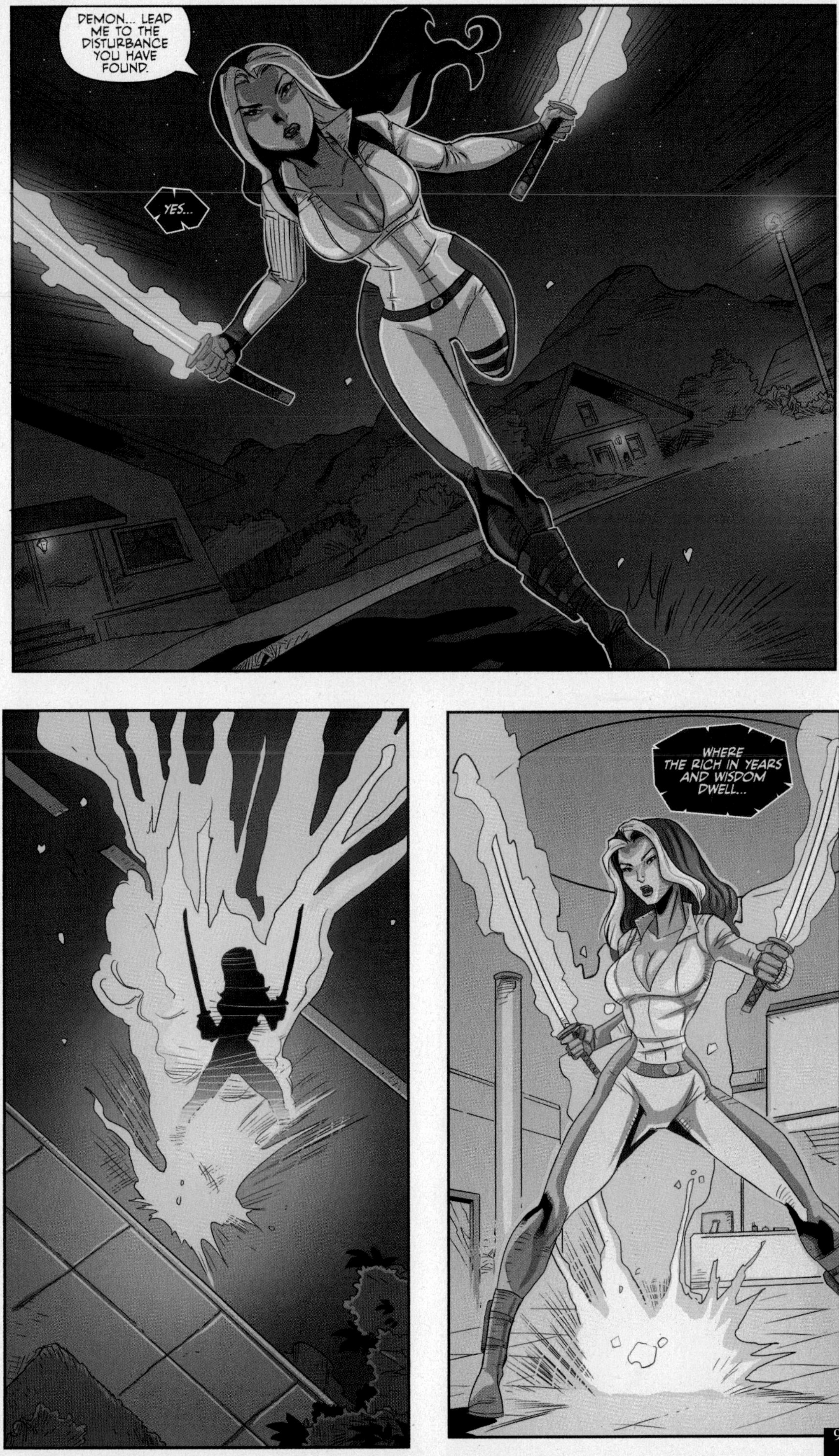
DEMON... LEAD ME TO THE DISTURBANCE YOU HAVE FOUND.
YES...
WHERE THE RICH IN YEARS AND WISDOM DWELL...

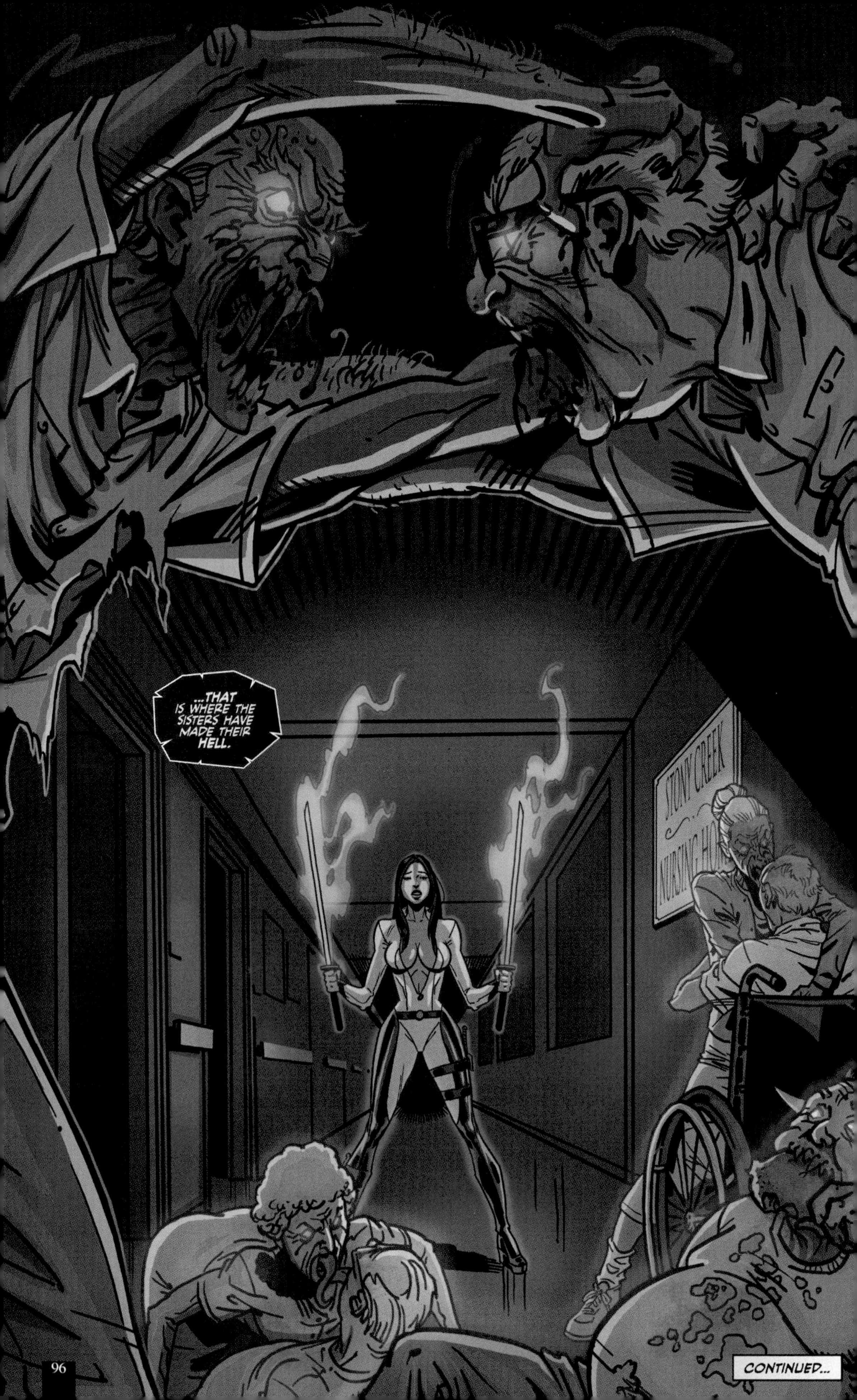
...THAT IS WHERE THE SISTERS HAVE MADE THEIR HELL.
STONY CREEK NURSING HO
CONTINUED...

Grimm Fairy Tales presents:

ZOMBIES & DEMONS

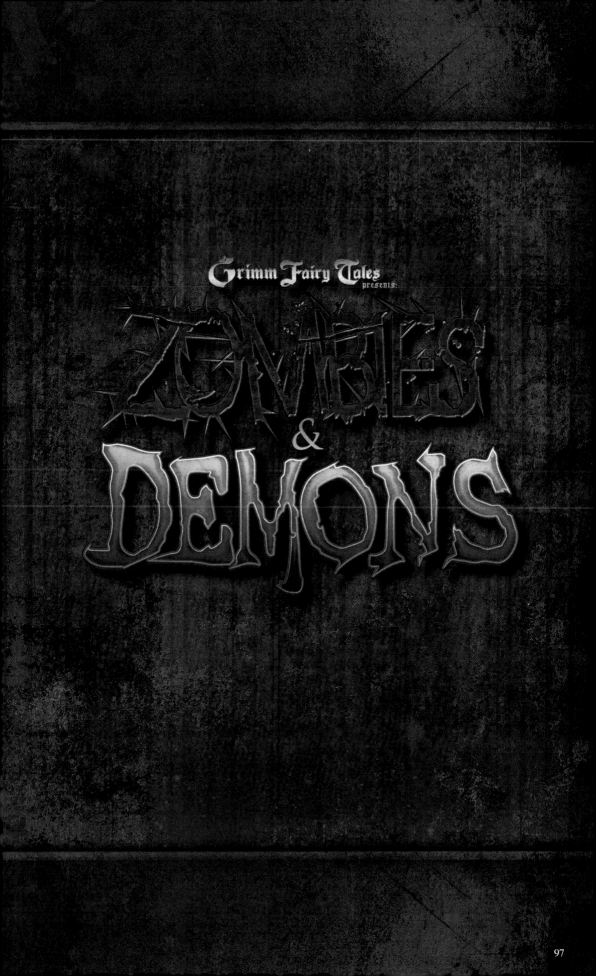

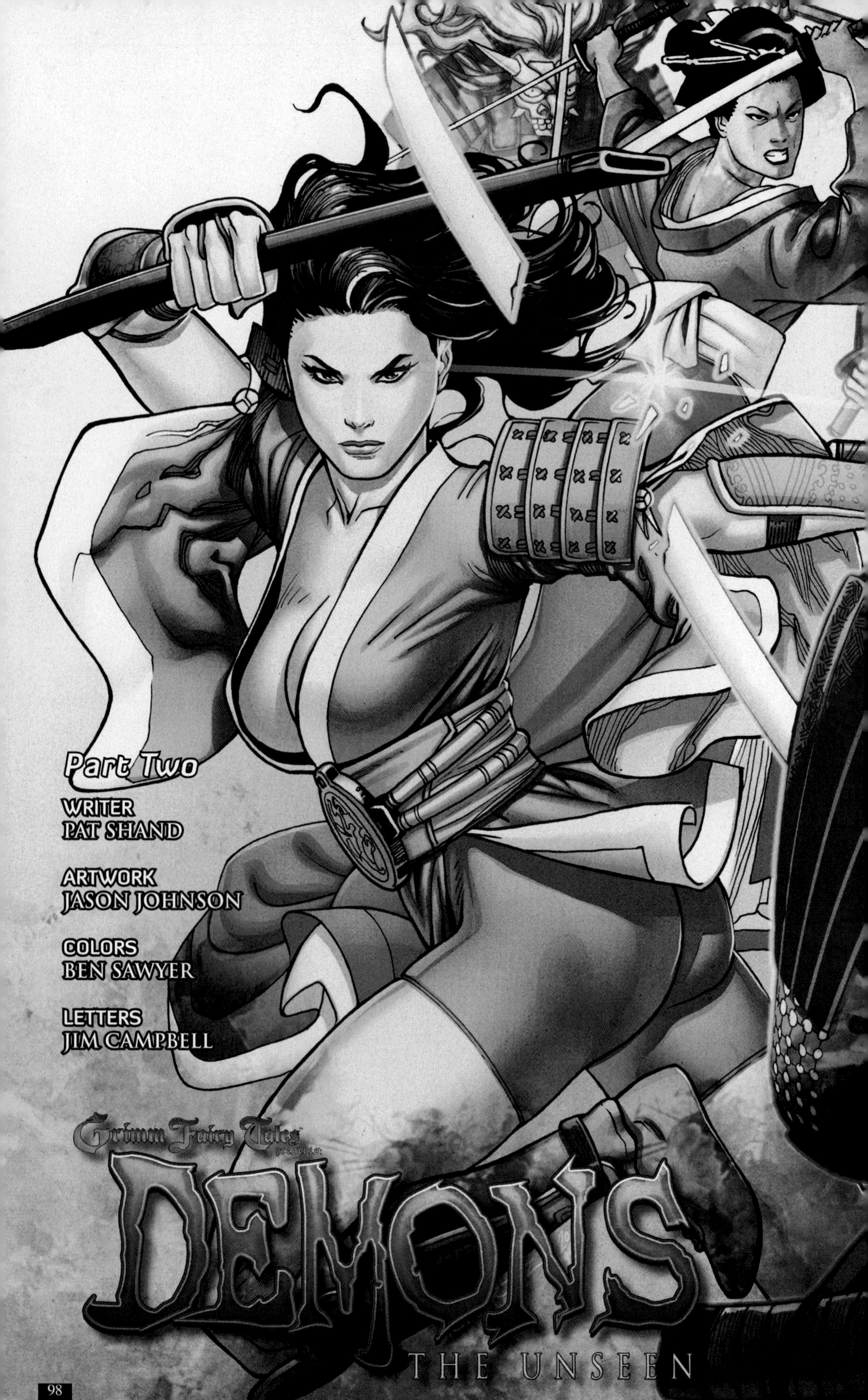
Part Two
WRITER
PAT SHAND
ARTWORK
JASON JOHNSON
COLORS
BEN SAWYER
LETTERS
JIM CAMPBELL
Grimm Fairy Tales presents:
DEMONS
THE UNSEEN

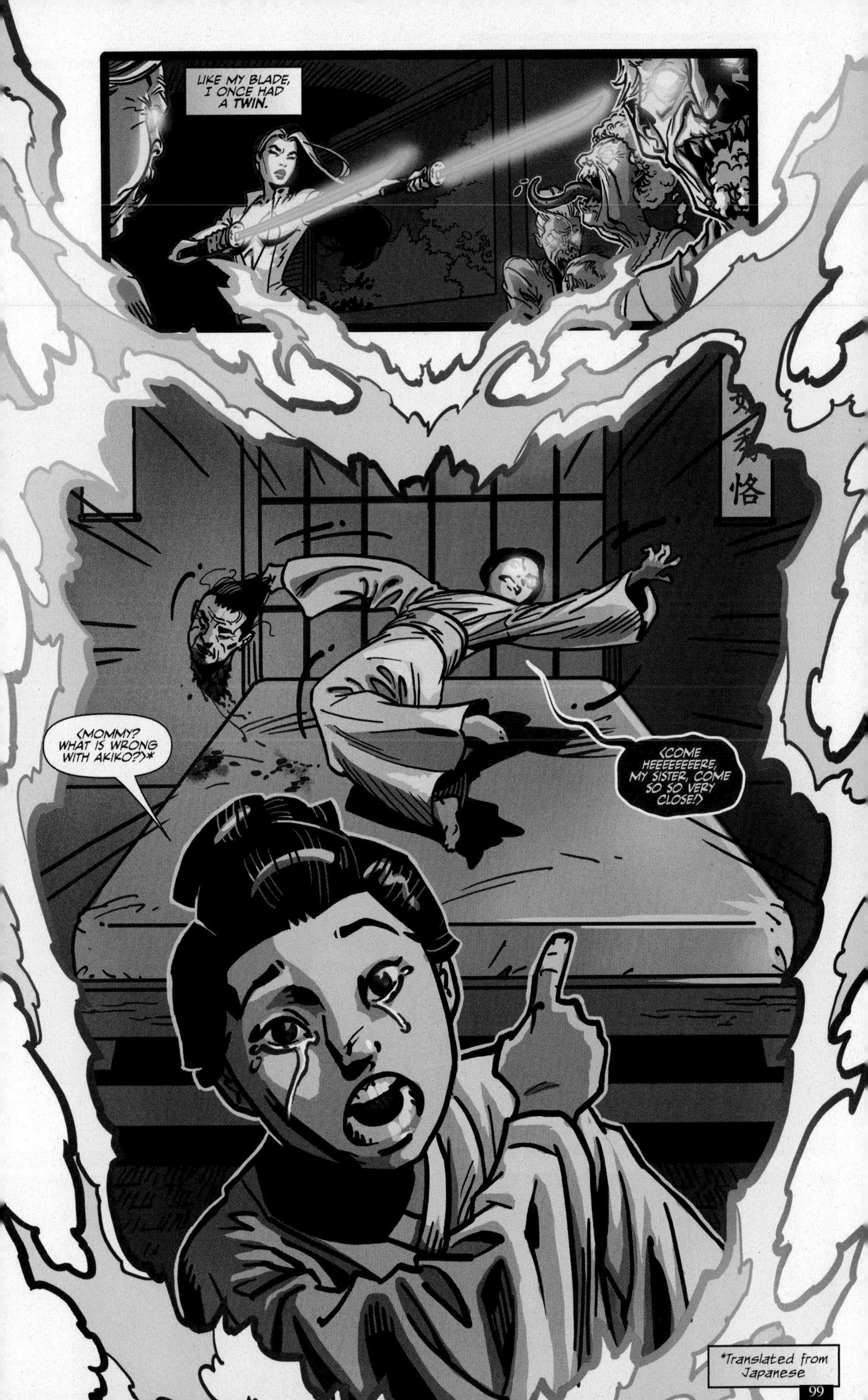
LIKE MY BLADE, I ONCE HAD A TWIN.
<MOMMY? WHAT IS WRONG WITH AKIKO?>*
<COME HEEEEEEEERE, MY SISTER, COME SO SO VERY CLOSE!>
*Translated from Japanese

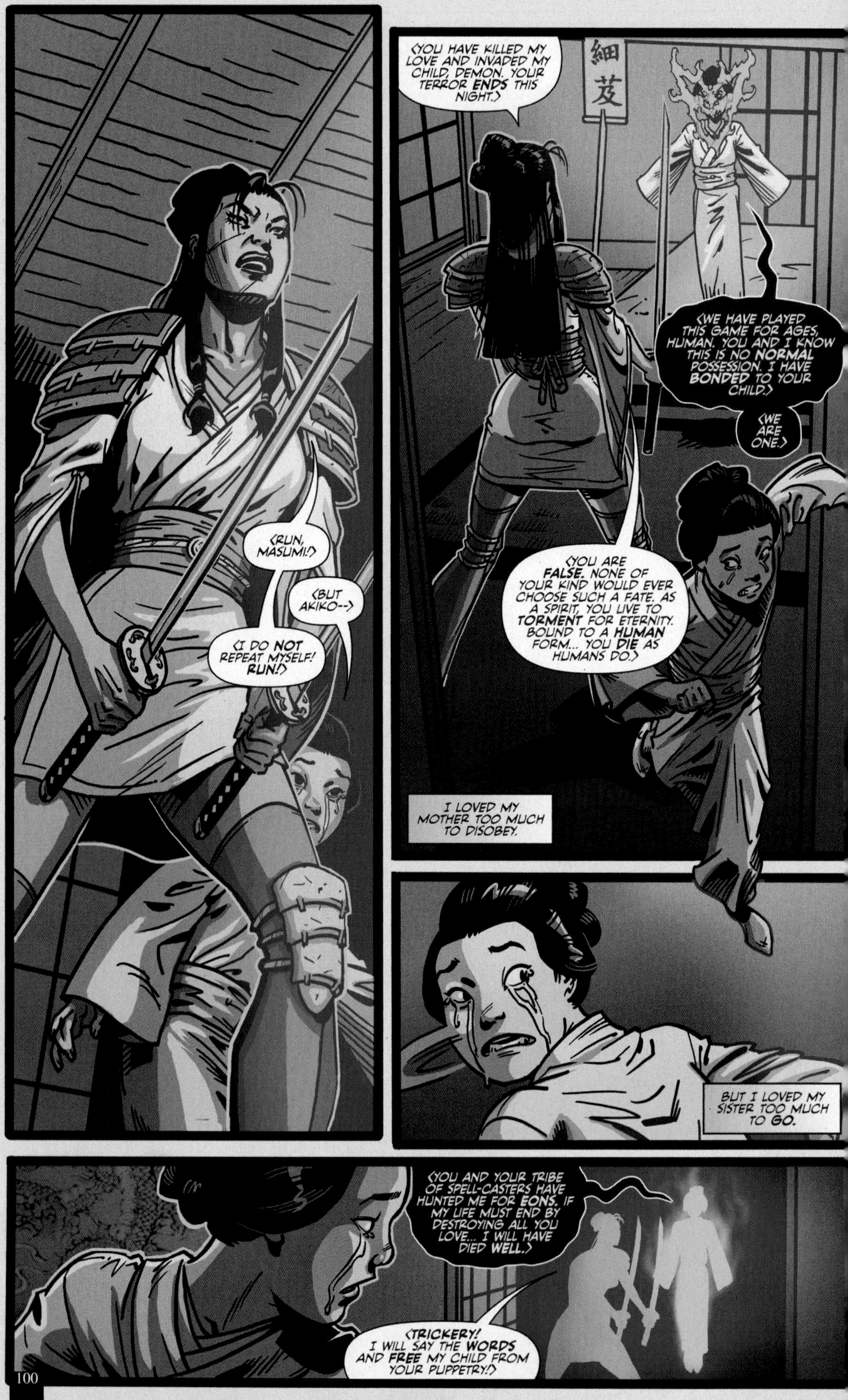

<RUN, MASUMI!>
<BUT AKIKO-->
<I DO NOT REPEAT MYSELF! RUN!>
<YOU HAVE KILLED MY LOVE AND INVADED MY CHILD, DEMON. YOUR TERROR ENDS THIS NIGHT.>
細 芨
<WE HAVE PLAYED THIS GAME FOR AGES, HUMAN. YOU AND I KNOW THIS IS NO NORMAL POSSESSION. I HAVE BONDED TO YOUR CHILD.>
<WE ARE ONE.>
<YOU ARE FALSE. NONE OF YOUR KIND WOULD EVER CHOOSE SUCH A FATE. AS A SPIRIT, YOU LIVE TO TORMENT FOR ETERNITY. BOUND TO A HUMAN FORM... YOU DIE AS HUMANS DO.>
I LOVED MY MOTHER TOO MUCH TO DISOBEY.
BUT I LOVED MY SISTER TOO MUCH TO GO.
<YOU AND YOUR TRIBE OF SPELL-CASTERS HAVE HUNTED ME FOR EONS. IF MY LIFE MUST END BY DESTROYING ALL YOU LOVE... I WILL HAVE DIED WELL.>
<TRICKERY! I WILL SAY THE WORDS AND FREE MY CHILD FROM YOUR PUPPETRY!>

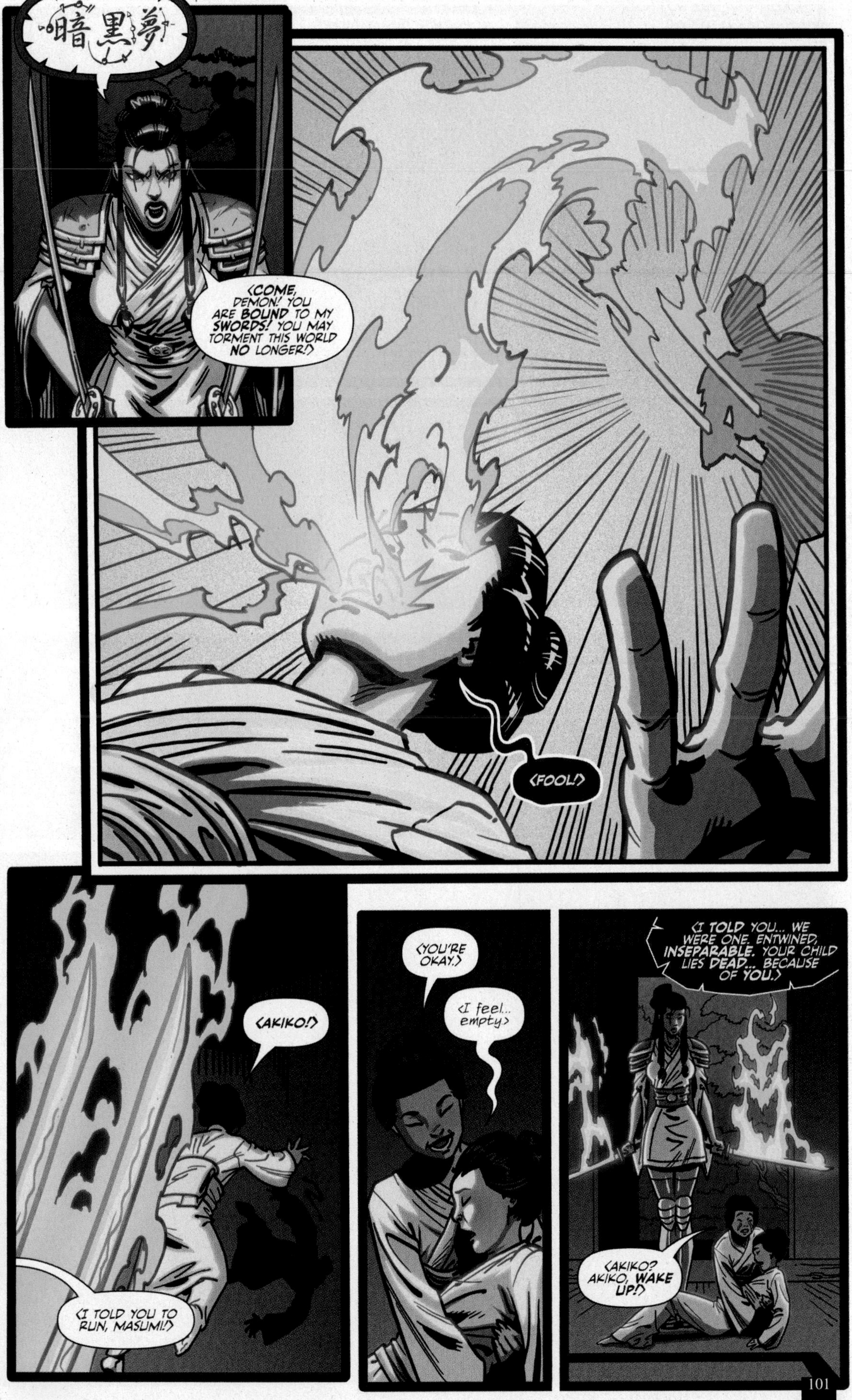
暗黒夢
<COME, DEMON! YOU ARE **BOUND** TO MY **SWORDS!** YOU MAY TORMENT THIS WORLD **NO** LONGER!>
<FOOL!>
<AKIKO!>
<I TOLD YOU TO RUN, MASUMI!>
<YOU'RE OKAY.>
<I feel... empty>
<I **TOLD** YOU... WE WERE ONE. ENTWINED, **INSEPARABLE.** YOUR CHILD LIES **DEAD**... BECAUSE OF **YOU.**>
<AKIKO? AKIKO, **WAKE UP!**>

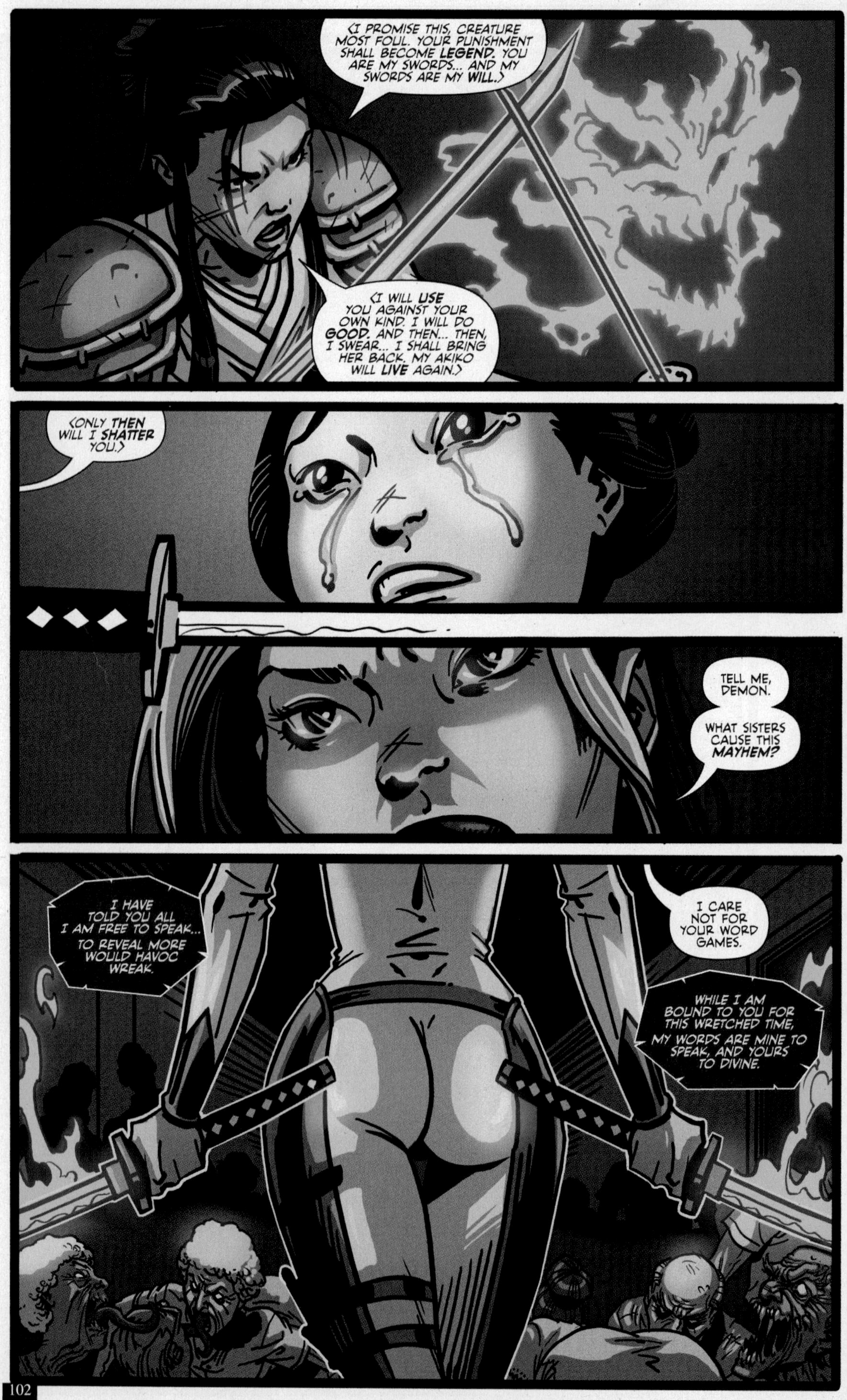

<I PROMISE THIS, CREATURE MOST FOUL. YOUR PUNISHMENT SHALL BECOME LEGEND. YOU ARE MY SWORDS... AND MY SWORDS ARE MY WILL.>
<I WILL USE YOU AGAINST YOUR OWN KIND. I WILL DO GOOD. AND THEN... THEN, I SWEAR... I SHALL BRING HER BACK. MY AKIKO WILL LIVE AGAIN.>
<ONLY THEN WILL I SHATTER YOU.>
TELL ME, DEMON.
WHAT SISTERS CAUSE THIS MAYHEM?
I HAVE TOLD YOU ALL I AM FREE TO SPEAK... TO REVEAL MORE WOULD HAVOC WREAK.
I CARE NOT FOR YOUR WORD GAMES.
WHILE I AM BOUND TO YOU FOR THIS WRETCHED TIME, MY WORDS ARE MINE TO SPEAK, AND YOURS TO DIVINE.

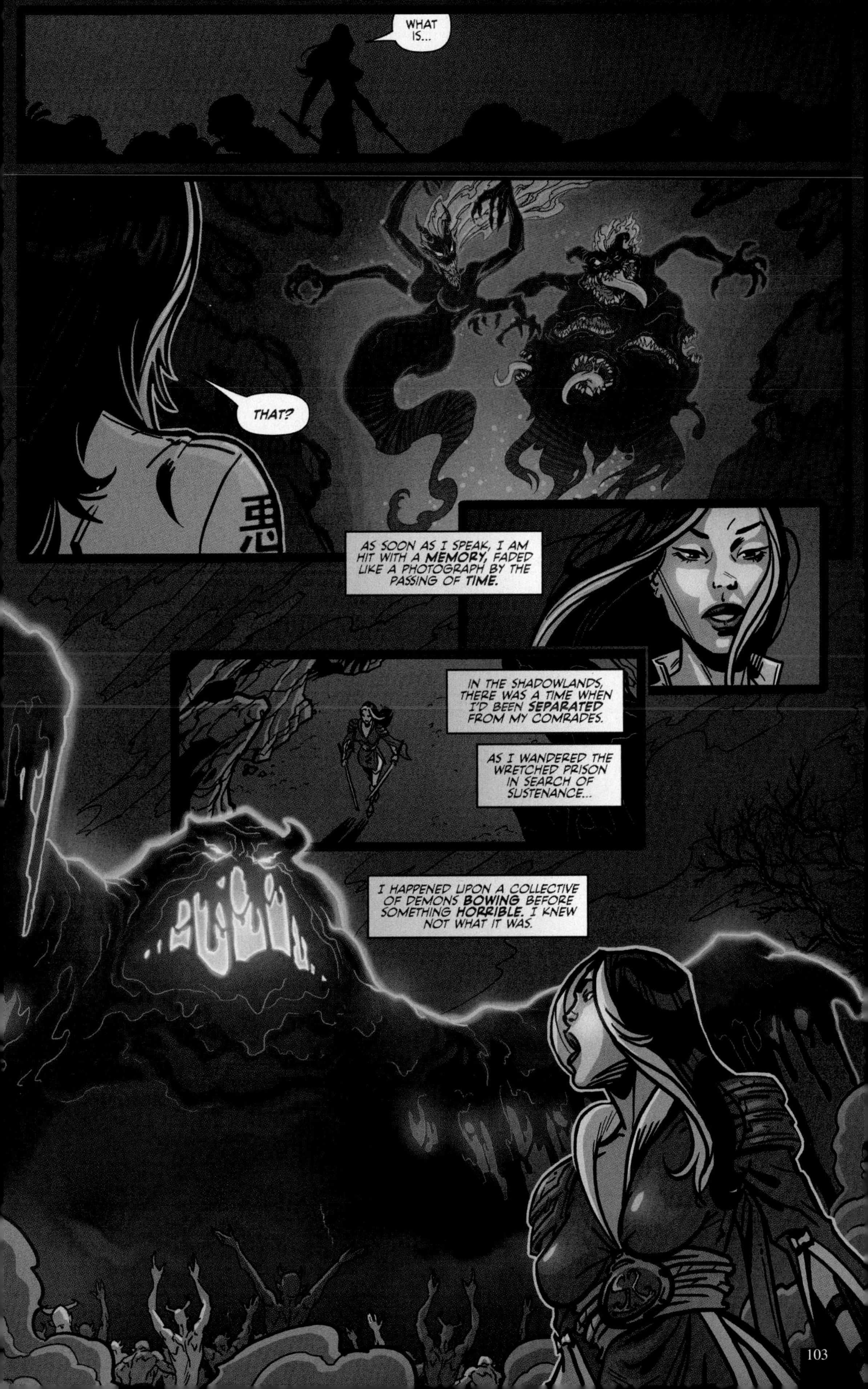

WHAT IS...
THAT?
AS SOON AS I SPEAK, I AM HIT WITH A **MEMORY,** FADED LIKE A PHOTOGRAPH BY THE PASSING OF **TIME.**
IN THE SHADOWLANDS, THERE WAS A TIME WHEN I'D BEEN **SEPARATED** FROM MY COMRADES.
AS I WANDERED THE WRETCHED PRISON IN SEARCH OF SUSTENANCE...
I HAPPENED UPON A COLLECTIVE OF DEMONS **BOWING** BEFORE SOMETHING **HORRIBLE.** I KNEW NOT WHAT IT WAS.

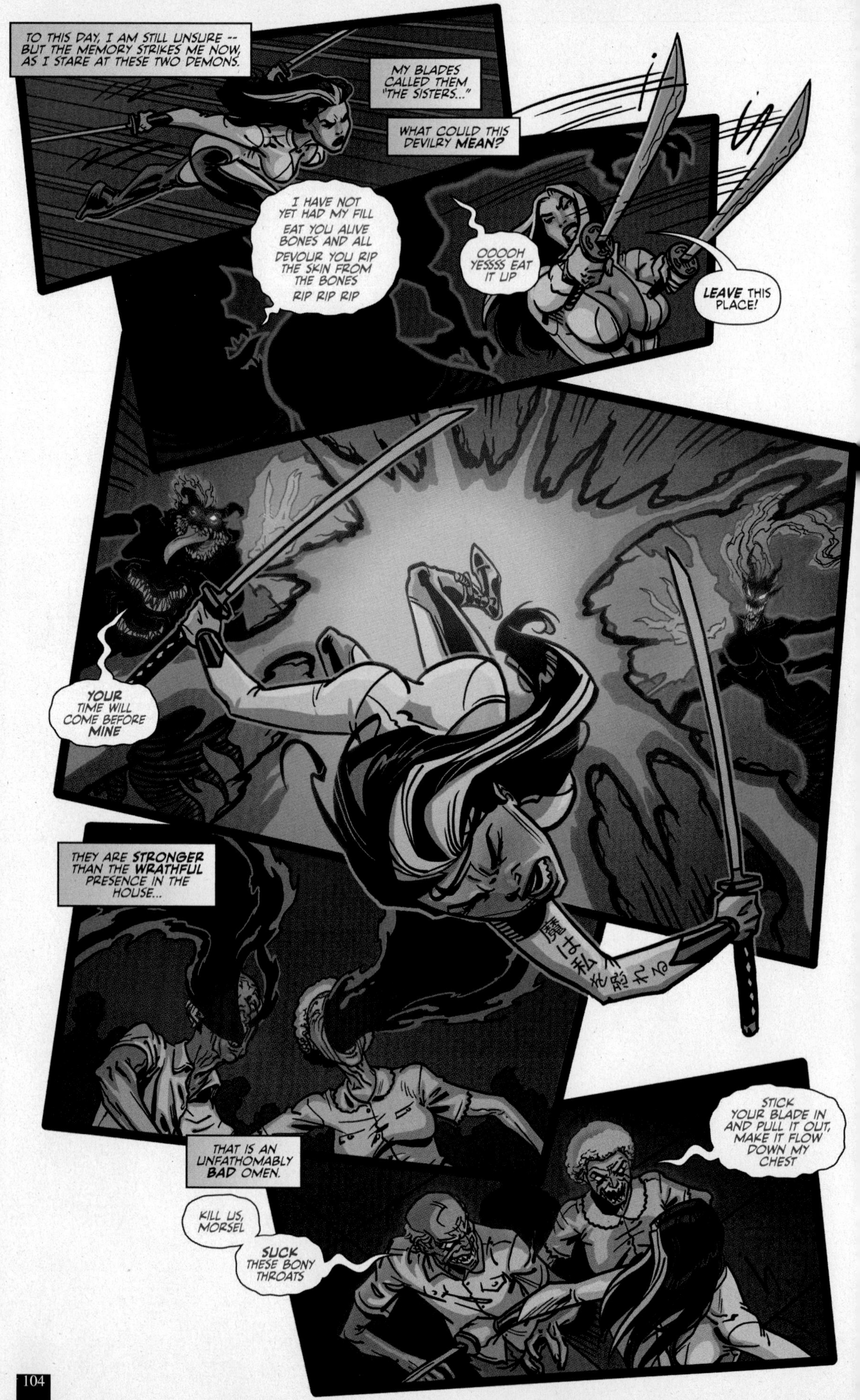
TO THIS DAY, I AM STILL UNSURE -- BUT THE MEMORY STRIKES ME NOW, AS I STARE AT THESE TWO DEMONS.
MY BLADES CALLED THEM "THE SISTERS..."
WHAT COULD THIS DEVILRY MEAN?
I HAVE NOT YET HAD MY FILL
EAT YOU ALIVE BONES AND ALL
DEVOUR YOU RIP THE SKIN FROM THE BONES
RIP RIP RIP
OOOOH YESSSS EAT IT UP
LEAVE THIS PLACE!
YOUR TIME WILL COME BEFORE MINE
THEY ARE STRONGER THAN THE WRATHFUL PRESENCE IN THE HOUSE...
THAT IS AN UNFATHOMABLY BAD OMEN.
STICK YOUR BLADE IN AND PULL IT OUT, MAKE IT FLOW DOWN MY CHEST
KILL US, MORSEL
SUCK THESE BONY THROATS

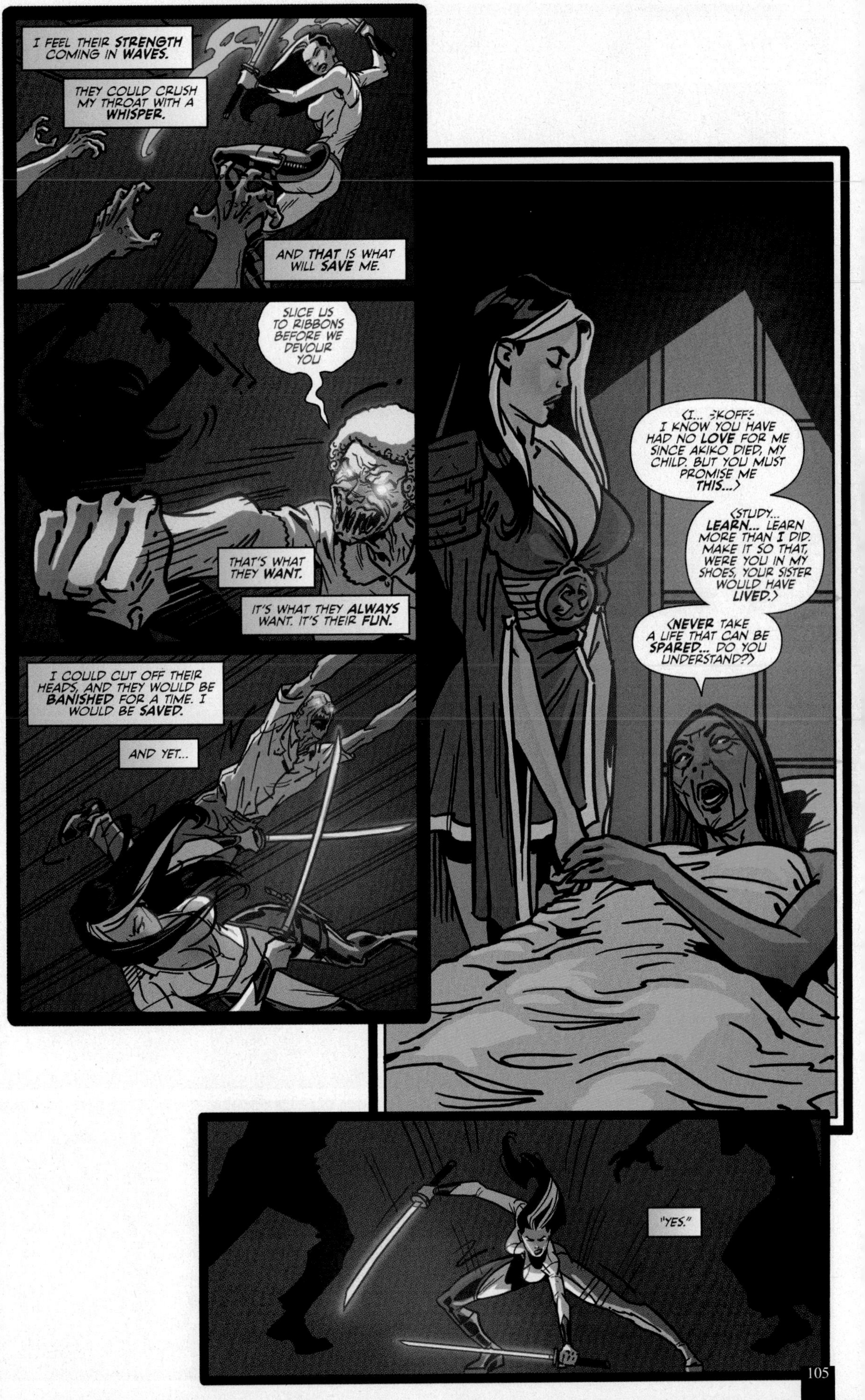

I FEEL THEIR STRENGTH COMING IN WAVES.
THEY COULD CRUSH MY THROAT WITH A WHISPER.
AND THAT IS WHAT WILL SAVE ME.
SLICE US TO RIBBONS BEFORE WE DEVOUR YOU
THAT'S WHAT THEY WANT.
IT'S WHAT THEY ALWAYS WANT. IT'S THEIR FUN.
I COULD CUT OFF THEIR HEADS, AND THEY WOULD BE BANISHED FOR A TIME. I WOULD BE SAVED.
AND YET...
<I... SKOFF: I KNOW YOU HAVE HAD NO LOVE FOR ME SINCE AKIKO DIED, MY CHILD. BUT YOU MUST PROMISE ME THIS...>
<STUDY... LEARN... LEARN MORE THAN I DID. MAKE IT SO THAT, WERE YOU IN MY SHOES, YOUR SISTER WOULD HAVE LIVED.>
<NEVER TAKE A LIFE THAT CAN BE SPARED... DO YOU UNDERSTAND?>
"YES."

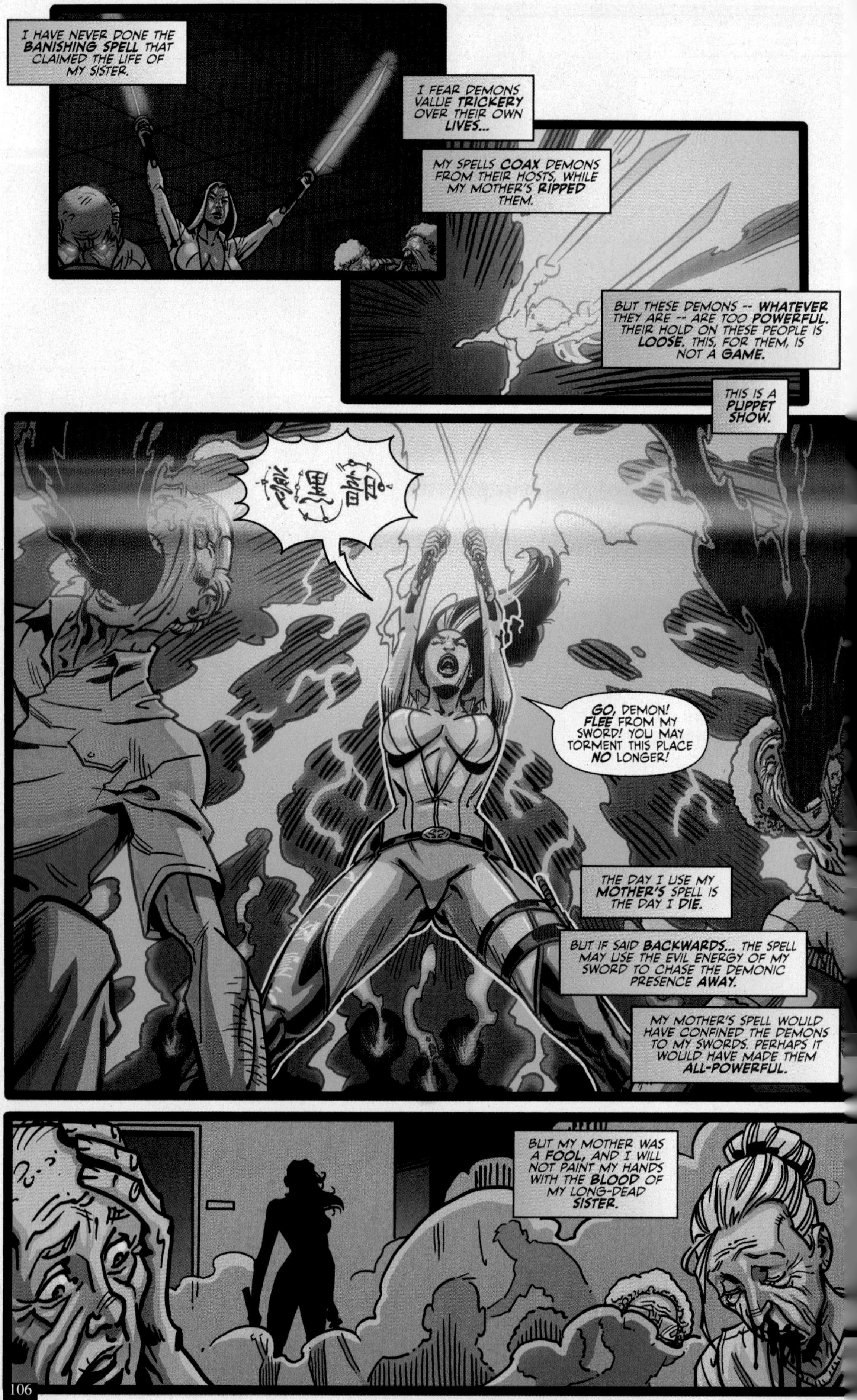
I HAVE NEVER DONE THE BANISHING SPELL THAT CLAIMED THE LIFE OF MY SISTER.
I FEAR DEMONS VALUE TRICKERY OVER THEIR OWN LIVES...
MY SPELLS COAX DEMONS FROM THEIR HOSTS, WHILE MY MOTHER'S RIPPED THEM.
BUT THESE DEMONS -- WHATEVER THEY ARE -- ARE TOO POWERFUL. THEIR HOLD ON THESE PEOPLE IS LOOSE. THIS, FOR THEM, IS NOT A GAME.
THIS IS A PUPPET SHOW.
GO, DEMON! FLEE FROM MY SWORD! YOU MAY TORMENT THIS PLACE NO LONGER!
THE DAY I USE MY MOTHER'S SPELL IS THE DAY I DIE.
BUT IF SAID BACKWARDS... THE SPELL MAY USE THE EVIL ENERGY OF MY SWORD TO CHASE THE DEMONIC PRESENCE AWAY.
MY MOTHER'S SPELL WOULD HAVE CONFINED THE DEMONS TO MY SWORDS. PERHAPS IT WOULD HAVE MADE THEM ALL-POWERFUL.
BUT MY MOTHER WAS A FOOL, AND I WILL NOT PAINT MY HANDS WITH THE BLOOD OF MY LONG-DEAD SISTER.

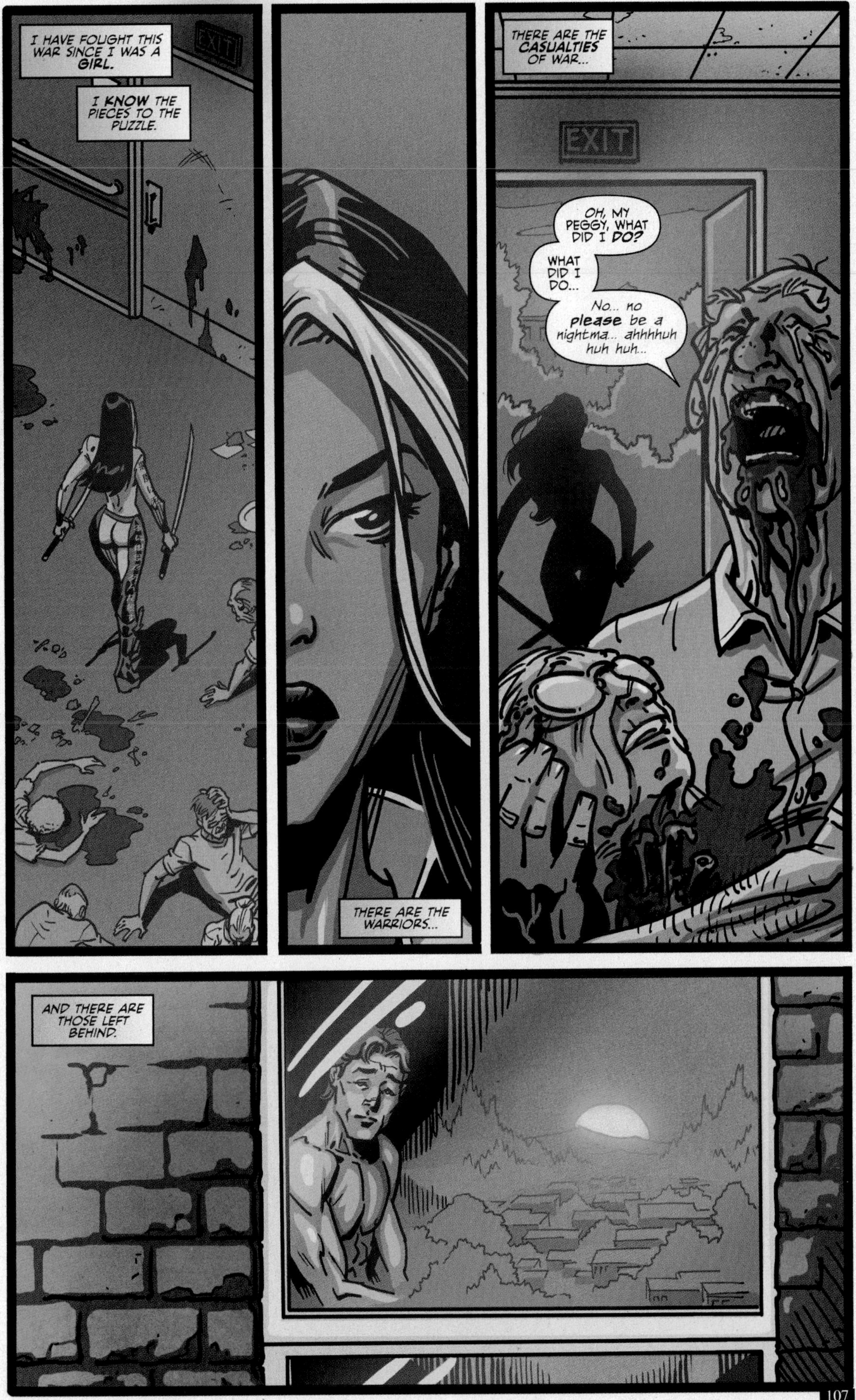
I HAVE FOUGHT THIS WAR SINCE I WAS A **GIRL.**
I **KNOW** THE PIECES TO THE PUZZLE.
EXIT
THERE ARE THE WARRIORS...
THERE ARE THE **CASUALTIES** OF WAR...
EXIT
OH, MY PEGGY, WHAT DID I **DO?**
WHAT DID I DO...
No... no **please** be a nightma... ahhhhuh huh huh...
AND THERE ARE THOSE LEFT BEHIND.

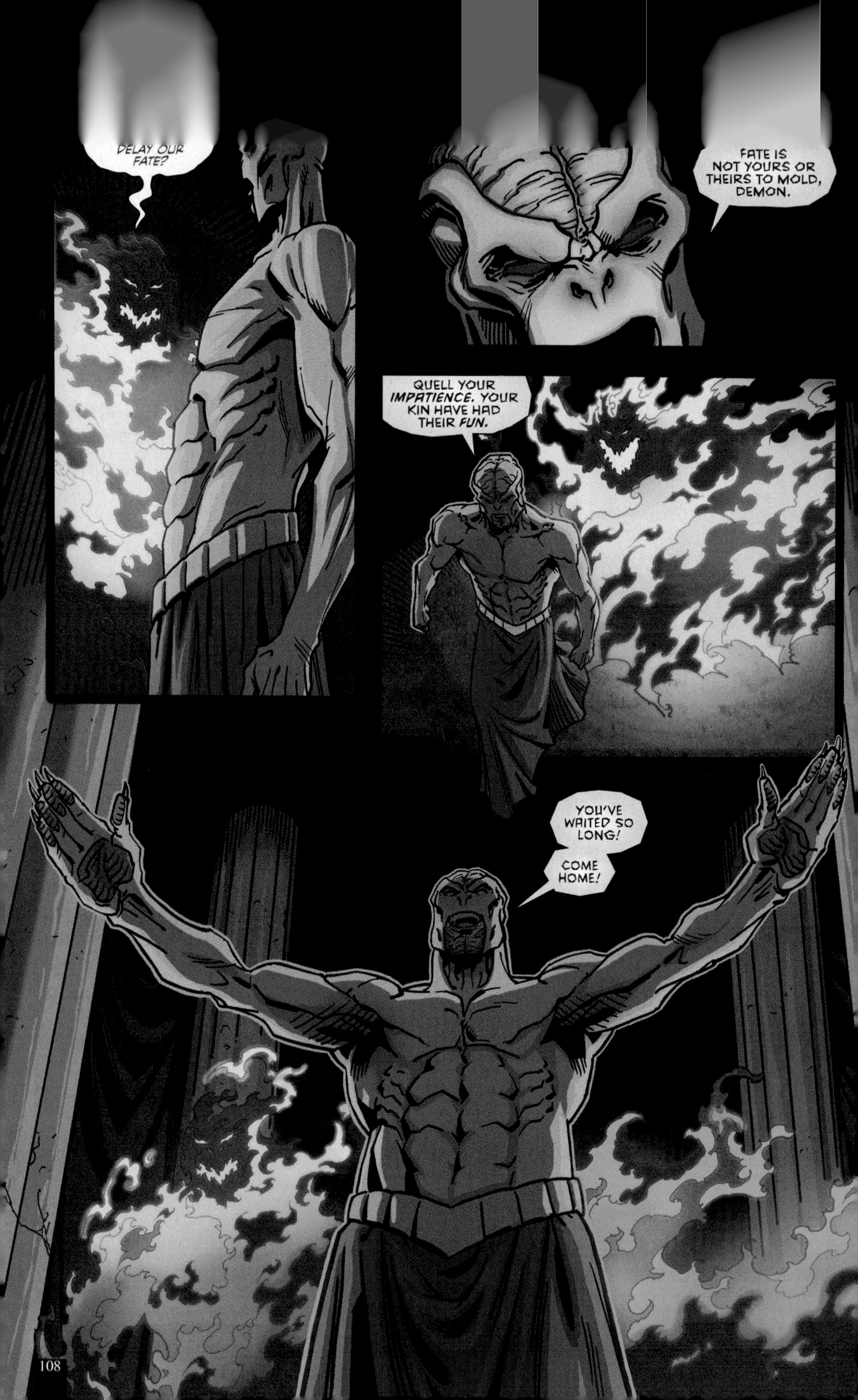
DELAY OUR FATE?
FATE IS NOT YOURS OR THEIRS TO MOLD, DEMON.
QUELL YOUR IMPATIENCE. YOUR KIN HAVE HAD THEIR FUN.
YOU'VE WAITED SO LONG!
COME HOME!

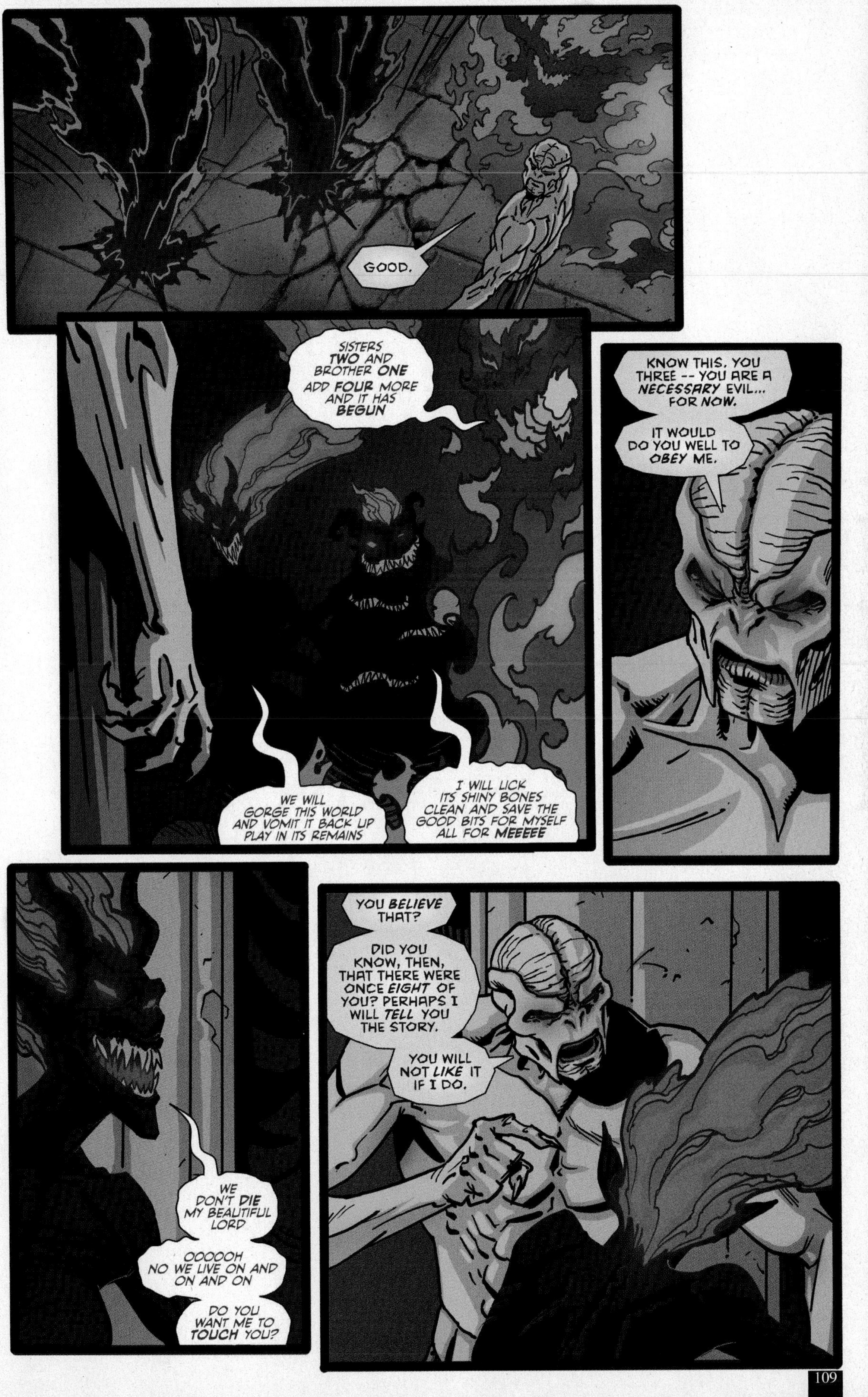
GOOD.
SISTERS TWO AND BROTHER ONE ADD FOUR MORE AND IT HAS BEGUN
WE WILL GORGE THIS WORLD AND VOMIT IT BACK UP PLAY IN ITS REMAINS
I WILL LICK ITS SHINY BONES CLEAN AND SAVE THE GOOD BITS FOR MYSELF ALL FOR MEEEEE
KNOW THIS. YOU THREE -- YOU ARE A NECESSARY EVIL... FOR NOW.
IT WOULD DO YOU WELL TO OBEY ME.
WE DON'T DIE MY BEAUTIFUL LORD
OOOOOH NO WE LIVE ON AND ON AND ON
DO YOU WANT ME TO TOUCH YOU?
YOU BELIEVE THAT?
DID YOU KNOW, THEN, THAT THERE WERE ONCE EIGHT OF YOU? PERHAPS I WILL TELL YOU THE STORY.
YOU WILL NOT LIKE IT IF I DO.

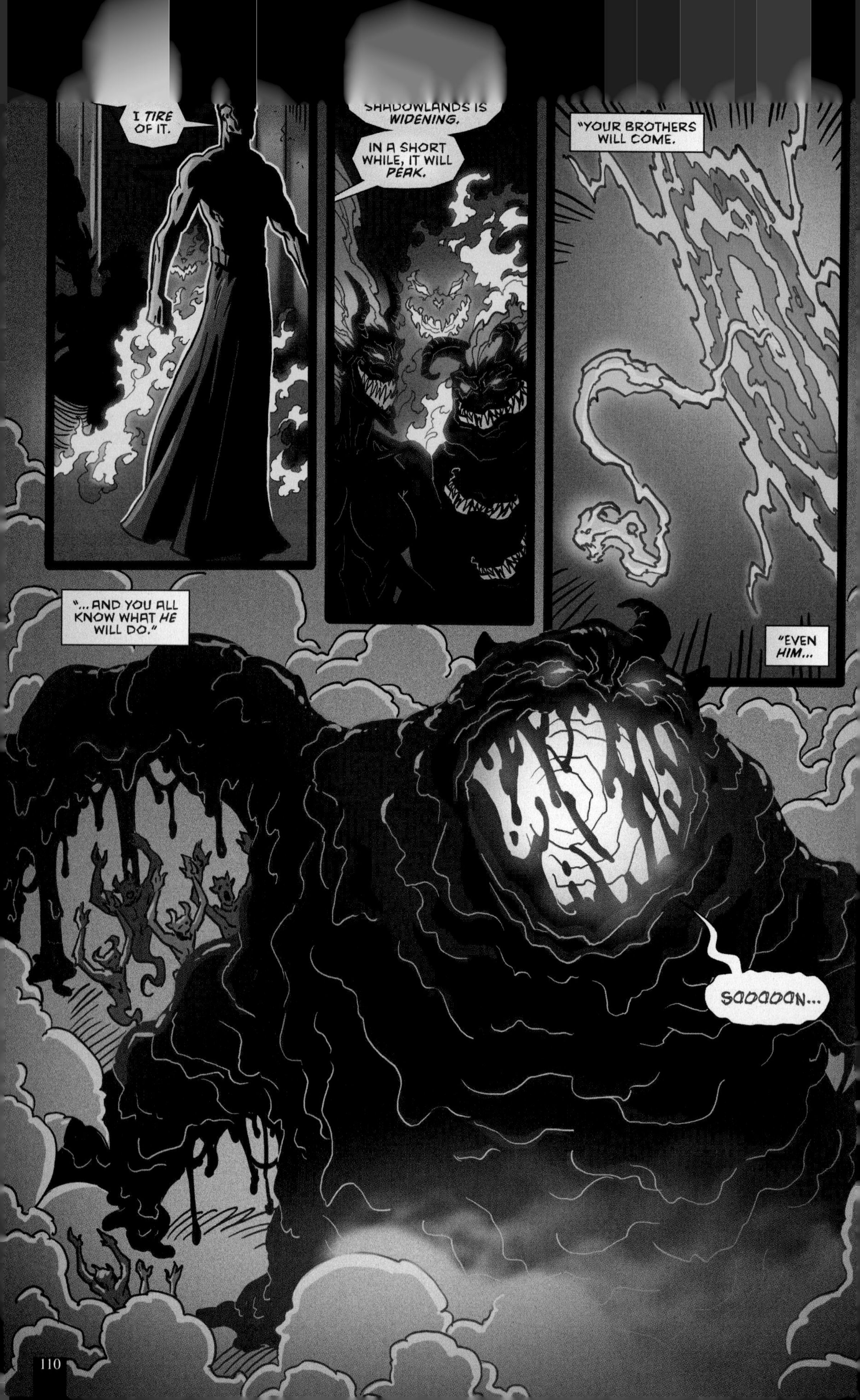
I TIRE OF IT.
SHADOWLANDS IS WIDENING.
IN A SHORT WHILE, IT WILL PEAK.
"YOUR BROTHERS WILL COME.
"EVEN HIM...
"...AND YOU ALL KNOW WHAT HE WILL DO."
SOOOOON...

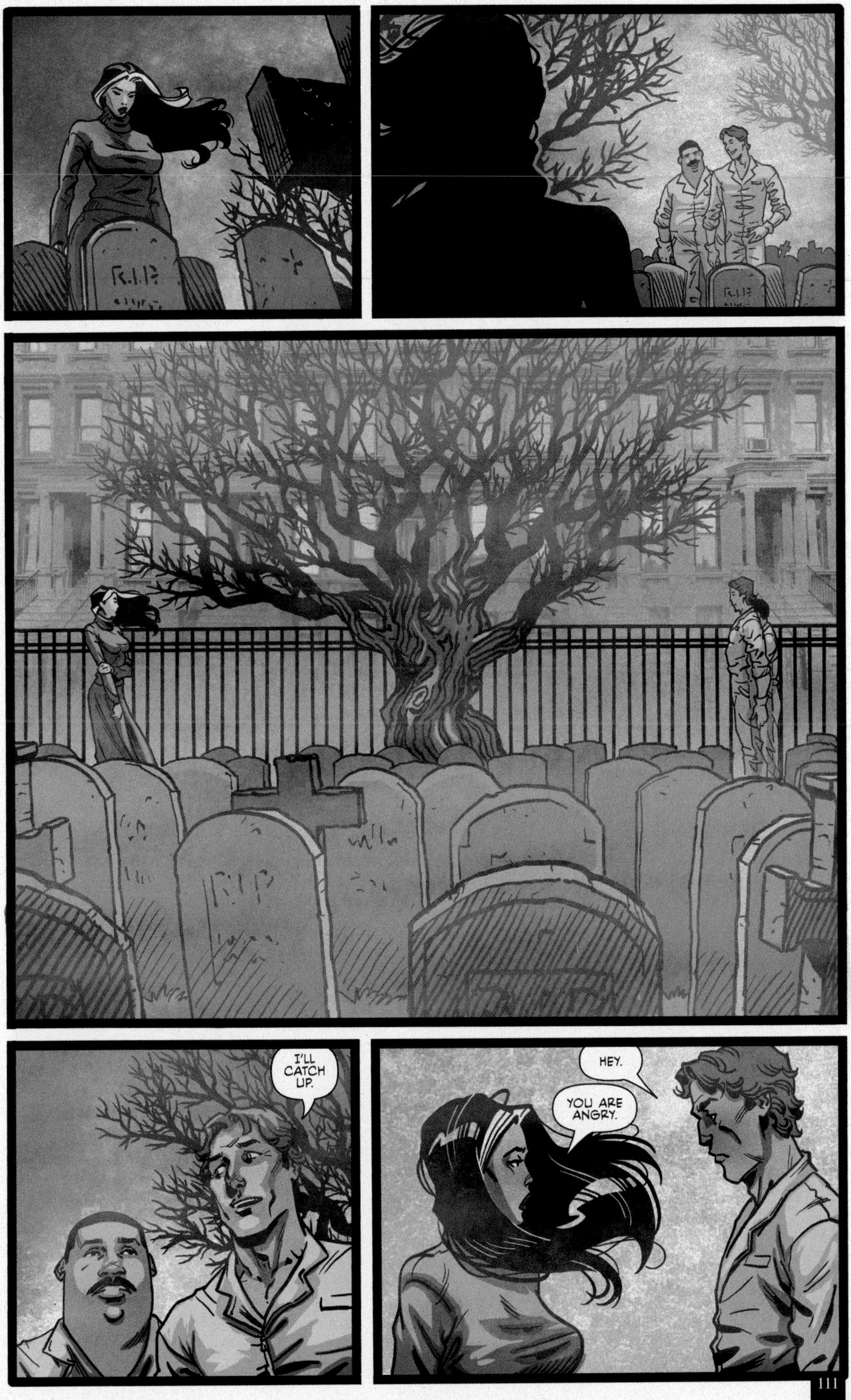
R.I.P.
R.I.P.
R.I.P.
I'LL CATCH UP.
HEY.
YOU ARE ANGRY.

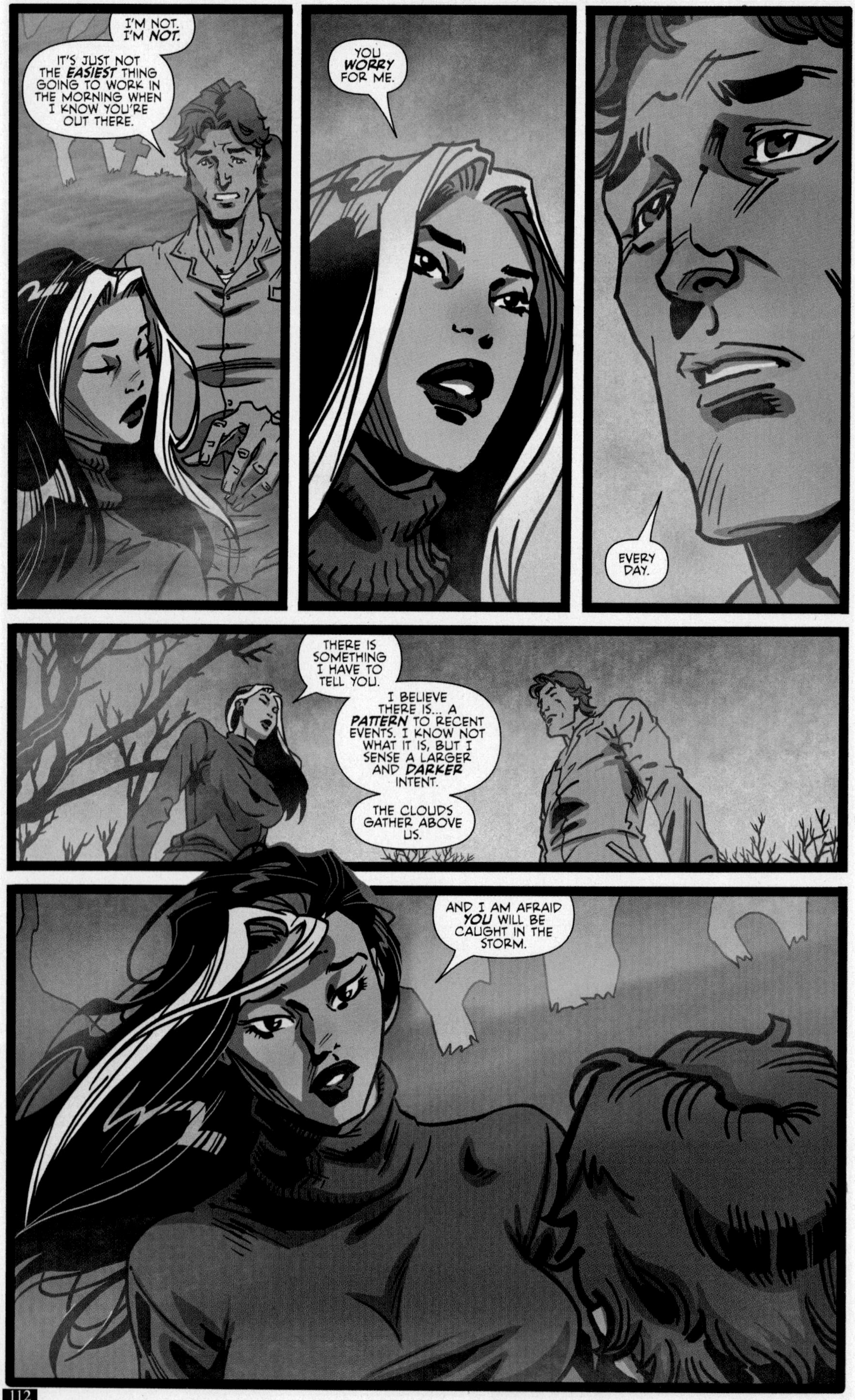
I'M NOT. I'M NOT.
IT'S JUST NOT THE EASIEST THING GOING TO WORK IN THE MORNING WHEN I KNOW YOU'RE OUT THERE.
YOU WORRY FOR ME.
EVERY DAY.
THERE IS SOMETHING I HAVE TO TELL YOU.
I BELIEVE THERE IS... A PATTERN TO RECENT EVENTS. I KNOW NOT WHAT IT IS, BUT I SENSE A LARGER AND DARKER INTENT.
THE CLOUDS GATHER ABOVE US.
AND I AM AFRAID YOU WILL BE CAUGHT IN THE STORM.

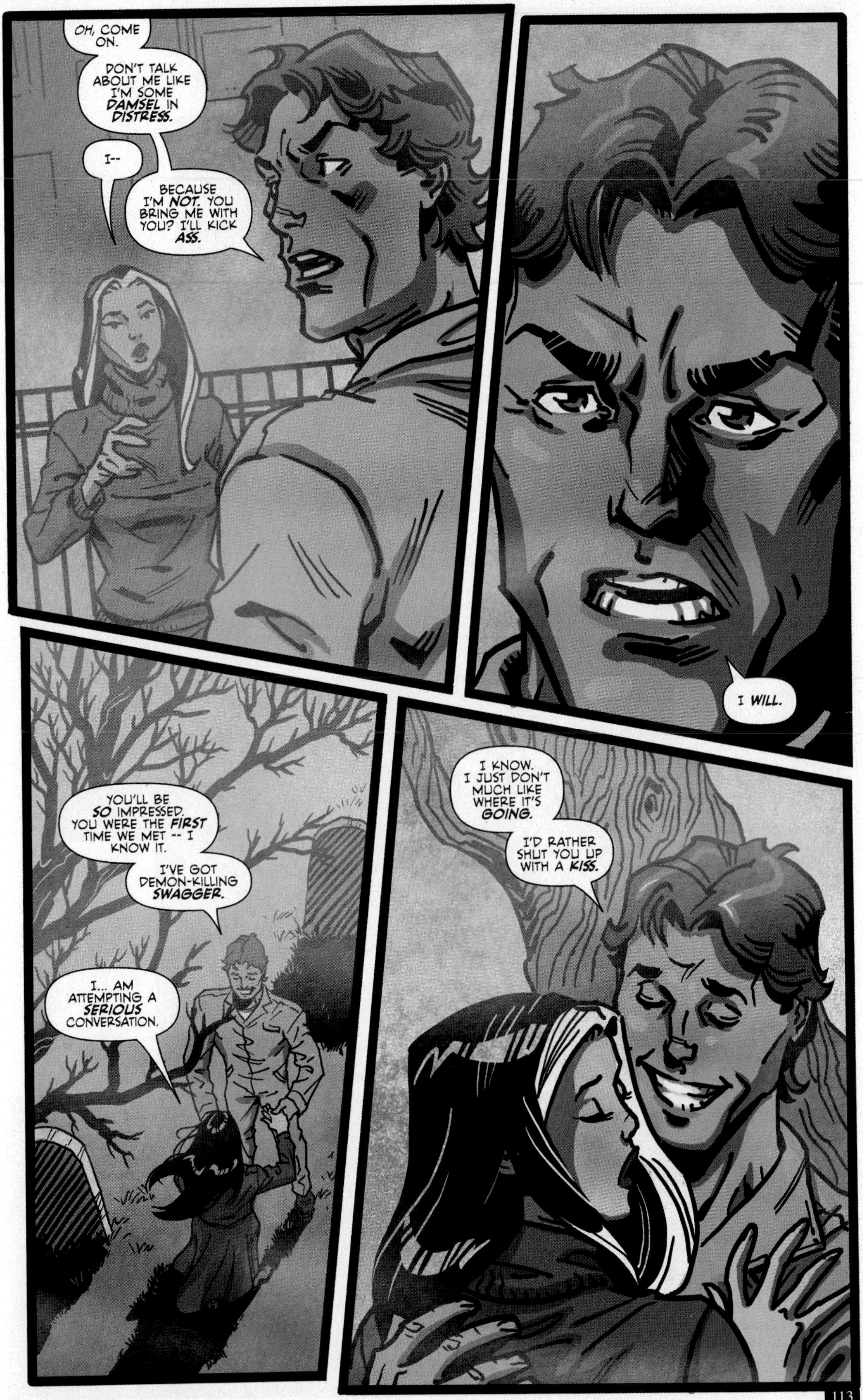

OH, COME ON.
DON'T TALK ABOUT ME LIKE I'M SOME DAMSEL IN DISTRESS.
I--
BECAUSE I'M NOT. YOU BRING ME WITH YOU? I'LL KICK ASS.
I WILL.
YOU'LL BE SO IMPRESSED. YOU WERE THE FIRST TIME WE MET -- I KNOW IT.
I'VE GOT DEMON-KILLING SWAGGER.
I... AM ATTEMPTING A SERIOUS CONVERSATION.
I KNOW. I JUST DON'T MUCH LIKE WHERE IT'S GOING.
I'D RATHER SHUT YOU UP WITH A KISS.

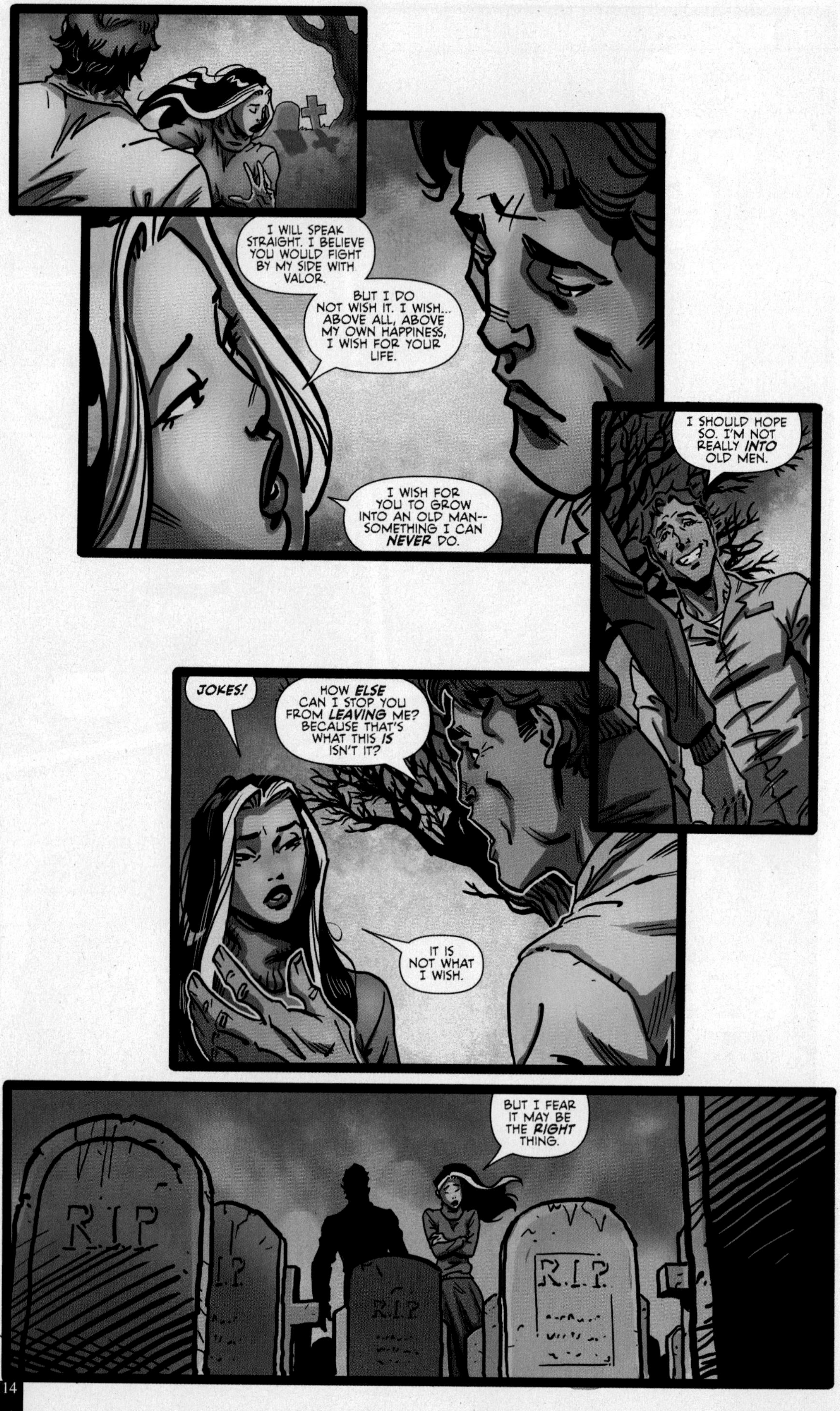
I WILL SPEAK STRAIGHT. I BELIEVE YOU WOULD FIGHT BY MY SIDE WITH VALOR.
BUT I DO NOT WISH IT. I WISH... ABOVE ALL, ABOVE MY OWN HAPPINESS, I WISH FOR YOUR LIFE.
I WISH FOR YOU TO GROW INTO AN OLD MAN-- SOMETHING I CAN NEVER DO.
I SHOULD HOPE SO. I'M NOT REALLY INTO OLD MEN.
JOKES!
HOW ELSE CAN I STOP YOU FROM LEAVING ME? BECAUSE THAT'S WHAT THIS IS ISN'T IT?
IT IS NOT WHAT I WISH.
BUT I FEAR IT MAY BE THE RIGHT THING.
R.I.P
R.I.P
R.I.P
R.I.P

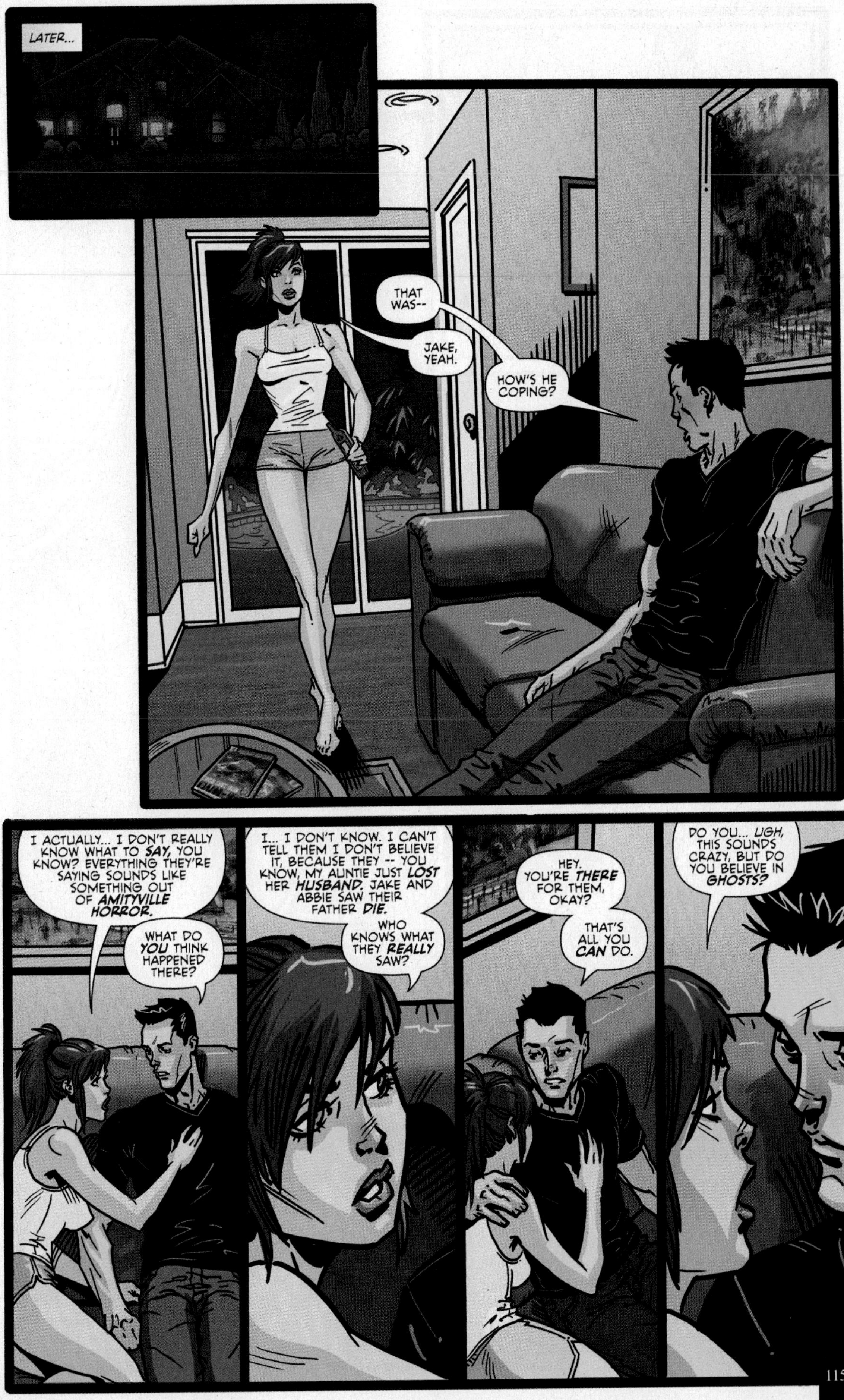
LATER...
THAT WAS--
JAKE, YEAH.
HOW'S HE COPING?
I ACTUALLY... I DON'T REALLY KNOW WHAT TO SAY, YOU KNOW? EVERYTHING THEY'RE SAYING SOUNDS LIKE SOMETHING OUT OF AMITYVILLE HORROR.
WHAT DO YOU THINK HAPPENED THERE?
I... I DON'T KNOW. I CAN'T TELL THEM I DON'T BELIEVE IT, BECAUSE THEY -- YOU KNOW, MY AUNTIE JUST LOST HER HUSBAND. JAKE AND ABBIE SAW THEIR FATHER DIE.
WHO KNOWS WHAT THEY REALLY SAW?
HEY. YOU'RE THERE FOR THEM, OKAY?
THAT'S ALL YOU CAN DO.
DO YOU... UGH, THIS SOUNDS CRAZY, BUT DO YOU BELIEVE IN GHOSTS?

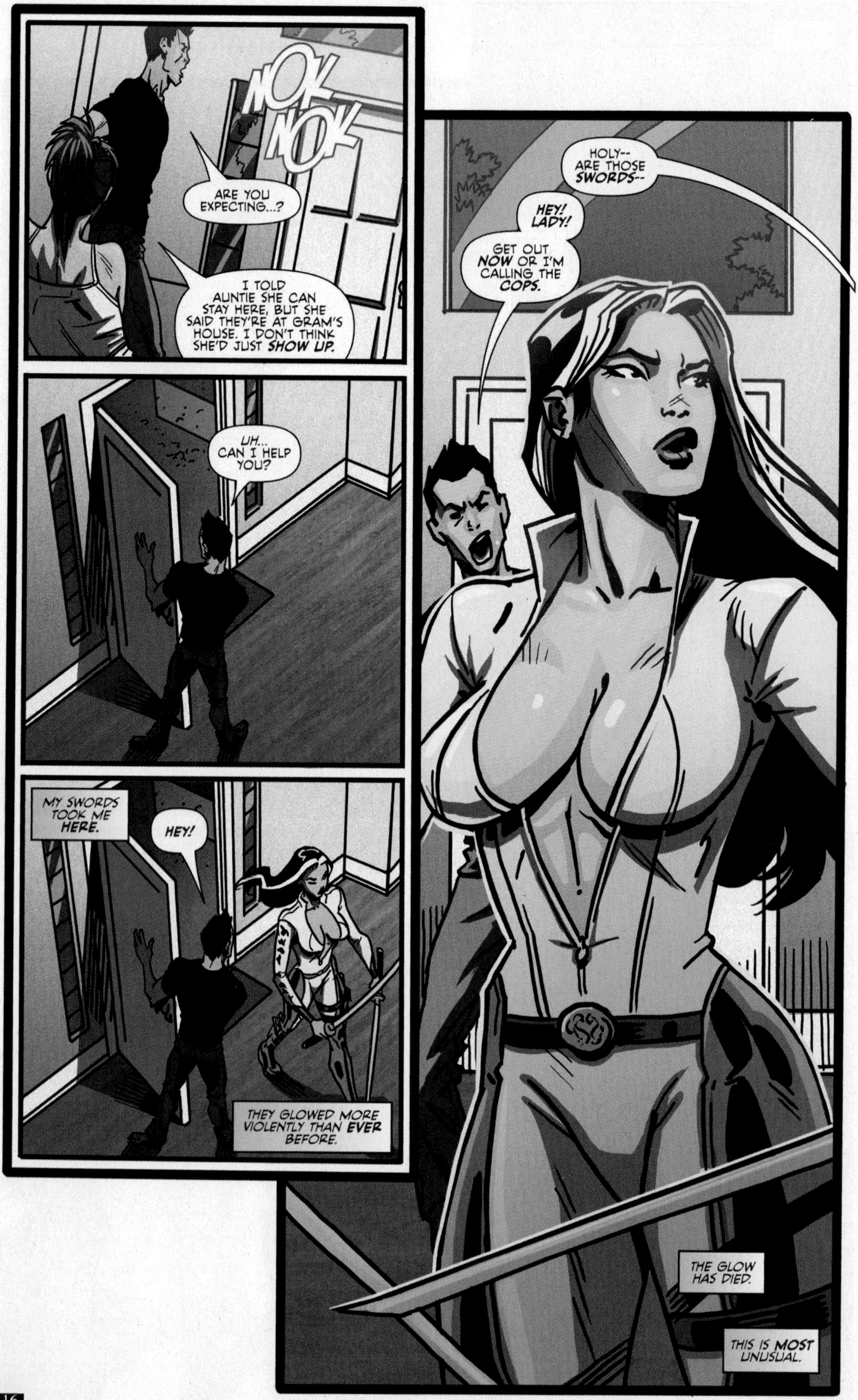
NOK NOK
ARE YOU EXPECTING...?
I TOLD AUNTIE SHE CAN STAY HERE, BUT SHE SAID THEY'RE AT GRAM'S HOUSE. I DON'T THINK SHE'D JUST SHOW UP.
UH... CAN I HELP YOU?
MY SWORDS TOOK ME HERE.
HEY!
THEY GLOWED MORE VIOLENTLY THAN EVER BEFORE.
HOLY-- ARE THOSE SWORDS--
HEY! LADY!
GET OUT NOW OR I'M CALLING THE COPS.
THE GLOW HAS DIED.
THIS IS MOST UNUSUAL.

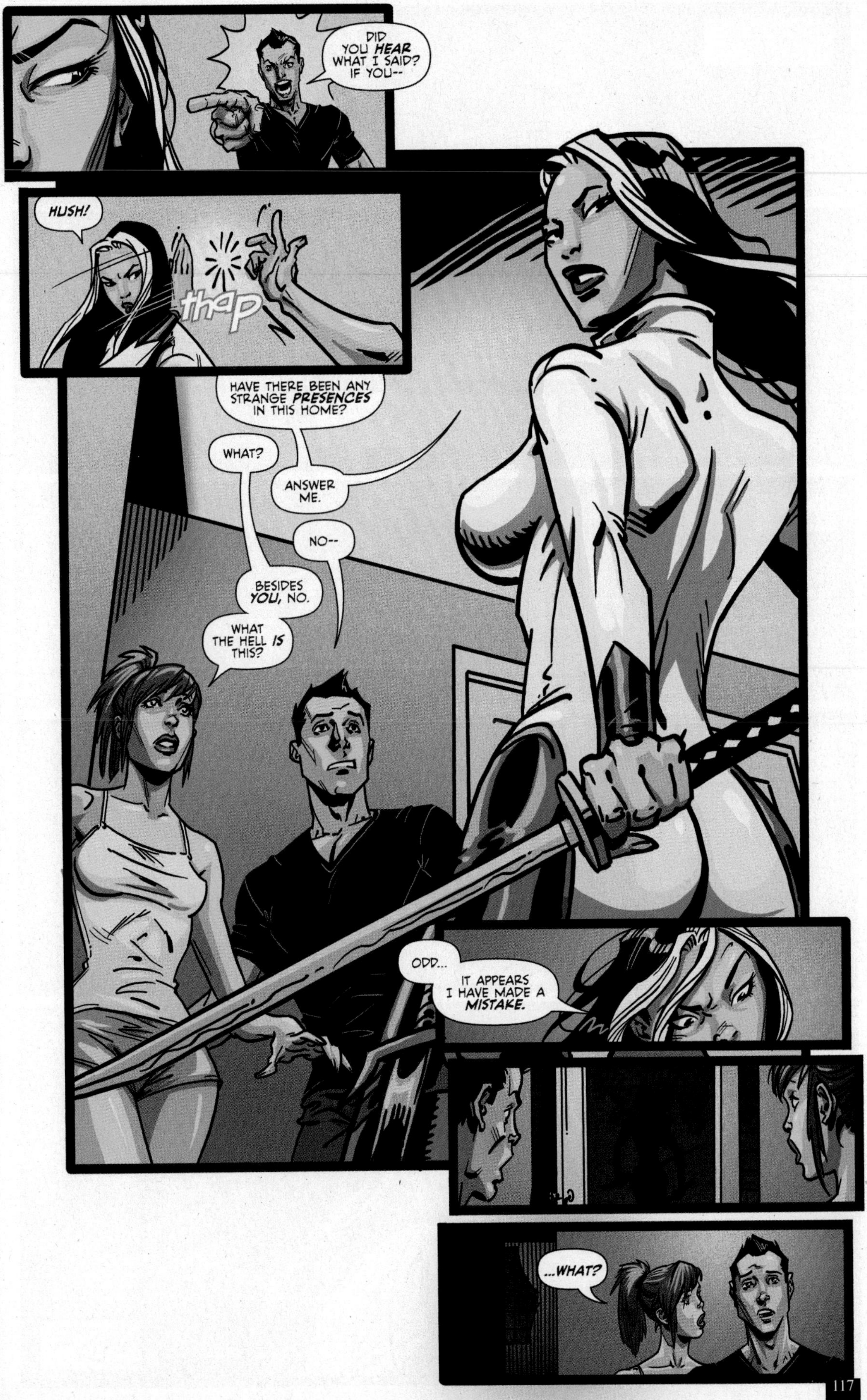
DID YOU HEAR WHAT I SAID? IF YOU--
HUSH!
thap
HAVE THERE BEEN ANY STRANGE PRESENCES IN THIS HOME?
WHAT?
ANSWER ME.
NO--
BESIDES YOU, NO.
WHAT THE HELL IS THIS?
ODD...
IT APPEARS I HAVE MADE A MISTAKE.
...WHAT?

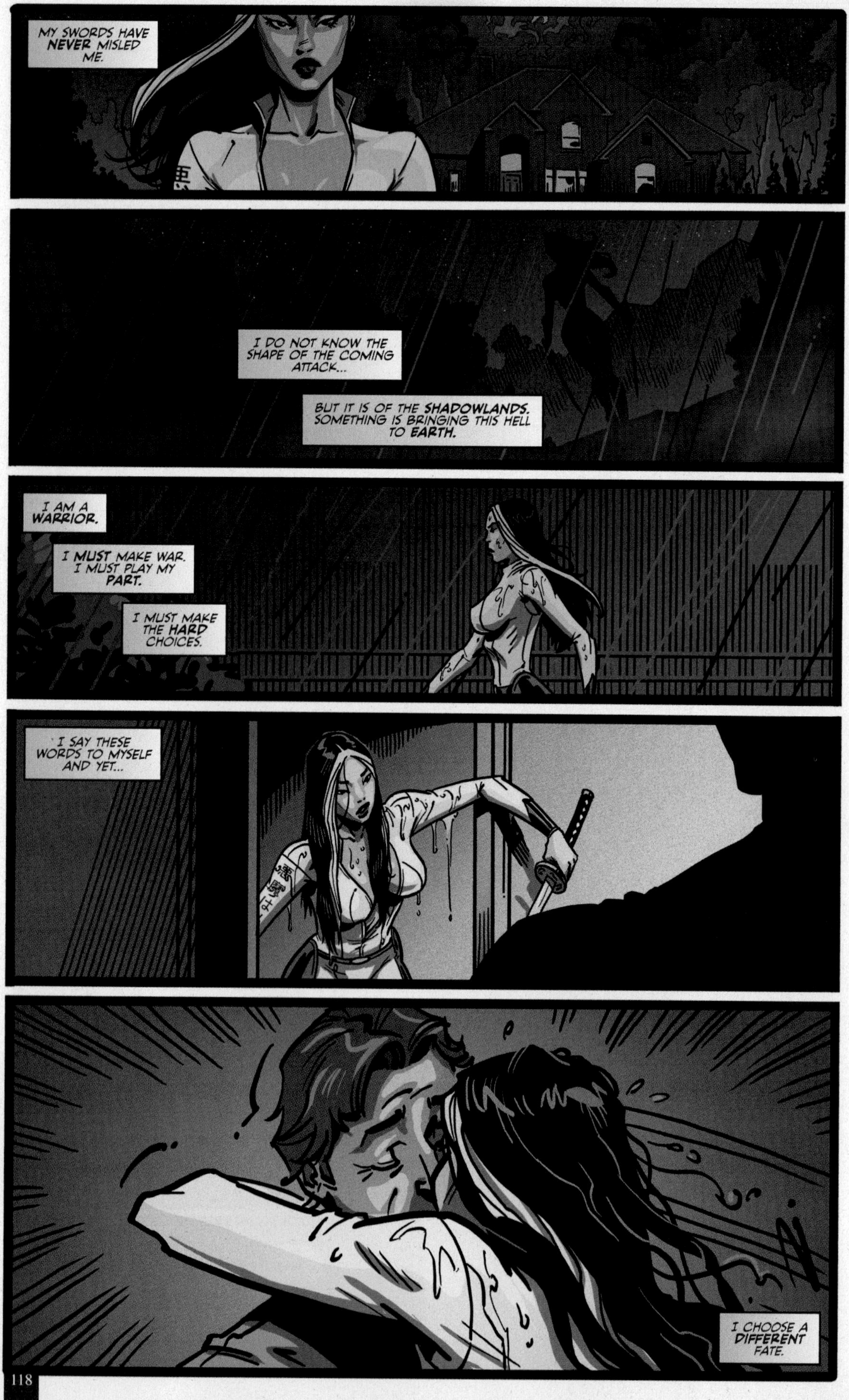
MY SWORDS HAVE NEVER MISLED ME.
I DO NOT KNOW THE SHAPE OF THE COMING ATTACK...
BUT IT IS OF THE SHADOWLANDS. SOMETHING IS BRINGING THIS HELL TO EARTH.
I AM A WARRIOR.
I MUST MAKE WAR. I MUST PLAY MY PART.
I MUST MAKE THE HARD CHOICES.
I SAY THESE WORDS TO MYSELF AND YET...
I CHOOSE A DIFFERENT FATE.

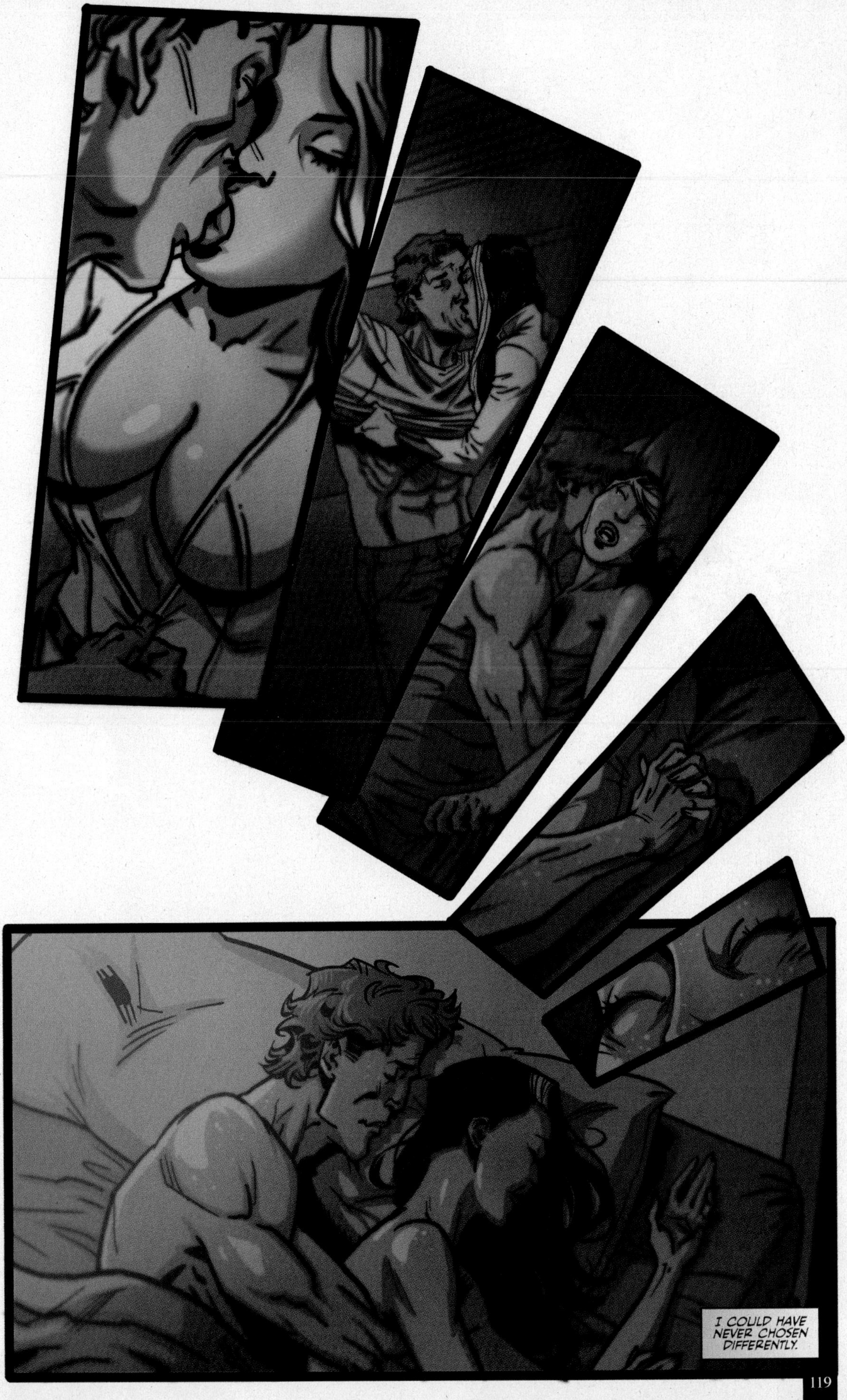
I COULD HAVE NEVER CHOSEN DIFFERENTLY.

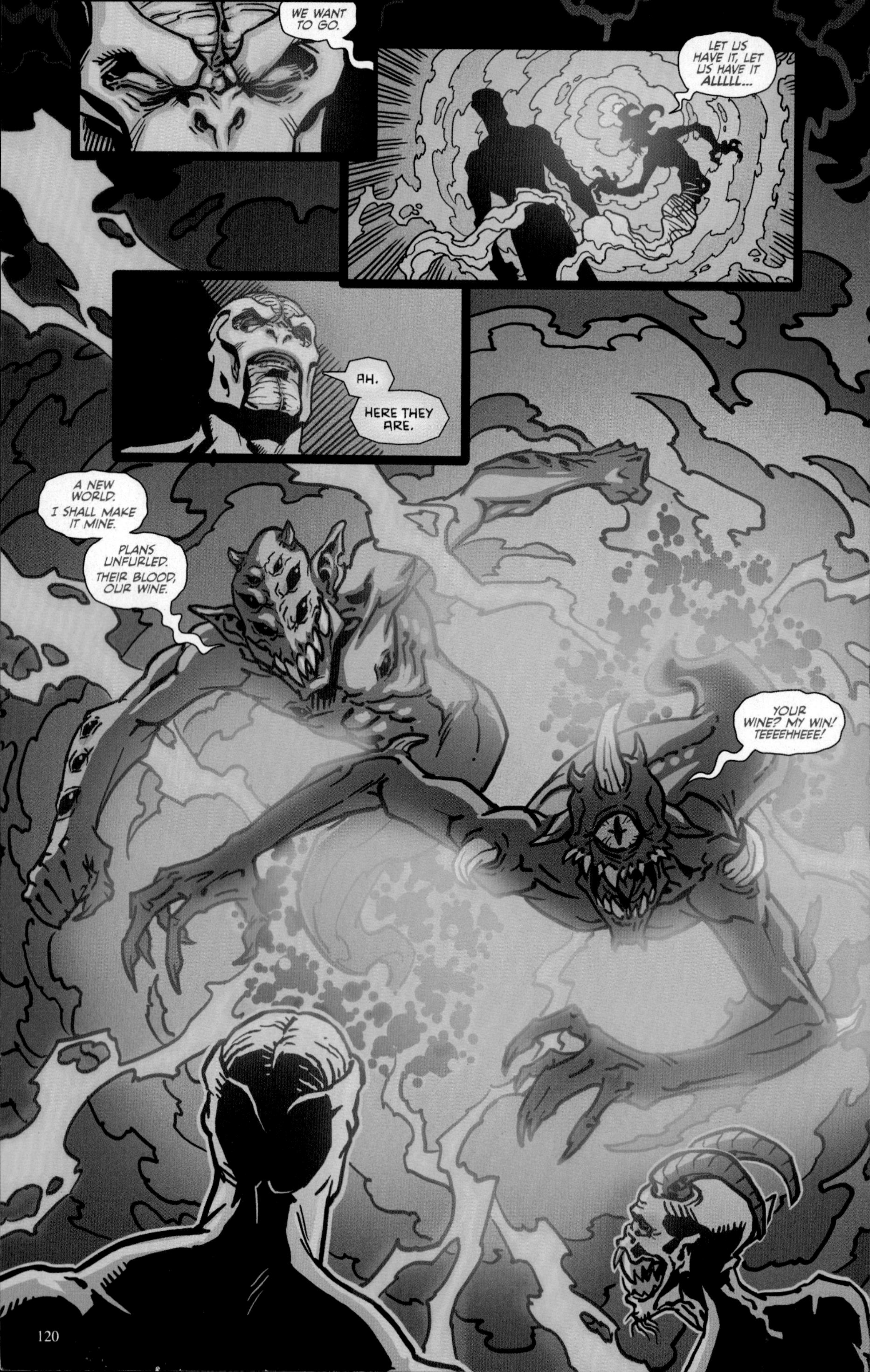
WE WANT TO GO.
LET US HAVE IT, LET US HAVE IT ALLLLL...
AH.
HERE THEY ARE.
A NEW WORLD. I SHALL MAKE IT MINE.
PLANS UNFURLED. THEIR BLOOD, OUR WINE.
YOUR WINE? MY WIN! TEEEEHHEEE!

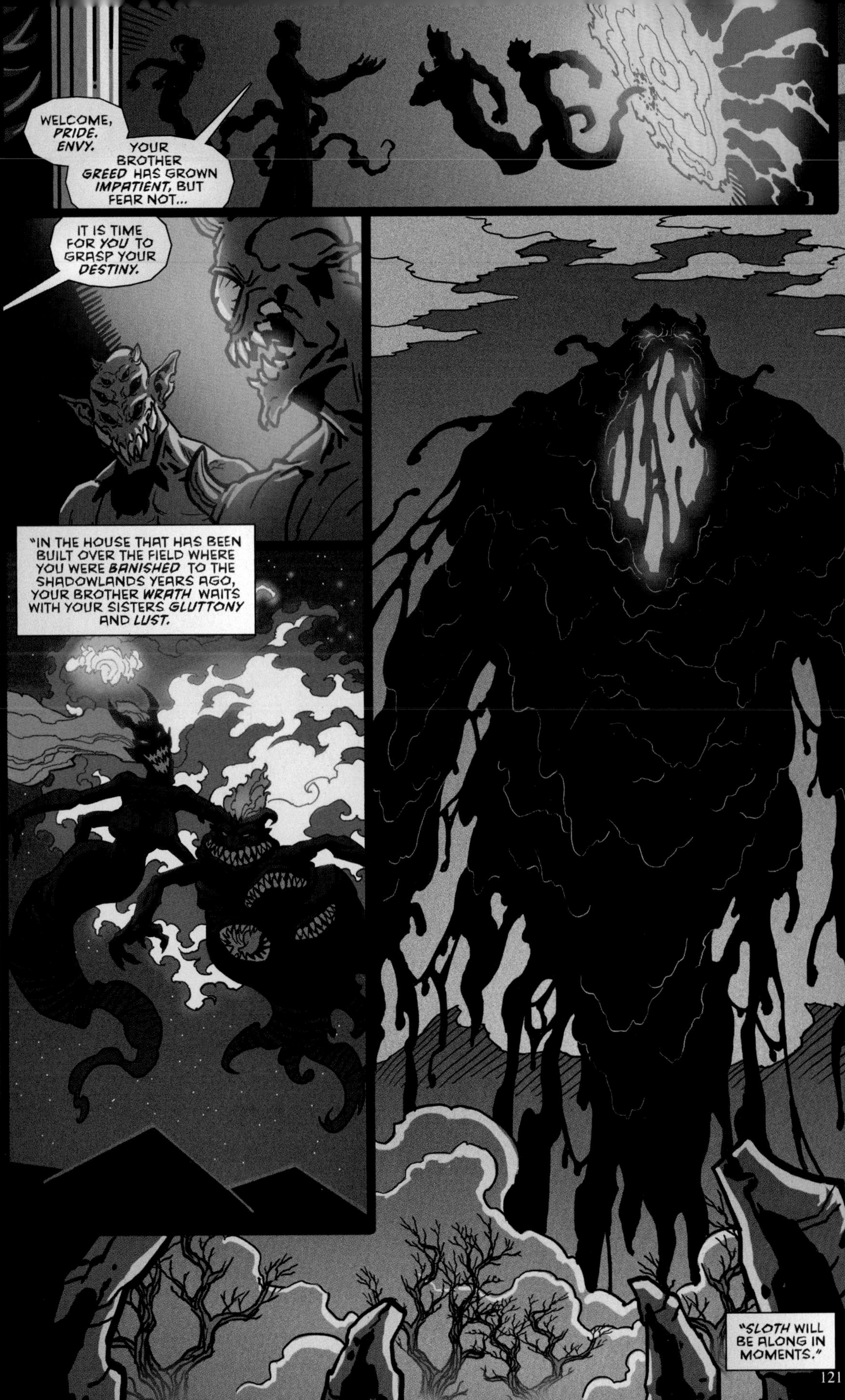

WELCOME, PRIDE. ENVY.
YOUR BROTHER GREED HAS GROWN IMPATIENT, BUT FEAR NOT...
IT IS TIME FOR YOU TO GRASP YOUR DESTINY.
"IN THE HOUSE THAT HAS BEEN BUILT OVER THE FIELD WHERE YOU WERE BANISHED TO THE SHADOWLANDS YEARS AGO, YOUR BROTHER WRATH WAITS WITH YOUR SISTERS GLUTTONY AND LUST.
"SLOTH WILL BE ALONG IN MOMENTS."

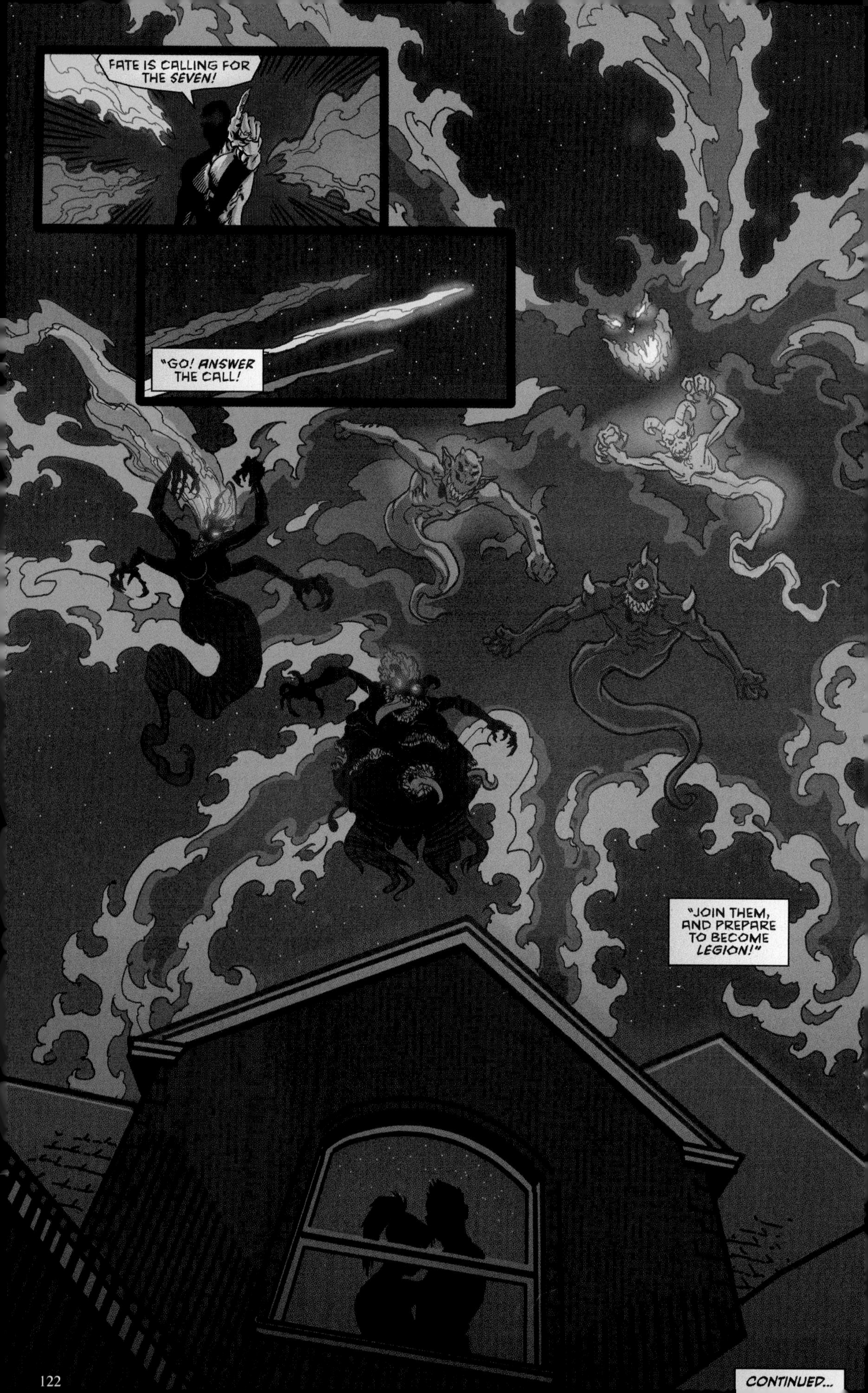
FATE IS CALLING FOR THE *SEVEN!*
"GO! *ANSWER* THE CALL!
"JOIN THEM, AND PREPARE TO BECOME *LEGION!*"
CONTINUED...

Grimm Fairy Tales presents:

Zombies & Demons

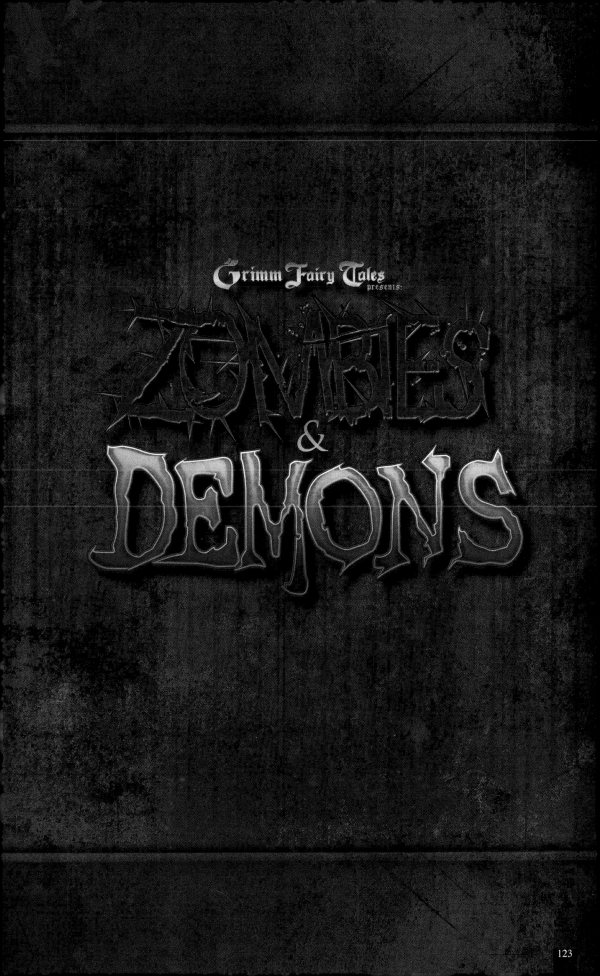

DEMONS
THE UNSEEN

Grimm Fairy Tales presents

GERARD
FERGUSON
1985-2013

Part Three

WRITER
PAT SHAND

ARTWORK
MATIAS BERGARA

COLORS
BEN SAWYER

LETTERS
JIM CAMPBELL

FARMER

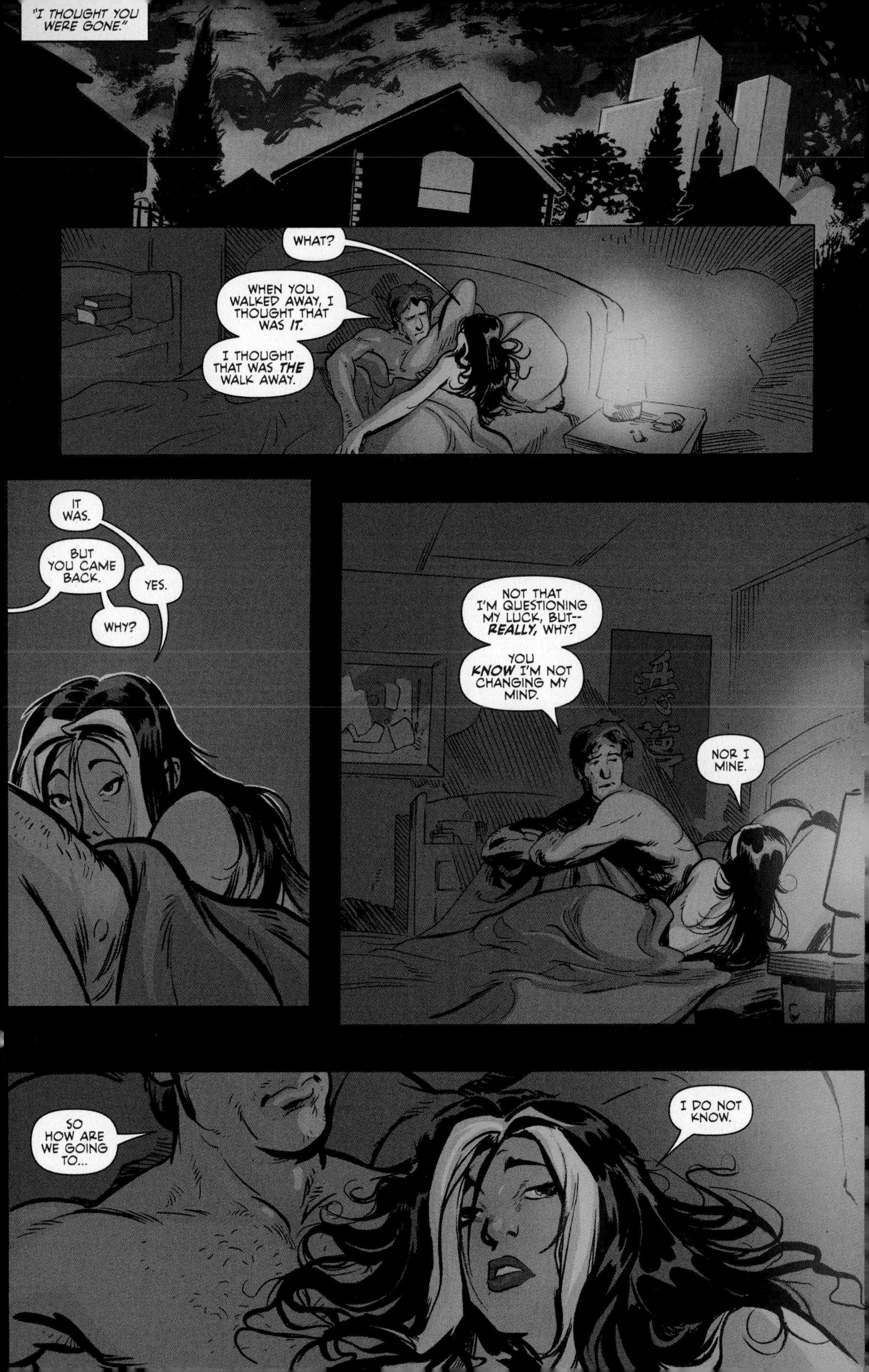
"I THOUGHT YOU WERE GONE."
WHAT?
WHEN YOU WALKED AWAY, I THOUGHT THAT WAS *IT.*
I THOUGHT THAT WAS ***THE*** WALK AWAY.
IT WAS.
BUT YOU CAME BACK.
YES.
WHY?
NOT THAT I'M QUESTIONING MY LUCK, BUT-- ***REALLY,*** WHY?
YOU ***KNOW*** I'M NOT CHANGING MY MIND.
NOR I MINE.
SO HOW ARE WE GOING TO...
I DO NOT KNOW.

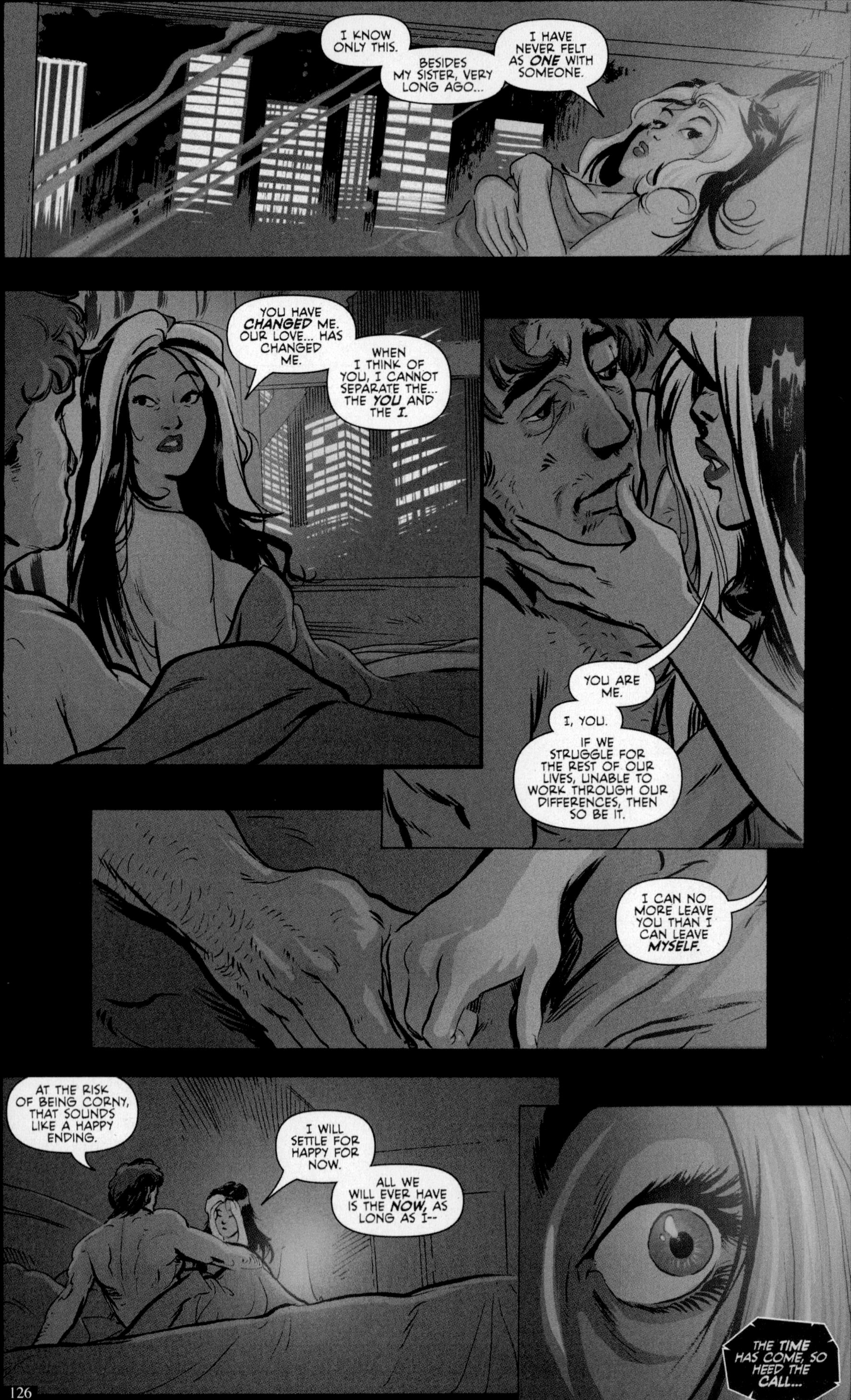
I KNOW ONLY THIS.
BESIDES MY SISTER, VERY LONG AGO...
I HAVE NEVER FELT AS *ONE* WITH SOMEONE.
YOU HAVE *CHANGED* ME. OUR LOVE... HAS CHANGED ME.
WHEN I THINK OF YOU, I CANNOT SEPARATE THE... THE *YOU* AND THE *I.*
YOU ARE ME.
I, YOU.
IF WE STRUGGLE FOR THE REST OF OUR LIVES, UNABLE TO WORK THROUGH OUR DIFFERENCES, THEN SO BE IT.
I CAN NO MORE LEAVE YOU THAN I CAN LEAVE *MYSELF.*
AT THE RISK OF BEING CORNY, THAT SOUNDS LIKE A HAPPY ENDING.
I WILL SETTLE FOR HAPPY FOR NOW.
ALL WE WILL EVER HAVE IS THE *NOW,* AS LONG AS I--
THE *TIME* HAS COME, SO HEED THE *CALL...*

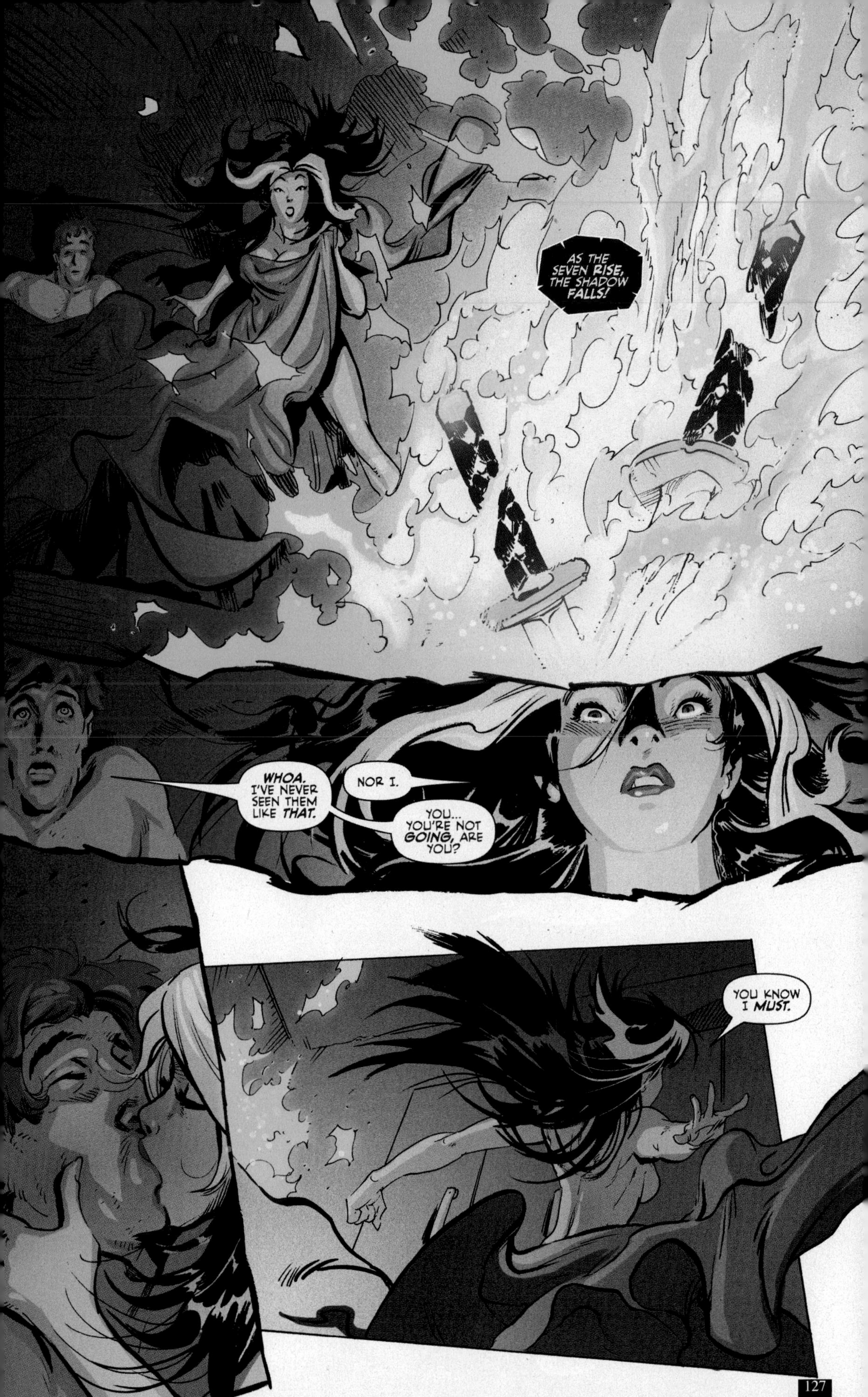
AS THE SEVEN RISE, THE SHADOW FALLS!
WHOA. I'VE NEVER SEEN THEM LIKE THAT.
NOR I.
YOU... YOU'RE NOT GOING, ARE YOU?
YOU KNOW I MUST.

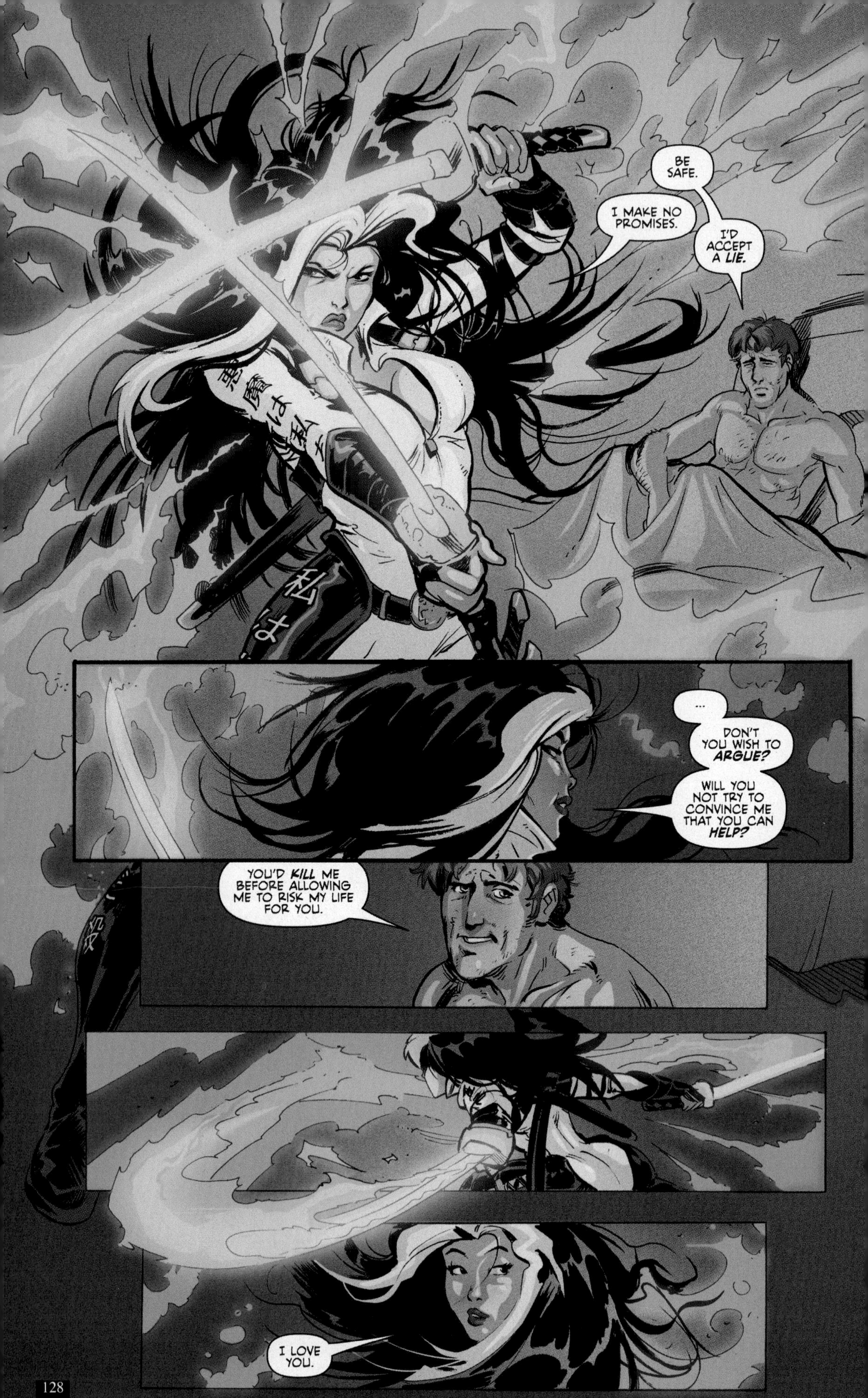
BE SAFE.
I MAKE NO PROMISES.
I'D ACCEPT A LIE.
...
DON'T YOU WISH TO ARGUE?
WILL YOU NOT TRY TO CONVINCE ME THAT YOU CAN HELP?
YOU'D KILL ME BEFORE ALLOWING ME TO RISK MY LIFE FOR YOU.
I LOVE YOU.

I LOVE YOU, TOO.

ENOUGH TO *LIE* TO YOU...

DEMONIC
TELEPORTATION

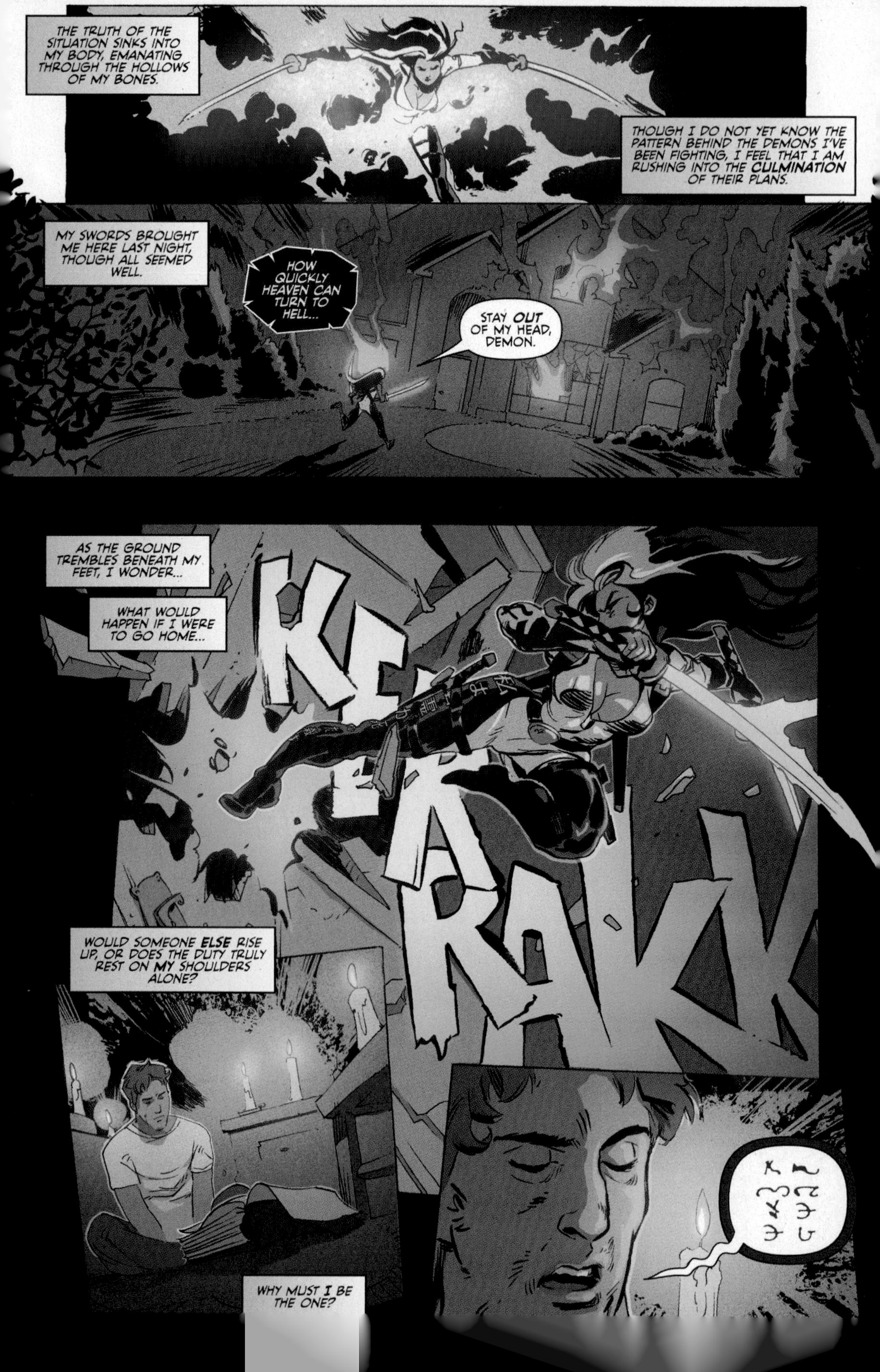
THE TRUTH OF THE SITUATION SINKS INTO MY BODY, EMANATING THROUGH THE HOLLOWS OF MY BONES.
THOUGH I DO NOT YET KNOW THE PATTERN BEHIND THE DEMONS I'VE BEEN FIGHTING, I FEEL THAT I AM RUSHING INTO THE CULMINATION OF THEIR PLANS.
MY SWORDS BROUGHT ME HERE LAST NIGHT, THOUGH ALL SEEMED WELL.
HOW QUICKLY HEAVEN CAN TURN TO HELL...
STAY OUT OF MY HEAD, DEMON.
AS THE GROUND TREMBLES BENEATH MY FEET, I WONDER...
WHAT WOULD HAPPEN IF I WERE TO GO HOME...
WOULD SOMEONE ELSE RISE UP, OR DOES THE DUTY TRULY REST ON MY SHOULDERS ALONE?
WHY MUST I BE THE ONE?

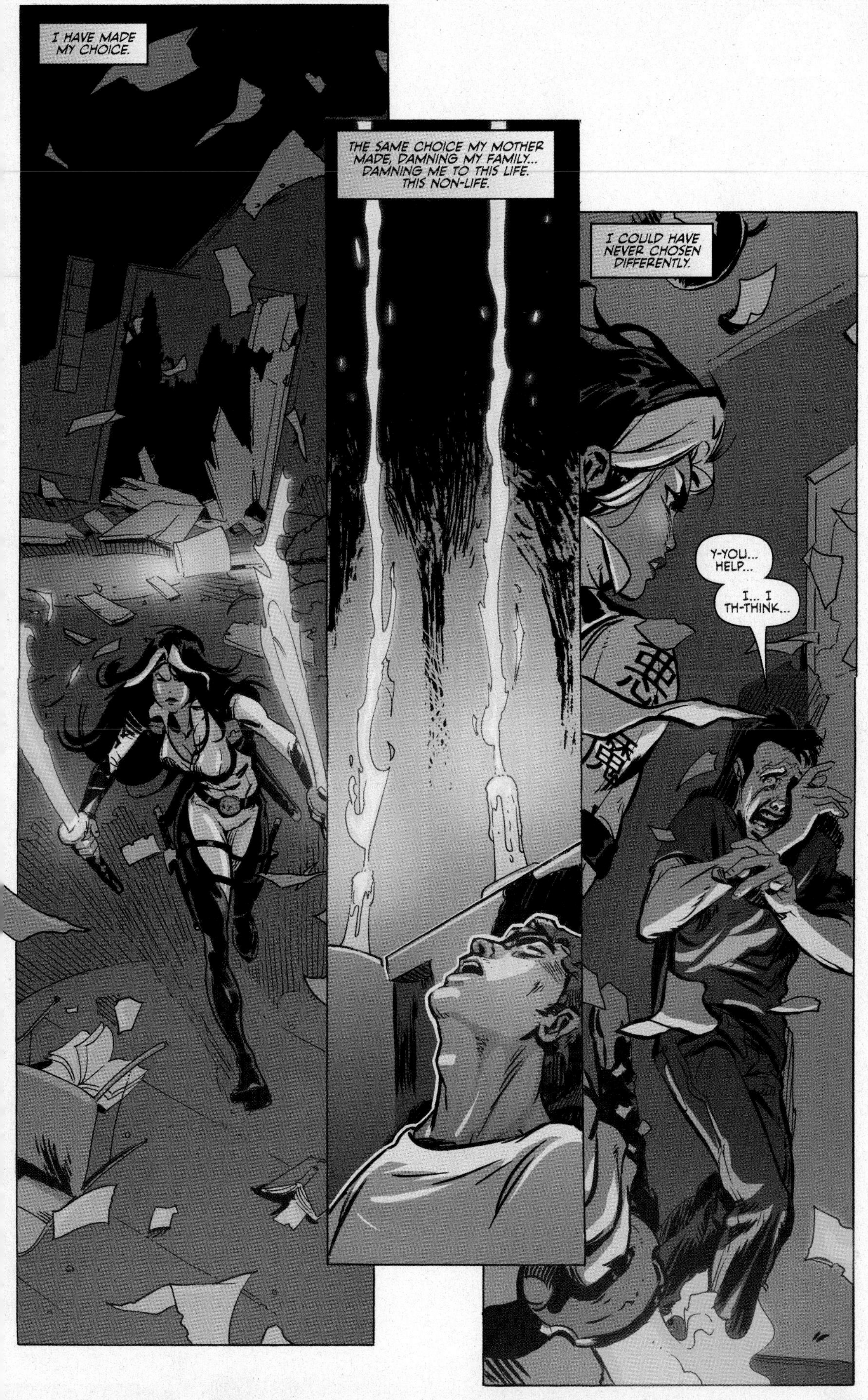
I HAVE MADE MY CHOICE.
THE SAME CHOICE MY MOTHER MADE, DAMNING MY FAMILY... DAMNING ME TO THIS LIFE. THIS NON-LIFE.
I COULD HAVE NEVER CHOSEN DIFFERENTLY.
Y-YOU... HELP...
I... I TH-THINK...

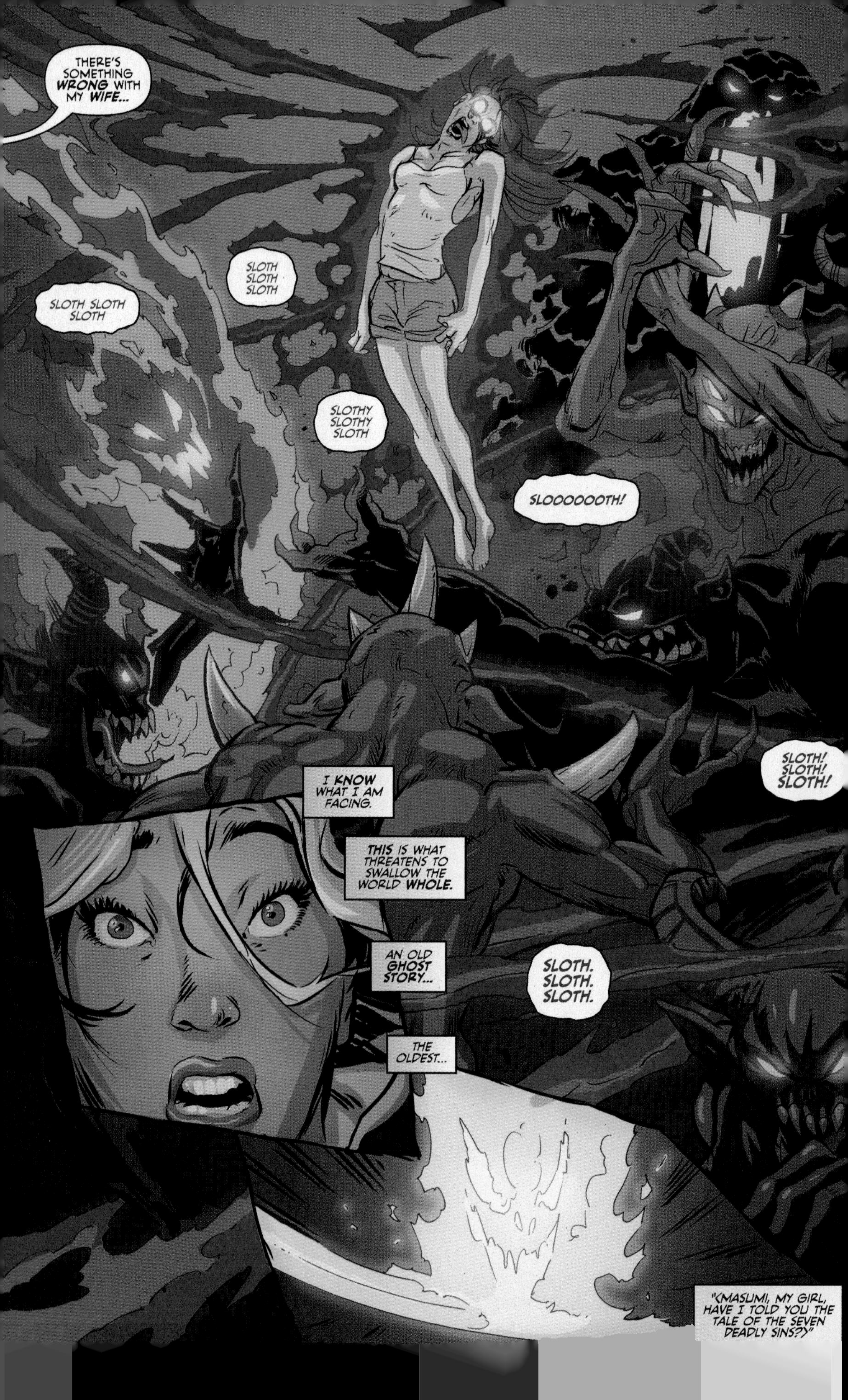
THERE'S SOMETHING WRONG WITH MY WIFE...
SLOTH SLOTH SLOTH
SLOTH SLOTH SLOTH
SLOTHY SLOTHY SLOTH
SLOOOOOOTH!
SLOTH! SLOTH! SLOTH!
I KNOW WHAT I AM FACING.
THIS IS WHAT THREATENS TO SWALLOW THE WORLD WHOLE.
AN OLD GHOST STORY...
SLOTH. SLOTH. SLOTH.
THE OLDEST...
"<MASUMI, MY GIRL, HAVE I TOLD YOU THE TALE OF THE SEVEN DEADLY SINS?>"

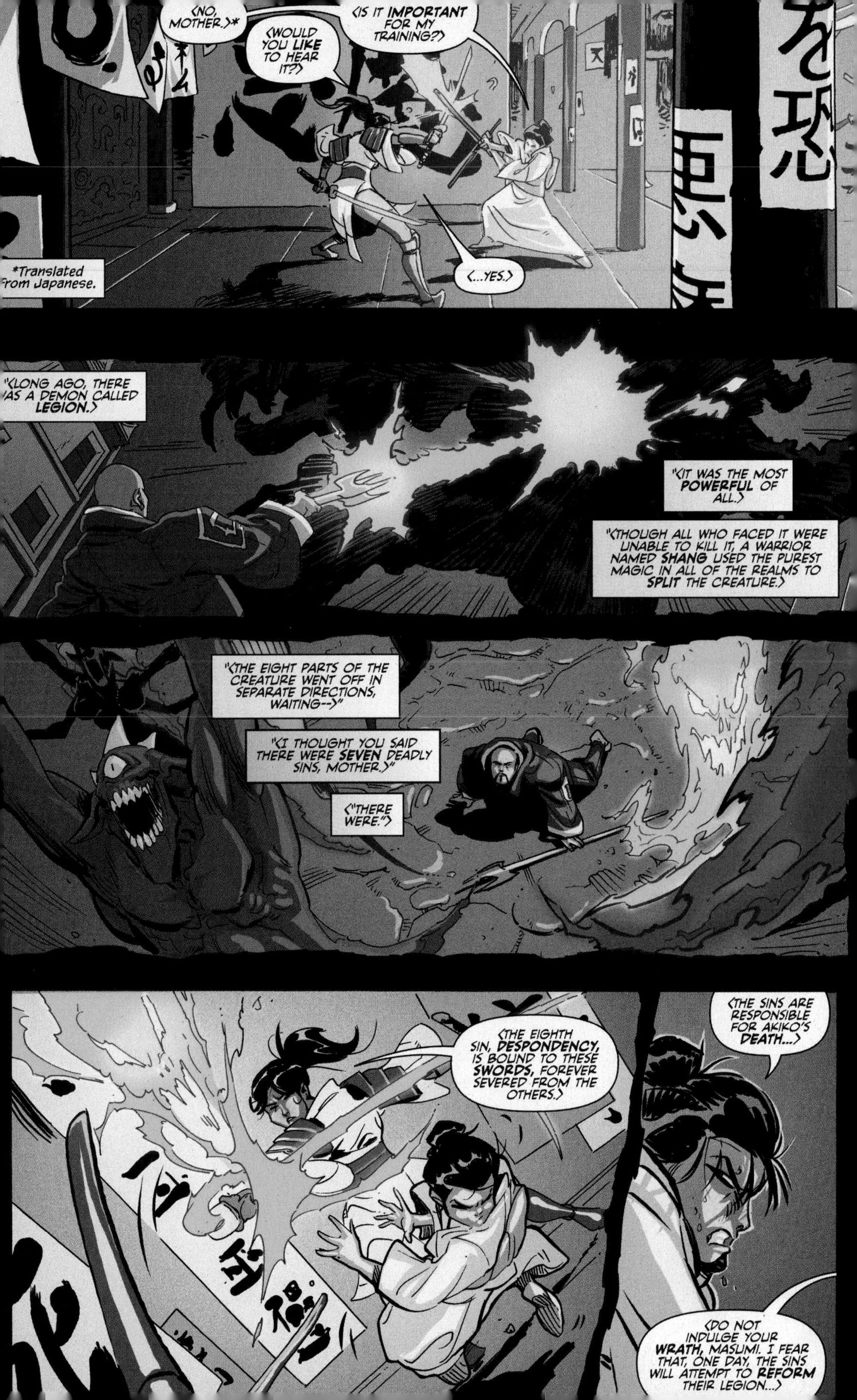
<NO, MOTHER.>*
<WOULD YOU LIKE TO HEAR IT?>
<IS IT IMPORTANT FOR MY TRAINING?>
*Translated from Japanese.
<...YES.>
"<LONG AGO, THERE WAS A DEMON CALLED LEGION.>
"<IT WAS THE MOST POWERFUL OF ALL.>
"<THOUGH ALL WHO FACED IT WERE UNABLE TO KILL IT, A WARRIOR NAMED SHANG USED THE PUREST MAGIC IN ALL OF THE REALMS TO SPLIT THE CREATURE.>
"<THE EIGHT PARTS OF THE CREATURE WENT OFF IN SEPARATE DIRECTIONS, WAITING-->"
"<I THOUGHT YOU SAID THERE WERE SEVEN DEADLY SINS, MOTHER.>"
<"THERE WERE.">
<THE EIGHTH SIN, DESPONDENCY, IS BOUND TO THESE SWORDS, FOREVER SEVERED FROM THE OTHERS.>
<THE SINS ARE RESPONSIBLE FOR AKIKO'S DEATH...>
<DO NOT INDULGE YOUR WRATH, MASUMI. I FEAR THAT, ONE DAY, THE SINS WILL ATTEMPT TO REFORM THEIR LEGION...>

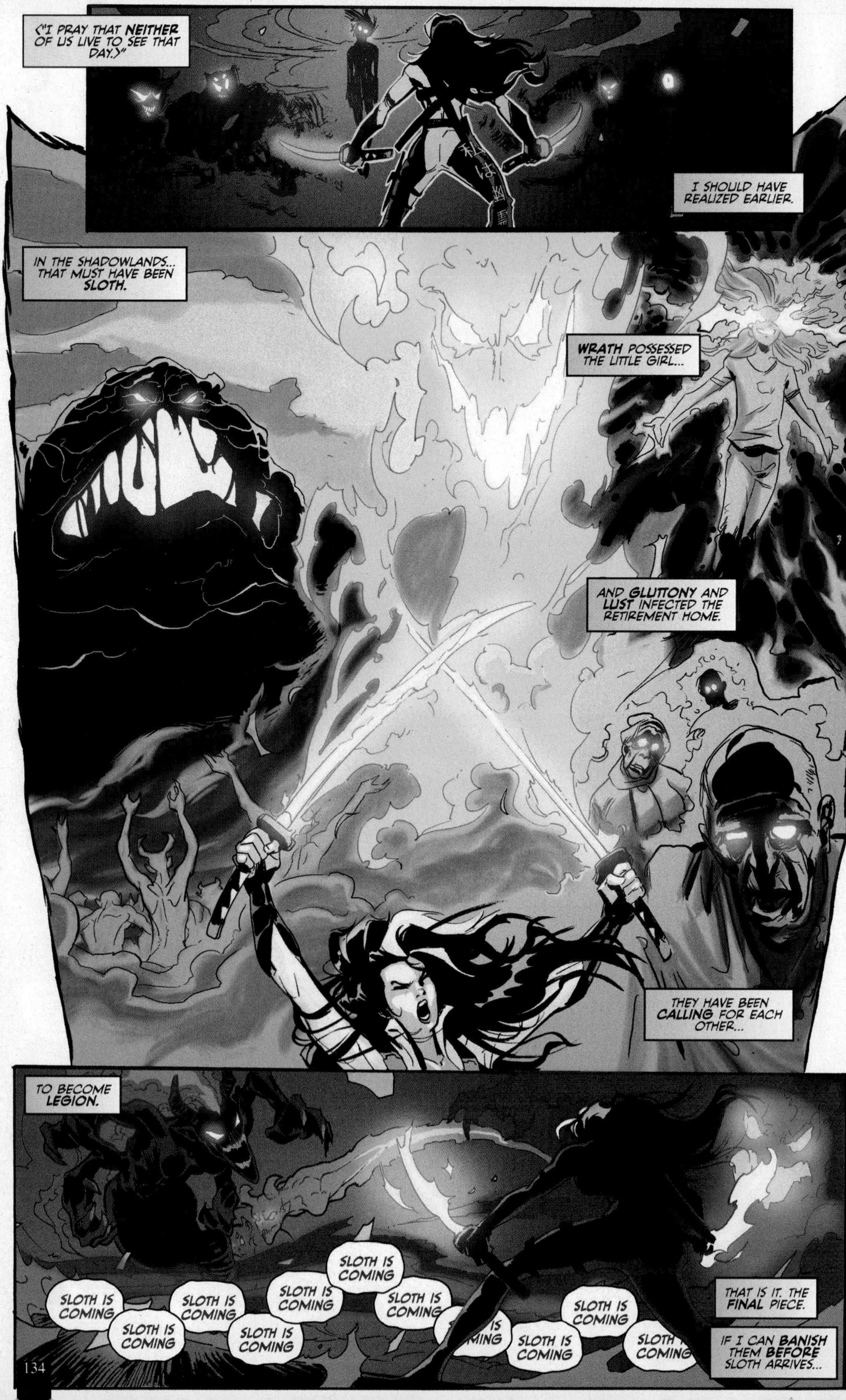

<"I PRAY THAT NEITHER OF US LIVE TO SEE THAT DAY.>"
I SHOULD HAVE REALIZED EARLIER.
IN THE SHADOWLANDS... THAT MUST HAVE BEEN SLOTH.
WRATH POSSESSED THE LITTLE GIRL...
AND GLUTTONY AND LUST INFECTED THE RETIREMENT HOME.
THEY HAVE BEEN CALLING FOR EACH OTHER...
TO BECOME LEGION.
SLOTH IS COMING
SLOTH IS COMING
SLOTH IS COMING
SLOTH IS COMING
SLOTH IS COMING
SLOTH IS COMING
SLOTH IS COMING
SLOTH IS COMING
SLOTH IS COMING
THAT IS IT. THE FINAL PIECE.
IF I CAN BANISH THEM BEFORE SLOTH ARRIVES...

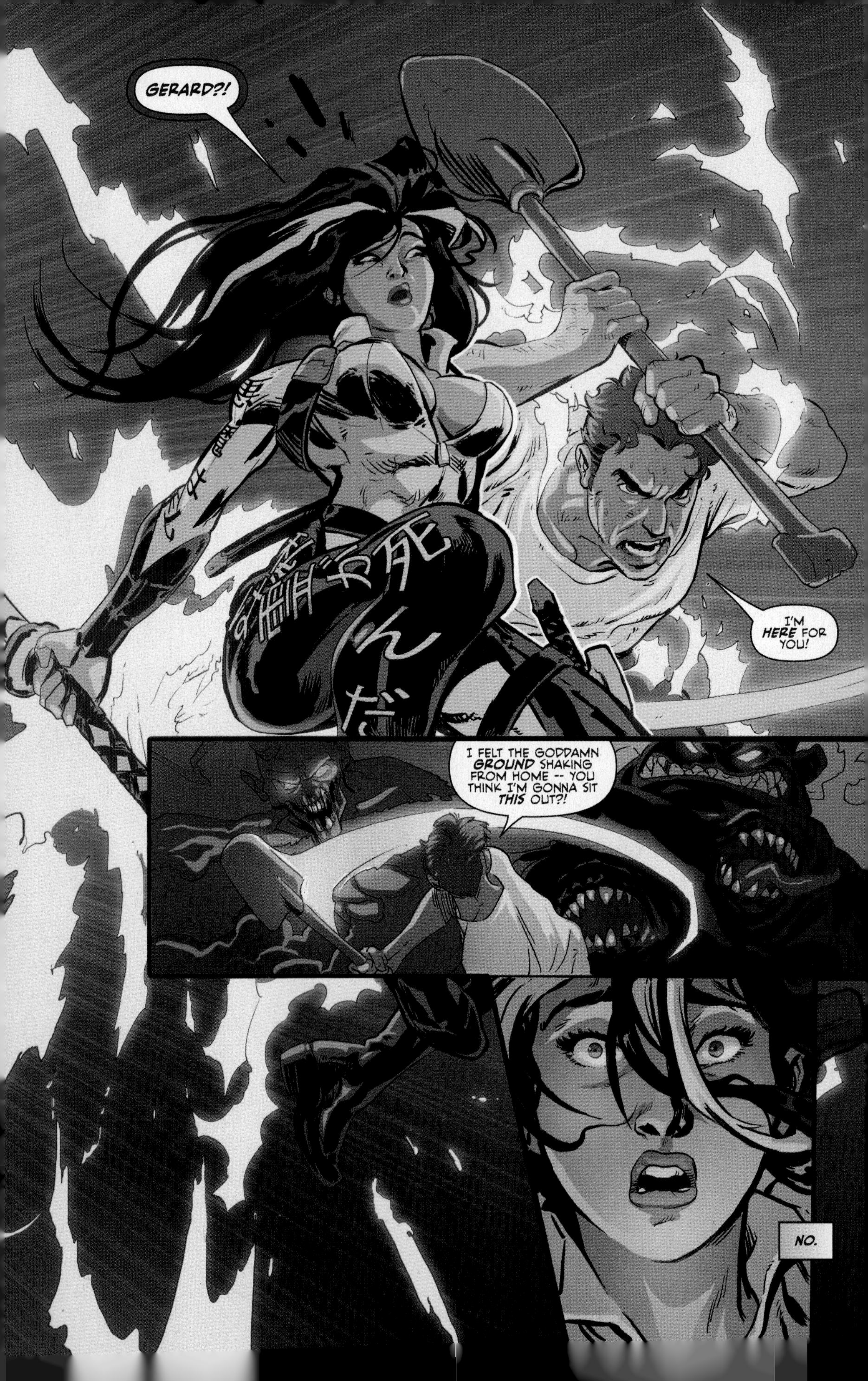
GERARD?!
I'M HERE FOR YOU!
I FELT THE GODDAMN GROUND SHAKING FROM HOME -- YOU THINK I'M GONNA SIT THIS OUT?!
NO.

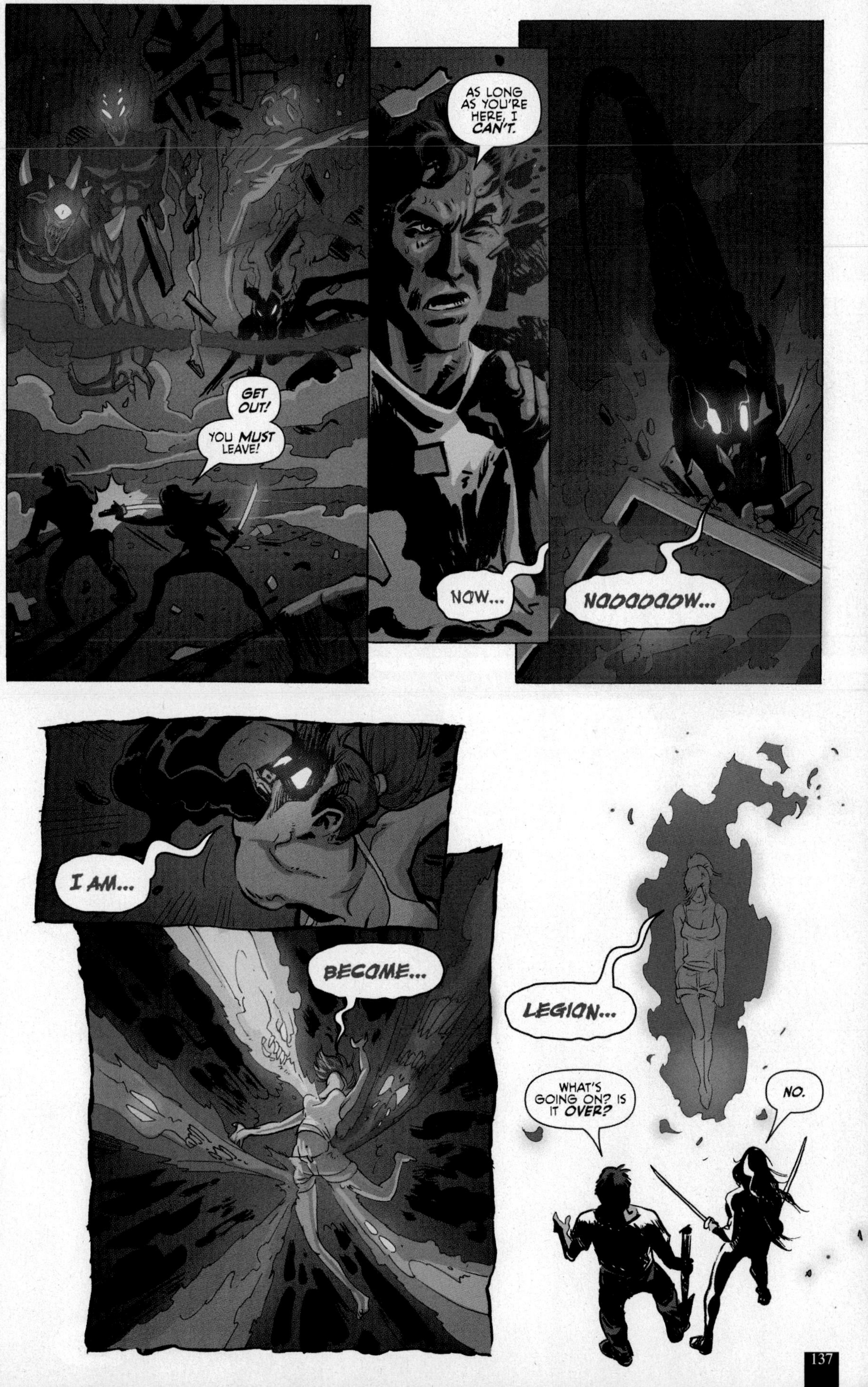
GET OUT!
YOU MUST LEAVE!
AS LONG AS YOU'RE HERE, I CAN'T.
NOW...
NOOOOOOW...
I AM...
BECOME...
LEGION...
WHAT'S GOING ON? IS IT OVER?
NO.

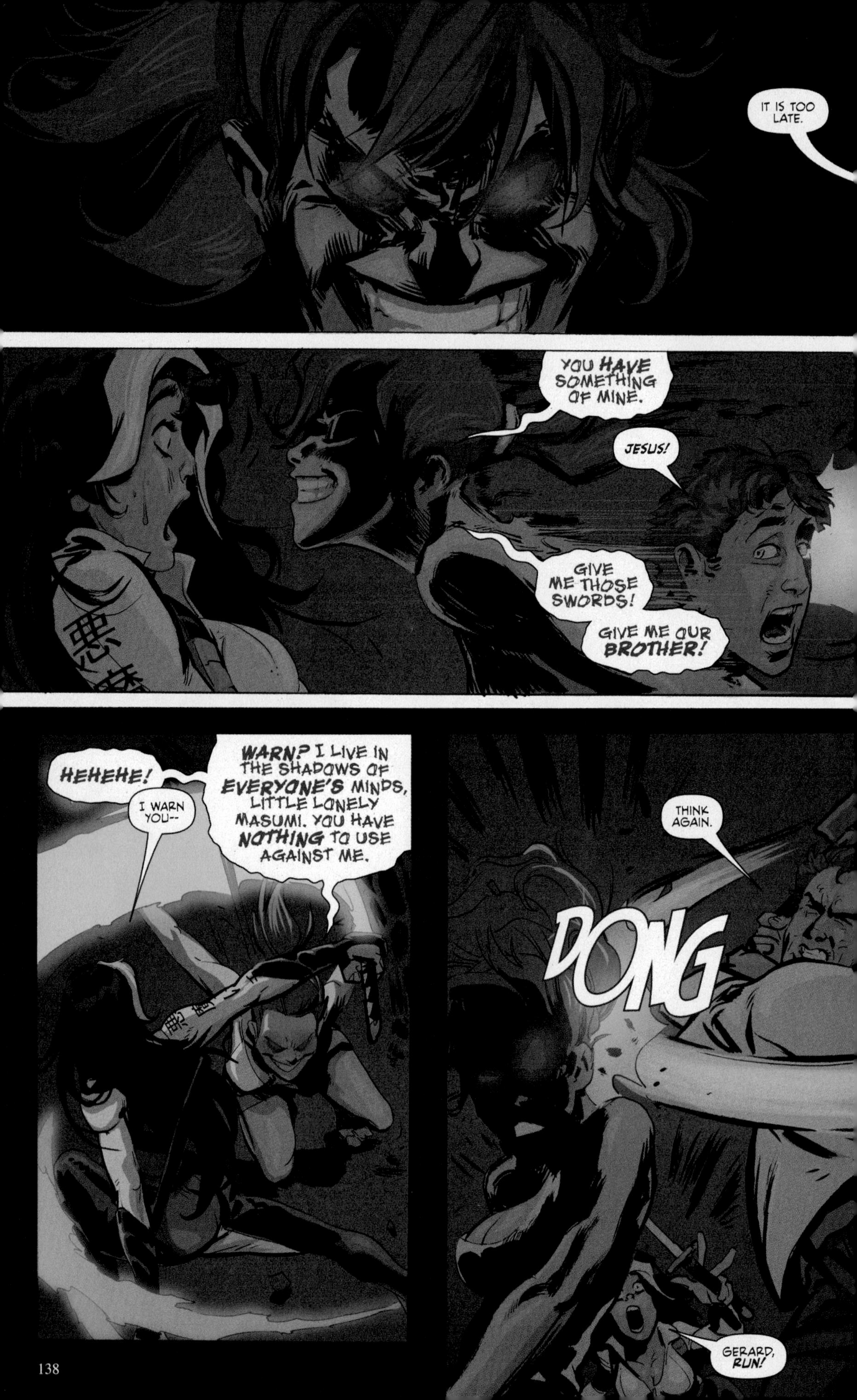

IT IS TOO LATE.
YOU HAVE SOMETHING OF MINE.
JESUS!
GIVE ME THOSE SWORDS!
GIVE ME OUR BROTHER!
HEHEHE!
I WARN YOU--
WARN? I LIVE IN THE SHADOWS OF EVERYONE'S MINDS, LITTLE LONELY MASUMI. YOU HAVE NOTHING TO USE AGAINST ME.
THINK AGAIN.
DONG
GERARD, RUN!

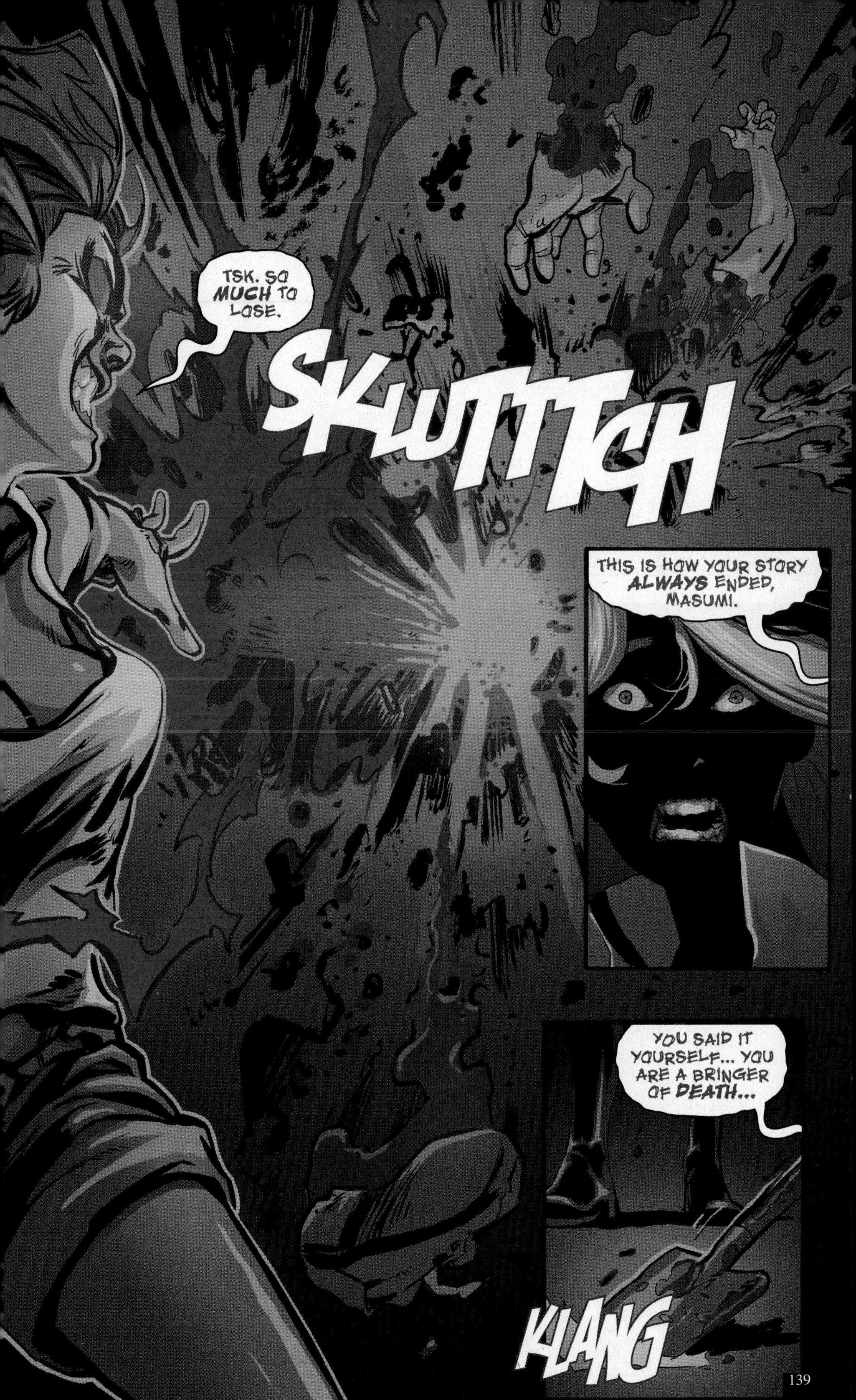
TSK. SO MUCH TO LOSE.
SKUTTTCH
THIS IS HOW YOUR STORY ALWAYS ENDED, MASUMI.
YOU SAID IT YOURSELF... YOU ARE A BRINGER OF DEATH...
KLANG

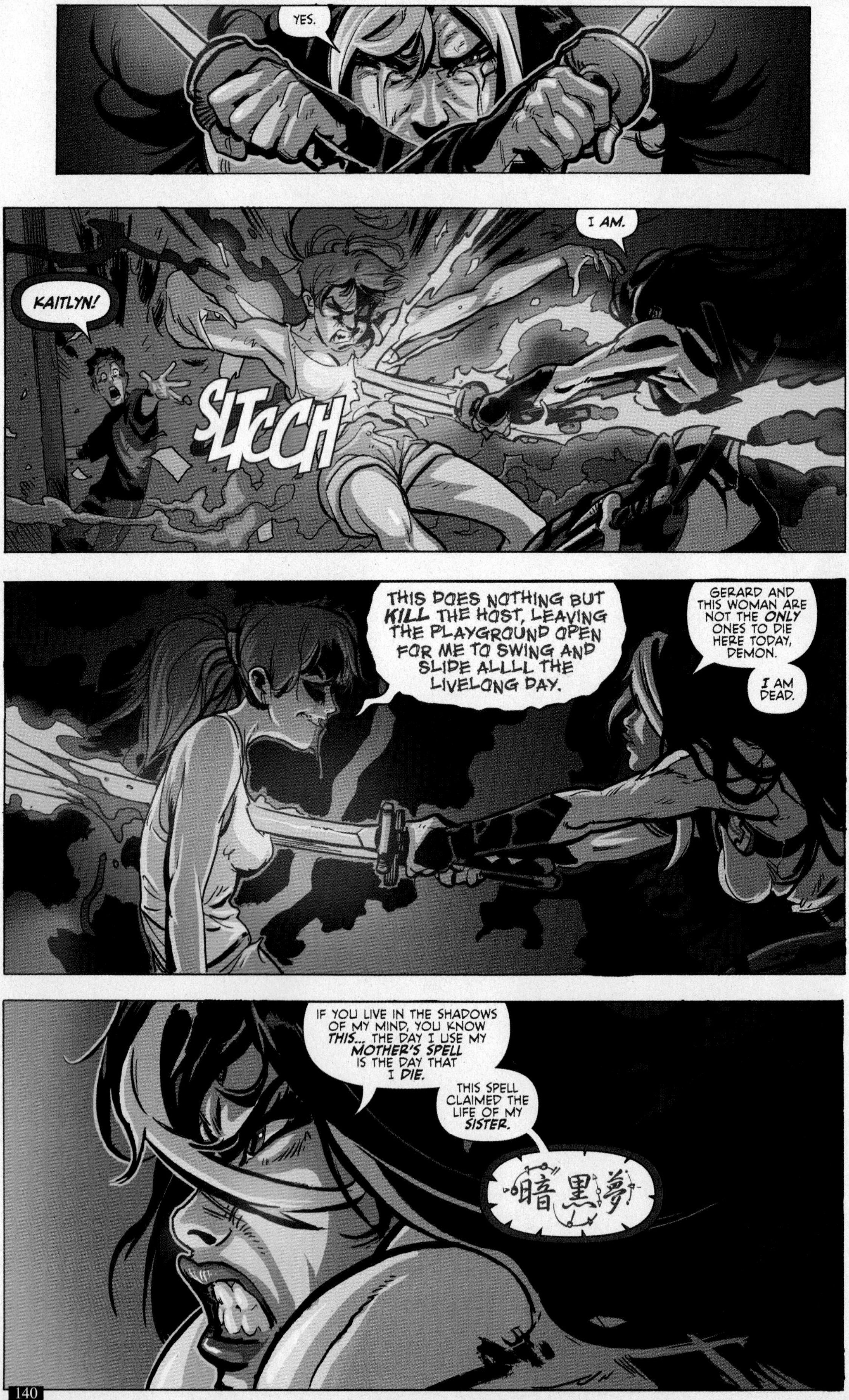
YES.
I AM.
KAITLYN!
SLTCCH
THIS DOES NOTHING BUT KILL THE HOST, LEAVING THE PLAYGROUND OPEN FOR ME TO SWING AND SLIDE ALLLL THE LIVELONG DAY.
GERARD AND THIS WOMAN ARE NOT THE ONLY ONES TO DIE HERE TODAY, DEMON.
I AM DEAD.
IF YOU LIVE IN THE SHADOWS OF MY MIND, YOU KNOW THIS... THE DAY I USE MY MOTHER'S SPELL IS THE DAY THAT I DIE.
THIS SPELL CLAIMED THE LIFE OF MY SISTER.
暗黒夢

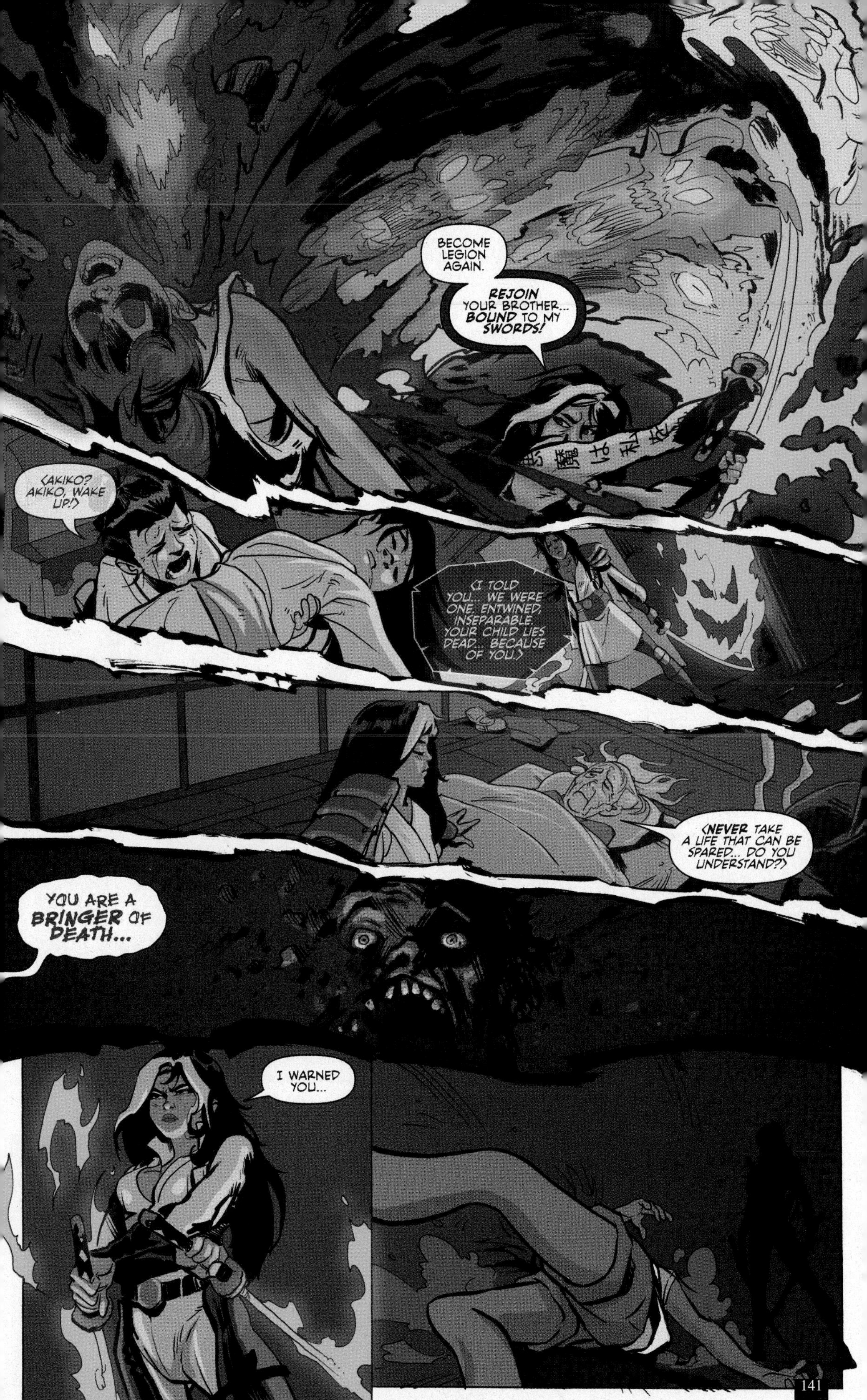
BECOME LEGION AGAIN.
REJOIN YOUR BROTHER... BOUND TO MY SWORDS!
<AKIKO? AKIKO, WAKE UP!>
<I TOLD YOU... WE WERE ONE. ENTWINED, INSEPARABLE. YOUR CHILD LIES DEAD... BECAUSE OF YOU.>
<NEVER TAKE A LIFE THAT CAN BE SPARED... DO YOU UNDERSTAND?>
YOU ARE A BRINGER OF DEATH...
I WARNED YOU...

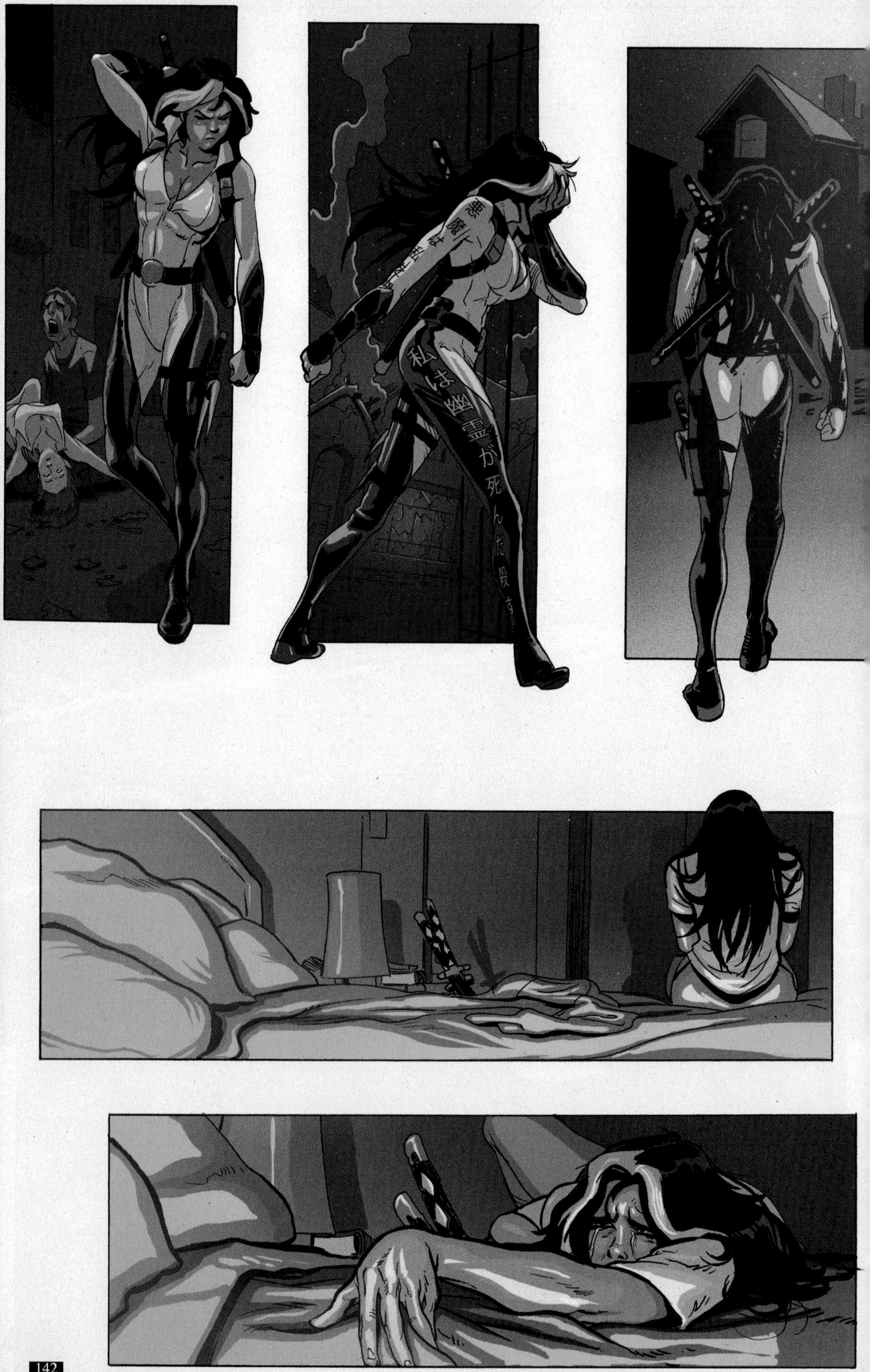
私は幽霊が死んだ殺す

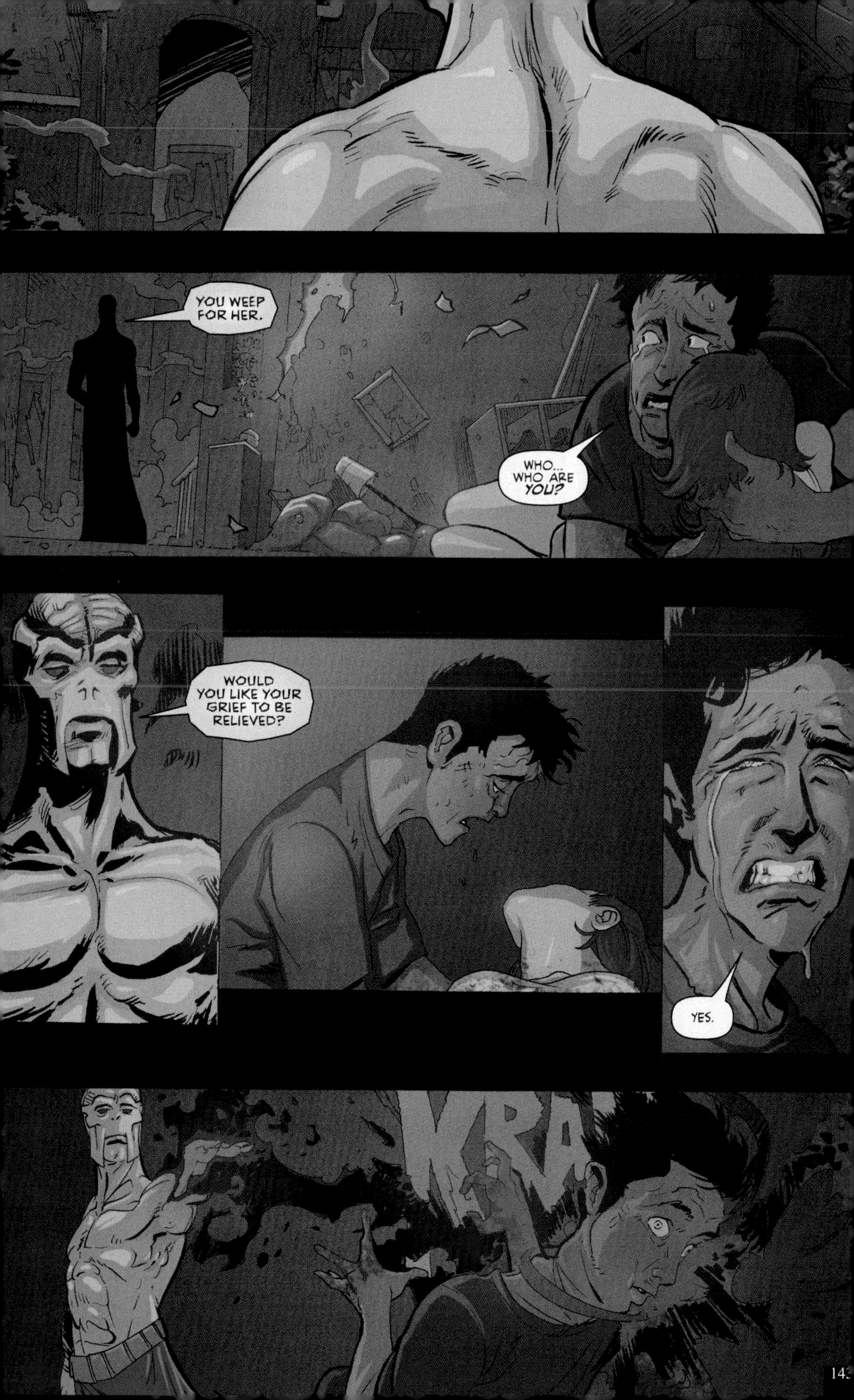
YOU WEEP FOR HER.
WHO... WHO ARE *YOU*?
WOULD YOU LIKE YOUR GRIEF TO BE RELIEVED?
YES.
KRA

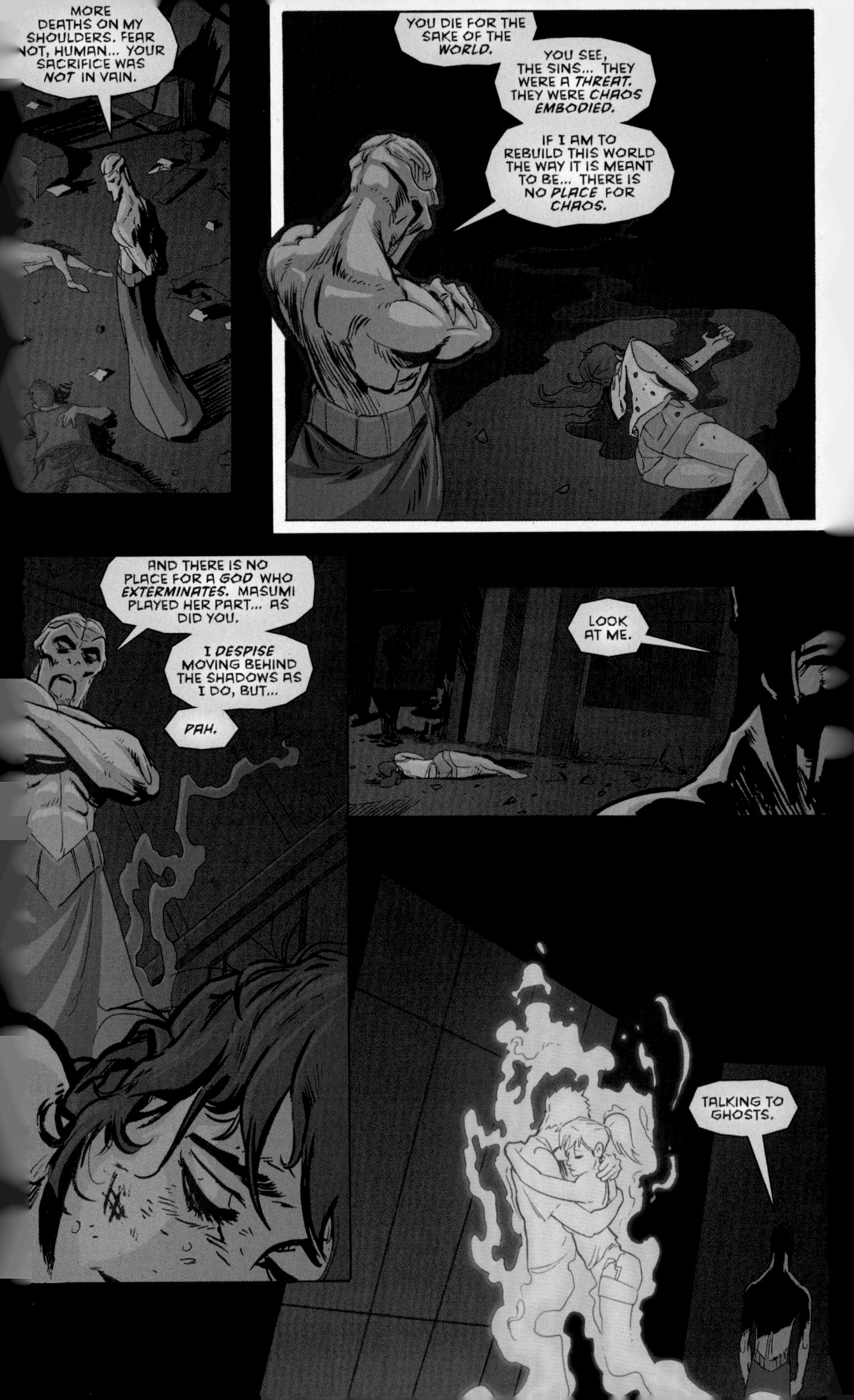
MORE DEATHS ON MY SHOULDERS. FEAR NOT, HUMAN... YOUR SACRIFICE WAS NOT IN VAIN.
YOU DIE FOR THE SAKE OF THE WORLD.
YOU SEE, THE SINS... THEY WERE A THREAT. THEY WERE CHAOS EMBODIED.
IF I AM TO REBUILD THIS WORLD THE WAY IT IS MEANT TO BE... THERE IS NO PLACE FOR CHAOS.
AND THERE IS NO PLACE FOR A GOD WHO EXTERMINATES. MASUMI PLAYED HER PART... AS DID YOU.
I DESPISE MOVING BEHIND THE SHADOWS AS I DO, BUT...
PAH.
LOOK AT ME.
TALKING TO GHOSTS.

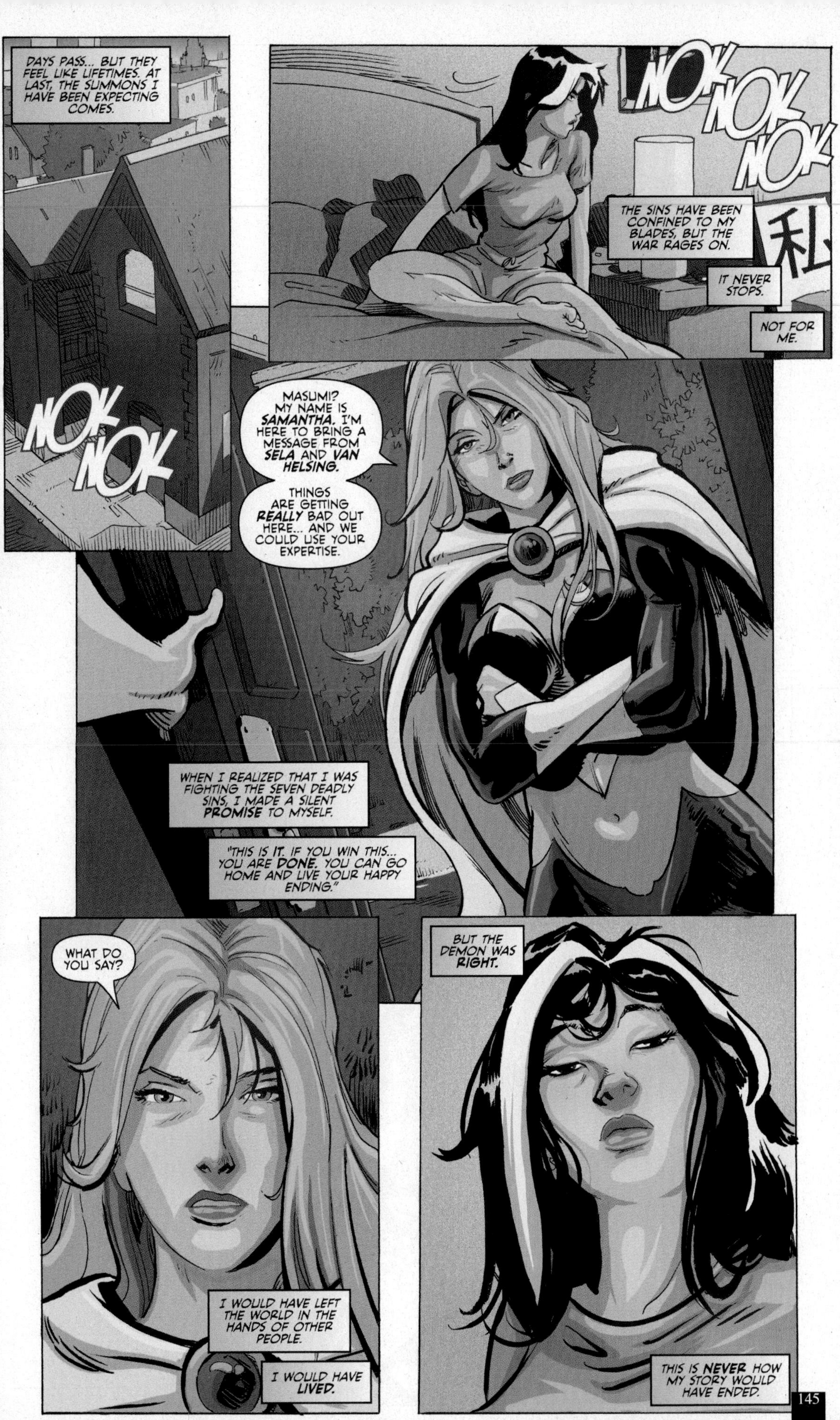
DAYS PASS... BUT THEY FEEL LIKE LIFETIMES. AT LAST, THE SUMMONS I HAVE BEEN EXPECTING COMES.
NOK NOK NOK
THE SINS HAVE BEEN CONFINED TO MY BLADES, BUT THE WAR RAGES ON.
私
IT NEVER STOPS.
NOT FOR ME.
NOK NOK
MASUMI? MY NAME IS SAMANTHA. I'M HERE TO BRING A MESSAGE FROM SELA AND VAN HELSING.
THINGS ARE GETTING REALLY BAD OUT HERE... AND WE COULD USE YOUR EXPERTISE.
WHEN I REALIZED THAT I WAS FIGHTING THE SEVEN DEADLY SINS, I MADE A SILENT PROMISE TO MYSELF.
"THIS IS IT. IF YOU WIN THIS... YOU ARE DONE. YOU CAN GO HOME AND LIVE YOUR HAPPY ENDING."
WHAT DO YOU SAY?
I WOULD HAVE LEFT THE WORLD IN THE HANDS OF OTHER PEOPLE.
I WOULD HAVE LIVED.
BUT THE DEMON WAS RIGHT.
THIS IS NEVER HOW MY STORY WOULD HAVE ENDED.

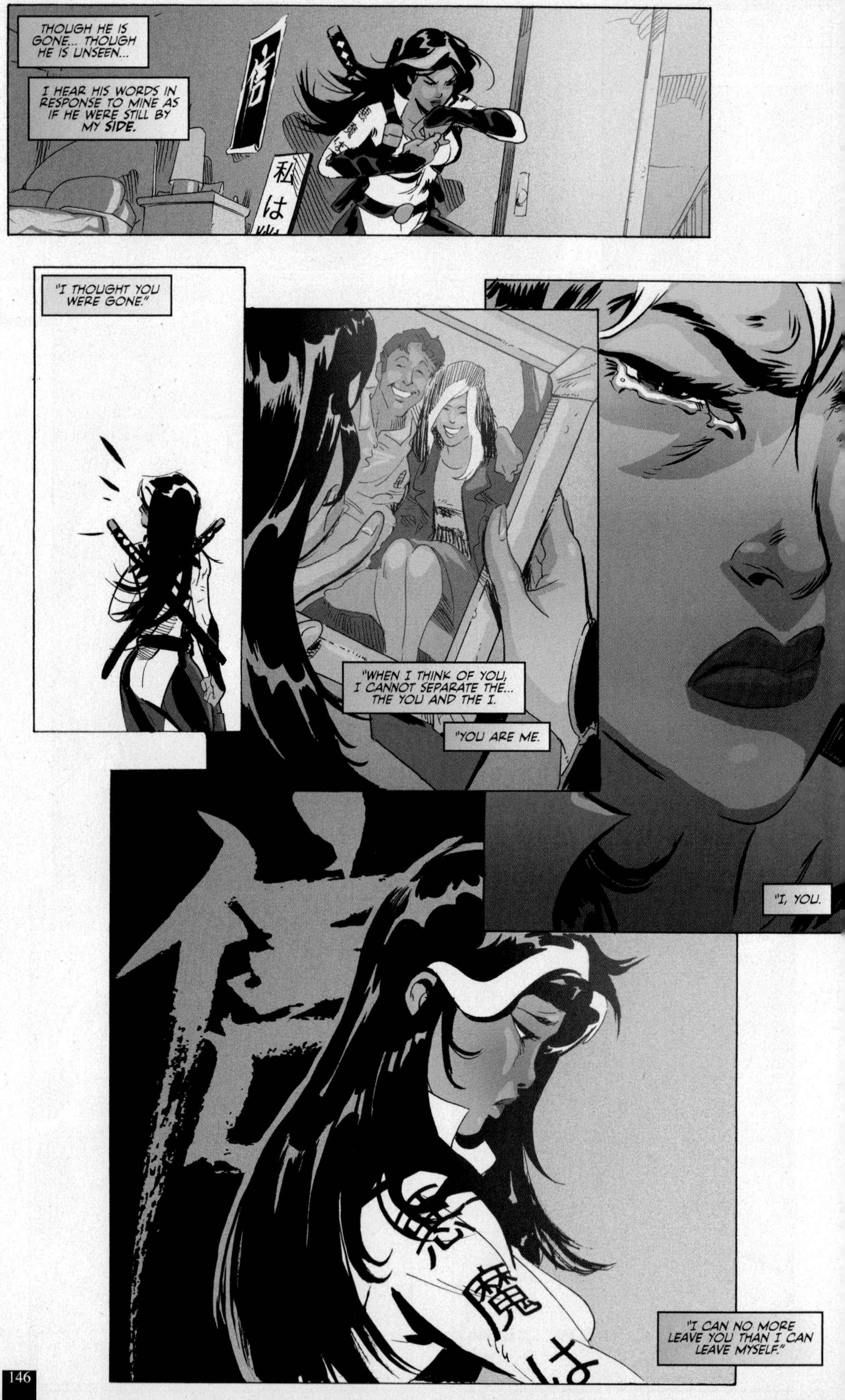
THOUGH HE IS GONE... THOUGH HE IS UNSEEN...
I HEAR HIS WORDS IN RESPONSE TO MINE AS IF HE WERE STILL BY MY SIDE.
私は
"I THOUGHT YOU WERE GONE."
"WHEN I THINK OF YOU, I CANNOT SEPARATE THE... THE YOU AND THE I.
"YOU ARE ME.
"I, YOU.
"I CAN NO MORE LEAVE YOU THAN I CAN LEAVE MYSELF."

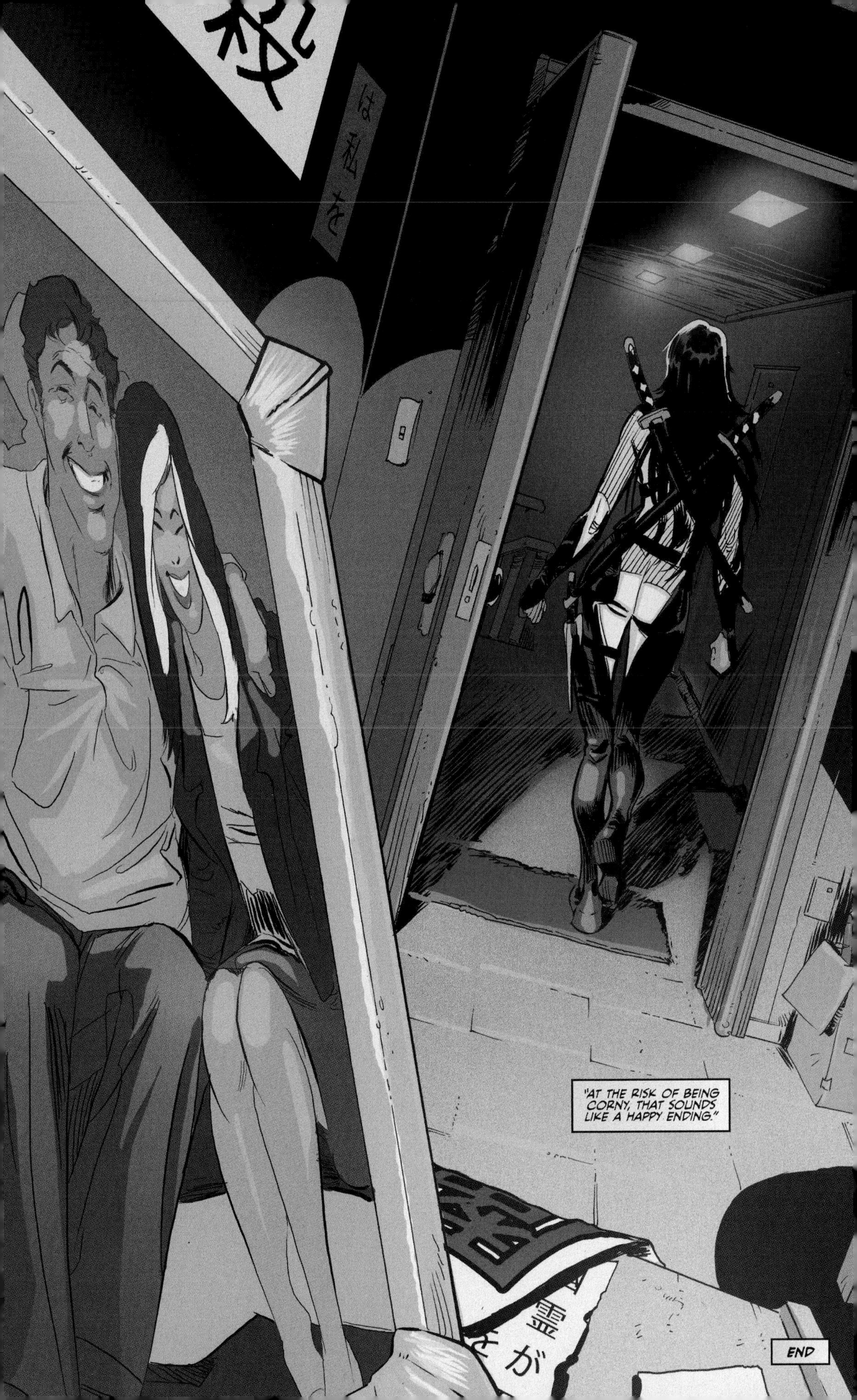

は私を
"AT THE RISK OF BEING CORNY, THAT SOUNDS LIKE A HAPPY ENDING."
END

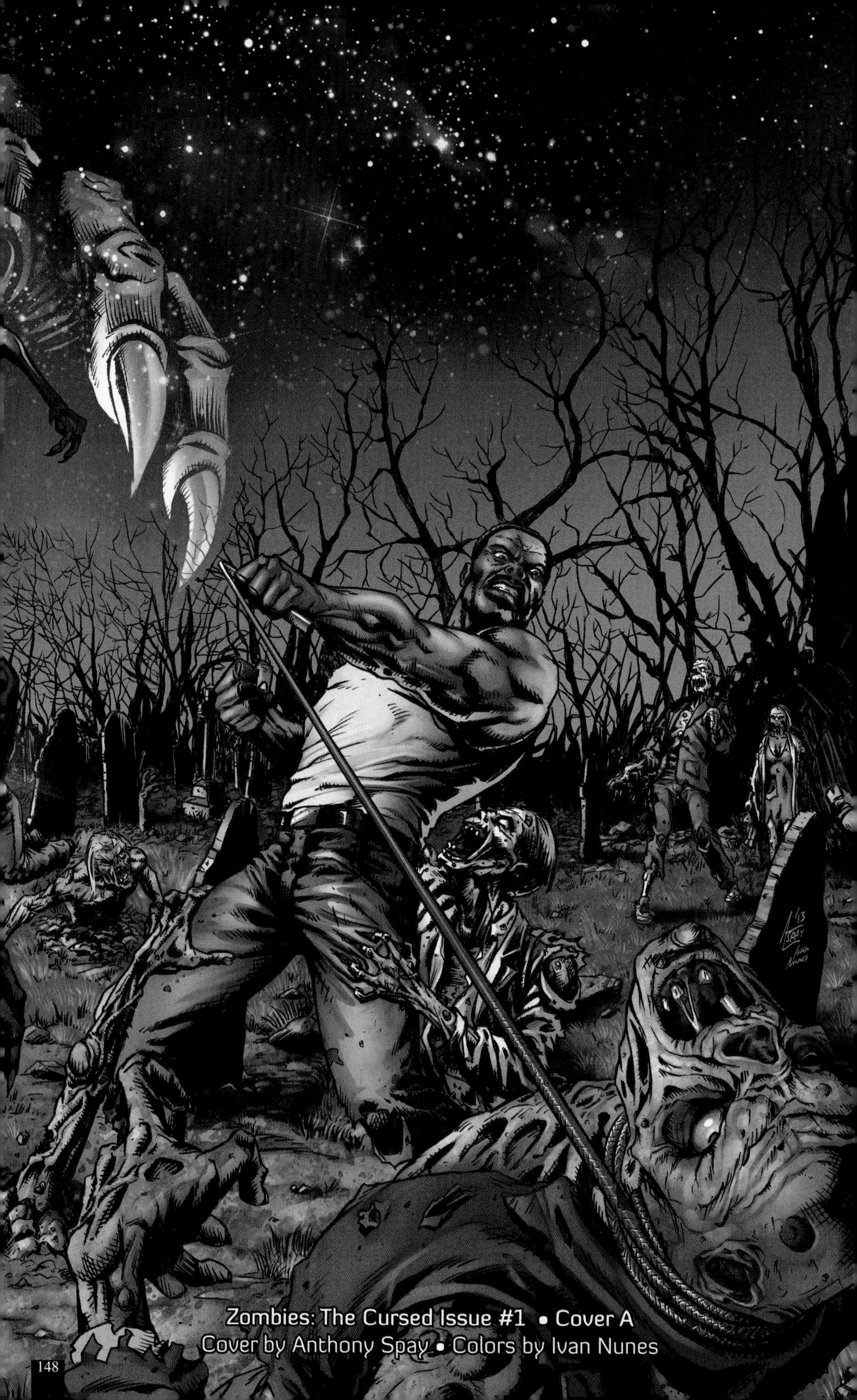

Zombies: The Cursed Issue #1 • Cover A
Cover by Anthony Spay • Colors by Ivan Nunes

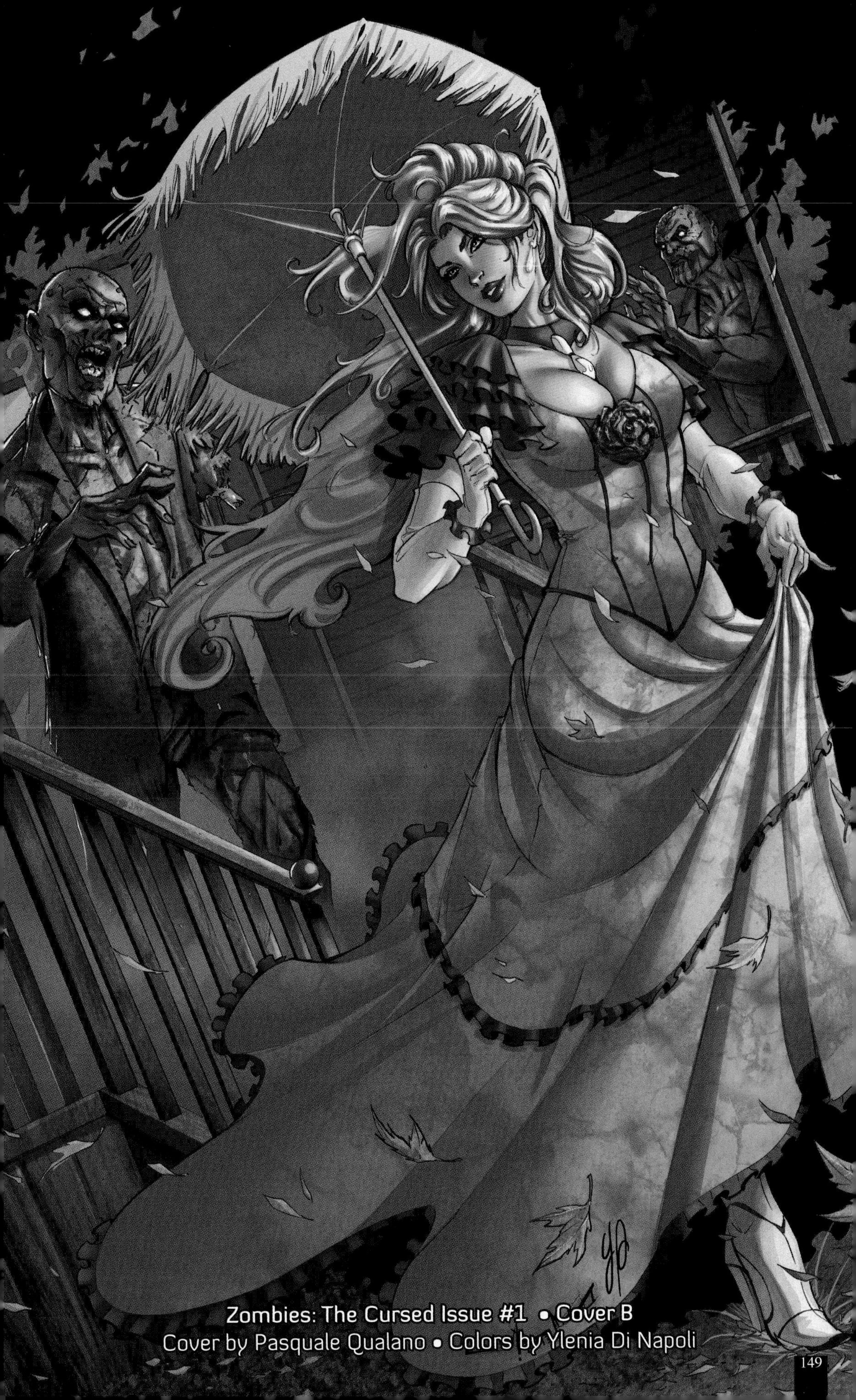

Zombies: The Cursed Issue #1 • Cover B
Cover by Pasquale Qualano • Colors by Ylenia Di Napoli

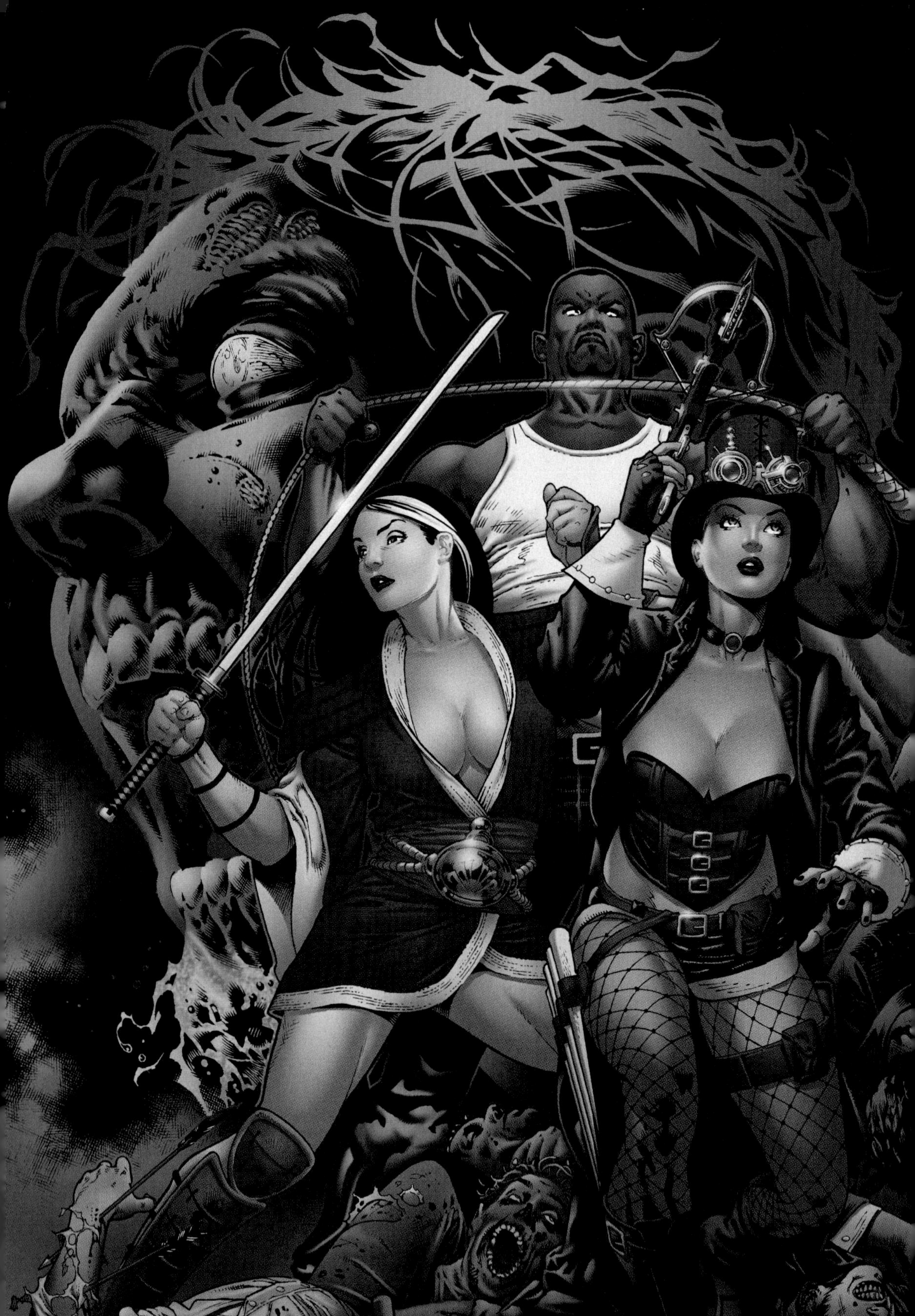

Zombies: The Cursed Issue #2 • Cover A
Cover by Paulo Siqueira • Colors by Sean Ellery

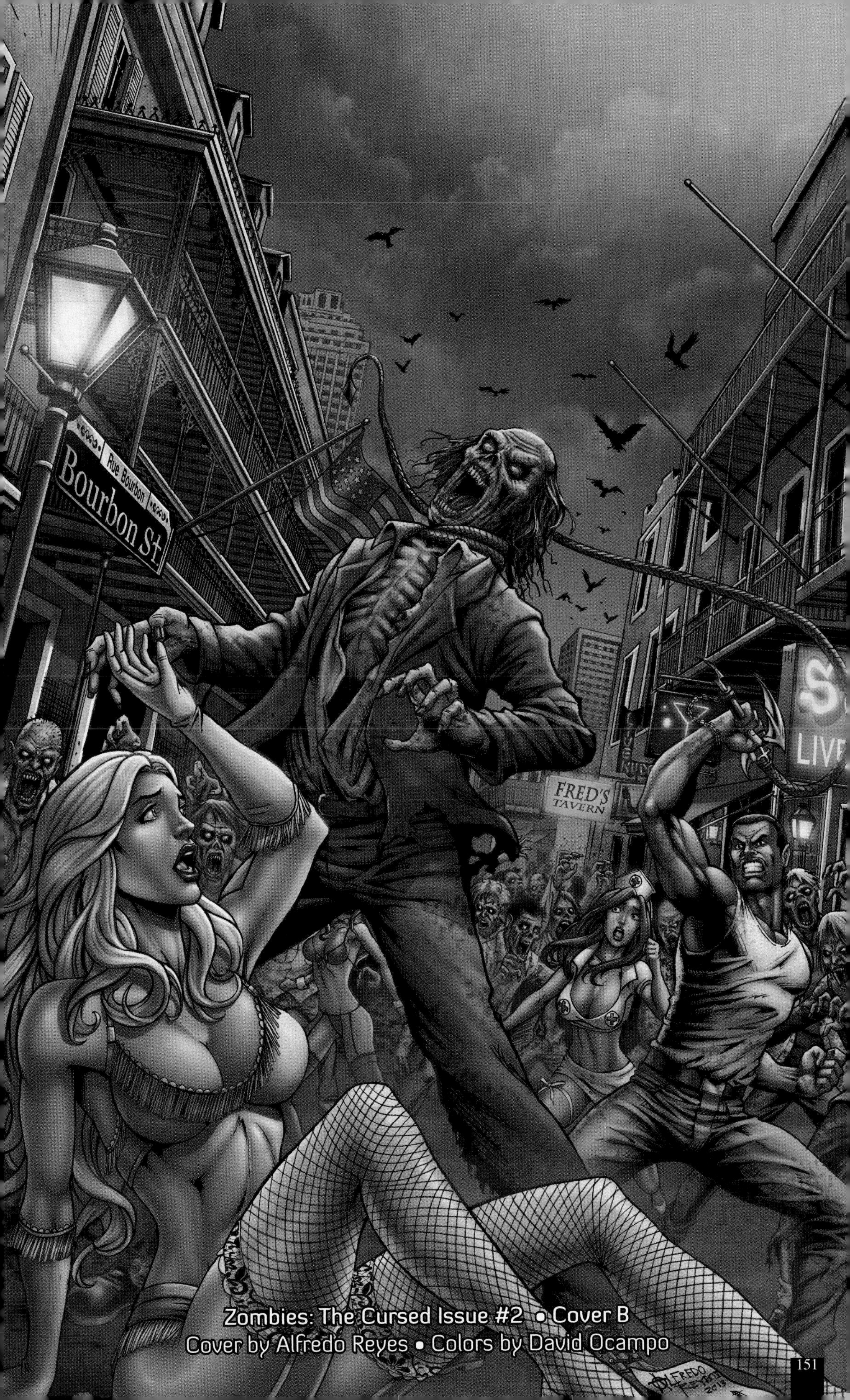

Rue Bourbon
Bourbon St.
FRED'S TAVERN
LIVE

Zombies: The Cursed Issue #2 • Cover B
Cover by Alfredo Reyes • Colors by David Ocampo

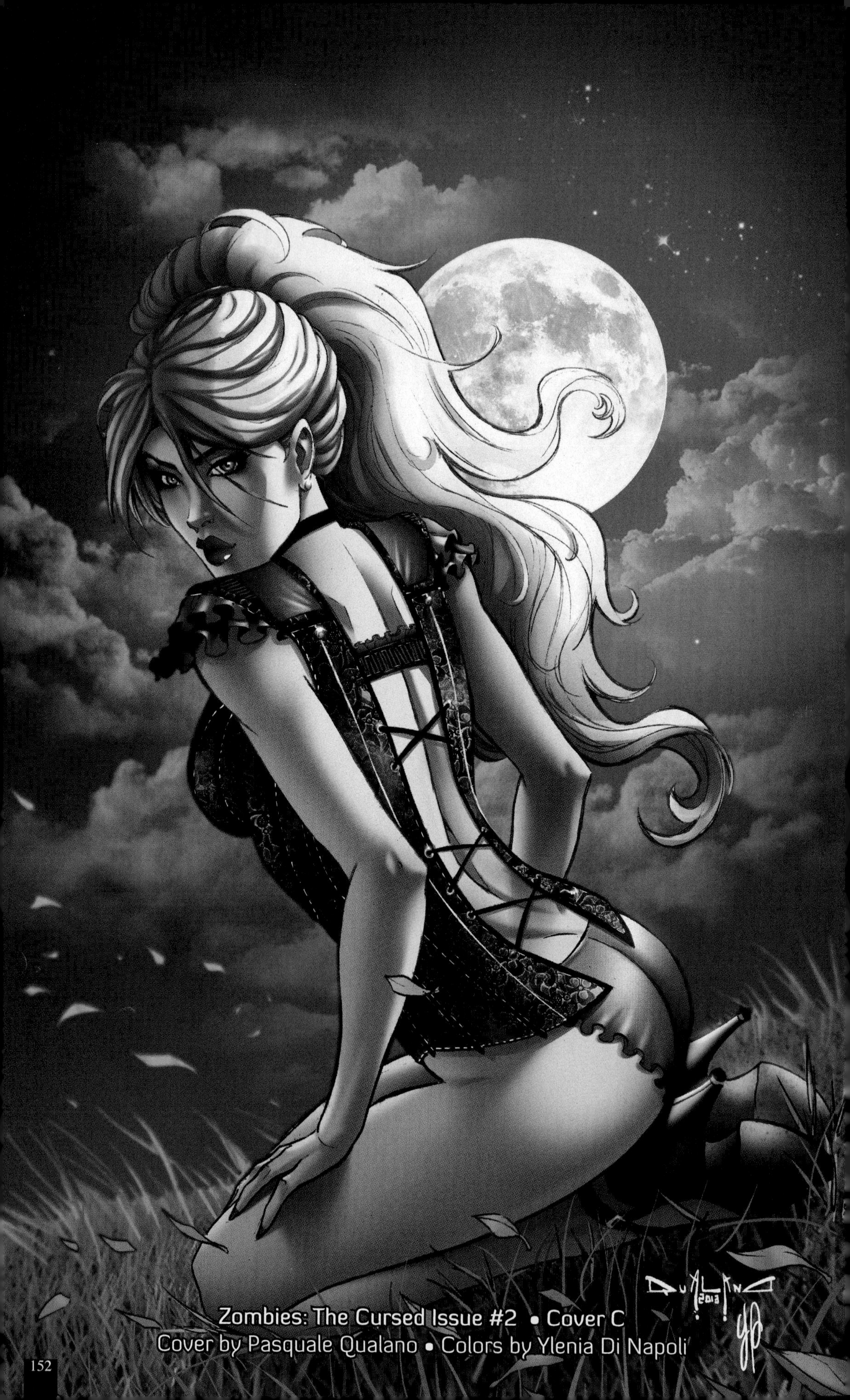

Zombies: The Cursed Issue #2 • Cover C
Cover by Pasquale Qualano • Colors by Ylenia Di Napoli

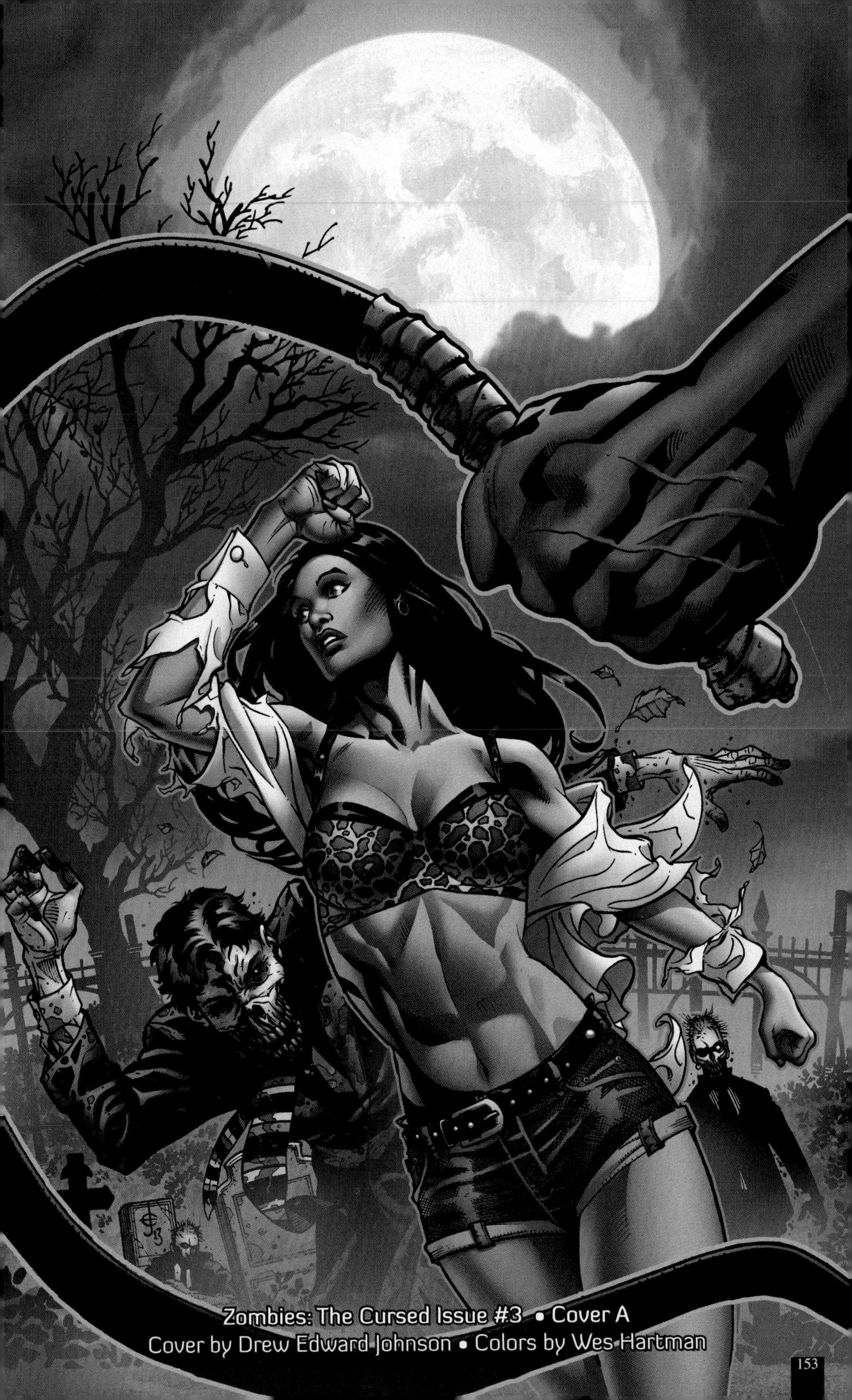

Zombies: The Cursed Issue #3 • Cover A
Cover by Drew Edward Johnson • Colors by Wes Hartman

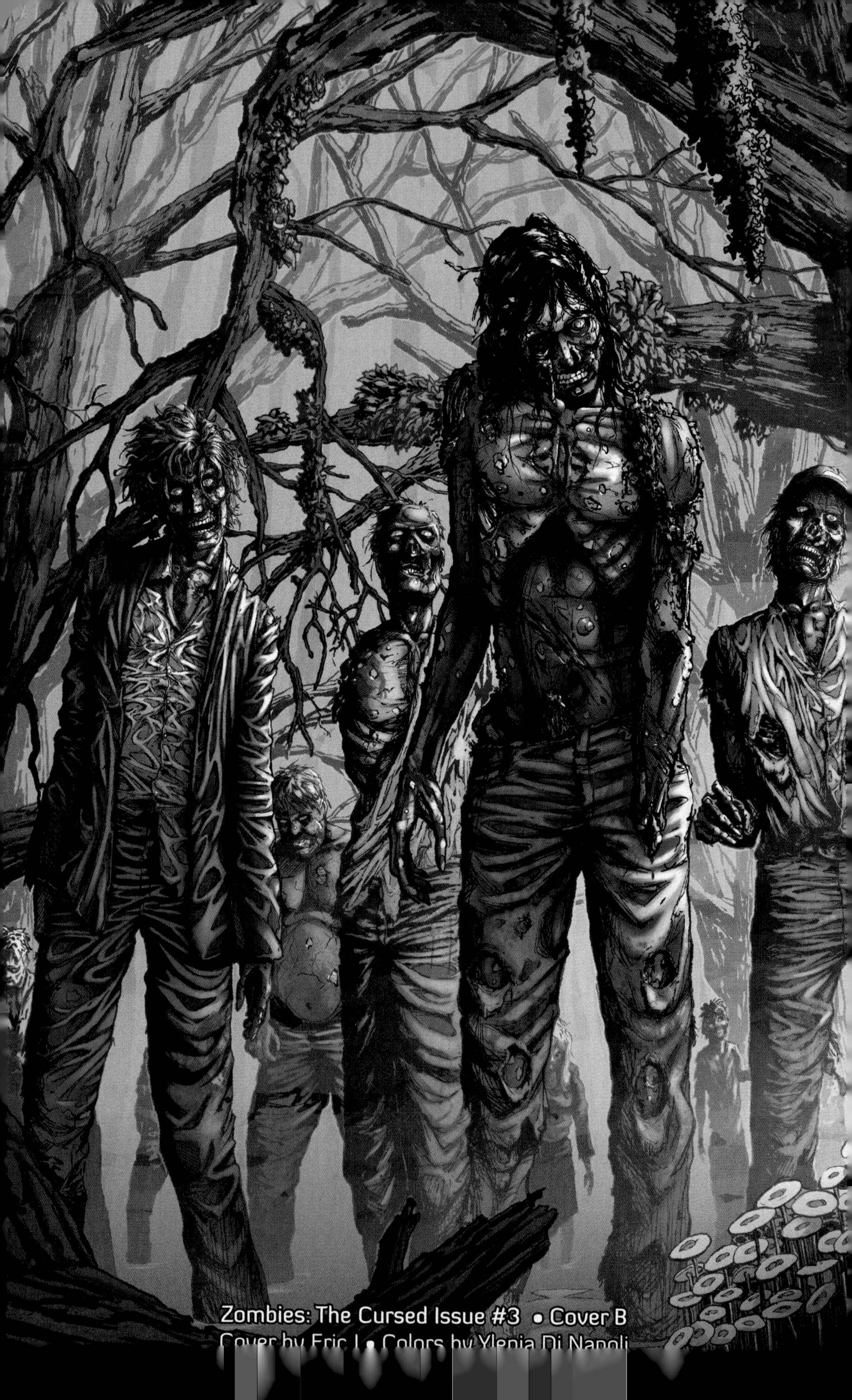

Zombies: The Cursed Issue #3 • Cover B
Cover by Eric J • Colors by Ylenia Di Napoli

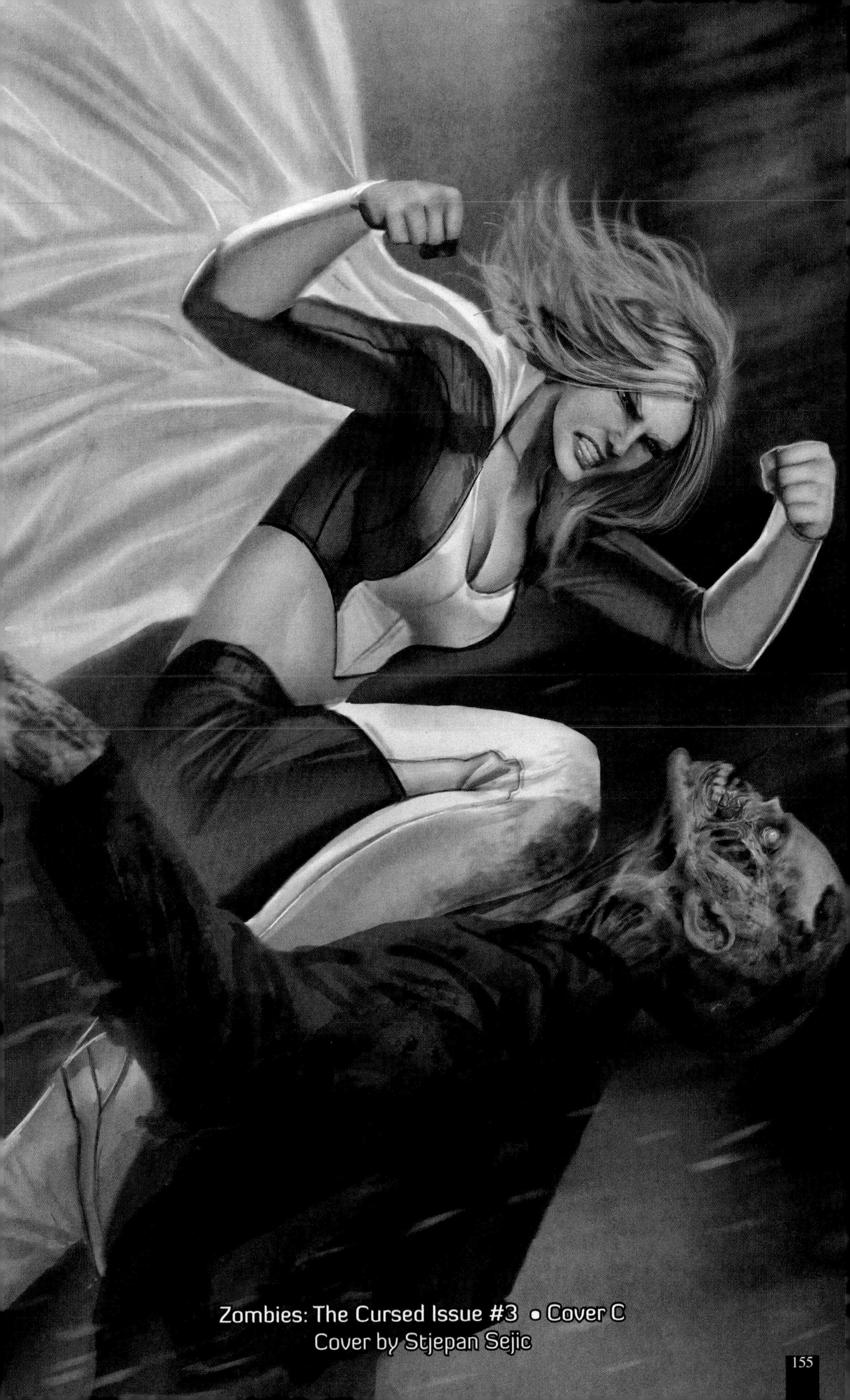

Zombies: The Cursed Issue #3 • Cover C
Cover by Stjepan Sejic

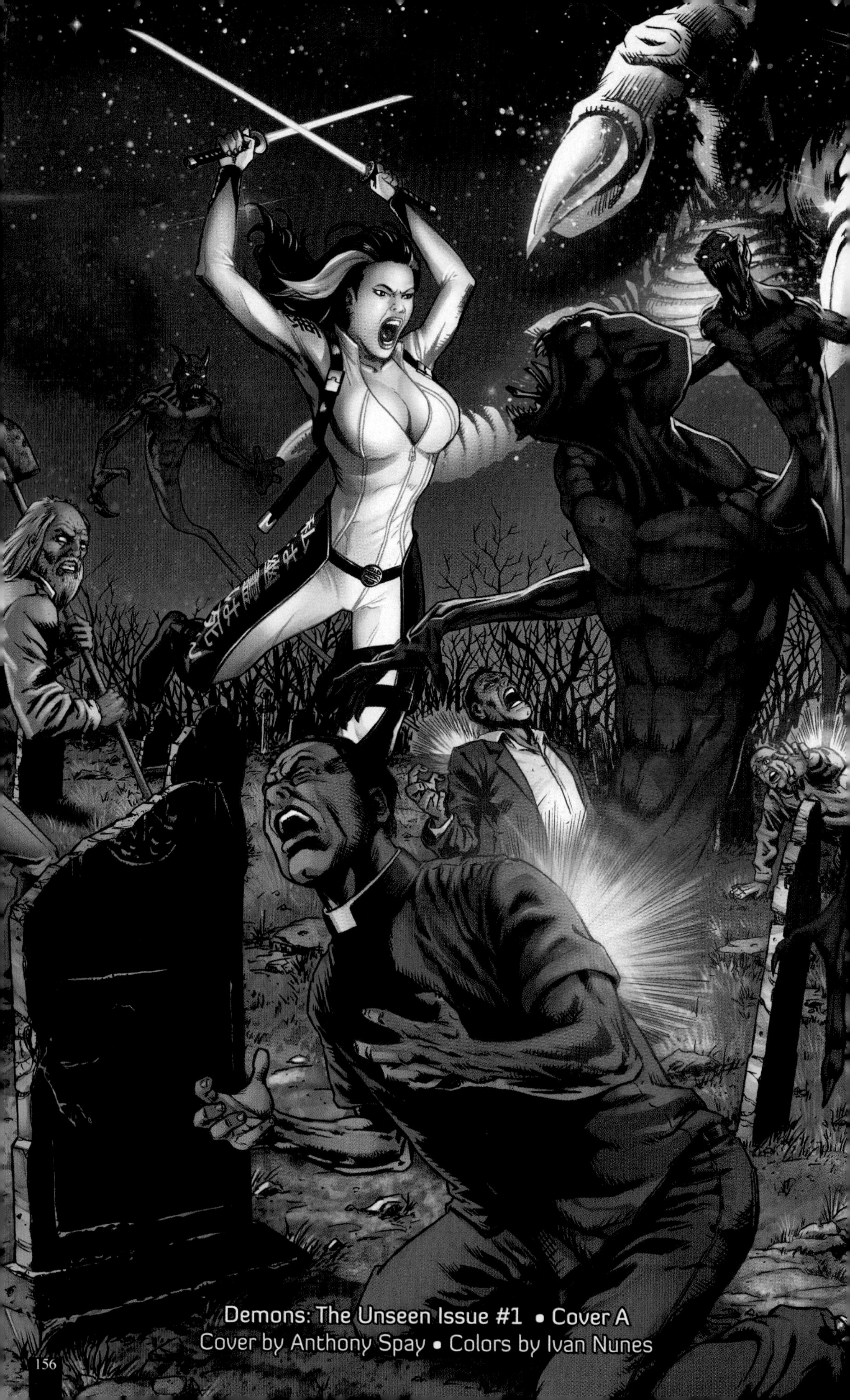

Demons: The Unseen Issue #1 • Cover A
Cover by Anthony Spay • Colors by Ivan Nunes

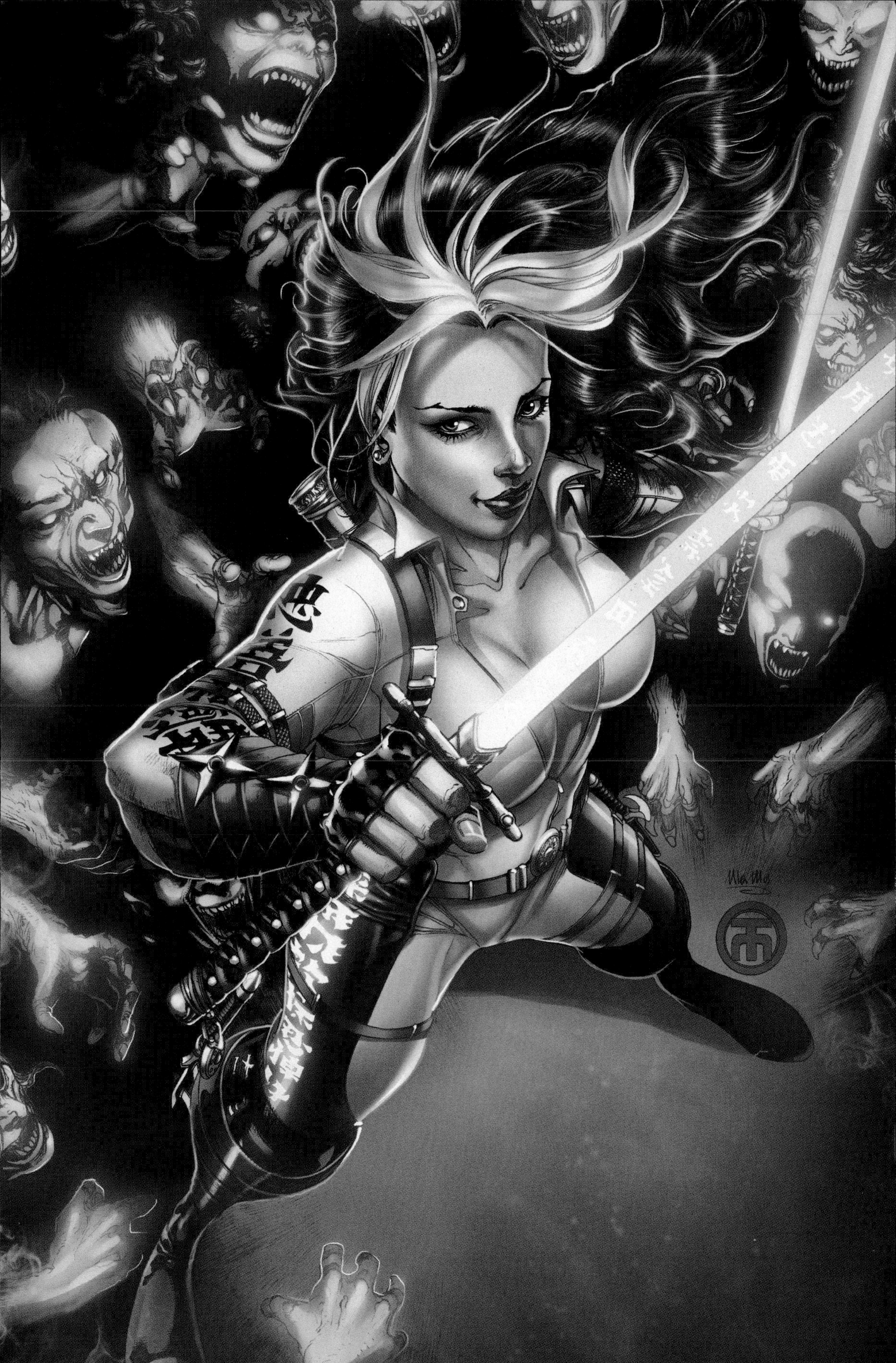

Demons: The Unseen Issue #1 • Cover B
Cover by Harvey Tolibao • Colors by Ula Mos

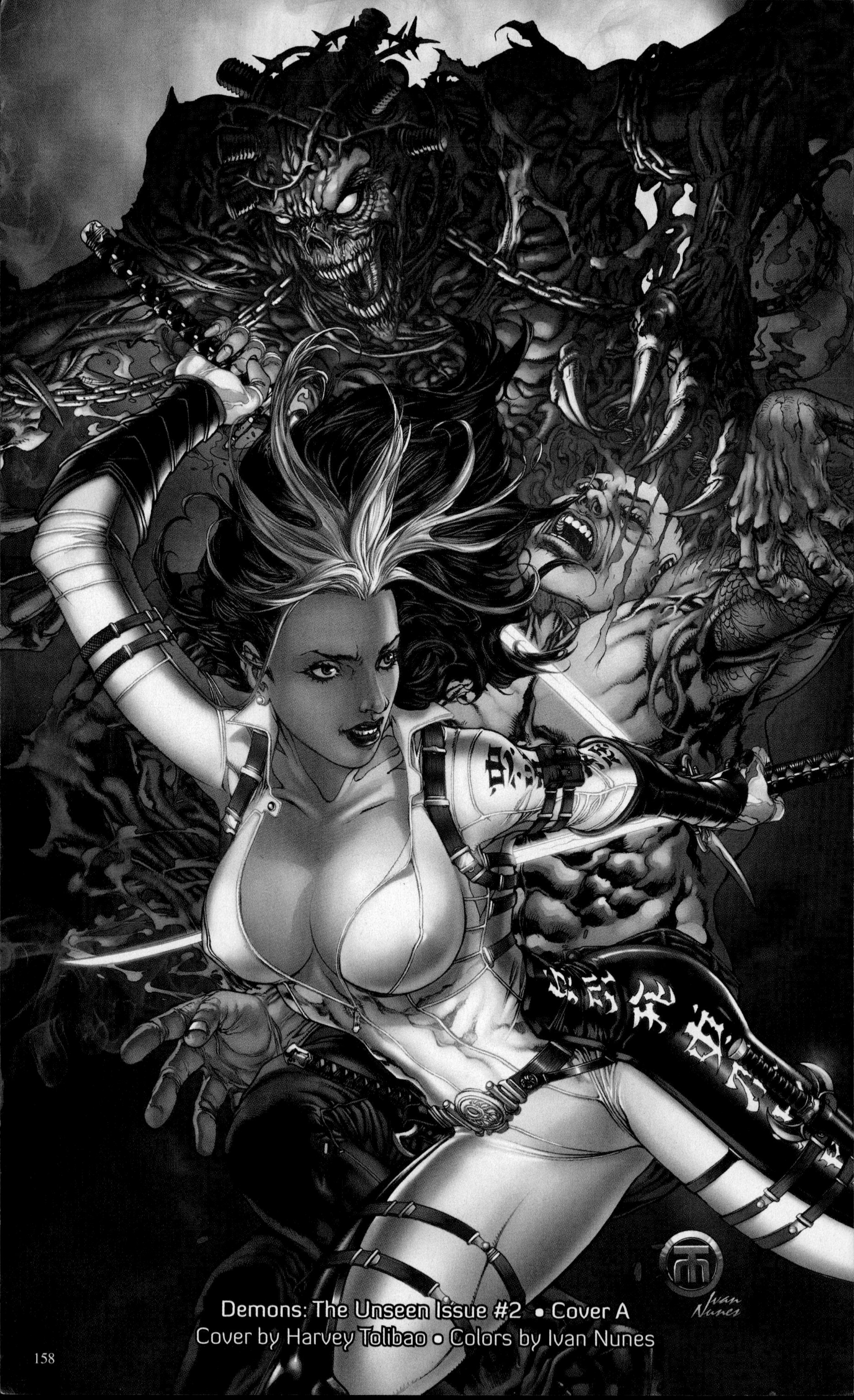
Ivan Nunes

Demons: The Unseen Issue #2 • Cover A
Cover by Harvey Tolibao • Colors by Ivan Nunes

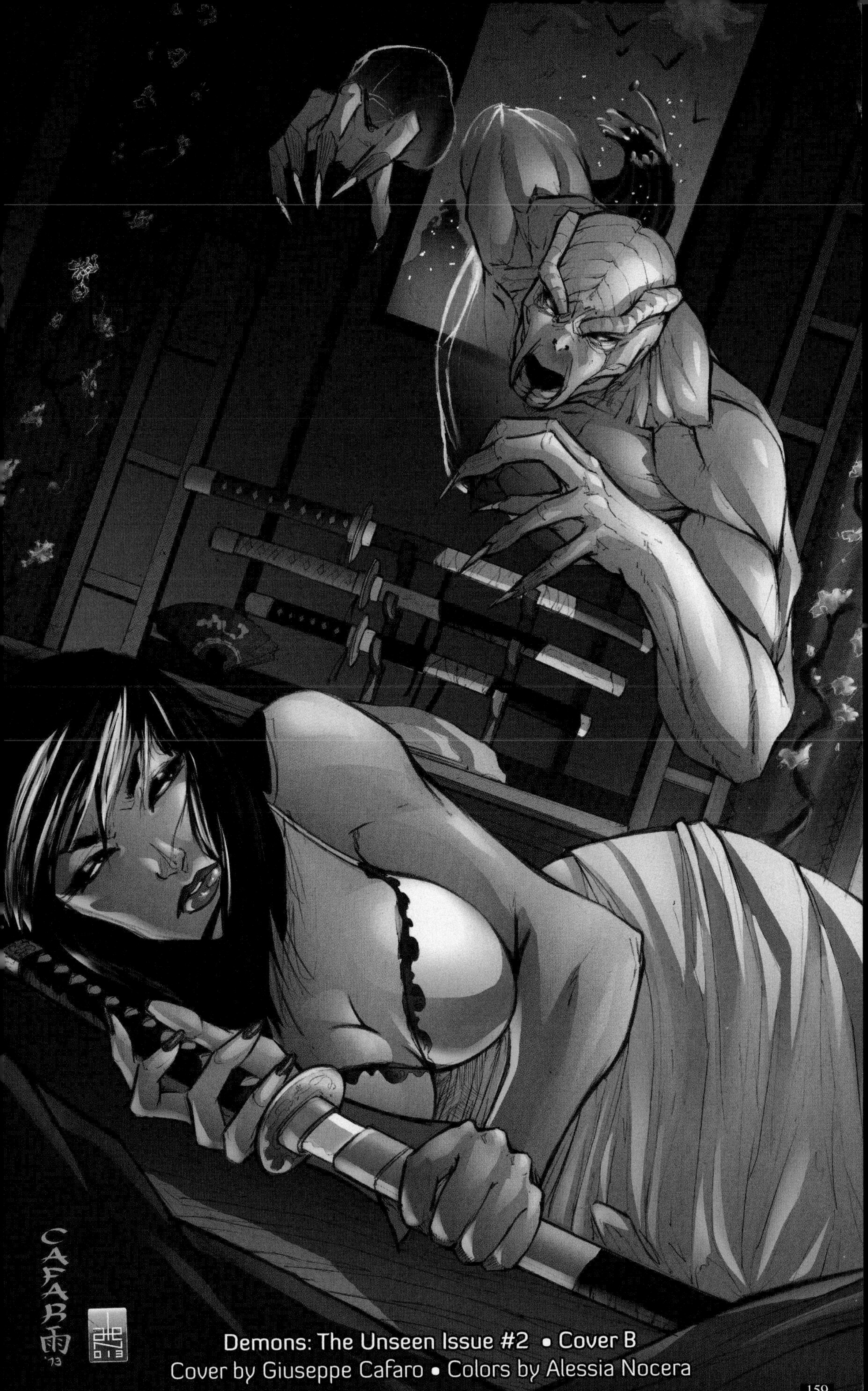

Demons: The Unseen Issue #2 • Cover B
Cover by Giuseppe Cafaro • Colors by Alessia Nocera

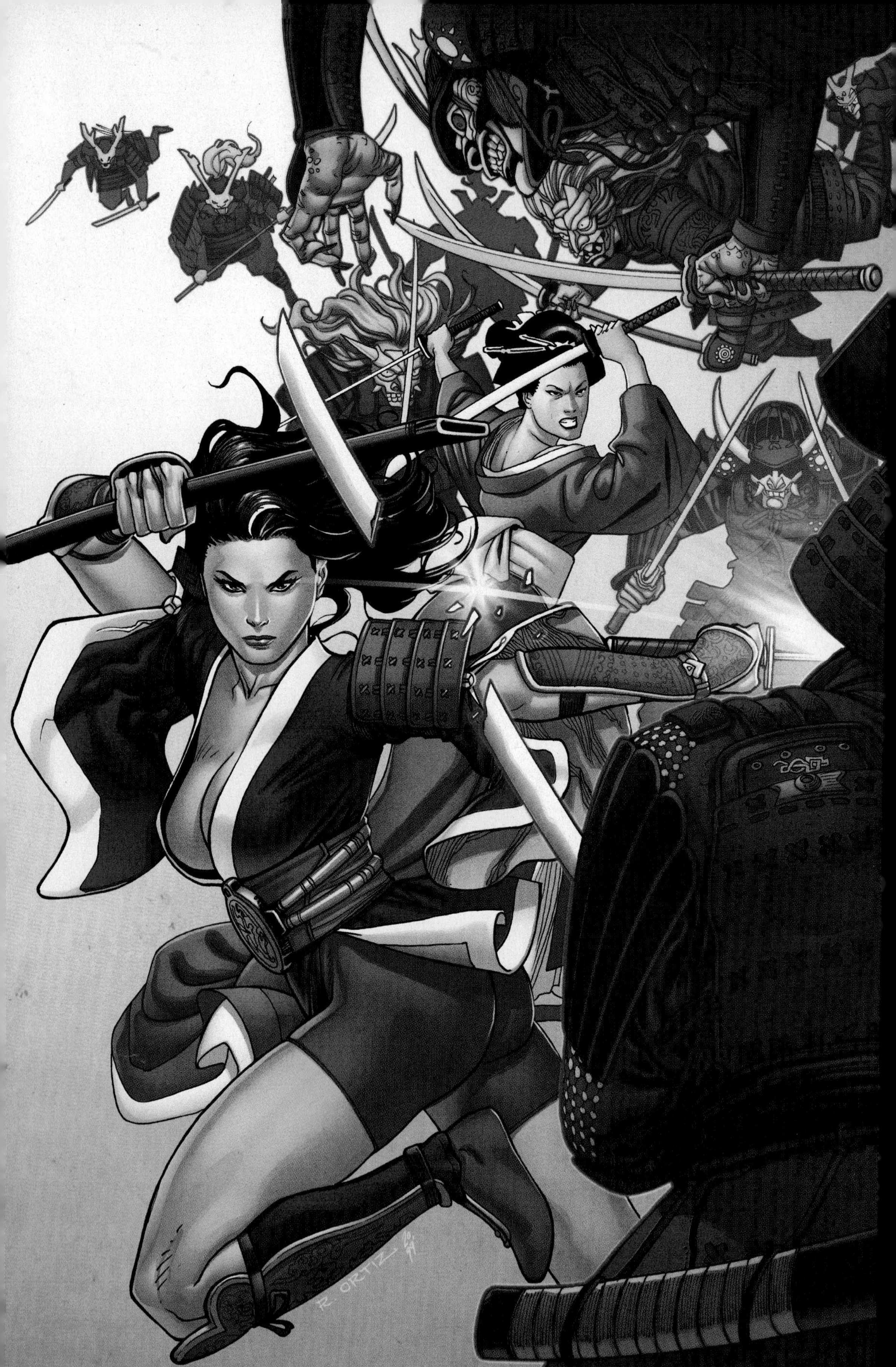
R. ORTIZ

Demons: The Unseen Issue #2 • Cover C
Cover by Richard Ortiz • Colors by Simon Gough

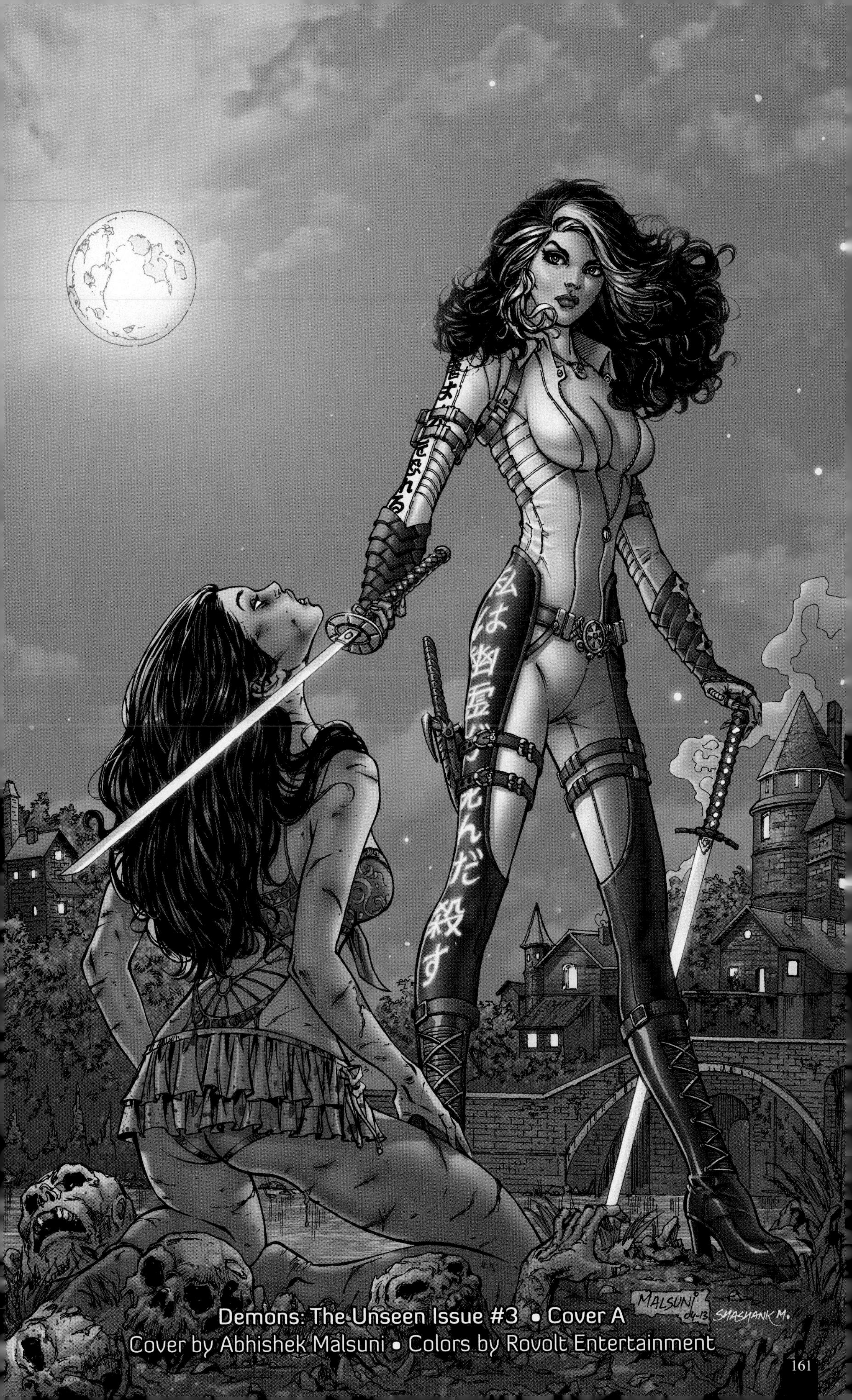
MALSUNI
SHASHANK M.

Demons: The Unseen Issue #3 • Cover A
Cover by Abhishek Malsuni • Colors by Rovolt Entertainment

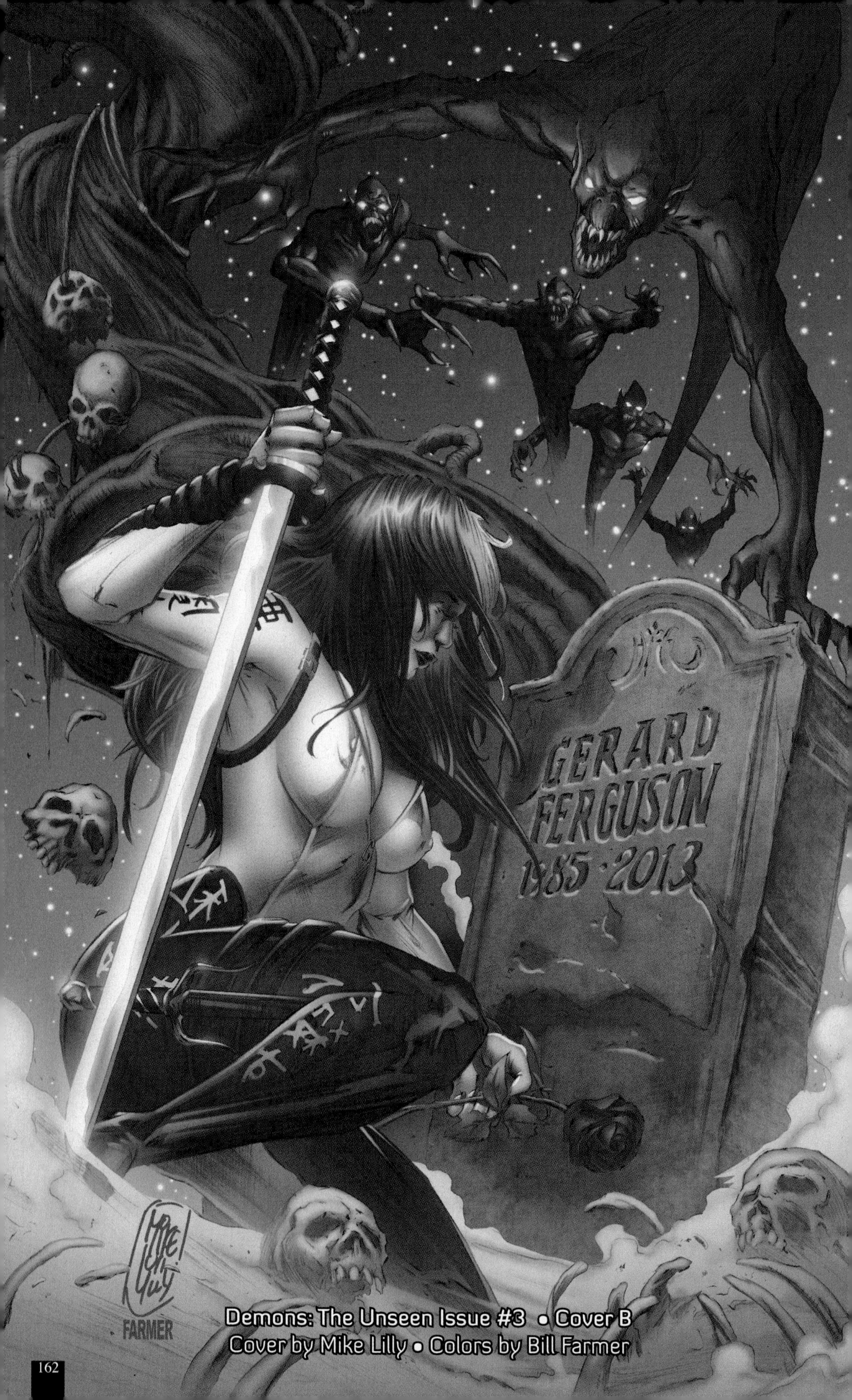
GERARD
FERGUSON
1985 - 2013
FARMER

Demons: The Unseen Issue #3 • Cover B
Cover by Mike Lilly • Colors by Bill Farmer

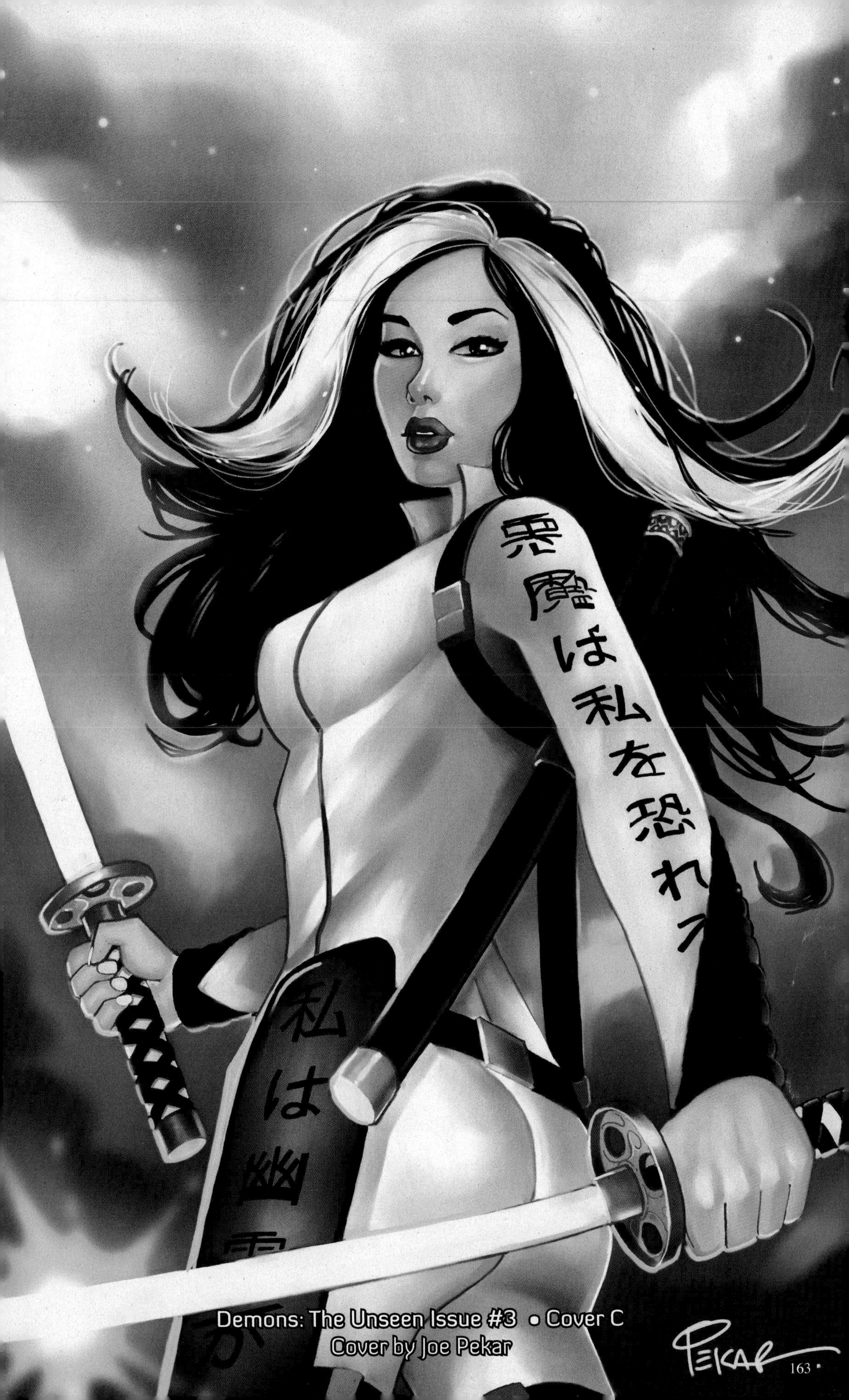
悪魔は私を恐れ
私は幽
PEKAR

Demons: The Unseen Issue #3 • Cover C
Cover by Joe Pekar

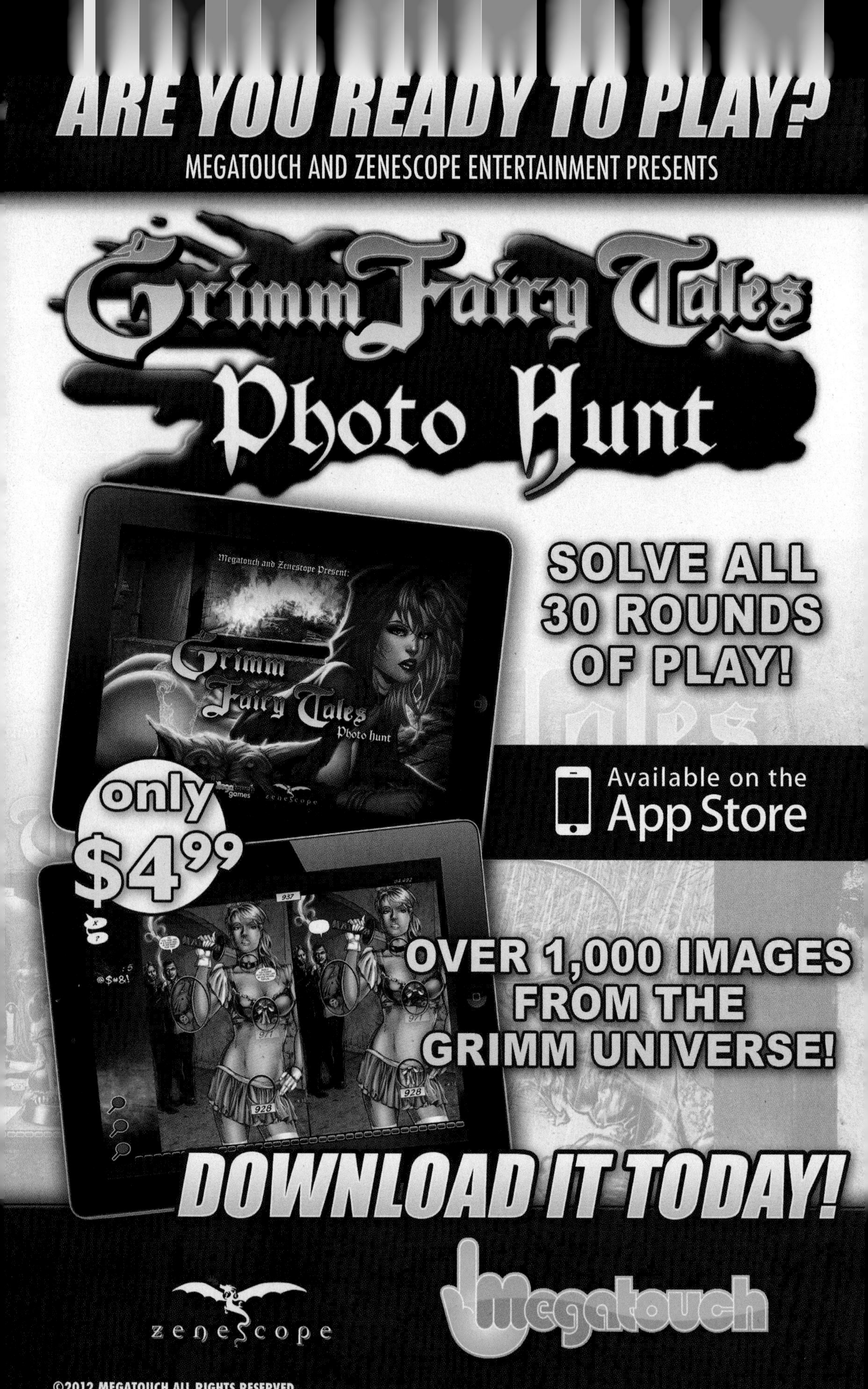
ARE YOU READY TO PLAY?
MEGATOUCH AND ZENESCOPE ENTERTAINMENT PRESENTS
Grimm Fairy Tales
Photo Hunt
Megatouch and Zenescope Present:
Grimm Fairy Tales
Photo hunt
SOLVE ALL 30 ROUNDS OF PLAY!
Available on the
App Store
only
$4.99
OVER 1,000 IMAGES FROM THE GRIMM UNIVERSE!
DOWNLOAD IT TODAY!
zenescope
Megatouch

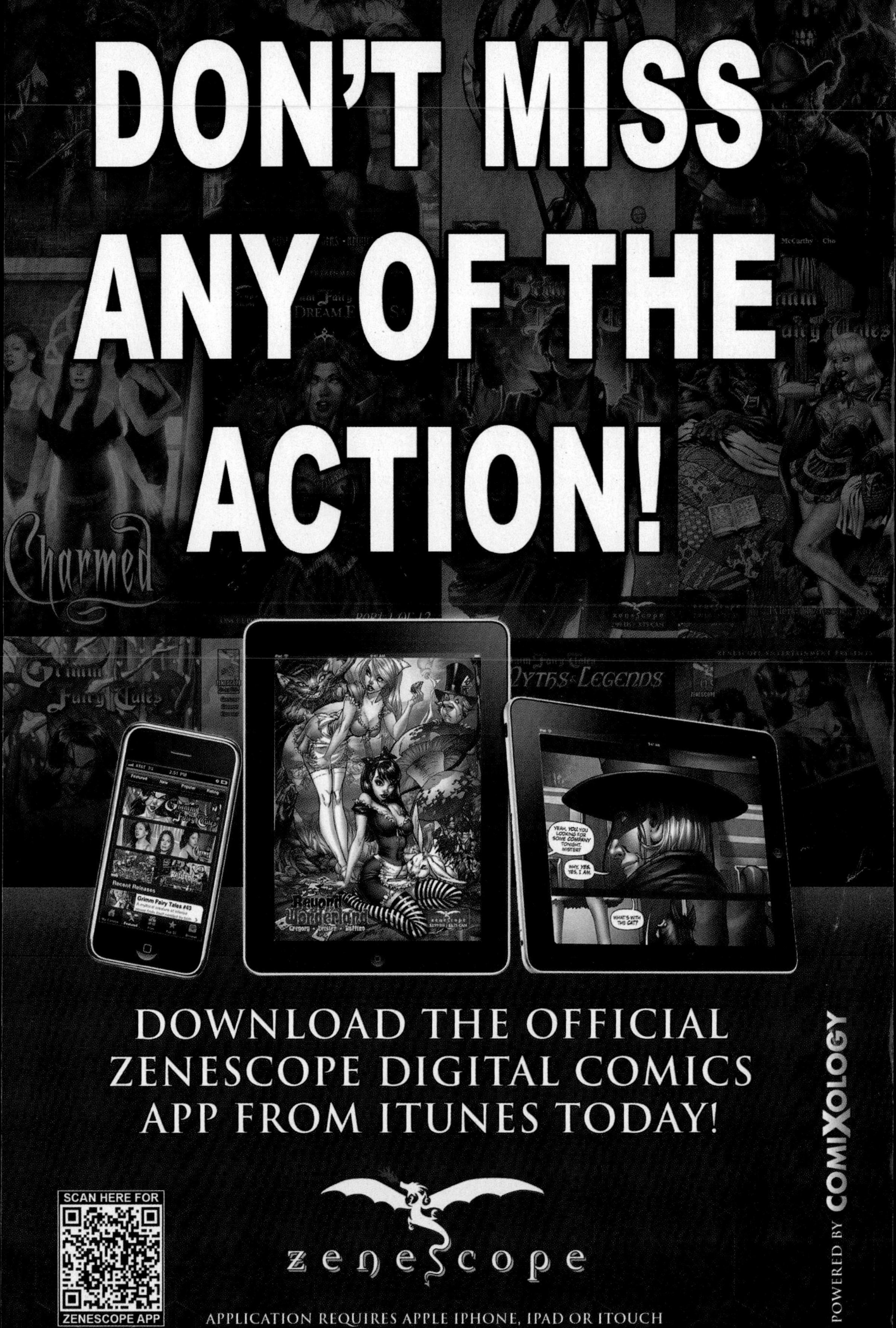
DON'T MISS
ANY OF THE
ACTION!
Charmed
Grimm Fairy Tales
Myths & Legends
Beyond Wonderland
YEAH, YOU. YOU LOOKING FOR SOME COMPANY TONIGHT, MISTER?
WHY, YES. YES, I AM.
WHAT'S WITH THE CAT?
DOWNLOAD THE OFFICIAL
ZENESCOPE DIGITAL COMICS
APP FROM ITUNES TODAY!
SCAN HERE FOR
ZENESCOPE APP
zenescope
APPLICATION REQUIRES APPLE IPHONE, IPAD OR ITOUCH
POWERED BY COMIXOLOGY

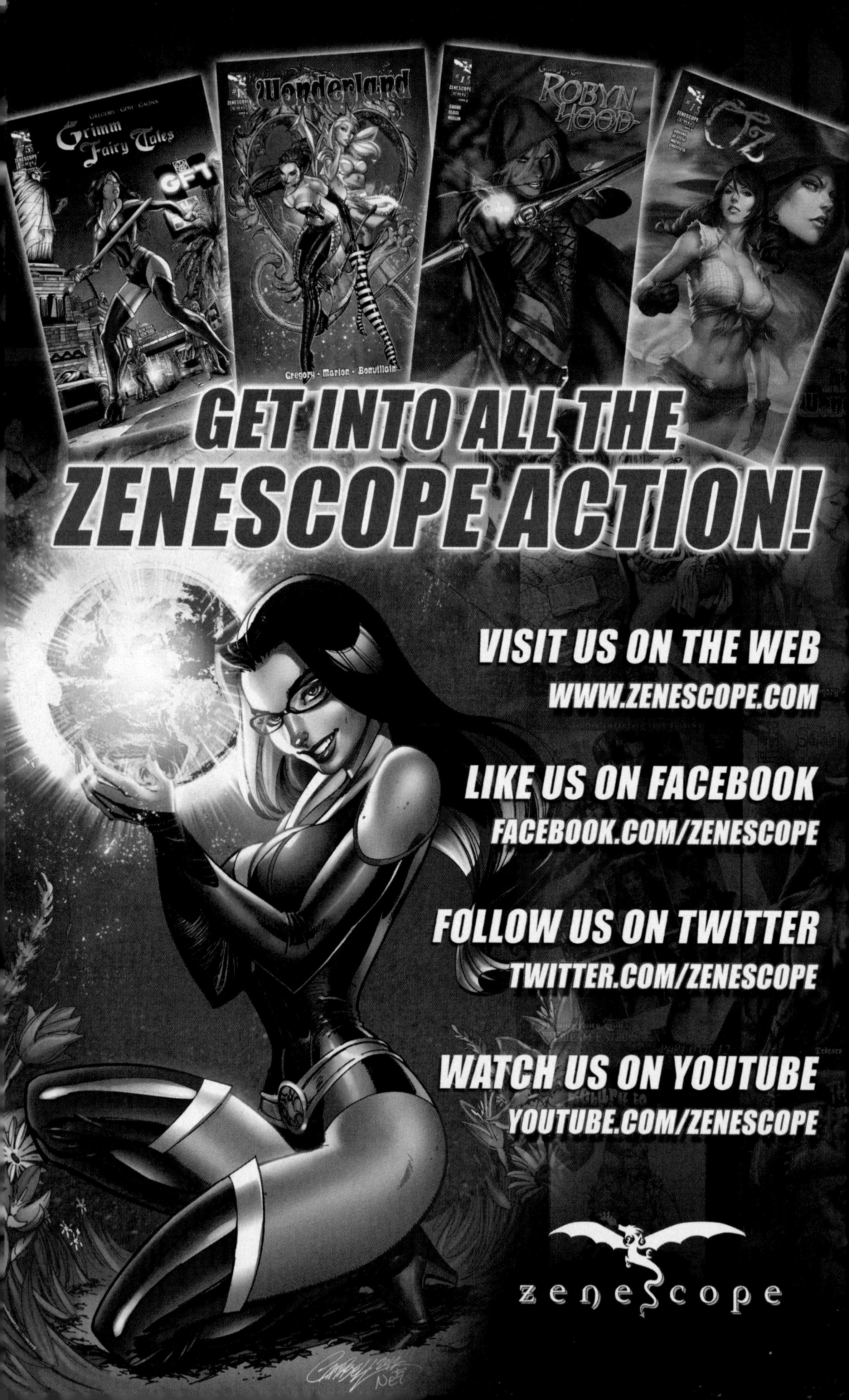
Grimm Fairy Tales
Wonderland
Gregory · Marion · Bonvillain
Robyn Hood
Oz
GET INTO ALL THE
ZENESCOPE ACTION!
VISIT US ON THE WEB
WWW.ZENESCOPE.COM
LIKE US ON FACEBOOK
FACEBOOK.COM/ZENESCOPE
FOLLOW US ON TWITTER
TWITTER.COM/ZENESCOPE
WATCH US ON YOUTUBE
YOUTUBE.COM/ZENESCOPE
zenescope

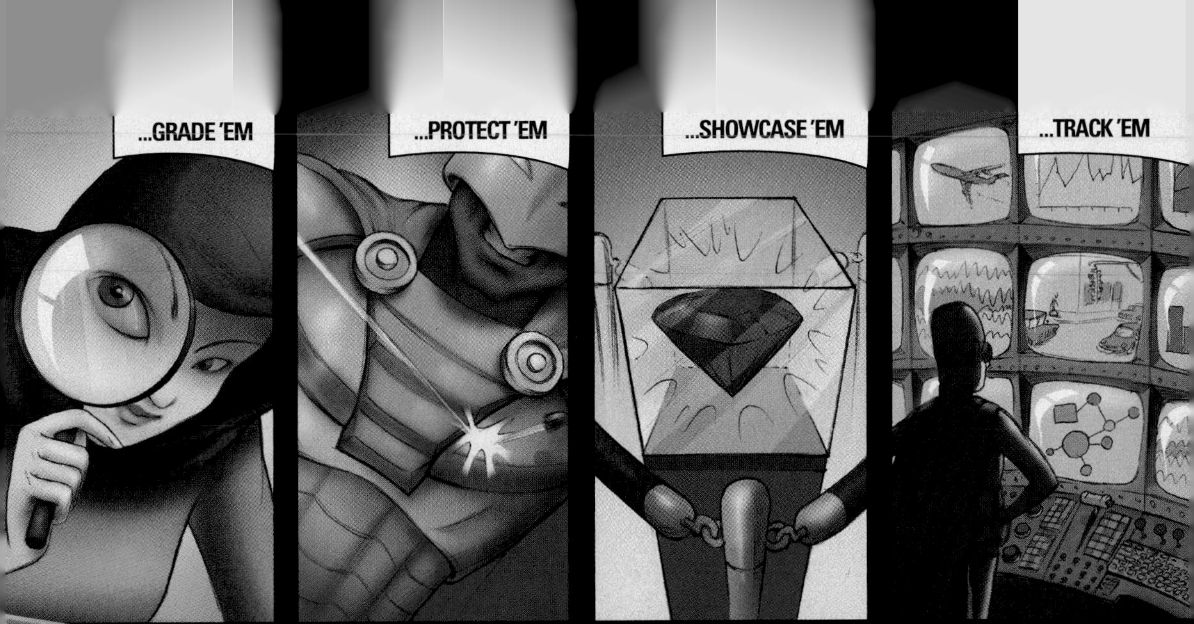
...GRADE 'EM
...PROTECT 'EM
...SHOWCASE 'EM
...TRACK 'EM

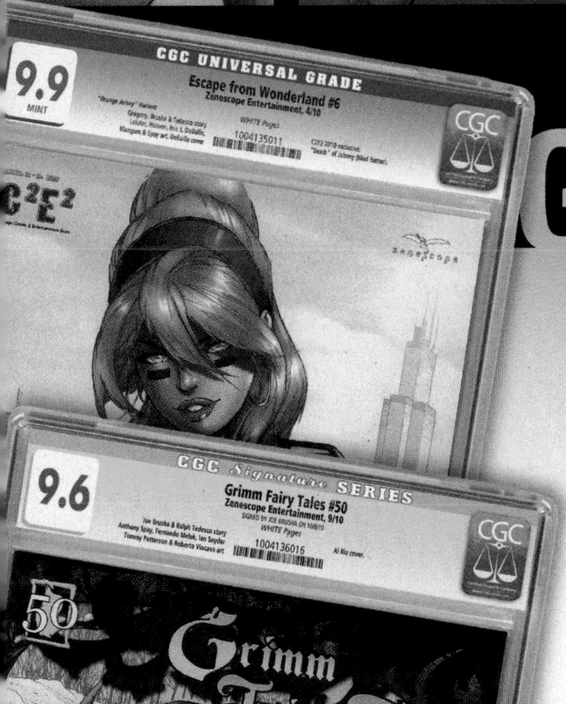
9.9
MINT
CGC UNIVERSAL GRADE
Escape from Wonderland #6
Zenescope Entertainment, 4/10
CGC
9.6
CGC Signature SERIES
Grimm Fairy Tales #50
Zenescope Entertainment, 9/10
CGC
Grimm Fairy Tales

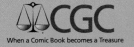

Grimm Fairy Tales presents:

ZOMBIES & DEMONS

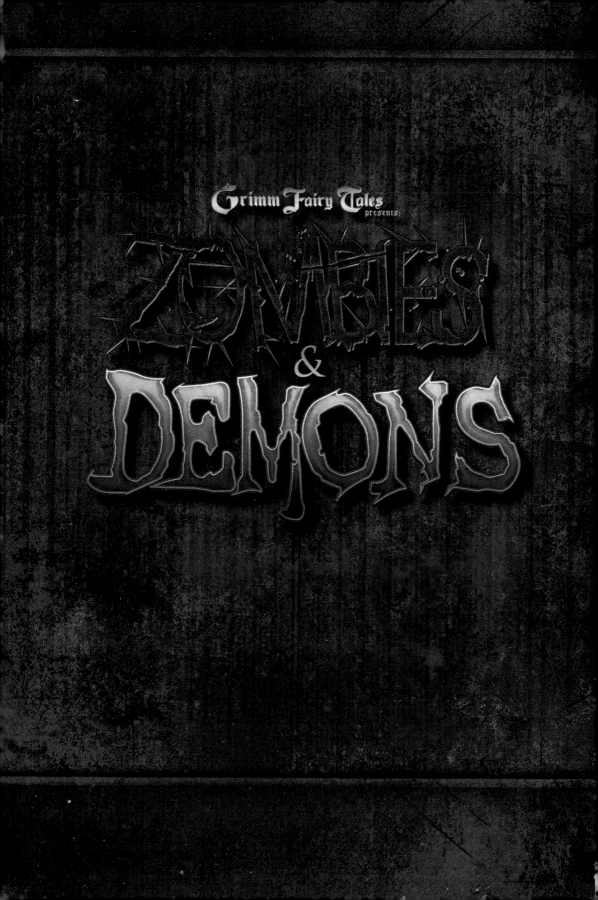